WITHDRAWN

DATE DUE

MAR 27 2003		
SEP 0 8 2010		
MAY 0 2 2013		
FEB 2 0 2014		

#47-0108 Peel Off Pressure Sensitive

Virtues of the mind

Almost all theories of knowledge and justified belief employ moral concepts and forms of argument borrowed from moral theories, but none of them attends to the current renaissance in virtue ethics. This remarkable book is the first attempt to establish a theory of knowledge based on the model of virtue theory in ethics. The book develops the concept of an intellectual virtue, and then shows how the concept can be used to give an account of the major concepts in epistemology, including the concept of knowledge.

A highly original work of philosophy for professionals, the book will also provide students with an excellent introduction to epistemology, virtue theory, and the relationship between ethics and epistemology.

Virtues of the mind

An inquiry into the nature of virtue
and the ethical foundations of knowledge

LINDA TRINKAUS ZAGZEBSKI

Loyola Marymount University

CAMBRIDGE
UNIVERSITY PRESS

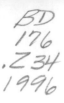

Published by the Press Syndicate of the University of Cambridge
The Pitt Building, Trumpington Street, Cambridge CB2 1RP
40 West 20th Street, New York, NY 10011-4211, USA
10 Stamford Road, Oakleigh, Melbourne 3166, Australia

First published 1996

Printed in the United States of America

Library of Congress Catalog-in-Publication data applied for.

A catalog record for this book is available from the British Library.

ISBN 0-521-57060-3 hardback
ISBN 0-521-57826-4 paperback

For Walter and Sander

Contents

Contents

Contents

Acknowledgments

This book has benefited from generous institutional support and the help of many individuals. I am indebted to Loyola Marymount University for granting me a summer research grant in 1991 to begin work on the project; for a College Fellowship in the spring semester of 1992, which permitted me to do a substantial amount of writing; and for a sabbatical leave in the fall of 1994 during the last stages of the book's preparation. I am also grateful to the National Endowment for the Humanities for a summer stipend in 1993 and for a Fellowship for College Teachers in 1995, which permitted me to complete the book.

I have also profited from the many public presentations of material from this project. These included two talks at the University of Saint Thomas, Saint Paul, Minnesota, in October 1993; three talks at the University of Colorado, Boulder; one at Bethel College, Saint Paul; one at Rhodes College, Memphis, Tennessee; and two at the University of Notre Dame. A version of Part III, section 3.1, was published as "The Inescapability of Gettier Problems" in *Philosophical Quarterly*, January 1994; it is used here with permission. A paper taken from Part II, section 3, was presented at the conference on norms and reasoning at the University of Glasgow in July 1995. A version of that talk was previously presented in a symposium on belief at the Claremont Graduate School, and I thank CGS for inviting me to participate in an experimental bulletin board course in which students read and discussed the manuscript.

Acknowledgments

I wish to extend special thanks to the people who generously read and commented on earlier versions of the manuscript, and whose suggestions immensely improved it. They include Charles Young, John Greco, William P. Alston, Hilary Kornblith, Dewey Hoitenga, Thomas D. Sullivan, Ernest Sosa, Carroll Kearley, and an anonymous referee. I also profited from the suggestions of Michael Slote, Mary Beth Ingham, George Pappas, and Amelie Rorty, all of whom read portions of the manuscript.

Finally, I wish to thank research assistants Doris Doss and Dan Speak for their patient work on bibliographical references.

Los Angeles
16 September 1995

Introduction

The deepest disputes in epistemology focus on concepts that are quite obviously ethical and often are borrowed directly from theoretical moral discourse. We frequently find references to epistemic *duty* or epistemic *responsibility*, to the fact that we *ought* to form beliefs in one way rather than another, to the fact that one way of believing is *good*, or at least better than some other, and more recently to the idea of intellectual *virtue*. But these concepts are often used with little reflection, and rarely with any concern for the fact that they may be borrowed from a particular *type* of moral theory. Any problems in the theory may adversely affect the epistemological inquiry. On the other hand, the theory's advantages may be advantages for epistemology as well.

Almost all epistemological theories are modeled on act-based moral theories. When their model is deontological ethics, that is usually readily apparent. Less obvious is the fact that the popular theory of reliabilism is structurally parallel to consequentialism. To my knowledge, no epistemological theory is closely modeled on a pure virtue theory. The idea of intellectual virtue was introduced into the epistemological literature by Ernest Sosa, but Sosa does no more than mention an association with virtue ethics, and subsequently "virtue epistemology" has been used as another name for reliabilism. The works of Lorraine Code and James Montmarquet come closer to linking epistemology with virtue ethics, but neither one derives the concept of epistemic virtue from a background aretaic ethics or pushes the similarities between intellectual virtue and moral virtue very far. This is too bad because interest in virtue ethics has blossomed in the last few decades after a long period of neglect. If a virtue-based ethical theory has advantages over an act-based theory, it ought to be illuminating to look closely at this kind of theory for help in developing the concepts needed in analyzing knowledge and justified belief. In any case, because the use of the act-based model in analyzing justification has resulted in an impasse between internalists and externalists, it may now be a good time to investigate a new approach.

The focus of the theory I will propose is the concept of intellectual virtue. Unfortunately, philosophers have rarely given the intellectual virtues much notice, and this neglect is not limited to contemporary philosophy; it has occurred throughout the entire history of philosophy. Of course, moral philosophers have examined *virtue* at length, but on those few occasions in which they mention an intellectual virtue, it is almost always the Aristotelian virtue of *phronesis,* or practical wisdom, but that has aroused interest only because of the way Aristotle connects *phronesis* with the traditional moral virtues. Other intellectual virtues are usually ignored altogether. Clearly, a true aretaic approach to epistemology requires a theory of virtue that gives the intellectual virtues their proper place. I will develop here a virtue theory that is inclusive enough to handle the intellectual as well as the moral virtues within a single theory, and I will then show how such a theory can be used in analyzing some of the principal concepts in normative epistemology, including the concepts of knowledge and of justified belief.

In the work that follows I will argue that the relationship between the evaluation of cognitive activity and the evaluation of acts in the overt sense usually reserved to ethics is more than an analogous one. I will argue that the intellectual virtues are so similar to the moral virtues in Aristotle's sense of the latter that they ought not to be treated as two different kinds of virtue. Intellectual virtues are, in fact, forms of moral virtue. It follows that intellectual virtue is properly the object of study of moral philosophy. This claim is intended, not to reduce epistemic concepts to moral concepts in the way that has sometimes been attempted, but to extend the range of moral concepts to include the normative dimension of cognitive activity. At the same time, this thesis is not simply a semantical quibble about the meaning of the word "moral." If I am right, normative epistemology is a branch of ethics. Either discipline ignores the other at its peril.

Finally, I will argue that intellectual virtue is the primary normative component of both justified belief and knowledge. The justifiedness of beliefs is related to intellectual virtue as the rightness of acts is related to moral virtue in a pure virtue ethics. In both cases it is the latter that is more fundamental. I define knowledge as cognitive contact with reality arising from what I call "acts of intellectual virtue." The theory gives a prominent place to the virtue of *phronesis*, a virtue whose primary function is to mediate between and among the whole range of moral and intellectual virtues. My hope is that this project will show how a virtue-based epistemology is preferable to a belief-based epistemology for some of the same reasons that a virtue-based moral theory is preferable to an act-based moral theory.

The book is divided into three parts. Part I is on metaepistemology. Part II is on normative ethics. Part III is on normative epistemology. In Part I, I examine some problems in contemporary epistemology and show the advantages of the virtue approach I take in the rest of the book. In Part II, I develop a theory of virtue and vice that is broad enough to handle the evaluation of cognitive activity. In this part I attempt to advance the analysis of the structure of virtue beyond its present point in the contemporary literature and to make a case for a view of human psychology in which cognitive activity cannot be sharply separated from feeling states and motivations. In this part I also argue for the thesis that intellectual virtues are forms of moral virtue. I then show how the deontic epistemic concepts of justified belief and epistemic duty can be defined in terms of intellectual virtue in the same way that the deontic concepts of right act and moral duty can be defined in terms of the traditional concept of moral virtue. In Part III I apply my account of intellectual virtue to the primary question of epistemology, namely, when is a person in a state of knowledge? I offer criticisms of some major recent theories that have been labeled "virtue epistemology," answer anticipated objections to my theory, show how the theory I propose is immune to Gettier problems, and end with some conjectures on the connections among the sciences of ethics, epistemology, and cognitive theory.

In this inquiry I do not investigate such time-honored questions of epistemology as: What does a rational doxastic structure look like? That is to say, how are we to decide among the competing models offered by foundationalism, coherentism, and their variants? Neither do I attempt to answer the question: What is the origin of knowledge? That is to say, how are we to decide among empiricism, rationalism, and other theories on the basis for obtaining knowledge? Nor do I say very much about the kind of knowledge that cannot be subsumed under the category of knowing-that. Accounts of knowledge are often distorted by ignoring forms of knowledge other than knowing-that, and I will attempt to be sensitive to the dangers. A comprehensive theory of knowledge would have to include both the propositional and the nonpropositional, but the inquiry of this book will not go very far into the latter.

In my approach I take seriously the treatment of the concept of knowledge throughout the history of philosophy, but at the same time I connect it with the main concerns of contemporary epistemology (e.g., the internalism/externalism dispute, Gettier problems). In my approach to the analysis of virtue I attempt the same combination of concern for the historical tradition with an awareness of the theoretical questions lately considered most interesting in ethics (e.g., moral luck, the scope of the moral). My illustrations and counterexamples are not limited to the singularly peculiar world of philosophers' fiction but may be drawn from literature, from the history of philosophy, or from ordinary experience. My aim is to show how it is possible for a pure virtue theory to be rich enough to provide the foundations of normative epistemology.

— Endless is the search of Truth.

Laurence Sterne, *The Life and
Opinions of Tristram Shandy*

Part I

The methodology of epistemology

The nature of knowledge is arguably the central concern of epistemology and unarguably one of the major interests of philosophy from its beginning. Ever since Plato and no doubt long before, knowledge has been held in high regard. Plato called knowledge the most important element in life (*Protagoras* 352d) and said that the only thing truly evil is to be deprived of it (*Protagoras* 345b). Even today, few deny that it is the chief cognitive state to which we aspire, and some claim that it is the chief state of any kind to which we aspire. The possession of knowledge is one of life's great joys – or, at least, one of its benefits. In short, knowledge is valuable.

The valuational aspect of knowledge and of the related states of justified, rational, or warranted belief has led to numerous parallels between moral and epistemic discourse. As Roderick Chisholm observed years ago, "many of the characteristics philosophers have thought peculiar to ethical statements also hold of epistemic statements" (1969, p. 4). Since then epistemologists have routinely referred to epistemic *duty* and *responsibility*, to epistemic *norms* and *values*, and to intellectual *virtue*. On occasion they also use forms of argument that parallel arguments in ethics. In some cases this is done consciously, but in other cases it appears to be unnoticed, and the epistemological discussion is carried on without attention to the fact that the corresponding

1

discussions in ethics have by now become more advanced.[1] Section 1 will be devoted to an examination of these parallels. In 1.1 I argue that when epistemologists borrow moral concepts, they implicitly borrow the types of ethical theory in which these concepts are embedded. An awareness of the fact that moral concepts function in different ways in different types of moral theory can illuminate their use in epistemology. Almost all contemporary epistemic theories take an act-based moral theory as their model, even most of those that use the concept of intellectual virtue. But I argue in 1.2 that a virtue-based epistemic theory has certain advantages over a belief-based theory that parallel some of the advantages of a virtue-based ethical theory over an act-based ethical theory.

In section 2 I defend the desirability of a virtue approach from a different direction – from problems in contemporary epistemology. First, there are the problems surrounding the concept of justification, which have led to the present impasse between internalism and externalism. I suggest that since justification is a property of a belief, it is very difficult to adjudicate disputes over this concept if the belief is treated as the bottom-level object of evaluation. Instead, if we focus on the deeper concept of an intellectual virtue and treat the justifiability of a belief as derivative, these problems no longer loom so large and we may hope that the internalism/externalism dispute will lose much of its sting. Another problem in epistemology is the worry that making the single belief state of a single person the locus of evaluation is too narrow. For one thing, it has led to the neglect of two epistemic values that have been very important in the history of philosophy: understanding and wisdom. For another, the social basis for knowledge and justification needs to be recognized, as well as the

---

[1] Jonathan Dancy has made a similar point in discussing the analogies between ethics and epistemology: "In general, ethics as a subject has been more exhaustively investigated, and the tendency has been for epistemologists to use for their own purposes results which they take to have been established on the other side. Since they are commonly ill-informed about the solidity of these 'results,' the resulting epistemology is often unstable" (Dancy and Sosa 1992, p. 119). Dancy goes on to mention virtue epistemology in particular and the desirability of its being informed by results in ethics.

connection between epistemic states and noncognitive states of the believer. These concerns can be handled more readily by a virtue approach. Then in section 3 I look at a particular form of the connection between cognitive and noncognitive states: the connection between believing and feeling. There are numerous ways in which believing includes or is caused by feeling in the broad sense, including emotion and desire, and this gives us another reason to use ethics, particularly virtue ethics, in analyzing the normative aspect of belief states.

I will make a close association between theoretical ethics and normative epistemology in this book. But before that can be done convincingly, one objection to connecting moral and epistemic evaluation should be considered. This is the claim that whereas acts are voluntary, beliefs are not, so there is an important disanalogy between the primary object of moral evaluation – the act – and the primary object of epistemic evaluation – the belief. In 4.1 I argue that since the point of a virtue approach is to shift the locus of evaluation from the act/belief to the virtue, it follows that this objection largely misses the point, but I then go on to argue in 4.2 and 4.3 that in any case, beliefs and acts are sufficiently similar in voluntariness in a wide range of cases to permit similar types of evaluation.

1 USING MORAL THEORY IN EPISTEMOLOGY

The relationship between ethics and normative epistemology is both close and uneasy. The so-called ethics of belief debate has called attention to the idea that we can be commended or criticized for our beliefs and other cognitive states, but it is disputable whether the sense of evaluation intended is distinctively moral. As we have already seen, moral terminology is often used, but epistemic evaluation is conducted within practices that do not include some of the characteristic components of moral evaluation, most significantly, a system of rewards and punishments. Still, it is worth considering the indications that we think of ourselves as responsible for our epistemic states in a sense at least close to that of the moral. Michael Stocker (1982) has presented a prima facie case for the affirmative, arguing that responsibility for physical acts is linked with responsibility for mental goings-on, including beliefs, but this position is controversial, and since it makes responsibility for cognitive activity derivative from responsibility for overt acts, it limits the scope of cognitive responsibility in a way I believe seriously underrates the true extent of our cognitive responsibility. More recently, Christopher Hookway (1994) has argued that epistemic evaluation ought to focus on the activity of inquiry rather than on beliefs, and that the ethics of inquiry will show the proper place of self-controlled personal responsibility in epistemic evaluation.[2] This approach seems to me a promising one.

The ambivalence about our responsibility for having knowledge or justified belief is dramatically exemplified in the present impasse between internalism and externalism. The internalism/externalism distinction can be applied either to theories of justification or to theories of knowledge. Clearly, no matter how we define knowledge and justified belief, they will turn out to be highly desirable and important cognitive states, and this means there is something good about these states. But the type of good intended is not always clear, and this confusion is at the root of the internalist/externalist debate. Internalists about justification require that the factors needed for justification be cognitively accessible and internal to the believer, whereas externalists deny this, maintaining that the believer need not be aware of the feature or features that make her belief justified. A parallel distinction has been made in the account of the normative component of knowledge.[3] Internalists think of knowledge or justified belief as

---

[2] In this connection Kenneth W. Kemp has told me that he thinks that the root of the difference between me and Aristotle is that the form of intellectual activity which is my paradigm is that of inquiry, while for Aristotle the paradigm is that of contemplation. The work that follows may serve to confirm Kemp's appraisal.

[3] There are many different ways of drawing the distinction between internalism and externalism. Probably the most common one is to define internalism as the view that *all* justifying features of a belief be cognitively accessible and internal to the agent, whereas externalists claim that *some* justifying features are external or inaccessible. But it is clear from the discussion of reliabilism, the most popu-

good in a sense similar to the way we think of acts, motives, and persons as good. These are the objects of praise when they are good and blame when they are bad. Externalists think of knowledge or justified belief as good in the sense we think of eyesight, hearing, intelligence, or musical talent as good. We may, in some circumstances, praise very high quality in these faculties, but we tend not to blame deficiencies in them and generally neither praise nor blame them when they are normal. Given this fundamental difference in the senses in which epistemic states can be good, it is not surprising that the internalism/externalism dispute has so far been intractable.

Later we will consider the problem of the extent to which our behavior of any kind is under our control, but at the outset it is worth remarking that we do think our cognitive behavior as well as our overt behavior can be favorably affected by effort and training on our part. Some of the most important questions we ask about our lives include "What should I think about?" and "What should I believe?" as well as "What should I want?" and "What should I do?" Furthermore, we criticize others for their beliefs as well as for their actions, and we probably are even more inclined to criticize their beliefs than their feelings and desires. For example, a person who cannot help feeling envious but attempts to control such feelings is not criticized as much as someone who permits his envy to influence his beliefs on the morality of social and economic arrangements. The same point applies to beliefs formed, not out of undue influence by the passions, but by a more obviously "mental" error. So we blame a person who makes hasty generalizations or who ignores the testimony of reliable authority. Such criticism is much closer to *moral* criticism than the criticism of bad eyesight or poor blood circulation. When people call others shortsighted or pigheaded, their criticism is as much like moral criticism as when they call them offensive or

lar version of externalism, that externalists generally believe that the most important or salient justifying features typically are inaccessible to the agent's consciousness. This permits hybrid positions according to which some important justifying features are and some are not cognitively accessible. See Laurence BonJour's contribution to Dancy and Sosa 1992, p. 132, for an explanation of the way this distinction is used in the contemporary literature.

obnoxious; in fact, what is obnoxious about a person can sometimes be limited to a certain pattern of thinking. The same point
can be made, in differing degrees, of a variety of other names
people are called for defects that are mostly cognitive: mulish,
stiff-necked, pertinacious, recalcitrant, or obstinate; wrong-
headed, vacuous, shallow, witless, dull, muddleheaded, thick-
skulled, or obtuse. Of course, the connotation of blame in the use
of these terms may be partly conveyed by tone of voice, but their
usage definitely differs from that of the purely nonmoral labels
given to the brain damaged or congenitally mentally retarded.
What's more, the association of praise and blame is explicitly
extended to states of knowledge and ignorance when we use such
expressions as "She should have known better."

It will take most of this book to demonstrate that epistemic
evaluation is a form of moral evaluation, but I hope these few
considerations explain in part the strong attraction to concepts
and forms of argument from ethics in epistemological discourse,
even in discourse on the nature of knowledge. I believe the way
ethics is used in epistemology should be taken very seriously
since much depends upon it: the choice of concepts used and their
theoretical interconnections, what is taken for granted and what
is assumed to need close argument, and even the social practices
that the background ethical theory promotes. Epistemologists use
ethical theory anyway. I suggest that it be done self-consciously
and advisedly. In 1.1 and 1.2 I will look at the ethical theories that
provide contemporary epistemologists with their models and
will defend the use of a true virtue theory in epistemology.

1.1 Contemporary epistemic theories and their ethical models

A significant way in which contemporary epistemic theory parallels moral theory is that the locus of evaluation is the individual
belief, just as the locus of evaluation in most modern ethics has
been the individual act. Epistemologists assume that the normative concepts of interest to their inquiry are properties of beliefs in
one of two senses of "belief": either they are properties of the
psychological states of believing, or they are properties of the

propositional objects of such states. Disputes between foundationalists and coherentists and between externalists and internalists are disputes about the nature of such properties.

There are several epistemic analogues of the concept of a right act, and all of them are categories of belief. Perhaps most important for contemporary discussion is the concept of a justified belief. To be justified is a way of being right. Alternatively, epistemologists may speak of a warranted, rational, or well-founded belief, and in each case the concept used may or may not be understood as a component in the concept of knowledge. So there may be more than one way of being right epistemically. Having a belief that is justified or rational or well founded is one way of being right. Another way is to have whatever it takes to convert a true belief into knowledge. In each case the epistemological concept is the analogue of the right act. So just as the right act is usually the primary concept for moral philosophers, the justified (rational, warranted, well-founded) belief is the primary concept for epistemologists. Even when the question addressed is the nature of knowledge, the focus is still on the belief and its normative properties. As Roderick Firth puts it, "The ultimate task of a theory of knowledge is to answer the question, 'What is knowledge?' But to do this it is first necessary to answer the question, 'Under what conditions is a belief warranted?'" (1978, p. 216). Firth calls this "the unavoidable first step," but in practice the first step is generally the major part of the theory. So whether the epistemologist is concerned with rational belief or with knowledge, the theory virtually always focuses on the belief and it makes the evaluation of belief conceptually basic.

Since contemporary epistemology is belief-based, it is no surprise that the type of moral theory from which these theories borrow moral concepts is almost always an act-based theory, either deontological or consequentialist. So we generally find that epistemologists refine their inquiry into one of two types of questions: (1) Does the belief violate any epistemic *rules* or any epistemic *duties*? Is it epistemically *permissible,* within one's epistemic *rights*? Theories of this sort take deontological moral theories as their normative model. (2) Was the belief formed by a reliable process for obtaining the truth? Theories of this sort are the forms of reliabilism, structurally parallel to consequentialism. In reliabilist theories the epistemic goal is to bring about true beliefs and to avoid bringing about false beliefs, just as on consequentialist theories the moral goal is to bring about good states of affairs and to avoid bringing about bad states of affairs. And like most consequentialist ethics, reliabilism understands the good as quantitative. Whereas the utilitarian aims to maximize the balance of pleasure over pain, the reliabilist aims to maximize the balance of true over false beliefs.

So both deontological and reliabilist theories in epistemology have structural similarities with act-based ethics. An interesting variant is the theory of Ernest Sosa, who, in his well-known paper "The Raft and the Pyramid" (1980), proposed that epistemologists focus on intellectual virtue, a property of a person, rather than on properties of belief states, and argued that the concept of intellectual virtue can be used to bypass the dispute between foundationalists and coherentists on proper cognitive structure. I find Sosa's suggestion illuminating but have been disappointed that he has not adapted his concept of virtue from a virtue theory of morality. Rather, his model of a moral theory is act-based, and his definition of virtue is consequentialist: "An intellectual virtue is a quality bound to help maximize one's surplus of truth over error" (1985, p. 227; reprinted in Sosa 1991, p. 225). On the other hand, Sosa's idea of justification is more deontological, involving the adoption of a belief through "cognizance of its according with the subject's principles, including principles as to what beliefs are permissible in the circumstances as viewed by that subject" (1991, p. 144). Sosa's theory, then, combines consequentialist and deontological approaches with an informal concept of virtue that is not embedded in aretaic ethics. Like a virtue ethicist, he is sensitive to the importance of the social environment in his understanding of intellectual virtue, but Sosa does not go very far to connect his use of the concept of intellectual virtue with its use in ethics, and he apparently believes Aristotelian ethics to be generally inapplicable to his concerns.[4] In any case, he makes no attempt to integrate

---

[4] In "Intellectual Virtue in Perspective" (1991, p. 271) Sosa dissociates his use of the concept of a virtue from the Aristotelian sense. In referring to the faculty of

intellectual virtue into the broader context of a subject's psychic structure in the way that has been done by many philosophers for the moral virtues. What's more, Sosa's examples of intellectual virtues are faculties such as eyesight and memory, which are not virtues at all in traditional virtue theory. It turns out, then, that his plea for a turn to the concept of intellectual virtue actually has little to do with the concept of intellectual virtue *as* a virtue in the classical sense.

In fairness to Sosa, however, it ought to be pointed out that virtue ethicists have had little to say about intellectual virtue either. Generally the only intellectual virtue that gets any attention is *phronesis*, or practical wisdom, but that is examined only because of Aristotle's connection of *phronesis* with the distinctively *moral* virtues. The intellectual virtues that have direct relevance to epistemic evaluation are typically ignored altogether, so it is no wonder that Sosa has not found much help in virtue ethics for the analysis of the concept he believes is central to epistemology. Virtue theory simply has not kept pace with the needs of epistemology if Sosa is right. I think, then, that Sosa's insight that it would be fruitful for epistemology to make the primary object of evaluation intellectual virtues and vices and to

sight, he says, "Is possession of such a faculty a 'virtue'? Not in the narrow Aristotelian sense, of course, since it is not a disposition to make deliberate choices. But there is a broader sense of 'virtue,' still Greek, in which anything with a function – natural or artificial – does have virtues. The eye does, after all, have its virtues, and so does a knife. And if we include grasping the truth about one's environment among the proper ends of a human being, then the faculty of sight would seem in a broad sense a virtue in human beings; and if grasping the truth is an intellectual matter then that virtue is also in a straightforward sense an intellectual virtue." In this passage Sosa seems to treat sight as the virtue of the eye, but in Plato and Aristotle sight is the function of the eye, not its virtue. Plato (*Republic* 352e–353c) and Aristotle (*Nicomachean Ethics* [hereafter abbreviated *NE*] II.6.1106a14–27) both accept an analogy according to which a person's (or soul's) virtue is related to his function as the eye's virtue is to the eye's function. The eye's virtue is a trait that enables the eye to see well. Extending the analogy in the way Sosa desires, we should say that grasping the truth is a function of the intellect, not its virtue. The virtues would be those traits whereby the intellect is enabled to grasp the truth well. I thank Charles Young for noticing this problem in the way Sosa relates the concept of virtue to that of a function.

attach secondary justification to individual beliefs because of their source in intellectual virtues is a significant contribution to the field. In addition, his suggestion that "[w]e need to consider more carefully the concept of a virtue and the distinction between moral and intellectual virtues" (1980, reprinted in Sosa 1991, p. 190) strikes me as exactly right and is advice I am following in this book.

In the years since Sosa introduced the concept of intellectual virtue into the epistemological literature, the term "virtue epistemology" has become known as another name for reliabilism and related theories such as Plantinga's theory of proper function (Greco 1992, 1993; Kvanvig 1992). But as we have seen, reliabilism is structurally parallel to consequentialism, not virtue theory, and although Plantinga's theory does not have a consequentialist structure, it is not modeled on a virtue theory either, and, like Sosa, Plantinga focuses on faculties, not virtues.

Like Sosa, Greco defines an intellectual virtue in terms of its propensity to achieve a certain consequence:

> What is an intellectual virtue or faculty? A virtue or faculty in general is a power or ability or competence to achieve some result. An intellectual virtue or faculty, in the sense intended above, is a power or ability or competence to arrive at truths in a particular field and to avoid believing falsehoods in that field. Examples of human intellectual virtues are sight, hearing, introspection, memory, deduction and induction. (1992, p. 520)

It is quite obvious that sight, hearing, and memory are faculties, and (as mentioned in n. 4), the Greeks identified virtues, not with faculties themselves, but with the excellences of faculties. The sense in which Greco's examples can be considered virtues, then, is misapplied if it is intended to reflect the way the concept of virtue has been used in ethics. In fact, it has little connection with the history of the concept of intellectual virtue, although that history is quite sparse, as already noted. Aristotle's examples of intellectual virtues include theoretical wisdom (*sophia*), practical wisdom (*phronesis*), and understanding or insight (*nous*). Hobbes's list includes good wit and discretion; Spinoza's primary intellectual virtue is understanding. Many more examples of intellectual virtues will be discussed in what follows. None of these qualities are faculties like sight or hearing.

Kvanvig (1992) also treats reliabilism as the primary example of virtue epistemology, giving special attention to the theories of Armstrong, Goldman, and Nozick. None of these theories attempts to analyze intellectual virtue on the model of the concept of virtue operative in an aretaic moral theory, nor do they make much, if any, use of the work of moral philosophers in understanding the nature of virtue. Even when Kvanvig traces the roots of virtue epistemology to Aristotle, it is to Aristotle's epistemology that he briefly turns, not to Aristotle's theory of virtue. Kvanvig's attack on the turn to virtues in structural epistemology therefore has no bearing on the project I am developing here any more than do the objections offered by Greco.

Ironically, although Kvanvig devotes most of his book to establishing the bankruptcy of what *he* calls "virtue epistemology," the position he urges at the end of his book is one with which I wholeheartedly agree. There Kvanvig urges us to give up the "Cartesian perspective" that evaluates beliefs singly, attempting to cement them together to form a cognitive structure, and ignoring the social conditions of believing and the importance of intellectual models. What is needed, he says, is a paradigm shift from the atomistic approach to one that focuses on knowledge as a communal effort, extended in time and embedded in all the theoretical and practical activities that characterize human life. When such a shift is made, he argues, the true importance of the virtues will emerge. I find this suggestion agreeable and have made an independent attempt to carry out such a shift in the theory that follows. But, unlike Kvanvig, I will argue that a virtue-based epistemology is well suited to analyze the traditional concepts of epistemology, namely, justification and knowledge.

Two theories that come closer to the one I wish to develop are those of Lorraine Code and James Montmarquet. In her book *Epistemic Responsibility* (1987), Code gives a provocative account of intellectual virtue, stressing a "socialized" approach to epistemology, pointing out the connections between epistemology and moral theory, and exhibiting a sensitivity to the epistemological importance of aspects of human nature other than the purely cognitive. Code credits Sosa with the insight that epistemology ought to give more weight to the knowing subject, her environment, and her epistemic community than it had previously, but Code argues that Sosa's reliabilism does not go far enough in that direction. She urges a move to what she calls a "responsibilist epistemology":

> I call my position "responsibilism" in contradistinction to Sosa's proposed "reliabilism," at least when *human* knowledge is under discussion. I do so because the concept "responsibility" can allow emphasis upon the active nature of knowers/believers, whereas the concept "reliability" cannot. In my view, a knower/believer has an important degree of choice with regard to modes of cognitive structuring, and is accountable for these choices; whereas a "reliable" knower could simply be an accurate, and relatively passive, recorder of experience. One speaks of a "reliable" computer, not a "responsible" one. (Pp. 50–1)

This suggestion is promising and there are insights in Code's treatment of the intellectual virtues to which we will turn again in what follows. Still, Code looks only at consequentialist and deontological ethics for analogies with epistemology rather than at virtue theory (1987, pp. 40–2). And even that much she does not pursue very far, saying, "Despite the analogy I argue for . . . between epistemological and ethical reasoning, they are not amenable to adequate discussion under the rubric of any of the traditional approaches to ethics, nor under any reasonable amalgam thereof" (p. 68). Code's account supports the rejection of the atomistic approach to epistemology, seen in the later book by Kvanvig, but she neither makes such a rejection explicit nor sees the problem in using act-based moral theory as the analogue for epistemic theory when such a rejection is made. This leads her to identify with Sosa's theory more than she should, given the insights she develops in her book. *Her* examples are virtues in the sense of classical ethics; she does not seem to notice that his are not.

A very interesting defense of the claim that epistemology ought to focus on the epistemic virtues in a sense that is at least similar to the moral virtues is given by James Montmarquet (1986a, 1993). He takes seriously the idea that an epistemic virtue is a virtue in the classical sense of a trait for which we can be held responsible, and his examples are clearly intended to connect with the literature on moral virtue. Montmarquet says:

> First, there are what I will call the virtues of *impartiality*. These include such particular qualities as an openness to the ideas of others, the willingness to exchange ideas with and learn from them, the lack of jealousy and personal bias directed at their ideas, and the lively sense of one's own fallibility. A second class might be termed – with due respect to alleged connection between "vino" and "veritas" – the virtues of *intellectual sobriety*. These are the virtues of the sober-minded inquirer, as opposed to the "enthusiast" who is disposed, out of sheer love of truth, discovery, and the excitement of new and unfamiliar ideas, to embrace what is not really warranted, even relative to the limits of his own evidence. A third I would term the virtues of *intellectual courage*. These include most prominently the willingness to conceive and examine alternatives to popularly held beliefs, perseverance in the face of opposition from others (until one is convinced one is mistaken), and the determination required to see such a project through to completion. (1993, p. 23)

Persons who desire the truth would desire to have these traits, says Montmarquet, but they are not simply traits that are truth conducive in any straightforward way. In fact, epistemic virtues are virtues even when or if they are not truth conducive. Furthermore, he says, since persons with such intellectual vices as closed-mindedness or prejudice may not be deficient in the *desire* for truth, some of the epistemic virtues function as regulators of that desire (1993, p. 25). I will question later whether either of these two claims is true. I will argue that truth conduciveness is an essential component of intellectual virtues and I will attempt to ground these virtues in the motivation for knowledge. But the pertinent point for our discussion of methodological motivation is that Montmarquet has identified some virtues that operate on

13

the formation of beliefs and that are connected in one way or another with either the desire for truth or its regulation. This is an important insight.

Montmarquet's approach is vaguely Aristotelian, but like the others, his epistemology is belief-based. In his book, he stresses the ways in which the moral evaluation of acts is dependent upon the moral evaluation of beliefs, and he offers his analysis of epistemic virtue as his contribution to the ethics of belief debate. But Montmarquet does not develop his proposals out of an ethical virtue theory, and he takes pains to make the idea of an epistemically virtuous person "broad enough to embrace either a strict deontological approach or a less strict, qualified consequentialism" (1993, p. 44). So Montmarquet does not connect his theory with aretaic moral theory, nor does he associate the concept of intellectual virtue with the traditional epistemological concepts except for a brief proposal to define justification in terms of epistemic virtue: "A person S is justified in believing p insofar as S is epistemically virtuous in believing p" (p. 99). This proposal has the potential to link Montmarquet's project with the concerns of contemporary epistemology, but he does not pursue it. Still, there are a number of insights in his book that I will discuss in later sections.

Alvin Goldman in one place (1992) appears to accept a form of "virtue epistemology" similar to that of Sosa. Goldman explicitly links the concepts of justification and intellectual virtue, saying, "The basic approach is, roughly, to identify the concept of justified belief with the concept of belief acquired through the exercise of intellectual virtues" (p. 157). But the resulting theory remains a form of reliabilism and is belief-based. Goldman's and Sosa's treatments of justification are structurally close to mine, but they arise at a stage of analysis later than the development of the concept of intellectual virtue, which I believe is best examined first. When we get to the derivation of the concept of justified belief at the end of Part II, I will briefly return to their views in order to point out that there may be ways their theories and mine can be merged. These theories are important and subtle. I do not intend my lack of thorough investigation into their intricacies to indicate a lack of appreciation for the contribution they have made to epistemology. My aim is to develop an independent approach to epistemology that can be connected at critical points with other, more familiar approaches. I will have to leave to others the task of working out the details of such a connection.

I conclude that no epistemological theory is based on a carefully developed virtue theory. We have seen that several theories recognize, or at least come close to recognizing, the desirability of such a theory, but they do not consciously connect normative epistemological concepts with virtue ethics in any great detail. To make this connection, the concept of intellectual virtue should be analyzed sufficiently to show its status as a virtue and its relationship to moral virtue.

1.2 *Some advantages of virtue-based theories*

Until recently contemporary moral theories were almost exclusively act-based, with more and more subtle forms of consequentialism vying with more and more subtle deontological theories for the allegiance of philosophers. Lately there has been a resurgence of interest in virtue theories, as well as some strong and well-known attacks on contemporary act-based theories, although the latter are not always associated with the former.[5]

The mark of a virtue theory of morality is that the primary object of evaluation is persons or inner traits of persons rather than acts. To describe a good person is to describe that person's virtues, and it is maintained that a virtue is reducible neither to the performance of acts independently identified as right nor to a disposition to perform such acts.[6] There is both more and less to a moral virtue than a disposition to act in the right way. There is more because a virtue also includes being disposed to have characteristic emotions, desires, motives, and attitudes. There is less because a virtuous person does not invariably act in a way

---

[5] A good example of this is Susan Wolf's paper "Moral Saints" (1982). Wolf's provocative attack on both utilitarian and Kantian theories is not accompanied by a call to bring back classical Aristotelianism. In fact, she explicitly denies that our conception of the moral will permit this move.

[6] Gregory Trianosky (1987) makes a distinction, discussed below. What he calls primary and secondary actional virtues are conceptually or causally tied to right action respectively, but what he calls spiritual virtues are not so tied.

that can be fully captured by any set of independent normative criteria.[7] The common approach of act-based moral theories to begin the analysis with right and wrong acts and to subsequently define virtues and vices in terms of a conceptual or causal connection to such acts is insufficient to capture the nature of virtues and vices as they are understood by such theories.

Within this framework there are several varieties of virtue theories. Some theories do not define a virtue in terms of a right act, but neither do they define a right act in terms of virtues. They focus on the agent and her traits as a way of determining what is right but do not maintain that what is right is right because it is what a virtuous person would do; they say only that what a virtuous person would do is the best *criterion* for what is right. These theories are what Michael Slote calls agent-focused (1993 and forthcoming), and they are what I call weak virtue theories. By a pure virtue theory, in contrast, I mean a theory that treats act evaluation as derivative from the character of an agent. Roughly, an act is right *because* it is what a virtuous person might do. In such theories aretaic concepts are conceptually more fundamental than deontic concepts.

Since, as far as I know, no one has yet proposed an epistemological theory that is closely modeled on any form of virtue theory, it is worth investigating as many forms of the virtue approach as possible. Much of what follows will not require a position on the preferability of one form over another, and my hope is that most of what I do in this book will be agreeable to the adherents of most versions of virtue ethics and of interest to adherents of other types of ethical theory. When we get to the relation between virtues and acts/beliefs in Part II, I will propose a way to define the evaluative properties of both acts and beliefs in terms of moral and intellectual virtue, the approach of a pure virtue theory, and

---

[7] Some virtue ethicists go farther and claim that not only is it impossible to reduce a virtue to a disposition to act in a way that can be fully captured by some set of normative criteria, but a virtue is not reducible to a disposition to act in a way that can be captured by any set of *descriptive* criteria either. So a virtue is not an act disposition of any sort. Von Wright (1963) and Wallace (1978) take this position.

one of my aims is to show that even the strongest form of virtue ethics can be plausibly extended to handle epistemic evaluation.

Let us now consider several respects in which a virtue approach to ethics has been considered superior to an act-based approach. Each of these points has already been made in the literature and my present purpose is not to endorse them but to call attention to the fact that in each case a parallel point can be made about a virtue approach to epistemology. These points are not equally plausible, but they do show us how concerns in ethical theory have counterparts in normative epistemology.

Probably the first major attempt in recent philosophy to call attention to the advantages of focusing ethics on virtues rather than on acts was Elizabeth Anscombe's important paper "Modern Moral Philosophy," which appeared in 1958. There Anscombe argues that the principal notions of modern moral discourse – namely, *right, wrong, obligation,* and *moral duty* – lack content. On the other hand, concepts such as *just, chaste, courageous,* and *truthful* are conceptually rich. A similar point was made by Bernard Mayo in the same year (1958, p. 209). In addition, Anscombe argues, *obligation, right, wrong,* and *duty* are legal concepts that make no sense without a lawgiver and judge. Traditionally, such a legal authority was God, and it is no accident that these concepts entered Western philosophical discourse with the Judeo-Christian religion. Given the modern absence of an ethic grounded in theism, however, legalistic ethics is incoherent. It would be far better to return to an Aristotelian virtue ethics, which contains neither a blanket concept of wrong nor a concept of duty, Anscombe argues.

Moral philosophers have not generally accepted Anscombe's position that the concepts favored by legalistic, act-based ethics are incoherent or unnatural in the absence of a divine lawgiver, but it is not uncommon to accept her claim that virtue concepts have the advantage of greater richness; in fact, Bernard Williams's distinction between "thin" and "thick" moral concepts is now well known.[8] Williams's examples of thick ethical concepts in-

---

[8] Bernard Williams makes this distinction throughout *Ethics and the Limits of*

clude *courage, treachery, brutality,* and *gratitude.* Such concepts are amalgams of the normative and the descriptive. That is, they both imply a positive or negative moral judgment about that to which they apply and have sufficient descriptive content to permit ordinary users of these concepts to pick out typical instances in everyday life. Clearly, not only are virtue concepts "thick" in Williams's sense, but virtue concepts are among the paradigm examples.

A second and more compelling set of considerations favoring a virtue approach to ethics is that more and more philosophers are becoming convinced that morality is not strictly rule governed. The idea is that there can be no complete set of rules sufficient for giving a determinate answer to the question of what an agent should do in every situation of moral choice. With the exception of act utilitarianism, act-based theorists have been faced with the problem that more and more complex sets of rules seem to be necessary to capture the particularity of moral decision making. Philosophers such as Martha Nussbaum have argued for a more particularist approach, using literature as the basis for a model that does not begin with the rule or principle but with the insight into the particular case.[9] While particularists are not necessarily virtue theorists,[10] dissatisfaction with attempts to force the making of a moral judgment into a strictly rule-governed model is one of the motivations for contemporary virtue ethics.[11]

A third reason favoring a virtue approach to ethics is that it can explain better than act-based theories the specifically moral value of such personal goods as love and friendship.[12] There are cases in which acting out of a motive of love or friendship seems to be morally preferable to acting out of duty, and when a motive of

---

Philosophy (1985), and Allan Gibbard also uses this distinction in *Wise Choices, Apt Feelings* (1990).

[9] Martha Nussbaum takes this position in numerous places. See especially *Love's Knowledge* (1990).

[10] W. D. Ross is an example of a particularist, nonabsolutist, act-based theorist.

[11] Although the objection that morality is not strictly rule governed has been leveled against strict deontological theories, it has been argued that not even Kant thought that moral reasoning is algorithmic. See O'Neill 1989, esp. chap. 1.

[12] Examples would be Stocker 1976 and Blum 1980.

love and a motive of duty conflict, it is not obvious that the latter ought to override the former. Although it is not impossible for an act-based ethical theory to account for such intuitions,[13] it is much easier on a virtue approach since the perspective of the individual agent can easily be worked into the concept of a virtue, whereas the major act-based theories approach morality primarily from an impersonal standpoint and can accommodate the distinctive values of individual persons only with difficulty.

A fourth reason favoring the focus of moral theory on virtues rather than on acts and principles is that there are virtues that are not reducible to specifiable acts or act dispositions. Gregory Trianosky (1987) has argued that there are higher-order moral virtues that cannot be analyzed in terms of relations to acts. For example, it is a virtue to have well-ordered feelings. A person with such a virtue has positive higher-order feelings toward her own emotions. Similarly, it is a virtue to be morally integrated, to have a positive higher-order evaluation of one's own moral commitments. These are virtues that cannot be analyzed in terms of some relation to right action. Furthermore, although Trianosky does not say so explicitly, such higher-order virtues are connected to the virtue of integrity since integrity in one of its senses is the virtue of having a morally unified self, and it is difficult to see how such a virtue can be explicated in terms of dispositions to perform acts of a specified kind.[14]

The resurgence of interest in virtue ethics in recent philosophy is certainly not due solely to these four sets of considerations. Nonetheless, these reasons are important, have generated considerable discussion, and all have analogues in the evaluation of cognitive activity. In fact, as we shall see, some of them are even stronger in epistemic evaluation than in moral evaluation.

I have said that contemporary epistemology is belief-based, just as modern ethics is act-based. Epistemic states are evaluated in terms of properties of beliefs or belief dispositions, just as moral evaluations are typically given in terms of properties of acts

---

[13] Again, W. D. Ross comes to mind.

[14] I surmise that the difficulty of an act-based theory in accounting for integrity in this sense is one of the reasons integrity is rarely discussed.

or act dispositions. Beliefs that are evaluated positively are called justified, just as acts evaluated positively are called right. Some epistemologists make the act-based moral analogy more obvious by making epistemic duty the primary normative concept.

Now if Anscombe is right that legalistic moral language makes no sense without a divine lawgiver, such language in epistemology is even more peculiar. We can at least find practical reasons for continuing to judge acts and to render verdicts in the moral case, but it is hard to see the point of such a system in the evaluation of beliefs and cognitive activities. What purpose is served by putting Jones up before an epistemic tribunal for believing in UFOs? Is she to be declared epistemically guilty? What follows from *that*? This is not to deny that there is a point to the concept of epistemic duty, as we shall see at the end of Part II, and perhaps even of epistemic guilt. What is doubtful, however, is that these concepts are to be understood in the hard-hitting sense typically associated with legalistic language, with heavy social sanctions, punishments, and the like.

More convincing is Anscombe's point that the concepts of *right, wrong, obligation,* and *duty* lack content, as well as Williams's related point on the preferability of thick over thin moral concepts. In epistemic evaluation we also see this distinction between thick and thin concepts. The reaction of ordinary people to epistemic impropriety is not simply to say that a person's belief is unjustified but to direct evaluation toward the person himself and to call him "narrow-minded," "careless," "intellectually cowardly," "rash," "imperceptive," "prejudiced," "rigid," or "obtuse." People are accused of "jumping to conclusions," "ignoring relevant facts," "relying on untrustworthy authority," "lacking insight," being "unable to see the forest for the trees," and so on. Of course, the beliefs formed as the result of such defects are evaluated negatively, but any blanket term for this negative evaluation, such as "unjustified" or "irrational," fails to convey any other information than the negative evaluation alone and is therefore a thin concept in Williams's sense. Concepts such as the ones just named have a much richer content. They are not only normative terms, conveying a negative evaluation, but indicate the *way* in which the believer acted improperly. All of these terms are names for either intellectual vices or for categories of acts exhibiting intellectual vice.

The second set of reasons for preferring a virtue approach in ethics also applies to epistemology. There is no reason to think that being in an epistemically positive state is any more rule governed than being in a morally positive state. Several philosophers have called attention to this problem.[15] Insight, for example, is an intellectual virtue that is not rule governed but differs significantly in the form it takes from one person to another and from one area of knowledge to another. Insight is necessary for another virtue, trust, which has an intellectual as well as a moral form. There is no algorithm for determining trustworthiness, even in principle. Not only does one need insight into the character of others to have trust in its virtuous form, but trust also involves certain affective qualities, and it is hard to see how these could be described procedurally. In addition, such intellectual virtues as adaptability of intellect, the ability to recognize the salient facts, sensitivity to detail, the ability to think up explanations of complex sets of data, and the ability to think up illuminating scientific hypotheses or interpretations of literary texts, as well as such virtues as intellectual care, perseverance, and discretion, are not strictly rule governed. In each case, the virtue involves an aspect of knowing-how that is partially learned by imitation and practice. John Henry Newman has a number of examples that support this view. In one, he discusses a medieval historian who asserts that the *Aeneid* could not be a thirteenth-century forgery.[16] The historian's conviction is built upon a lifetime of study of the differences between the classical and medieval minds. "We do not pretend to be able to draw the line between what the medieval intellect could or could not do; but we feel sure that at least it could not write the classics. An instinctive sense of this, and a faith in testimony, are the sufficient, but the undeveloped argument on which to ground our certitude" (1979, p. 237).

---

[15] See, e.g., Tiles and Tiles 1993; Wisdo 1993; Montmarquet 1993; and Kvanvig 1992, p. 192.
[16] This case is also discussed in Wainwright 1996, chap. 3.

If those philosophers who advise a more particularist approach to moral evaluation are right, it is reasonable to think that the same point applies to epistemic evaluation. An interesting consequence is that the recent turn to literature for help in understanding the right way to act might also help us in understanding the right way to think and to form beliefs. Good fiction can give us a vivid picture of the inner life of its characters, and this includes the intricacies of their methods of inquiry and processes of belief formation. If we can obtain a better sense of the morality of acts from fictional portrayal, it is also likely that we can obtain a better sense of the goodness and badness of ways of thinking and believing from fictional portrayals as well.

The third advantage of aretaic ethics also has a parallel in epistemic evaluation. Contemporary epistemology focuses on epistemic values that are impersonal: the value of possessing truth and the value of rationality and justified belief. Truth, like utility, is a good that does not depend upon the point of view of any given individual, and rationality and justifiability are typically understood in a way that also is impersonal. But there is one personal epistemic value so important that it is the one from which philosophy gets its name, and that is wisdom. Wisdom is a value that is at least difficult, probably impossible, to understand impersonally on the model of rationality. It is likely that wisdom, like friendship, takes a different form in each individual case, and it resists any analysis that does not make essential reference to the standpoint of the individual. This feature of wisdom is reflected in the fact that human knowledge is usually thought to increase over the ages, but few people would observe the same progress in human wisdom. This is presumably because there is no stock of wisdom possessed by the species comparable to the stock of knowledge. Each person has to begin at the beginning in developing wisdom, and the experience needed for wisdom requires a certain amount of time, whereas growth in knowledge can be accelerated by proper teaching of the most advanced knowledge of an age. A related reason for the difference is that much knowledge is propositional and can be learned a bit at a time, whereas wisdom unifies the whole of human experience and understanding. The unifying feature of wisdom explains another distinctive mark of wisdom, namely, that it cannot be misused, whereas knowledge surely *can* be misused. Wisdom not only unifies the knowledge of the wise person but unifies her desires and values as well. There is nothing incoherent or even surprising about a knowledgeable person who is immoral, but it is at least surprising, perhaps incoherent, to say that a wise person is immoral.

These considerations may explain how the focus on belief in epistemological theories has led to a neglect of the importance and value of wisdom. The fact that there is no stock of wisdom distinct from its integration into the psyche of the wise person shows that wisdom cannot be analyzed as a function of individual propositions believed or individual states of believing, nor can a belief-based approach explain the connection between wisdom and moral goodness. The way in which wisdom is acquired makes it similar to the way in which friendships develop, suggesting that the individual perspective of the wise person is part of what makes it valuable. And even if the claim that perspective is essential to wisdom is not convincing, it cannot be denied that a virtue approach is preferable in an account of wisdom if wisdom itself is a virtue, as the tradition has thought it to be. And even if wisdom is not a virtue but an epistemic value of a different sort, surely wisdom is connected more closely to virtues than to justified or rational believing as the latter is handled in contemporary epistemology.

We may even hope that a virtue epistemology would be in a position to deal with the epistemic analogue of conflicts between impersonal and personal values. If it is an advantage of virtue ethics that it can explain better than act-based theories the proper moral relationship between the motive of duty and the motive of friendship, it ought also to be an advantage of a virtue epistemology to explain better than belief-based theories the proper relationship between the motive of rationality or justifiability, on the one hand, and the motive for wisdom and other personal epistemic values such as understanding and insight, on the other. Just as the motivation for impersonal moral values can conflict with personal values (e.g., duty can conflict with friendship), impersonal epistemic values can conflict with personal epistemic values. Perhaps a person facing a conflict between rejecting a claim on the basis of a counterexample and accepting it because of the understanding it provides may be in a quandary of this sort. On the face of it, this conflict can be construed as a conflict between the desire for the impersonal value of rationality and the desire for the personal value of understanding or an increase of wisdom. This is not to deny that the presence of a putative counterexample requires us to give further thought to a proposal, but it does indicate an advantage of a virtue theory since such a theory can give a place to both values, whereas it is difficult to see how a belief-based theory can even properly formulate the conflict between rational believing and understanding or wisdom.

Consider finally the epistemic analogue of the fourth objection to act-based theories. The type of higher-order moral virtue identified by Trianosky has a cognitive parallel. It is an intellectual virtue to be cognitively integrated, just as it is a moral virtue to be morally integrated. A person who is cognitively integrated has positive higher-order attitudes toward her own intellectual character and the quality of the beliefs and level of understanding that such a character produces. Good belief-based theorists such as William Alston have sometimes attempted to identify this desirable quality, but Alston's way of doing so is to say that not only is it epistemically valuable to *be* justified in one's beliefs, but it is epistemically valuable to be justified in believing one's beliefs are justified (1993, p. 529). Unfortunately, this way of approaching the virtue of cognitive integration is inadequate because the quality in question is not a property of a single belief, not even a belief about all of one's beliefs. To have a good intellectual character, it is not sufficient to simply pile up justified beliefs and judge that they are justified. A person who is cognitively integrated has epistemic values that determine such things as the proportion of one's time spent gathering evidence or considering arguments for and against an unpromising theory, as well as the epistemic worth of one belief over another and the way in which each belief fits into her overall belief structure and is conducive to understanding. Cognitive integration is partially constitutive of intellectual integrity, the virtue of having an intellect with an identity. I conclude that at least some intellectual virtues cannot be analyzed in terms of a relation to good (justified, warranted) beliefs. The virtue of intellectual integrity requires a virtue approach to at least some aspects of epistemic evaluation.

In addition to the objections to act-based theories in general, arguments against consequentialism have been given in the recent literature, some of which have analogues in problems with reliabilism and other externalist theories of knowledge or justification.[17] Consequentialism is an externalist moral theory. Whether or not the consequentialist identifies good with utility, good is seen as something that is *produced*. The moral value of an act is determined by something external to the act and external to the thoughts, feelings, and motives that produce the act. The way a person thinks or feels may have moral value, but it is only derivative – the value of a means to an end. Even when the consequentialist identifies good with a state of a person such as pleasure or knowledge, good is conceptually external to the nature of persons as such. Further, good is quantitatively measurable. It is, then, always at least conceptually possible, and often causally possible, that more good is produced when people act with no awareness of what they are doing or when they act from motives that are commonsensically vicious – motives such as vindictiveness, cruelty, or hatred. A world in which this is always the case is possible and it would be morally preferable to the one we have. The objection here is that there are goods such as love, friendship, and loyalty that are good in themselves, not only insofar as they produce a high level of good as identified from the external, impersonal viewpoint. In addition, some of these values are not quantifiable, nor is it most natural to treat them as the external products of acts that are right because of their production.

Reliabilism is structurally parallel to consequentialist ethics. According to reliabilism the epistemic goal is to form true beliefs and not to form false beliefs, just as on consequentialist theories the moral goal is to produce good states of affairs and not to produce evil states of affairs. And it has already been remarked

---

[17] We shall see in Part II that reliability is a component of intellectual virtue, so the differences between my theory and reliabilism are not as great as might be implied by the discussion of this section.

that like most consequentialist ethics, externalist epistemic theories are quantitative. Since truth is assumed to be a property of propositions, the objects of belief, the goal of gaining truth is increased with each succeeding true proposition believed. So just as the utilitarian aims to maximize the balance of pleasure over pain, the reliabilist aims to maximize the balance of true over false beliefs. The aim is to have as many true beliefs as possible while paying the price of as few false beliefs as can be managed. The human faculties, abilities, and feelings that lead a person to form true beliefs have epistemic value only insofar as they are means to such an end. There is nothing intrinsically epistemically valuable about human reason, memory, and the senses. It is conceptually and sometimes causally possible for people to gain more true beliefs without any cognitive effort or awareness of what they are doing, or when their beliefs are formed out of motives that are commonsensically vicious, such as a narrow-minded disregard for the views of others. A world in which this always happens would be an epistemically better world than the one we have. Furthermore, it has already been pointed out that truth is an impersonal value. We see, then, that each of the features of consequentialist ethics identified above has a parallel in reliabilist epistemology.

I wish to propose an objection to the reliabilist approach just described that parallels an objection sometimes made by virtue ethicists to utilitarianism. I will begin by considering two ways of being omniscient posed by Charles Taliaferro (1985) in a completely different context. Taliaferro compares two omniscient beings he calls Dennis and Christopher. Both Dennis and Christopher believe all and only true propositions, but Dennis believes them because he has learned them from Christopher, who we will suppose has "seen" the truths for himself or has learned them by his own power. Notice that from the reliabilist viewpoint the two omniscient believers are equal in knowledge. Both use perfectly reliable truth-producing mechanisms, and both end up with exactly the same set of beliefs. Dennis is an ideal cognizer as much as is Christopher, at least with respect to the goal of truth acquisition. But Taliaferro points out that Dennis is cognitively inferior to Christopher because of the way in which he gets his knowledge.

We might say that in this case what Dennis is like and what he does is only accidentally connected to his acquiring the truth, and his cognitive worth is the worth of the perfect computer. This problem is structurally similar to the problem of the ideal utilitarian moral agent, where the kind of person he is and even what he does is only accidentally related to the moral evaluation of his acts. Although Taliaferro is concerned in this example with the concepts of omniscience and cognitive perfection, his reason for claiming that standard accounts of omniscience are defective is just that knowledge implies cognitive power. Clearly, Christopher has more cognitive power than Dennis, and the analysis of knowledge, not just omniscience, should account for this.

If Taliaferro is right, his point should hold in the case of ordinary human knowledge as well, although that is not Taliaferro's interest in this article. Compare, then, the human counterparts of Dennis and Christopher. Let us suppose that they both believe a large set of true propositions T. Assume that the differences in their other beliefs are insignificant since they believe the same number of true propositions and the same number of false propositions, and there is no difference in the importance of their respective beliefs. The only epistemic difference between them is that Christopher believes the propositions in T by the direct use of his own perceptual and cognitive powers, whereas Dennis believes them on the authority of Christopher. Let us assume also that Christopher is a perfectly reliable authority, so that Dennis's belief-forming process is just as truth conducive as Christopher's. According to reliabilism, the normative property of the beliefs of Dennis is equal to that of Christopher. On the assumption that this property is also the property that converts true belief into knowledge, Dennis and Christopher are equal in their knowledge of T. But intuitively Christopher is superior in knowledge to Dennis because he possesses greater cognitive power. But since he does not know more true propositions than Dennis does, his superiority in knowledge must involve superior quality.

Christopher's superiority might be explicated by a more detailed description of the case. Perhaps his superiority is due to the greater clarity or understanding that accompanies the acquisition of true beliefs by the exercise of one's own powers, but it might also be that we attach greater value to Christopher's mode of acquiring the truth quite apart from the extra value of such things as clarity and understanding. One thing that is bothersome about reliabilism, like what is bothersome about consequentialism, is the fact that on these theories self-consciousness and the power of directing the activities of the self that self-consciousness allows are only incidentally related to the good under consideration. Just as a utility-calculating machine would be the ideal moral agent according to utilitarianism, a truth-producing machine would be the ideal epistemic agent according to reliabilism. The nature of the process leading to believing the truth and the extent of the agent's awareness of the process are only contingently related to the goal of knowledge, so something like the Oracle at Delphi (minus the riddles and with infallibility) would be epistemically ideal. Although I know of no actual argument against the acceptability of such a consequence, I find it unpalatable and imagine that others will too. It follows, then, that there are worries about reliabilism that parallel worries about utilitarianism. This gives us another reason to look for an alternative ethical model for epistemology.

I will conclude this section with one final advantage of a virtue theory that applies both to ethical and to epistemological evaluation. The basic evaluative concept in act-based ethics is that of the right act, where right means not wrong, or permissible. The focus of this type of ethics is on avoiding blameworthiness rather than on achieving moral praiseworthiness. Virtue ethics, in contrast, allows for a greater range of evaluative levels and gives due regard to the fact that our moral aim is not only to avoid the bottom level of the moral scale but to end up as high on the scale as possible. Similarly, the basic evaluative concept in belief-based epistemology is that of the justified belief, and again, to be justified is to do the minimum necessary to avoid the epistemic equivalent of blame; it is not to achieve a high level of epistemic worth. But presumably our epistemic aim is to reach as high a level of epistemic evaluation as we can. A virtue theory does justice to the full range of evaluative states, whereas an act-based ethics and a belief-based epistemology do not. The full exposition of this point must await an account of the way these concepts operate in each kind of theory, a matter that will be examined at the end of Part II, but we can say at least this much at this stage of the inquiry: It is an advantage in a theory if it can give a clear and unified account of the full range of human evaluative levels, both ethically and epistemically. The notions of virtue, vice, and their intermediate states are intended to apply to the full range of evaluative levels, whereas the concepts of right/wrong and justified/unjustified are not. We will need to see whether a virtue theory can live up to its promise of handling the full range of levels of evaluation after such a theory has been developed.

2 DIFFICULTIES IN CONTEMPORARY EPISTEMOLOGY

In section 1 we looked at reasons for using a virtue theory in the evaluation of epistemic states that arise within ethics. In this section we will look at reasons for preferring a virtue approach that arise within epistemology. I will investigate the current problems in resolving the nature of justification, as well as the complaints that contemporary epistemology is too atomistic and that the value of understanding has been neglected. I will argue that these problems should lead us to investigate a virtue theory of normative epistemology.

2.1 *Problems in the notion of justification*

One of the most intractable problems in contemporary epistemology is the dispute between internalists and externalists. This problem has now become the focus of the analysis of both the concept of knowledge and the concept of justification. The latter concept in particular seems to be in a conceptual muddle, and it is here that we will begin looking at the problems in contemporary epistemic theory.

Justification has been for some time a key concept in the Anglo-American epistemological literature. It fact, it has received more analytical attention than knowledge itself. This is partly due to the fact that it is commonly held that knowledge is justified true belief (JTB), and since the concept of true belief was thought to be relatively clear until recently, attention turned to an account of justification. Of course, ever since Gettier's famous paper over thirty years ago, there have been misgivings about this project, but much of the motivation for the research involving Gettier cases has been the conviction that there is (or ought to be) an important connection between justification and knowledge. So many philosophers have thought that the JTB account of knowledge is more or less correct that it is virtually impossible to list its adherents. In fact, Roderick Chisholm (1989, p. 90) says its popularity extends far beyond the present, calling JTB "the traditional definition of knowledge," existing as far back as Plato's *Theaetetus*. An early-twentieth-century example of the same analysis can be found in C. I. Lewis, who says, "Knowledge is belief which is not only true but also is justified in its believing attitude" (1946, p. 9).

A second motivation for making justification central in epistemology is virtually the opposite of the first. Some epistemologists have thought it necessary to separate the concept of knowledge from an egocentric concept identified by Richard Foley (1993) with rationality and have focused their attention on the latter. Justification in at least one of its senses is an egocentric concept, associated more with rationality than with knowledge. So even when knowledge is removed from the center of discourse in epistemology, justification does not necessarily go with it. In short, the concept of justification is a highly important one in contemporary epistemology, and its importance is not limited to a narrow range of theories.

It is gradually becoming apparent, however, that there are so many notions of justification in the literature that it is difficult to identify a single target of dispute. Sometimes "justification" is used to name attributively whatever it is that, added to true belief, equals knowledge, but often it is connected with substantive notions such as basing beliefs on evidence or doing one's epistemic duty (Feldman and Conee 1985, p. 15; Firth 1978, p. 219), or being epistemically responsible (Kornblith 1983; BonJour 1985, p. 8), or doing any number of other things that are good or right from the believer's perspective or from the perspective of a rational person in the believer's circumstances.

30

Noting this plethora of views, both William Alston and Alvin Plantinga have recently argued that there is mischief in the idea of justification, and we will turn to their arguments next.[18] The problem as they see it is not simply that more than one concept has been analyzed under the name "justification," although that would be bad enough. More serious is the fact that conceptual confusion over justification has led to the present impasse between internalists and externalists. Internalists claim, roughly, that the believer must have cognitive access to the justifying condition of a belief, and externalists deny this. Although both sides have heaps of supporting arguments, it is remarkably difficult to resolve the differences between them. The heart of the problem is that the two approaches are working with different kinds of valuation. If Alston and Plantinga are right, it is impossible with the present confusion in the concept of justification to resolve these differences. We will turn first to Plantinga's argument since he believes the internalism/externalism dispute can be resolved by splitting the concept of justification. I will argue that this move will not work because the disagreement on the normative dimension of knowledge that has led to the internalism/externalism controversy is deeper than Plantinga recognizes.

Plantinga claims that (1) "the traditional view," originating with Locke and Descartes, identifies justification with both the component of knowledge in addition to true belief and the idea of doing one's epistemic duty, (2) the traditional view is an incoherent equivocation and is to blame for the impasse between internalism and externalism, and (3) the remedy is to separate the two concepts. Justification is connected with the idea of doing one's duty, which is the source of the attraction to internalism. Warrant is the element that converts true belief into knowledge and should be analyzed in an externalist fashion with a different type of normative dimension. Justification is neither necessary nor sufficient for warrant and it is a mistake to connect the two.

---

[18] See Plantinga 1990; Alston 1993. Large portions of Plantinga's 1990 paper now appear in the first chapter of his book *Warrant: The Current Debate*. In the book Plantinga stresses the deontological associations with the idea of justification and drops the claim made in the paper that the idea of justification is ambiguous.

The concept of knowledge is well rid of deontological associations.

Plantinga's point is both historical and conceptual and I will address both points. I will argue that although Plantinga appreciates the fact that the pretheoretical notion of knowledge includes a normative aspect, he is too quick to identify moral concepts with deontological ones, and he does not recognize the fact that internalism has a broader association with valuation than with deontology, both conceptually and historically. This leads Plantinga to underestimate the hold of internalism on accounts of knowledge.

It is clear from Plantinga's recent work that he identifies moral concepts with deontological ones, a view that is so common as to seem obvious to many post-Kantians. He says straightforwardly, "Most of us will agree that a person is guilty, properly blamed, properly subject to censure and moral disapproval, if and only if she fails to do her duty" (1990, p. 52).[19] But many philosophers past and present would deny that morality is coextensive with the realm of duty, not the least of whom is Aristotle. Nonetheless, Plantinga goes on to use the claim just quoted to attack internalism via an attack on the idea that knowledge is true belief that is dutiful or within one's epistemic rights or conforming to one's intellectual obligations. But as we shall see next, internalism is associated with moral concepts generally, not just with deontological notions. If so, Plantinga cannot refute internalism by arguing that the normative aspect of knowledge is not like the deontological. Instead, he must show that it is not like the moral.

Suppose that we were to take seriously the idea of investigating the normative component in knowledge on the analogy with moral virtue as proposed in section 1. Aristotle says we can be praised and blamed for our moral virtues and vices and for the voluntary actions that issue from these qualities (*NE* III.1.1109b30–1). We do not need to go into the intricacies of Aristotle's notion of the voluntary to understand his confidence that this area of our lives is one for which we are responsible. But one cannot be blamed for something that is inaccessible to one's con-

---

[19] The same sentence appears in Plantinga 1993a, p. 15.

sciousness and is not at least under one's indirect control. This internal accessibility need not be present at every moment at which a person is blameworthy, however, since Aristotle claims that the truly wicked person not only is no longer in control of his own nature but may no longer be even aware of his wickedness (*NE* VII.8.1150b30–6). Both consciousness and control were present at earlier stages of his decline, however. Aristotle's theory, then, contains an internalist aspect, and this is true in spite of the fact that notions of duty, obligation, or rights do not arise at all in his account. If, then, the normative element in knowledge were like Aristotelian moral virtue, there would be an internalist constraint on the account of knowledge that is not associated with deontology. Since Plantinga gives no arguments at all for the claim that internalism is associated only with deontology, he must be mistaken in the implied answer to his question, "Once one gives up the deontology, however, what is the reason or motivation for retaining the internalism?" (1990, p. 67).

Plantinga's point, however, is historical as well as conceptual. He claims that the source of internalist theories of knowledge is the deontology of Descartes and Locke. So even if he is wrong that deontology is the only imaginable source of internalism, he could still be right that deontology is what has in fact attracted epistemologists to internalism. However, Plantinga's discussion misconstrues both Descartes and Locke.

First, consider his quotation from Locke:

> Faith is nothing but a firm assent of the mind: which if it be regulated, as is our duty, cannot be afforded to anything, but upon good reason; and so cannot be opposite to it. He that believes, without having any reason for believing, may be in love with his own fancies; but neither seeks truth as he ought, nor pays the obedience due his maker, who would have him use those discerning faculties he has given him, to keep him out of mistake and error. He that does not this to the best of his power, however he sometimes lights on truth, is in the right but by chance; and I know not whether the luckiness of the accident will excuse the irregularity of his proceeding. This, at least is certain, that he must be accountable for whatever mistakes he

runs into: whereas he that makes use of the light and faculties God has given him, and seeks sincerely to discover truth, by those helps and abilities he has, may have this satisfaction in doing his duty as a rational creature, that though he should miss truth, he will not miss the reward of it. For he governs his assent right, and places it as he should, who in any case or matter whatsoever, believes or disbelieves, according as reason directs him. He that does otherwise, transgresses against his own light, and misuses those faculties, which were given him.[20]

In this passage Locke does indeed make much of the idea of epistemic duty, but as Plantinga himself points out, Locke is not here talking about knowledge at all but only about belief. But since Locke thought knowledge and belief to be mutually exclusive states,[21] there should be no temptation to think that Locke identified the normative element in *knowledge* with duty. Instead, knowledge is defined by Locke as "the perception of the connection and agreement, or disagreement and repugnancy, of any of our ideas" (*Essay concerning Human Understanding*, ed. Nidditch, IV.1.2). The perception of agreement or disagreement is an act of judgment to Locke, so where there is knowledge there is judgment. What is important for the present discussion is that in making such a judgment the mind perceives its own act. The primary condition for knowledge, then, is something internal to the mind and accessible to it. This is an internalist theory if anything is, yet there is no question of following duty, doing what is permitted, etc. No deontological concept applies.

Let us now look at Descartes, the other source of the deontological tradition according to Plantinga. The quotation Plantinga uses is from Descartes's discussion of the origin of error in *Meditation IV*:

---

[20] Plantinga 1990, p. 51. Quoted from Locke's *Essay concerning Human Understanding* IV. 17.24.

[21] In "Justification in the Twentieth Century" (1990) Plantinga does not even mention that Locke thought knowledge and belief are mutually exclusive states, but he remedies the error in 1993a, p. 14, where he presents an argument that is otherwise the same.

But if I abstain from giving my judgment on any thing when I do not perceive it with sufficient clearness and distinctness, it is plain that I act rightly. . . . But if I determine to deny or affirm, I no longer make use as I should of my free will, and if I affirm what is not true, it is evident that I deceive myself; even though I judge according to truth, this comes about only by chance, and I do not escape the blame of misusing my freedom; for the light of nature teaches us that the knowledge of the understanding should always precede the determination of the will. It is in the misuse of the free will that the privation which constitutes the characteristic nature of error is met with.[22]

Notice that in this passage Descartes does not even mention duties or rights, although he does use a lot of moral terminology, including "should," "act rightly," and "escape blame." But again, such terminology can be found in Plato and Aristotle, neither of whom connected these concepts with a concept of duty. Furthermore, Descartes himself never speaks of duty, obligation, or epistemic rights anywhere else in *Meditation IV*. But then if Descartes was not thinking in terms of duties, the passage quoted by Plantinga merely calls attention to a moral component in knowledge or belief, rather than a deontological one, and, as we have seen, that is quite a different matter. So while Locke associates deontological concepts with believing, he does not do so with knowing, and while Descartes associates moral concepts with knowing, they are not specifically deontological. The connection between knowledge and internalism, then, cannot be due to an association of knowledge with deontology in Locke and Descartes.

The sources of the attraction to internalism are more ancient than Descartes and Locke anyway. As we have already seen, it has been claimed by Roderick Chisholm and others that the origin of the idea that justification is an ingredient in knowledge can be found in Plato (*Theaetetus* 201c–210b), who proposed, and then rejected, the suggestion that knowledge is true belief plus an account or explanation (*logos*). M. F. Burnyeat (1980b) and Gail Fine (1990, p. 107) have disputed the identification of Plato's no-

---

[22] Quoted from *Philosophical Works of Descartes*, trans. Haldane and Ross, p. 50.

tion of *logos* with justification. In any case, the notion of *logos* is normative and is quite obviously internalist, although it is certainly not deontological. It is true that internalism in contemporary epistemology has been strongly influenced by the important work of Chisholm, the preeminent epistemological deontologist. Still, it is very unlikely that Chisholm bears the principal responsibility for the hold that internalism has had in epistemology, even for recent writers.

Plantinga's solution is to use the term "warrant" for the normative element in knowledge, for which he gives an externalist account, and he reserves "justification" for an internalist normative aspect of beliefs that is independent of knowledge and presumably not as important.[23] I have one major misgiving about this approach apart from the considerations I have already given on the desirability of using a virtue approach to epistemology. Although the concept of justification is in a conceptual muddle, it at least has a history of usage in philosophical discourse, whereas the concept of warrant has virtually no history at all. It is not clear to me that much is gained by removing the muddled concept of justification from center stage in epistemology and letting another term fill one of the roles of "justification," one not previously in common usage.

It may be argued that Plantinga's target in this paper is *pure* internalism, and Aristotelian virtue theory is not purely internalist. But if this is Plantinga's intent, there would be no reason for him to conclude from an argument rejecting pure internalism that pure externalism ought to be accepted. So either he intends to attack weaker forms of internalism in his argument connecting internalism with deontology, in which case the argument fails at the step at which he makes the connection, or he intends to attack only pure internalism, in which case he has given no reason to reject theories that have stronger internalist elements than his own.[24]

---

[23] The evidence that justification is not as important as warrant for Plantinga is simply that he has written two volumes on warrant and is now writing a third, whereas he discusses justification mostly in the context of anticipated objections to his own theory.

[24] I thank John Greco for getting me to see the point of this paragraph.

In short, I believe Plantinga is right that the tradition assigns an internalist element to knowledge, but he is mistaken in thinking that the attraction to internalism is due solely to the association of deontological concepts with knowledge. He is right again that the concept of justification is in a muddle and that there appears to be an impasse between internalists and externalists, but he exaggerates the ease with which internalist intuitions can be removed from the concept of knowledge and assigned to a distinct territory of justification. Finally, the use of the new term "warrant" for the normative element of knowledge may not be illuminating if it simply replaces one of the previous senses of the word "justification."

Let us now look briefly at the problem as seen by William Alston in "Epistemic Desiderata" (1993). Alston goes farther than Plantinga. He identifies six candidates for necessary conditions for justification, all of which can be found in the contemporary literature, and he concludes that there is no uniquely identifiable concept about which competing accounts differ. The problem as Alston sees it cannot simply be solved by settling on one candidate and eliminating the rest.

The six candidates are as follows: (1) A justified belief must be *based on* an adequate ground. (2) What justifies a belief must *probabilize* it. (3) A justifier must be cognitively accessible to the subject. (4) A justified belief must satisfy certain higher-level conditions, in particular, not only must a justified belief be held only in circumstances in which it is permitted, but the believer must hold the belief in the knowledge (or justified belief) that it is permitted. (5) A justified belief must fit into a coherent total system of beliefs. (6) The believer must satisfy intellectual obligations in forming and maintaining the belief.

Like Plantinga, Alston focuses on the apparent irresolvability of the dispute between internalists and externalists over these conditions, and he proposes that they are working with different concepts, different selections of epistemic desiderata, not just different views on the proper application of a common concept (see esp. 1993, pp. 532–4). If Alston is right, there simply is not enough of a pretheoretical notion of justification to give us any confidence that all these accounts are aiming to elucidate the same concept. Alston goes on to suggest that perhaps the most honest course would be to abandon the concept of justification altogether, although he says he doubts that this is feasible (p. 533).

In this paper Alston makes a strong case for the claim that justification cannot bear all the conceptual weight that has been assigned to it, even if it is not a component of knowledge. But my interest here is not in whether the concept of justification can survive Alston's attack; the point is that the concept is in trouble. Unlike the concept of knowledge, the concept of justification is somewhat artificial and it is questionable how far we can get if we look for a pretheoretical notion of justification as a starting point for analysis. My response to this situation is to start elsewhere. We already have a number of motivations for using a virtue approach to epistemology, and the confusion in the notion of justification gives us one more. Since justifiedness is a property of a belief, we might bypass the problems in analyzing it if we can succeed in focusing on the deeper concept of an intellectual virtue and showing how justification is best treated as a derivative concept. I will show how the justifiedness of a belief can be defined in terms of intellectual virtue in the same way the rightness of an act can be defined in terms of moral virtue in Part II.

One of the implications of Alston's concerns about the confusion over the notion of justification is that it may be impossible to resolve the dispute between internalists and externalists on justification because there is no common target of debate. And, of course, we could raise the same doubts about knowledge since there is also an internalism/externalism dispute about knowledge. Is there a single notion of knowledge about which competing accounts differ? Alston thinks that there is,[25] and I am inclined to agree with him. But we still need some way of resolving the internalism/externalism controversy. It is interesting that David Brink (1989) maintains that there are two senses of knowl-

[25] Alston says (1993, n. 15) that he thinks there is more commonality in the notion of knowledge than in the notion of justification.

edge, one internalist, one externalist. So not everybody thinks that the controversy *can* be resolved in a way that retains a unitary concept of knowledge. We should, then, look at the way this controversy dominates epistemology to see if there might not be an advantage in a different approach.

The dispute between externalists and internalists looms large mostly because of ambivalence over the place of luck in normative theory. Theorists who resist the idea that knowledge or justification is vulnerable to luck are pulled in the direction of internalism, and their account is egocentric. Externalists are more sanguine about luck. Ironically, one of the attractions of externalism is that it is supposed to be antiskeptical and thus bypasses the threat of the worst sort of epistemic luck. That is, it is not necessary to have an answer to the skeptical hypotheses in order to have knowledge on these theories. But, of course, there is lots of room for luck in externalist theories since the conditions that make it the case that the knower is in a state of knowledge are independent of her conscious access. So the idea seems to be that luck can work *for* us as well as against us, and under ordinary circumstances, we can assume that it works for us. Thus, externalism is attractive.

Internalists and externalists in epistemology selectively borrow lines of argument in ethics to bolster their respective positions, an observation we have already noted in a comment by Jonathan Dancy (Dancy and Sosa 1992, p. 119). Externalists attach themselves to the view that ignores the agent's motives and even intentions in discussing the rightness of acts, whereas internalists connect their arguments with the tradition in ethics that makes the agent central to moral evaluation. Dancy objects that epistemologists are prematurely siding with views that are very contentious in ethics, and he is right that epistemologists should not ignore the deep divisions in ethical traditions that stress one form of ethical evaluation over another. But it is interesting to consider the fact that the ethical analogue of the internalism/externalism dispute in epistemology does not seem to assume the level of importance that it has in epistemology. In fact, what is called internalism and externalism in ethics is a rather different dispute.[26] This is not to say that ethicists have not thought of the exact analogue of the distinction in epistemology; they just have not been as much taken by it as have epistemologists.

To see this, consider a brief but interesting argument given by Hilary Kornblith to the effect that the same distinction is made in ethics:

> One kind of moral evaluation has us ask, "Was the agent's action one which the correct moral theory would have him perform?" A second kind of moral evaluation has us ask, "Was the agent's action one which was morally correct by his own lights?" In the moral realm, we overlook an important kind of evaluation if we fail to ask either of these questions. If we ask only the former question, then we have no idea whether the action manifested moral integrity. If we ask only the latter question, we have no idea whether the agent acted in a morally acceptable manner. By the same token, if we ask only whether an agent's beliefs are formed in a reliable manner, we have no idea whether the belief is appropriately integrated in the agent's cognitive scheme. If we ask only whether the agent's belief is arrived at in a way which seems right to him, we have no idea whether the belief is formed in a way which is actually conducive to the agent's epistemic goals. (1985, p. 269)

To my mind what is most striking about Kornblith's argument in this passage is the fact that ethicists generally do *not* separate the two kinds of evaluation in the way he describes. And to the extent that they do, they do not see themselves as representing

[26] The positions in ethics that are called internalist and externalist have to do with the connection between motives and justifications for action. Robertson and Stocker (1991) identify at least three positions concerning the relation between moral justification and motivation that have been characterized by the terms "externalism" and "internalism." Whereas externalism in ethics would be recognizably externalist on the epistemological use of the term "externalist," the internalist positions are more narrowly internalist than is internalism in epistemology. I do not see that these various disputes have been sorted out well enough in ethics to be of use to the internalism/externalism dispute as it is carried on in epistemology. It is even possible that this is one matter in which the epistemologists are ahead of ethicists in clarifying a normative dispute.

opposing sides of a dispute on the grounds for moral evaluation. The arguments on the internalist side of the epistemological dispute are selectively borrowed from moral arguments, yet a moral philosopher would not give the parallel argument. Consider, for example, an argument for internalism offered by Carl Ginet:

> Assuming that S has the concept of justification for being confident that p, S *ought* always to possess or lack confidence that p according to whether or not he has such justification. At least he ought always to withhold confidence unless he has justification. This is simply what is meant by having or lacking *justification*. But if this is what S ought to do in any possible circumstance, then it is what S *can* do in any possible circumstance. That is, assuming that he has the relevant concepts, S can always tell whether or not he has justification for being confident that p. But this would not be so unless the difference between having such justification and not having it were always directly recognizable to S. And that would not be so if any fact contributing to a set that minimally constitutes S's having such justification were not either directly recognizable to S or entailed by something directly recognizable to S (so that its absence would have to make a directly recognizable difference). (1975, p. 36)

Ginet's argument utilizes the well-known ethical dictum "'ought' implies 'can.'" But beyond that, the argument would be very peculiar if used by a moral philosopher in analyzing the concept of a right act rather than a justified belief. The parallel argument would run something like the following:

> Assuming that S has the concept of rightness in doing A, S *ought* always to do A according to whether or not A is right (not wrong). But if this is what S ought to do in any possible circumstance, then it is what S *can* do in any possible circumstance. That is, assuming that he has the relevant concepts, S can always tell whether or not it is right to do A. But this would not be so unless the difference between being right and not being right were always directly recognizable to S. And that would

41

not be so if any fact contributing to a set that minimally constitutes S's being right were not either directly recognizable to S
or entailed by something directly recognizable to **S** (so that its
absence would have to make a recognizable difference).

A number of features of this argument make it odd enough that
we would never expect it to be offered by a moral philosopher,
but one of the most striking is that moral requirements are almost
always assumed to be as accessible to all normal moral agents as
they need be to have moral force. Moral philosophers would not
give an argument that rightness must be recognizable to the
agent, not because they typically *deny* that rightness need be recognizable, but because it is taken for granted that it *is* recognizable. So if S is incapable of recognizing the rightness of A, that fact
demands explanation. That explanation *might* excuse S, but again,
it might not. Only certain kinds of ignorance are acceptable ex-
cuses; ignorance of the moral law is not one of them. In any case, it
would be unusual for an ethicist to argue that rightness must
always be *directly* recognizable to the agent.

Ethicists are generally very hesitant to relativize moral rightness to the perspective of the agent, and yet that is what epistemological internalists are concerned to do with the concept of epistemic justification. When Laurence BonJour argues against
externalism, he says:

> One reason why externalism may seem initially plausible is
> that if the external relation in question genuinely obtains, then
> Norman will in fact not go wrong in accepting the belief, and it
> is, *in a sense*, not an accident that this is so. But how is this
> supposed to justify Norman's belief? From his subjective per-
> spective, it *is* an accident that the belief is true. (1980, p. 63)

Notice that BonJour refers to Norman's "subjective perspective"
as that which is the primary locus of evaluation, a position that
few moral philosophers would take.

The moral analogue of epistemological externalism is more
common. We have already seen that the externalist theory of
reliabilism is structurally identical to consequentialism. What
consequentialists would not do, however, is to offer their theory

as the contender to the internalist view that moral rightness must be accessible to the consciousness of the agent. On the contrary, to the extent that the consequences of an act are not accessible to the consciousness of the agent, that is considered a *problem* for consequentialism, perhaps an answerable one, but never a feature that would be touted as reason to think that there is something *wrong* with the view that moral rightness must be recognizable to human agents.

It seems to me, then, that before taking sides on the internalism/externalism dispute in epistemology, we ought to reexamine some of the assumptions that have led to the split in the first place. The fact that theoretical ethics proceeds for the most part without forcing such a split is some reason to think that it might be possible to do the same thing in epistemology. We will not be able to determine whether or not this can be done, however, without going back to foundational moral concepts. If we leave the concept of justification aside for the time being and start with the analysis of virtues and vices, we may find that an account of justification falls out naturally. After that account has been given, I will have more to say about the internalism/externalism dispute.

2.2 *The neglect of understanding and wisdom*

Lately, contemporary epistemology has been criticized on a number of other grounds that would make a virtue approach promising. I will not go through these in any great detail but will merely call attention to them. For one thing, some philosophers have complained that contemporary epistemology is insufficiently attentive to the social aspects of cognitive activity, and this complaint is not limited to those outside mainstream epistemology, because Sosa and Goldman have made much the same point. It seems to me, though, that other things being equal, the social component in cognitive activity is handled more easily by the traditional concept of virtue than by either the concept of a reliable belief-forming mechanism (Goldman) or that of a reliable belief-forming faculty (Sosa). Mechanisms and faculties can be contextualized into a social framework only with quite a bit of

43

artificiality, whereas a social context is intrinsic to the nature of a virtue as traditionally understood. On such accounts most virtues are traits that enable individuals to live well in communities. This is the position of Alasdair MacIntyre and is arguably the view of Aristotle. In addition, the way Aristotle understands the acquisition of virtue is fundamentally social since virtue is acquired primarily through imitation of those in one's society who already have it. Of course, this is no demonstration that the degree and kind of sociality to be found in the traditional concept of a virtue are sufficient to give epistemologists what is wanted in the social aspects of belief, but I suggest that at least some of the work of making the normative property of epistemic states more social is already done for us in the historical use of the concept of a virtue.

Jonathan Kvanvig's critique of recent epistemology is broader in its attack. Kvanvig objects both to the widespread focus on a single belief of a single person at a single time and also to the fact that the object of a belief is presumed to be a discrete proposition. Kvanvig calls this "the Cartesian perspective" and urges that it be abandoned. If a belief cannot be separated from other beliefs of the same person or from beliefs of other persons, then it is a mistake to attempt to evaluate beliefs singly, and this makes the belief-based approach to epistemology less attractive. In addition, Kvanvig argues, there are problems with the view that the objects of belief are discrete propositions having an isomorphic relation to sentences (1992, pp. 181–2). Since the present work is principally concerned with the normative aspects of epistemic states, the problem of the existence and nature of propositions and their individuation is too large a topic to be pursued here. However, I think it is worth mentioning that it may turn out that questions about the nature of the objects of knowledge can affect the way we approach the normative inquiry. Certainly, when we believe the truth, there is some sort of match between our mental state and reality, but it may not be necessary to think of the truth as itself dividing into countably many *truths,* and if so, the investigation into the way in which we *ought* to go about forming beliefs will not necessarily involve a search for an evaluatively positive connection between the believer's state and a discrete object. A virtue approach does not require any assumptions about the objects of knowledge and belief, whereas a belief-based approach usually operates under the assumption that beliefs are individuated in part by propositional objects. This may be another advantage of a virtue approach.

The emphasis on the proposition as the primary object of knowledge/belief is connected with other limitations of contemporary epistemology. Consider a famous quotation from Isaiah Berlin (1978) on the difference between what we might call "big" and "little" knowledge.

> There is a line among the fragments of the Greek poet Archilochus which says: "The fox knows many things, but the hedgehog knows one big thing." Scholars have differed about the correct interpretation of these dark words, which may mean no more than that the fox, for all his cunning, is defeated by the hedgehog's one defence. But, taken figuratively, the words can be made to yield a sense in which they mark one of the deepest differences which divide writers and thinkers, and, it may be, human beings in general. (p. 22)

The thrust of most contemporary epistemology is to make us like the fox. If the object of knowledge is a proposition, the person who is greatest in knowledge is the one who has amassed in his mind the highest number of true propositions that pass whatever test for warrant the theory has proposed. Of course, most epistemologists will remark in passing that some propositions are worth knowing more than others, but this is still compatible with the atomistic approach, the desire to be like the fox. There is a difference between the indisputable claim that knowledge puts the knower in cognitive contact with reality and the disputable claim that the object of knowledge is a true proposition. The former is compatible with being Isaiah Berlin's hedgehog, but the latter is not. If there is any doubt about this, consider two epistemic values that involve cognitive contact with reality and that do not aim to link the mind with a true proposition. These values are understanding and wisdom.

In post-Aristotelian ancient philosophy and throughout most of the modern age, certainty has been given more attention than understanding, whereas in Plato's and Aristotle's concept of *episteme,* in the philosophies they influenced in the Middle Ages, and in such modern philosophers as Spinoza and Locke, it was the reverse.[27] I will not present extensive evidence for the neglect of understanding in contemporary philosophy since I trust that this claim is not likely to be denied. Few contemporary epistemologists mention understanding except in passing, and even when it *is* mentioned, it is usually identified with that minimal grasp of the sense of a proposition necessary for believing it. Understanding in this sense is clearly not the major problem in attaining knowledge and so it gets little attention. An indication of the neglect of understanding is the fact that there usually is no listing for "understanding" in the indexes of major books in epistemology. The Macmillan *Encyclopedia of Philosophy* (1967) has no entry on understanding, nor is there one in the much more recent Blackwell reference book, *A Companion to Epistemology* (1992).

Generally the only philosophers who have anything to say about understanding are the historians of Greek philosophy. Julius Moravcsik (1979) tells us that the central epistemological aim of the Greek thinkers was to give an account of what it means to understand something (p. 53). Propositional knowledge was of secondary interest, he says. In one of his examples, Moravcsik considers the understanding of a proof, a case that vividly illustrates the difference between an epistemology focused on understanding and the contemporary approach:

[27] The concept of understanding was of central importance to Spinoza and Locke. Take, first, Spinoza: "Prop. XXVI. Whatsoever we endeavor in obedience to reason is nothing further than to understand; neither does the mind, in so far as it makes use of reason, judge anything to be useful to it, save such things as are conducive to understanding" (*Ethics;* trans. Elwes). Now consider John Locke, from "Epistle to the Reader," opening of the *Essay:* "He that hawks at larks and sparrows has no less sport, though a much less considerable quarry, than he that flies at nobler game: and he is little acquainted with the subject of this treatise – the UNDERSTANDING – who does not know that, as it is the most elevated faculty of the soul, so it is employed with a greater and more constant delight than any of the other. Its searches after truth are a sort of hawking and hunting, wherein the very pursuit makes a great part of the pleasure. Every step the mind takes in its progress towards Knowledge makes some discovery, which is not only new, but the best too, for the time at least."

What is it to understand a proof? It cannot be merely being able to reproduce it, or to know what it is, or to know lots of truths about it. One can conjure up possible cases in which someone can do all of the above and still not understand the proof. What elevates the above to understanding is the possessing of the right concepts, and the intuitive insight of the connection that makes the parts of the proof to be the proper parts of a sequence.

The same goes for explanations. It is not enough to know facts and generalizations concerning a certain subject; e.g. the respiratory system. It takes a certain insight to see why some accounts constitute adequate *explanations,* while others, though equally general, abstract, etc. do not. (P. 55)

Moravcsik goes on to say that in Plato propositional knowledge not only is secondary to the process of understanding but is derivative from it:

The only propositional knowledge that will be of interest will be that which is derived from the kind of theoretical understanding that Plato envisages. Mere knowledge of truths is of no interest to Plato; propositional knowledge figures in the dialogues only insofar as this may be, in some contexts, evidence for understanding, and needed for practical activity. (P. 60)

Moravcsik speculates that the increasing complexity of modern theories in both the social and the physical sciences has created a need to recapture the concept of understanding in epistemology.

In a more recent paper on Plato's epistemology, Gail Fine also argues that an account of knowledge (*episteme*) focused on understanding leads to a less atomistic approach, and that this ought to be of interest to contemporary epistemologists. Fine translates Plato's word "*episteme*" as "knowledge," but in a sense that includes understanding. In contrast, some commentators on Plato have inferred from the fact that *episteme* involves understanding that "*episteme*" should not be translated as "knowledge." Fine defends the position that Plato's account of *episteme is* an account of knowledge while at the same time connecting Plato's position with the recent turn away from justification:

> It is sometimes argued that if this is so, we ought not to say that Plato is discussing knowledge at all; rather, he is discussing the distinct phenomenon of understanding. For, it is said, understanding, but not knowledge, requires explanation and interrelated accounts; and knowledge, but not understanding, requires certainty, and allows one to know propositions individually, not only collectively. A more moderate version of this general sort of view claims that Plato is discussing knowledge – but an older concept of knowledge, according to which knowledge consists in or requires understanding, in contrast to "knowledge as knowledge is nowadays discussed in philosophy" [Burnyeat and Barnes 1980, p. 188].
>
> Now I agreed before that for Plato, knowledge typically requires explanation; but I argued too that this is only to say that for him, justification typically requires explanation. Similarly, I agree that, for Plato, knowledge does not require any sort of vision or certainty, but does require interrelating the elements of a field or discipline or . . . interrelating the elements of different disciplines in the light of the Form of the good. But, once again, I do not think this shows that he is uninterested in knowledge. We can say, if we like, that he believes knowledge consists in or requires understanding. But I would then want to add that this is not so different from "knowledge as knowledge is nowadays discussed in philosophy." To be sure, some contemporary epistemologists focus on conditions for knowing that a particular proposition is true, or believe that knowledge requires certainty, or that justification does not consist in or require explanation. But that is hardly characteristic of all contemporary epistemology. Indeed, concern with certainty is rather in disfavour these days; and many contemporary epistemologists defend holistic conceptions of knowledge, an appeal to explanatory connections to explicate the sort of coherence a justified set of beliefs must exhibit. Plato does indeed explicate *episteme* in terms of explanation and interconnectedness, and not in terms of certainty or vision; but we

should resist the inference that he is therefore not talking about knowledge, or that, if he is, he has an old-fashioned or unusual notion of knowledge. On the contrary, in this as in other matters, Plato is surprisingly up to date. (1990, pp. 114–15)

For the purpose of choosing an ethical model for normative epistemology, it does not matter whether Fine is right that the Platonic concept of knowledge included understanding or whether understanding was instead a distinct but even more important epistemic concept than knowledge. The important point is that understanding ought to be an important concept for us as well, it has clearly been neglected, and this neglect cannot be remedied if epistemology persists in making the locus of evaluation individual propositions or states of believing single propositions, as is the case with justification. Understanding is not a state directed toward a single propositional object at all. This is not to deny that there is a sense in which one can be said to understand a proposition p. But the understanding of p is not directed primarily at p itself. One understands p as part of and because of one's understanding of a system or network of truths, or to follow Kvanvig's advice in getting away from the atomistic terminology, we could say that one understands p as part of one's understanding of the pattern of a whole chunk of reality. This way of understanding understanding is not specifically Platonic, I suggest, even though we may have learned it from Plato. We can find a contemporary example of the same view in Nelson Goodman:

> Briefly, then, truth of statements and rightness of descriptions, representations, exemplifications, expressions – of design, drawing, diction, rhythm – is primarily a matter of fit: fit to what is referred to in one way or another, or to other renderings, or to modes and manners of organization. The differences between fitting a version to a world, a world to a version, and a version together or to other versions fade when the role of versions in making the worlds they fit is recognized. And knowing or understanding is seen as ranging beyond the acquiring of true beliefs to the discovering and devising of fit of all sorts. (1978, p. 138)

The ability to see the way bits of reality fit together is important in the conduct of our ordinary life, not just in theory construction and other areas of formal inquiry. In our private life this ability helps us in understanding another person. We each know in the propositional sense an enormous number of facts about a person with whom we are intimately acquainted, yet the knowledge of such facts does not constitute knowing the person. To understand a person's motivation or character we often need to be able to pick from the profusion of information about him stored in our memory certain facts that become salient in particular contexts. The juxtaposition of one bit of knowledge with another – say, his susceptibility to jealousy and fearfulness of other sorts – can produce insights that extend and deepen our understanding of his psychic makeup. And, of course, this same ability is crucially important in our knowledge of ourselves. It is very doubtful that an epistemology focused on the individual belief can explain the nature of such understanding if I am right that understanding involves the comprehension of structures of reality other than its propositional structure.

I will end this section with a brief mention of another neglected epistemic value that is the aim of the hedgehog rather than the fox. That value is wisdom, and its neglect is not trivial. The nature of wisdom may be elusive, but it is clear that whatever it is, wisdom is an epistemic value qualitatively different from the piling up of beliefs that have the property of justification, warrant, or certainty. Wisdom is neither a matter of the properties of propositional beliefs, nor is it a matter of the relations among such beliefs; it is a matter of grasping the whole of reality. We have already discussed wisdom in section 1.2 as an example of a personal value analogous to love and friendship, the importance of which moves us in the direction of a virtue theory. Wisdom may or may not be a state distinct from knowledge, just as understanding may or may not be distinct from knowledge. In any case, we should attempt as much as possible to get a unitary account of our epistemic life, so even if the goals of knowledge, understanding, and wisdom are distinct, it is reasonable to expect them to be interrelated in the way a person designs and conducts her cognitive life. If an approach to epistemic evaluation focused on the individual belief leads to the neglect of important goals related to knowledge, this is a problem that needs to be remedied. Wisdom and understanding have often been considered virtues themselves, and even if they are not, it is clear that they are closely associated with virtues. It follows that an approach to epistemology focused on the virtues offers the best hope of giving a unitary account of the goals of our epistemic life, including some that have been seriously neglected.

3 MORE REASONS TO TRY A VIRTUE APPROACH: THE RELATIONS BETWEEN BELIEVING AND FEELING

In the last two sections we have seen reasons for thinking a virtue approach to epistemic evaluation might be fruitful. One set of reasons arose within ethics and corresponded to the advantages of virtue ethics over act-based ethics. The second set of reasons arose from certain problems within epistemology itself. In this section I wish to look at some considerations arising from the philosophy of mind.

The treatment of belief as a psychic state independent of non-cognitive states is happily nearing its demise. In fact, recently problems have been raised with treating belief as an identifiable psychic state of any sort, but I will not get involved with that dispute.[28] My concern in this section is simply to point out that the psychic states conventionally assigned to epistemologists are by no means sharply distinguished from the psychic states conventionally assigned to ethicists. More specifically, I will point out some of the numerous ways states of believing are connected with feeling states and states of emotion. This by itself is not sufficient to lead us into a virtue epistemology, but since moral virtues are thought to govern the emotions while intellectual virtues govern the formation of beliefs, any preexisting interest in

---

[28] See particularly Stich 1983, where Stich argues that the concept of belief is a useless figment of folk psychology.

intellectual virtue ought to lead to an interest in ethical virtue theory if the considerations of this section are plausible.

Many people would probably think that the evidence for the influence of feeling on belief is too obvious to require comment, but philosophers have tended to think of any such influence as a defect, an embarrassment to be eliminated. An exception to the dominant view was William James:

> In its inner nature, belief, or the sense of reality, is a sort of feeling more allied to the emotions than to anything else. Mr. Bagehot distinctly calls it the "emotion" of conviction. I just now spoke of it as acquiescence. It resembles more than anything what in the psychology of volition we know as consent. Consent is recognized by all to be a manifestation of our active nature. It would naturally be described by such terms as "willingness" or the "turning of our disposition." What characterizes both consent and belief is the cessation of theoretic agitation, through the advent of an idea which is inwardly stable, and fills the mind solidly to the exclusion of contradictory ideas. (1981, vol. 2, pp. 913–14)

James has numerous examples that show that the emotive state of excitation and its forms such as desire, dread, and fear affect belief, and that we need not resort to any new principle of choice to explain this phenomenon: "Speaking generally, the more a conceived object *excites* us, the more reality it has" (1981, vol. 2, p. 935). One of James's examples is a man who has no belief in ghosts by daylight but temporarily believes in them when alone at night as he feels his blood curdle at a mysterious sound or vision. The man's fear leads to his belief. He also cites belief arising from dread:

> The thought of falling when we walk along a curbstone awakens no emotion of dread; so no sense of reality attaches to it, and we are sure we shall not fall. On a precipice's edge, however, the sickening emotion which the notion of a possible fall engenders makes us believe in the latter's imminent reality, and quite unfits us to proceed. (1981, vol. 2, p. 936)

Another form of excitation affecting belief is the emotion that accompanies religious conviction. James describes a particularly vivid example of this phenomenon, quoting Bagehot:

> The Caliph Omar burnt the Alexandrian Library, saying: "All books which contain what is not in the Koran are dangerous. All which contain what is in it are useless!" Probably no one ever had an intenser belief in anything than Omar had in this. Yet it is impossible to imagine it preceded by an argument. His belief in Mahomet, in the Koran, and in the sufficiency of the Koran, probably came to him in spontaneous rushes of emotion; there may have been little vestiges of argument floating here and there, but they did not justify the strength of the emotion, still less did they create it, and they hardly even excused it. . . . Probably, when the subject is thoroughly examined, conviction will be found to be one of the intensest of human emotions, and one most closely connected with the bodily state, . . . accompanied or preceded by the sensation that Scott makes his seer describe as the prelude of a prophecy:
>
> > At length the fatal answer came,
> > In characters of living flame –
> > Not spoke in words, nor blazed in scroll,
> > But borne and branded on my soul.
>
> A hot flash seems to burn across the brain. Men in these intense states of mind have altered history, changed for better or worse the creed of myriads, and desolated or redeemed provinces of ages. Nor is this intensity a sign of truth, for it is precisely strongest in those points in which men differ most from each other. John Knox felt it in his anti-Catholicism; Ignatius Loyola in his anti-Protestantism; and both, I suppose, felt it as much as it is possible to feel it. (James 1981, vol. 2, p. 936)[29]

James's sympathetic exposition of Bagehot's view of belief in this passage suggests that he might accept an even stronger thesis than the one we have been considering. In the case of the caliph,

---

[29] W. Bagehot, "The Emotion of Conviction," in *Literary Studies*, vol. 1, pp. 412–17.

his emotion *of* conviction appears to be more than a causal factor in the formation of a distinct belief state. Rather, the emotion seems to be an aspect of the belief itself; that is, belief is in part an emotive state.

As we have seen, James defines belief as "the sense of reality," and it is only one step to the famous claim of David Hume: to believe is to have a vivid impression.[30] This position has a feeling state as its dominant aspect – in fact, the *only* aspect that distinguishes it from mere thought. But even without going as far as Hume or James, we can find supporting evidence that vividness of conception is at least causally connected with belief in the way in which it is presupposed and exploited by propagandists. In an interview shortly after the release of his movie *JFK*, Oliver Stone talked about his use of MTV editing techniques to make the viewer form such a vivid conception of his (Stone's) interpretation of the Kennedy assassination that she finds herself believing it automatically:

> What's interesting about the movie [*JFK*] is that it's one of the fastest movies . . . It's like splinters to the brain. We have 2500 cuts in there, I would imagine. We had 2000 camera setups. We're assaulting the senses . . . in a sort of new-wave technique. We admire MTV editing technique and we make no bones about using it. We want to . . . get to the subconscious . . . and certainly seduce the viewer into a new perception of reality . . . [of] what occurred in Texas that day.[31]

Stone's approach in this movie is interesting because his assumption is that the combination of seductively vivid images and high speed leads the viewer inexorably to belief. The importance of vividness had been noted by Hume, but the use of speed is, of course, a contemporary innovation. The idea here is probably that

[30] Hume, *A Treatise of Human Nature* Book I.3.7. James mentions that Renouvier calls believing for no other reason than that we conceive it with passion "mental vertigo."

[31] Oliver Stone, quoted by Richard D. Heffner, "Last Gasp of the Gutenbergs," *Los Angeles Times*, 19 Feb. 1992. I do not think that the gaps I have made in the quotation affect the sense of Stone's remarks. I have left out several phrases because of the natural awkwardness of spontaneous oral discourse.

the assault by images at high speed leaves little time for the viewer to think critically. Whether it works is a matter for empirical investigation, but on the face of it, it would not be surprising if it does. Besides raising questions about the voluntariness of belief, to which we will turn in section 4, this example raises very interesting questions about the causal connections among graphic perceptual images, the emotional reaction to such images, and the formation of beliefs.

Let us next look at a homey example of the way in which believing is not clearly distinguishable from the affective states of hoping or wanting. Suppose Molly wants to speak to a friend, but she doubts that he is home; she somewhat disbelieves that he is home. However, she telephones anyway. After all, the effort of phoning is well worth the possible gain. Since she strongly hopes that he is home, she begins to look for a reason to believe it, a reason to make her hope reasonable. As her mind runs through reasons why he might be home after all, she finds that the strength of her assent to the proposition **John is home** increases both because she wants to believe it and because it is supported by the evidence she has considered in her ruminations. And these two reasons are not independent. At the first ring her hope surges and with it comes another surge of belief. Yes, she expects he *will* answer the telephone. At the second ring both her hope and her belief start to diminish, and at the third and fourth they diminish even more. She now begins to think that it is unlikely he is at home, and with each succeeding ring her belief that he is not home increases. Her assent to the proposition **John is not home** gets stronger and stronger.

This example illustrates two different things. First, it shows that belief comes in degrees due to degrees of assent, and second, it shows that belief is closely connected with such states as wanting, hoping, and expecting. Wanting and hoping are emotive or, at least, affective states; expecting and believing are usually thought not to be. But in the example just given, not only are there very close causal relations between wanting and hoping on the one hand and expecting and believing on the other, but it is not at all easy to distinguish between the emotive state and the cognitive state. Something like this might have been behind Wittgenstein's assertion that "the concepts of believing, expecting, hoping are less distantly related to one another than they are to the concept of thinking" (1967, sec. 574). The emotive aspect of believing, I would maintain, is in the component of assent, although "assent" is probably a rather anemic term for something that can range from the feeble to the robust.

The examples given by William James, the telephone example, and the Oliver Stone example all suggest that emotion is either a component of a belief or has a direct causal connection with a belief. If so, the causes of belief would include the causes that produce emotions, and the traits of character that regulate emotion would be properly applicable to the regulation of belief. These examples are also of processes that are common and presumably normal, although it is hard to know how to justify them to a critic of such processes. My point, though, is not to say that all such emotional influences on belief are justified but to call attention to the fact that emotions influence beliefs, that in some cases emotional states may not be clearly distinguishable from belief states, and that it follows that processes and habits within us that manage emotions and desires ought not to be examined independently of the processes and habits within us that manage the processes leading up to belief. Since the former are moral virtues and the latter intellectual virtues, the conclusion is that epistemologists ought to attend to accounts of the moral virtues.

Before leaving the consideration of the relation between belief and feeling, it may be worthwhile to consider an argument that the rationality or cognitive respectability of a belief requires that it be formed independently of the subject's desires or emotions. Richard Swinburne, for example, has presented such an argument:

> While beliefs may be influenced by desires, this is an irrational process and the agent cannot consciously allow this to happen. For . . . if we recognize that we believe something because we desire to, we will recognize that the belief is independent of the facts, and so we will cease to believe it. (1986, p. 270 n. 4)

C. S. Peirce presented almost exactly the same argument in "The Fixation of Belief" (1877). Peirce says there that "sentiments in their development will be very greatly determined by accidental causes," and once we recognize that a belief originates in sentiment, we will have reason to doubt it, for its origin in sentiment means that it has been acquired by something "extraneous to the fact" (1992, p. 119).

This argument is mistaken in at least two ways. First, beliefs may be influenced by feelings and desires in other ways than by the desire to believe a particular belief, as we have already seen in the Oliver Stone and William James examples. In fact, the James examples involve a desire to believe the contrary of what is believed (the existence of ghosts or falling off a ledge).[32] Second, it is false that the fact that a belief is influenced by desire makes it a belief acquired independently of the facts. Most of us know from experience that desire and other emotive states can aid as well as hurt information processing. A person enthusiastic about the subject of a lecture (or even the lecturer himself) will hear more and learn more than a bored or distracted person listening to the same talk. And Aristotle recognizes the attractive force of truth when he says, "Even Empedocles gets this right, drawn on by the truth itself" (*De Partibus Animalium* I.1.642a18–19).[33] But fear and other negative feelings also can aid the acquisition of true beliefs by sharpening one's attentiveness or imprinting a belief more vividly in one's memory.

Bernard Williams (1973) is no doubt right that to believe is to believe-true, and Swinburne is right that if we become aware that someone's belief was formed or sustained in a way that is independent of the facts, we will think that such a belief is irrational. But there is nothing in *that* thesis that should lead us to the conclusion that there is anything wrong or irrational if beliefs are affected by emotions and desires. It all depends upon whether a cognitive structure intimately connected with and affected by a

---

[32] Jenefer Robinson (1983) has argued that desires are more basic than emotions. If so, the primary causal factor underlying both emotions and beliefs would be desire, including, presumably, the desire for truth.

[33] Charles Young suggested this line from Aristotle.

feeling structure leads toward or away from knowledge. That question has not been settled, but I suggest that there is no hope of settling it if we persist in separating epistemic evaluation from the evaluation of emotive states and their influences on human behavior. A close study of virtue theory may not be the only way to accomplish this, but it is a way that gives us the advantage of using a type of theory that already has a long history. As we shall see in Part II, moral virtues regulate emotions and overt acts, and intellectual virtues regulate cognitive activity and the acquisition of beliefs. If beliefs and emotions are intimately connected, this should motivate us to look for connections between moral and intellectual virtues.

4 AN OBJECTION TO MODELING EVALUATION IN EPISTEMOLOGY ON ETHICS: THE DISPUTE OVER THE VOLUNTARINESS OF BELIEF

I have argued that normative epistemology uses concepts and forms of argument taken from theoretical ethics. Since epistemologists do this anyway, it might as well be done consciously and with attention to the ethical theories that provide the models of evaluation. I have also claimed that no one has pursued a virtue model in any detail, and that such a model may have advantages over act-based models, some arising from the nature of virtue theory itself, and others arising from within epistemology or the philosophy of mind. However, there is a common belief that could undermine any close association between theoretical ethics and normative epistemology, no matter what type of ethical theory is used. This is the widespread assumption that the human acts addressed in ethics are voluntary, but cognitive activity for the most part is involuntary, and since it is also assumed that the primary object of epistemic evaluation is the belief, it may be thought sufficient to argue that believing is involuntary in order to foil the attempt to model epistemic evaluation on moral evaluation. This is probably the most serious objection to evaluating persons for their beliefs in a way that is anything like moral evaluation. This problem will need to be surmounted before we can proceed further.

It should be recognized that beliefs often seem to be the outcome of instinctive processes, no more voluntary than our digestion, and even when they are produced by reflective thought, we may find our cognitive processes leading us inexorably to a particular belief – one that we may not even like – and that suggests that it is not *we* who direct the process but that we are more appropriately described as acted *upon*. The sense of being acted upon is probably even stronger in those cases in which a belief is influenced by emotion, as in William James's example of a belief formed out of a dread of falling from a high ledge. In at least some of these cases, beliefs appear to be involuntary, and if they are involuntary, it is inappropriate to make them objects of moral evaluation. For the same reason, it is inappropriate to blame a *person* for having the beliefs that she has. After all, a person is not blamed for something she cannot help, but at worst she is pitied the way a person with low native intelligence or a congenital physical disorder is pitied. So we are faced with the following challenge: When epistemologists use such concepts as epistemic *duty* or *responsibility*, epistemic *norms*, or intellectual *virtues* in analyzing justification and the normative aspect of knowledge, can the type of evaluation intended be anything more than a distant relative of moral evaluation since our beliefs lack the voluntary control necessary for being evaluated in the moral sense?

4.1 *The irrelevance of the objection to virtue theory*

I have several distinct points to make in response to this objection. First of all, the question of the voluntariness of beliefs has a much weaker force when used against a virtue theory than against other kinds of moral theory since the purpose of a virtue approach is to shift the locus of evaluation from the belief or act to the virtue or vice or other internal qualities of persons. The primary object of evaluation is inner traits of persons, and the evaluation of acts or beliefs is derivative. No one claims that our moral virtues and vices are under our complete control, but they are generally regarded as sufficiently voluntary to be the proper objects of moral evaluation, including moral praise and blame.[34] The appropriate question to ask about using a virtue approach in epistemology, then, is whether our intellectual virtues and vices are as voluntary as our moral virtues and vices.

On the face of it, there is no reason to think that intellectual courage, perseverance, honesty, or sincerity are any less voluntary than courage, perseverance, honesty, and sincerity considered as moral virtues. But virtues such as perceptiveness, the ability to think up coherent explanations of the facts, and insight into persons, problems, and theories seem to be less voluntary in that they depend more upon natural abilities and less on the sort of training that responds well to effort on our part, the training described by Aristotle in his account of the acquisition of the moral virtues. Still, it is doubtful that the degree of voluntariness of these virtues is any less than, say, that of compassion, generosity, or the virtue contrary to envy.[35] The voluntariness of none of these virtues is particularly striking, which is not to say that they are insufficiently voluntary for moral praise. Other examples help our case even more. The intellectual vice of conformity is surely as voluntary as greed; a person whose intellectual pride leads him to refuse to treat another fairly in an argument over a philosophical thesis has no less control over this trait than a person whose vengefulness leads him to refuse to treat another fairly in business dealings with him. Is a habit of intellectual prejudice any harder to overcome or less under one's control than the sorts of prejudices discussed in ethics? What about the intellectual virtue of open-mindedness? A person with such a trait shows adaptability of intellect, which is not significantly less voluntary than adaptability in overt behavior, as manifested in a person who reconsiders her moral positions when necessary and acts accordingly.

---

[34] Susan Sauve Meyer (1993) has argued that Aristotle does not in fact take the view that the virtues and vices are voluntary. Happily, we need not attempt to resolve this issue here since my claim is only that the voluntariness of intellectual virtues does not differ in any significant way from the voluntariness of the moral virtues.

[35] I do not know the name of the virtue contrary to envy, but presumably there is one.

The range of voluntariness of human traits, both intellectual and moral, is fairly wide, and there are probably good reasons to divide them in such a way that those on the lower end of the voluntariness scale are exempt from judgments of moral responsibility or any other sort of evaluation that is distinctively moral. This may be so, but there is no reason to think that such a division will split off the intellectual from the moral virtues. Therefore, if the moral virtues and vices are the primary objects of evaluation in ethics, there is no reason arising from lack of voluntariness to prevent the intellectual virtues and vices from being the primary objects of evaluation in epistemology, even if epistemic evaluation is closely connected to moral evaluation.

4.2 *The voluntariness of belief*

In spite of what has been said, it might be argued that if acts are voluntary in a wide and interesting range of cases whereas beliefs are not, this still makes the sense in which we hold persons responsible *for their beliefs* weaker than the sense in which we hold persons responsible *for their acts*, and this would make one kind of epistemic evaluation disanalogous with moral evaluation. After all, it can be argued, we blame a person more for an act that arises out of unfairness than for a belief that arises out of unfairness because quite apart from the voluntariness of the underlying vice, we think there is an additional element of voluntariness involved in the performance of the act that is lacking in the formation of the belief. So a professor who grades a student unfairly is more blameworthy than the same professor would be for merely believing unfairly that the student's philosophical position is unjustified. Even with the vice of unfairness, she was able to stop herself from the act of unfair grading, it is argued, whereas the belief is determined by involuntary processes once the vice is given. We should therefore look at a comparison of the voluntariness of beliefs and the voluntariness of acts. In doing so it will not be necessary to give an account of the voluntary since my purpose is to counter the claim of an alleged *difference* in voluntariness between acts and beliefs. Since moral evaluations of acts go on without a prior account of the voluntary, it should be sufficient to show that beliefs do not differ in their voluntariness from acts in a wide and interesting range of cases in order to show that the same kind of evaluations can be made about beliefs.

A survey of traditional and contemporary positions on cognitive voluntarism shows that the point at issue is interpreted in very different ways by different theorists. Some, particularly those who claim to be involuntarists, seem to think that the question is whether a belief is ever the direct object of choice.[36] It is highly doubtful that very many, if any, beliefs are in this category, but surely it is not necessary for a belief to be chosen in order to be voluntary. In fact, I think the frequency and importance of choice is vastly overrated even when the discussion is limited to acts, but I will not argue for that here. My point is that the issue cannot be settled by attempting to choose a belief at random, say, starting to believe it is Friday when you know very well it is Wednesday.[37]

The position that beliefs are straightforwardly involuntary is most notably represented by David Hume, who claims that "belief consists . . . in something, that depends not on the will, but must arise from certain determinate causes and principles, of which we are not masters" (1967, p. 624). Many recent philosophers take the position that beliefs are involuntary, but without the theoretical support of Hume's theory of ideas. This is one of the themes of Reformed Epistemology, influenced by Calvinist theology. Both Alvin Plantinga and George Mavrodes frequently speak of "finding myself believing" some proposition, as if I notice I have a belief the way I notice I am getting gray hair. And one of the elements of reliabilism is that it does not require any degree of cognitive voluntarism. To many observers of contemporary epistemology, this is an advantage of the theory, and that suggests that doubts about the voluntariness of belief are not uncommon.

One of the strongest views on the opposite side of the question of the voluntariness of belief is that of William James. After suffering through a series of emotional disorders, James came to the conclusion that the key to solving his problems was in the recog-

[36] Richard Swinburne (1986, p. 127) makes such an assumption, but so do many others.

[37] I have been asked this question in conversation as if that were the issue.

nition of the freedom of his own will. At that time in his life he wrote to his father, and what is most interesting for the present topic is that he indicated in that letter that he understood his primary exercise of free will to be in a belief rather than in an overt act:

> I think that yesterday was a crisis in my life. I finished the first part of Renouvier's second "Essais" and see no reason why his definition of Free Will – "the sustaining of a thought because I choose to when I might have other thoughts" – need be the definition of an illusion. At any rate, I will assume for the present – until next year – that it is no illusion. My first act of free will shall be to believe in free will. (1920, p. 148)[38]

This sentiment is familiar to most philosophers because it had already been expressed by Descartes (*Meditation IV*), whose cognitive voluntarism is one of the strongest in the philosophical tradition. Descartes claimed that belief is not purely an intellectual state or act since it is not the intellect that affirms or denies a proposition proposed for its consideration, but the will. This position had a long prior history in medieval philosophy, and James Montmarquet gives an interesting discussion of the parallels between the Cartesian view of the place of will in intellectual error and Augustine's account of sin (1993, App. 1, esp. pp. 116–17). The idea is that the will is attracted to truth and goodness and is never drawn to falsehood or sin as such. In the case of propositions that are proposed to the understanding without sufficient reason either to affirm or to deny, the will is able to act in virtue of its attraction to truth. While some proposition p is merely conjecture, the will is attracted to it by its possible truth. When the will recognizes that p is possibly untrue, it may then be led to reject p. The point seems to be that whichever feature of p is most salient to the mind of the subject – its possible truth or its possible untruth – is the one that leads to the affirmation or denial of p. In similar

---

[38] James develops his idea that the differences between the objects of believing and willing are immaterial with respect to our freedom in the *Principles of Psychology*, chap. 21, "The Perception of Reality." See the section on the relations of belief and will.

fashion, Augustine says that the will is always attracted by good, not evil as such. Even when a person sins, the will is attracted to the sinful deed "under the aspect of good"; that is, there is *something* good about it that becomes the focus of the sinner's attention. She concentrates on the fact that the act is, say, beneficial to a loved one or is pleasureful or causes less trouble in her community. She conveniently ignores the fact that it is also a violation of an important promise or that it causes serious harm to others for whom she has no special love or is a violation of moral duty in some other way. In a sense, of course, she is aware of the features of the act that would lead her to see its wrongfulness, all things considered, if she had been giving sufficient attention to these features. As a result of her inattention she does not weigh these features properly and is therefore guilty of a form of self-deception. Similarly, the believer focuses on those considerations that support the truth of the proposition believed and ignores or gives insufficient attention to contrary considerations. To the extent that the believer errs in focusing on certain considerations to the exclusion of others, the belief, like the wrongful act, arises out of self-deception and is voluntary in the same sense.

The Cartesian position that it is the will, not the intellect, that assents in one's believing (*credere*) was also the position of Aquinas, who thought that the fact that the intellect is under the control of the will is a necessary condition for the existence of intellectual virtues.[39] Since Aquinas, a long tradition of cognitive voluntarism has continued in Catholic philosophy, although I will not discuss these theories here.[40]

It is not surprising that the milder forms of cognitive voluntarism are more common than the extreme Cartesian–Jamesian variety, and some of them are remarkably similar to the Augustinian–Thomistic position, even if lacking the somewhat harsh associa-

---

[39] *Summa Theologica* (hereafter abbreviated *ST*) I-II, q. 56, a. 3. A good discussion of Aquinas on the relation between intellect and will appears in Stump 1994. Stump includes in that paper numerous examples of ways in which the will controls belief.

[40] See my edited book *Rational Faith: Catholic Responses to Reformed Epistemology* (1993). Some form of cognitive voluntarism is defended in a majority of the papers in this collection.

tions of the concepts of self-deception and blame. Consider, for example, the words of Pascal:

> The will is one of the chief organs of belief, not that it creates belief, but because things are true or false acording to the aspect by which we judge them. When the will likes one aspect more than another, it deflects the mind from considering the qualities of the one it does not care to see. Thus the mind, keeping in step with the will, remains looking at the aspect preferred by the will and so judges by what it sees there. (*Pensees,* trans. Krailsheimer, sec. II, p. 218)

In contemporary philosophy we find numerous examples of mild forms of cognitive voluntarism in such writers as Murray Clarke (1986), who argues for what he calls doxastic involuntarism and attention voluntarism, and Christopher Hookway (1981), who says we approach our beliefs, not as "alienated spectators," but with a sense of "engaged control" (p. 77). Jonathan Cohen (1992) distinguishes belief, which he defines as a disposition to feel that *p,* with no conceptual implications about the believer's reasoning, from acceptance, a mental act whereby *p* becomes one of the items one uses in one's reasoning, with no conceptual implications about feelings. Cohen then says that the latter but not the former is voluntary.

Another moderate view is expressed by Lorraine Code:

> When ethics of belief examples are taken as paradigmatic for the explanation of freedom in knowledge and belief in general, this suggests the conclusion that everything is a matter of choice: one can construct reality to suit one's purposes and passions. On the other hand, the kind of over-simplified paradigm that Stocker criticizes points to the opposite conclusion: that we are wholly passive with regard to our beliefs, hence no attribution of responsibility is warranted. The truth lies somewhere between these two points of view. This midposition is illustrated by examples of things people can choose to do: to stop being overweight, to be an informed opponent of apartheid, to stop being an alcoholic, to be a good driver. The results are reasonably described as voluntary outcomes of voluntarily

embarked upon courses of action. They are things one can be ordered to do and that one can approach diligently or otherwise. (1987, p. 84)

Eleonore Stump (1994) also defends a form of mild cognitive voluntarism. Some of her examples of the control of the will over belief concern the accessibility of a belief to the memory, such as willing oneself not to forget an important appointment or willing oneself to forget a past hurt. In these examples a belief is voluntary in the sense that we have indirect control over having it or recalling it.

My position is that beliefs, like acts, arrange themselves on a continuum of degrees of voluntariness, ranging from quite a bit to none at all. One of the major problems in comparing the voluntariness of beliefs and acts is that there appears to be a disanalogy between beliefs and acts at both the extreme upper and extreme lower ends of the continuum, and these putative disanalogies contribute to some confusion about the voluntariness of beliefs. A peculiarity of many discussions of the voluntariness of beliefs is that they take the paradigm case of an act for which we are morally responsible to be one at the extreme upper end of the voluntariness scale, the direct object of choice, whereas they take the paradigm case of a belief to be one at the lower end of the scale, such as a perceptual belief. It is no wonder that with such cases in hand beliefs and acts appear to differ significantly in voluntariness. So it often happens that the principal reason given for claiming that beliefs are involuntary and hence outside the range of moral responsibility is that they are not chosen. But this is to make the model of voluntariness unnecessarily restrictive and I do not intend to argue that we typically *choose* to believe something. For a fairer comparison, let us look instead at the whole range of beliefs and acts from the most to the least voluntary.

If we were to raise the question of whether acts are voluntary, the obvious answer would be that some are and some are not, and that there are degrees of voluntariness. At the upper end of the scale there are such acts as the choice of one of Wolfgang Puck's many culinary creations from the menu at Chinois. At the lower end of the scale there are such instinctive acts as sneezing, wincing, or scratching an itch. Moral philosophers ignore the acts in the latter category and tend to exaggerate the number and importance of the acts in the former category. But in between there is a lot of room for the voluntary.

Aristotle did not limit the voluntary to the chosen, and although his account of the voluntary is notoriously difficult, I think we might find something in that discussion useful to the question of the voluntariness of beliefs. One aspect of his discussion that many modern readers will find frustrating is that he makes the concept of moral responsibility more fundamental than the concept of the voluntary, the reverse of the typical contemporary approach. The idea seems to be that given that we hold persons responsible for certain acts (and it is assumed that we are right to do so), such acts must be voluntary. But in spite of the problems in Aristotle's theoretical account of the voluntary, his examples are hard to dispute. What is more to the point of the present discussion is that these examples aid the comparison of the voluntariness of acting and believing. It seems to me, for example, that believing is in general at least as voluntary as acts done out of passion or while drunk, for which Aristotle rightly says we are responsible. Consider also such acts (or omissions) as not noticing someone else's distress, taking out one's anger on an innocent bystander, laughing at someone's misfortune, impulsively making an envious remark, forgetting an important appointment, falling asleep in the presence of an important guest. In each case the act or pattern of acts exhibits a fault – boorishness, insensitivity, meanness, which are all moral faults – and the agent is to blame, not just for the underlying fault, but for the act or omission that results from that fault. Yet such acts and omissions are no more voluntary than typical cases of believing. The agent does not choose to act in such ways, nor *could* he have so chosen in many cases, so it is not like such unreflective habitual acts as tying one's shoes. Similarly, no choice immediately precedes the formation of a belief, nor could the believer have chosen to believe in relevant counterfactual circumstances, yet that is insufficient reason to draw the conclusion that believing is involuntary.

Furthermore, Aristotle distinguishes the vicious from the morally weak (akratic) person mostly by the fact that the vicious person has false beliefs that the akratic person does not have and that make him morally worse than the akratic individual. It takes bad will to have certain beliefs. Edmund Pincoffs defends this view well:

> If his beliefs are his justification for being dishonest, then he is blameable for holding a belief that, as he believes, justifies his being dishonest. For no belief can do this; and he cannot avoid blame by appeal to one. He is in this sense responsible for his beliefs, in that if he "chooses what is bad" as a consequence of them, he must either reject them or admit that they truly represent him, characterize him. (1986, p. 147)

Now there probably *is* something bothersome about the Aristotelian position that people are blameworthy for their false moral beliefs, but it is not the lack of voluntariness of beliefs in general that makes us worry. It is the fact that *some* people do not seem to meet the minimal conditions for control, even though they display vices, and so we may be inclined to pity them and to want to rehabilitate them rather than to blame them. And the farther their moral beliefs are from the norm, the more inclined we are to attribute them to involuntary processes. But this surely cannot be our standard response to cases of false moral beliefs, because Pincoffs is right in calling attention to the dependency of our responsibility for our acts on our responsibility for the beliefs providing our reasons for acting.

I conclude that we must reject the idea that the only element of the voluntary in acting is a distinct act of choice that occurs immediately before the act. Acts that follow a process of deliberation and choice are in a very select category, and if morality applied only to this class of acts, it would not apply to very much. Thus, the fact that few, if any, beliefs are the objects of choice does not threaten the claim that many beliefs are sufficiently voluntary to be subject to evaluation in the sense of moral evaluation.

I said earlier that beliefs and acts appear to be disanalogous at both the extreme upper end and the extreme lower end of the scale of voluntariness. I have considered the extreme upper end of the scale and have agreed that probably more acts than beliefs are the direct objects of choice, although many acts for which we are responsible are not in that category. At the lower end of the scale, however, I believe the difference is largely illusory. Many bodily acts are as involuntary as typical perceptual or memory beliefs, such as coughing or wincing. An important difference for the attribution of evaluative properties to acts and beliefs, however, is that epistemologists often treat involuntary perceptual or memory beliefs as paradigms of belief, and even of justified or rational belief. Sometimes these beliefs are treated as paradigms of knowledge as well. These cases seem to be disanalogous to acts as treated in ethics since nobody treats involuntary acts as the object of moral evaluation, much less as paradigms of right action. We will discuss perceptual and memory beliefs in Part III. Here my concern is not to deny that true perceptual beliefs in ordinary circumstances are rational or justified, nor do I wish to deny that they are cases of knowledge. Instead, I want to make the different point that it is a mistake to think of perceptual beliefs as paradigm cases of rationality and justifiability. Rationality has traditionally been understood as the property that makes us most distinctively human. Perceptual beliefs, however, admit of a number of different analyses, and on some accounts, a perceptual belief is no different when held by a human being than when held by many animals. If so, these beliefs are subhuman or, at least, subpersonal. To call beliefs that occur without the agency of the human agent "rational" or "justified" is a jarring use of such terms, given their historical usages. Moral philosophers would never use as paradigm cases of right acts such subpersonal involuntary acts as sneezing. This is not to say that there is no sense of "right act" in which sneezing is right, but only that it would distort the concept of a right act to begin the analysis of rightness with such an example as a paradigm case. Similarly, although I am not denying that there is a sense of "rational" and "justified" in which ordinary perceptual beliefs are rational and justified, it does not do justice to the history of the concept of rationality to lead off the investigation with these beliefs as paradigms.[41]

---

[41] It is probably true that the main reason epistemologists begin with cases of perceptual beliefs is their position that more complex and important beliefs

4.3 *Moral and epistemic luck*

I wish to conclude this section on the voluntariness of belief with a consideration on the significance of moral luck. Operating in the background of the complaint that epistemic evaluation cannot be closely modeled on moral evaluation because acts are voluntary and beliefs are not is the idea that there are distinct kinds of evaluation and that the primary mark of moral as opposed to other sorts of evaluation is that it is something that is completely under the control of the agent. People may not be able to control the extent to which they are strong or good-looking, make logical mistakes, or have good memories, but they can control the aspects in which they are *morally* evaluated, and, in fact, such control is largely what *distinguishes* moral evaluation from other sorts of evaluation, including the epistemic. This is the idea behind Kant's claim that it is only the good will that, properly speaking, has moral value. But the recent work on moral luck by Joel Feinberg (1970), Bernard Williams (1981), and Thomas Nagel (1979a) make the Kantian position highly problematic. Each has argued that the realm of the morally praiseworthy/blameworthy is not indisputably within one's voluntary control or accessible to one's consciousness. Nagel's paper "Moral Luck" offers an impressive set of examples of moral luck in consequences, in circumstances, and in constitution. The examples describe cases in which the moral praise or blame a person *should* have extends beyond that element which he controls. In some cases we blame an already blameworthy person more than we would otherwise because of the actual consequences of his act. In other cases we praise the

bear some interesting relation to perceptual beliefs. It must be admitted that moral philosophers have no such motivation to begin their analyses of the morality of typical human acts by beginning with cases of simple involuntary acts such as sneezing. The acts of interest to ethics simply do not relate to sneezing and scratching and itching in the way complex beliefs have often been thought to relate to perceptual beliefs. But this has no bearing on the question of voluntariness, the topic of this section. As an aside, it would be an interesting topic for investigation to see whether there are, in fact, involuntary acts that relate to typical cases of voluntary acts in a way analogous to the relation between perceptual beliefs and other beliefs in a typical empiricist theory.

person who actually performs a heroic act more than we would a person who would have done the same thing if she had been in the same circumstances. In still other cases, Nagel shows that the extent to which we praise and blame a person for her inner traits goes beyond the degree to which she controls the acquisition of those traits herself. Furthermore, Feinberg (1970) has shown that the Kantian attempt to ground moral evaluation in something luck free cannot succeed, because even a person's purely internal states, including the formation of intentions, can be affected by such things as a sneezing fit or other distractions.

The problem of moral luck is pertinent to our present discussion in two respects. First, although moral luck is a serious problem for ethics, it actually makes the attempt to model epistemic evaluation on moral evaluation easier to do. If moral evaluation cannot be distinguished from other types of evaluation on the basis of control, then the fact that we only partially control our cognitive processes and emotions leading up to the formation of beliefs is no objection to the attempt to model epistemic evaluation on moral evaluation. Of course, there are differences in the degree of luck both within the area of moral evaluation and within the area of epistemic evaluation, but it is much too facile to distinguish evaluation in the two areas on the grounds that we control the one but not the other. The similarities between moral and epistemic evaluation can easily be hidden by an assumed difference in the luck that is permitted in the two areas of evaluation.[42]

[42] A different way of responding to the existence of moral luck and assimilating moral and epistemic evaluation has been suggested by Michael Slote (1992a, 1992b). Slote gives up the concepts of praise and blame and bases evaluation on virtues in a sense that is not distinctively moral. Slote suggests such a move as a form of naturalizing both ethics and epistemology. Taking eliminative utilitarianism as his model, he proposes that we avoid the paradoxes of moral luck by adopting a kind of naturalized virtue ethics that is selectively eliminative. The distinctive moral sense of praise and blame would be eliminated in favor of a general form of assessment that assimilates moral evaluation to the type of assessment we do when we evaluate a person's physical strength, talents, beauty, or intelligence. Slote goes on to suggest that selective eliminativism may also be an attractive possibility for naturalizing epistemology. He suggests that we eliminate such controversial terms as "justified," "vindi-

Second, the rejection of the Kantian position that our moral status is completely within our control takes away one of the motivations for wanting a Kantian theory in the first place, and that makes a virtue approach more attractive. Aristotle was less embarrassed about the place of luck in moral assessment than most of us are because he never pretended to accept the Kantian dictum that desert is proportional to control.[43] It is worth noting, however, that the degree of luck in our virtues and vices is less than that in our intentions, our acts, and their consequences, as I have argued elsewhere (1994b). This is because moral luck has a cumulative effect. Internal traits of character give rise to dispositions in specific circumstances, which give rise to the formation of particular intentions, which lead to the performance of acts, which in turn lead to external consequences. New elements of luck are added at each succeeding stage, so that the greatest degree of luck exists in consequences, the least in traits of character. This may be one of the reasons Nagel spends much more time in his paper on examples of luck in consequences and only briefly mentions what he calls luck in constitution. A virtue approach to evaluation therefore reduces the component of luck, and this is one of its advantages.

I conclude that the worry that there is an important asymmetry between beliefs and acts with respect to voluntariness need not stop us from using moral theories as a way of understanding the nature of epistemic evaluation. Many beliefs are as voluntary as many acts and omissions for which we are morally responsible, although few, if any, beliefs are the objects of direct choice. There

cated," and "warranted" and talk instead of cognitive mechanisms or habits that "allow or cause *better or worse adaptation* to a creature's (or a person's or a species's) environment, or talk of *better or worse cognitive functioning*" (1992a, p. 370).

[43] See Martha Nussbaum's *The Fragility of Goodness* (1986), for the view that Aristotle's acceptance of moral luck is to be contrasted with Plato's nonacceptance of moral luck. Assuming that both Plato and Aristotle have virtue theories, it follows that an acceptance of moral luck is not a distinguishing characteristic of a virtue theory but only of certain forms of it. For an interesting account of the Aristotelian view on the luck of morality see also Kenny 1988.

is also a subset of involuntary beliefs that are commonly taken today to be paradigms of justified beliefs and/or paradigm cases of knowledge. These are perceptual beliefs. I have argued that because such beliefs are subpersonal, they should not be regarded as paradigm cases of rationality or justifiability, although this is not to say that they should be ruled out of the category of justifiability in advance. In addition, I have argued that because the point of a virtue theory is to shift the focus of evaluation from the act or belief to the trait of character, the dispute about the voluntariness of belief is somewhat beside the point. Intellectual virtues and vices are typically as voluntary as the traditional moral virtues and vices. Therefore, there is no reason to think that we are precluded from using a moral-theoretical model for epistemic evaluation on the grounds of a problematic difference in voluntariness.

5 CONCLUSION TO PART I: WHY CENTER EPISTEMOLOGY ON THE VIRTUES?

A major concern of contemporary epistemology is the analysis of the normative aspects of states of knowledge and belief, usually identified with justification, rationality, or warrant. I began with the observation that theories and argumentation about these matters are modeled on ethics, and the terminology is lifted from moral discourse. In some cases this is done consciously, but in other cases it is unnoticed, and the discussion is carried on with little regard for the history of the moral theories that provide the evaluative models and their comparative advantages and disadvantages. I suggested, then, that it would be advisable for epistemologists to use moral concepts in a more self-conscious fashion. Otherwise, any objections to the underlying moral theory can undermine the epistemic project as well. And even if the moral theory is not objectionable, it should be used in full awareness of alternatives. Virtue theories are enjoying a renaissance in ethics, and there are new forms of these theories, which I will discuss in Part II. I have urged epistemologists to examine these theories carefully for several reasons. First, no one has attempted to formulate a virtue theory for epistemology in any detail. Second, some of the reasons favoring a virtue approach in ethics have a parallel in reasons favoring a virtue approach in epistemology. Third, some of the difficulties in contemporary epistemology could be handled more easily by a virtue approach, including the confusion surrounding the notion of justification, the connections between belief and feeling, and the neglect of the values of understanding and wisdom.

There are also, of course, objections to virtue theory, but I hope that most readers will at least be intrigued enough to want to see what such a theory actually looks like. I do not, then, assume that all readers accept the superiority of virtue ethics over other approaches. For this reason I will make a dual appeal. First, to those who already believe that the most promising moral theory will be a form of virtue theory, I present my case directly. It will become necessary for me to do quite a bit of investigation into virtue ethics itself and to develop it in original ways in order to further the task of applying virtue to cognitive activity. This is because so little has been written on intellectual virtue and its connections with moral virtue. There is, in fact, a serious gap in virtue ethics in precisely that part of it that is most useful to epistemology, and it means that the virtue theory part of this book will not be acceptable to all virtue theorists. Nonetheless, I will attempt to present a range of options on these matters, and I hope that virtue ethicists as well as epistemologists will find something of interest in that account.

Second, for those readers who are not already convinced of the superiority of virtue theories, I suggest that my case be considered somewhat differently. It should by now be clear that no one has attempted an approach to normative epistemology that is closely modeled on virtue ethics in any of its forms. Given that almost everyone thinks the virtues are important in our moral life, I see no reason why they would deny that they are important in our cognitive life. The virtues of the mind are both interesting and too long ignored. I hope that an inquiry into their nature will be welcomed by epistemologists of all persuasions. At the very least, an account of the intellectual virtues can be adapted to many approaches in epistemology, just as an account of the moral virtues can be adapted to many approaches in ethics. Beyond that, I ask readers in the second group to adopt a "wait and see" attitude about virtue theory. It is likely that contemporary virtue theory is still too young to be the equal rival of deontological and consequentialist theories.[44] Part of its persuasiveness will undoubtedly be its fruitfulness in accounting for a broad range of human life, but I do not expect to have convinced readers of this yet. At the end of the book I will again ask the question of whether virtue theory can do what I am now proposing it has the promise of doing.

[44] See Slote 1992b for a defense of virtue theory as the equal rival of utilitarian and Kantian moral theories.

Part II

A theory of virtue and vice

We now begin the task of focusing epistemology on the concept of a virtue. In section 1, I distinguish several types of virtue theory by the ways they relate the fundamental moral concepts of a virtue, the good, and a right act. A pure virtue theory makes the concept of a right act derivative from the concept of a virtue, although there is more than one way such a theory can relate virtue to the good. Much of what I will do in Part II is compatible with many forms of aretaic ethics, but I am particularly interested in two forms of pure virtue theory: happiness-based and motivation-based theories. One of my aims in the rest of this book is to demonstrate that both forms of pure virtue theory, including the more radical, motivation-based theory, can be developed in ways that adequately handle epistemic evaluation. Incidentally, I expect moral philosophers will find something of interest in this part of the book, whether or not they have any interest in epistemology.

Section 2 will be devoted to a careful account of the nature of a virtue, distinguishing it from feeling states, from natural capacities, and from skills. I identify both a motivational component and a reliability component in virtue. In section 3 I turn to an investigation of the intellectual virtues. I argue that intellectual virtues are forms of moral virtue and that the many logical and causal connections among the moral and intellectual virtues make it important for a virtue theory to be broad enough in scope to account for the entire range of intellectual and moral virtues in a single theory. In section 4 I show how the motivational components of the particular intellectual virtues arise out of the motivation for knowledge, and how each virtue can be defined in terms of a combination of a motivation and reliable success in reaching the aim of that motivation. I then explain how the value of these components of virtue can be explained by each of the two forms of pure virtue theory, and show how to defend the motivation-based approach of basing the value of each intellectual virtue on the intrinsic value of the motivation for knowledge.

Section 5 focuses on the virtue of *phronesis*, or practical wisdom, which I argue is a higher-order, mediating virtue, operating over the entire range of moral and intellectual virtues. In section 6 I show how the basic deontic concepts in both ethics and epistemology can be defined in terms of aretaic concepts. This includes the concepts of right act, justified belief, wrong act, unjustified belief, and moral and epistemic duty. I then define the concept of what I call "an act of virtue," which is an act that is right in all respects. Part II concludes with considerations on the scope of the moral.

1 TYPES OF VIRTUE THEORIES

John Rawls has said that moral theory is "the study of how the basic notions of the right, the good, and moral worth may be arranged to form different structures" (1974–5, p. 5). If we substitute the concept of a virtue for that of moral worth, we may find it illuminating to classify moral theories by the ways they relate the fundamental moral concepts of a *virtue, the good,* and a *right* act. Most ethical theories have something to say about virtues, but what makes a theory a virtue theory is that it focuses analysis more on the concepts involved in the evaluation of persons than on act evaluation. The weakest form of virtue theory focuses on virtue, not because it maintains that the concept of a virtue is more fundamental than the concept of a right act, but because it contends that the concept of virtue offers the most useful *criterion* for the rightness of an act. So it is compatible with such a theory that a right act would be right whether or not it was chosen by a virtuous person, even though the best way to *determine* rightness is to look at the behavior of virtuous persons. Michael Slote (forthcoming) calls any such theory agent-focused and contends that arguably Aristotle's theory is of this kind. A theory that understands *phronesis* as a certain kind of moral insight into the right way to act in particular circumstances is merely agent-focused if it implies that what the agent has insight *into* is something more than the purely descriptive features of the situation and that these features exist prior to and independent of that kind of insight. Since act evaluation is not conceptually dependent upon agents and their traits in a merely agent-focused theory, it is not what I mean by a pure virtue theory. A thorough investigation into agent-focused epistemology would be interesting, and as far as I know, it has not yet been done. Most of what I will do in sections 2, 3, and 5 is compatible with such a theory, and I hope that those philosophers who are attracted to virtue theory but are unwilling to accept one of its stronger forms will find useful ideas in those sections.

By a pure virtue theory I mean a theory that makes the concept of a right act derivative from the concept of a virtue or some inner state of a person that is a component of virtue. This is a point both about conceptual priority and about moral ontology. In a pure virtue theory the concept of a right act is *defined* in terms of the concept of a virtue or a component of virtue such as a motivation. Furthermore, the *property* of rightness is something that emerges from the inner traits of persons. So according to a pure virtue theory an act would not have been right or wrong if it were not for its relation to certain inner personal traits.

I will not attempt a full defense of pure virtue theory in this book, but there is a short argument that I think shows its plausibility apart from the considerations given in Part I. The arguments there were supposed to show defects of act-based theories in comparison to which virtue theory has the advantage. The argument here is simply this. Persons are ontologically more fundamental than acts; acts are defined in terms of persons. It is reasonable to think, then, that the moral properties of persons are ontologically more fundamental than the moral properties of acts,

79

and the latter properties ought to be defined in terms of the former. Hence, virtues and vices are ontologically more fundamental than the rightness or wrongness of acts. The concept of right act ought to be defined in terms of the concept of virtue.

Two forms of pure virtue theory can be distinguished according to the different ways they relate the concept of a virtue and the concept of the good. If the concept of a good life (*eudaimonia*) or of good in the impersonal sense is the bottom-level moral concept, and the concept of a virtue is defined in terms of the concept of the good, the theory is what Michael Slote calls agent-prior and is what I will call good-based. Aristotle's ethics is most naturally interpreted as a theory of this kind. An interesting alternative is a new form of virtue ethics lately promoted by Slote, which he calls "agent-based." This type of theory makes the virtue, motivation, or other internal states of the agent ethically fundamental. A trait or motivation is good or bad in itself, not because its goodness or badness is *derived* from some prior concept of the good. The right is treated as a derivative concept, and the good in at least one of its senses may be treated as derivative as well.[1] Roughly, an act is right because it is an act a virtuous person would (or might) do, and a state of affairs is good because it is what virtuous persons are motivated to want or to pursue. In the strongest form of agent-basing (what Slote calls hyper-agent-basing), the good in the sense of well-being or the good life is derived from virtue as well as good in the impersonal sense. This theory not only denies that a virtue is a virtue because it is what a human person needs to live

---

[1] George Sher (1992) suggests a form of virtue ethics that he contrasts with both deontological and teleological approaches to the virtues and that seems to be very similar to what Slote calls agent-based. Sher says that it is possible that certain traits such as courage and wisdom are virtues, not because they lead to dutiful acts or because they are constituents of any further good, but simply because their own existence is a good. "It can be maintained, in other words, that a trait is a virtue whenever it, or its possession, has intrinsic value or worth" (p. 93). However, Sher does not go on to discuss the derivation of other moral concepts from virtue concepts, as an agent-based theory would do as I am describing it here. Sher calls this approach "perfectionist," but that term is misleading since it has also been used for a form of consequentialism. (See Hurka 1993, esp. pp. 58–9; Slote 1992b, pp. 245–7.)

well but goes on to say that a way of living counts as living well because it is the way virtuous persons want to live.[2]

I am interested in one form of good-based and one form of agent-based theory. In a common form of good-based theory the virtues are explained either as constituents of the good life or as means to the good life, where the good life is identified with happiness or the Aristotelian concept of *eudaimonia*. I call these theories *happiness-based*. Rosalind Hursthouse (1991) has a theory that is happiness-based. She defines a virtue as "a character trait a human being needs to flourish or live well" (p. 226). Hursthouse explicitly maintains the derivative character of right action and the foundational character of *eudaimonia*:

> [T]he theory is not trivially circular; it does not specify right action in terms of the virtuous agent and then immediately specify the virtuous agent in terms of right action. Rather, it specifies her in terms of the virtues, and then specifies these, not merely as dispositions to right action, but as the character traits (which are dispositions to feel and react as well as act in certain ways) required for *eudaimonia*. (P. 226)

According to Hursthouse (and Aristotle, on many interpretations), the order of the fundamental moral concepts is as follows. The good in the sense of *eudaimonia* is conceptually foundational.[3]

---

2 Lovers of theoretical classifications will notice that many variations of agent-basing can be developed. For example, a theory might be agent-based in the sense that it does not derive virtue concepts from other value concepts, but it might not derive the concept of a right act or the concept of the impersonal good from the concept of a virtue. Or it might derive one but not the other. Or again, it might derive some types of good but not others. Similar variations can be developed from the other kinds of virtue theory. In fact, act-based theories would also have the same kinds of permutations of these three concepts.

3 Charles Young has pointed out to me that Aristotle's position could be interpreted in such a way that it straddles the distinction between happiness-based and agent-based virtue ethics. Aristotle says: "Now we call that which is in itself worthy of pursuit more final than that which is worthy of pursuit for the sake of something else, and that which is never desirable for the sake of something else more final than the things that are desirable both in themselves and

The concept of virtue is derivative from the concept of *eudaimonia*, and the concept of a right act is derivative from the concept of a virtue.

In what follows I will also propose a form of agent-based theory I will call *motivation-based.* In that theory, the concept of a motivation will be treated as ethically fundamental, and the concept of a virtue will be constructed out of the concept of a good motivation. The concept of a right act will be defined in terms of the concept of a virtue. The structure of the theory will be left incomplete since I will not discuss the place of the concept of happiness or the good life.

The most important difference between happiness-based and motivation-based theories is that the former explain the good of a virtue teleologically. Virtue is good because of its connection to the thing that is more fundamentally good, namely, *eudaimonia*. In the motivation-based ethics I will present, virtues are not good because they lead to or are components of something else that is the primary good, so their goodness is not explained teleologically. So, for example, in happinesss-based ethics benevolence is good because of its connection with happiness. The difficulty for the theory, of course, is to give an account of happiness or *eudaimonia* that both sounds like the primary good and is such that benevolence and the other virtues are plausibly connected with happiness or *eudaimonia* as their end. In contrast, in a motivation-based ethics the goodness of benevolence is fundamental, and so is the goodness of justice and courage and all the rest of the virtues. The difficulty for this kind of theory is to make it plausible that each of the virtues is good in a fundamental, nonderivative way, and if the theory goes on to derive the con-

---

for the sake of that other thing, and therefore we call final without qualification that which is always desirable in itself and never for the sake of something else.

"Now such a thing happiness, above all else, is held to be; for this we choose always for itself and never for the sake of something else, but honour, pleasure, reason, and every virtue we choose indeed for themselves (for if nothing resulted from them we should still choose each of them) but we choose them also for the sake of happiness, judging that by means of them we shall be happy. Happiness, on the other hand, no one chooses for the sake of these, nor, in general, for anything other than itself" (*NE* I.7.1097a30–b6).

cepts of the good and of a right act from the concept of a virtue, the virtues must be such that they are capable of having such a function. One advantage of this type of theory is that many philosophers like the concept of virtue but are suspicious of teleology (e.g., Pincoffs 1986).

Clearly, the motivation-based approach to ethics requires some way of determining what makes a motivation a good one and what makes a trait a virtue. This is a daunting task, but perhaps no harder than the task of determining what makes a state of being a state of *eudaimonia*. One way of doing it, and to my mind a forceful one, is to appeal to experience. Many of us have known persons whose goodness shines forth from the depths of their being, and if we have not met them in person, we may have met them in literature, such as Dorothea Brooke in George Eliot's *Middlemarch*. Such an experience raises the question of whether we can know a person is good before we investigate her behavior, observe the outcome of her acts, or even see how her traits produce in her a state, such as happiness, which we determine to be good in advance. It is difficult to know the extent to which we can do this because in actual practice we already have and are used to using such concepts as a happy life and a right act before having the experiences I have described. Still, I believe it is possible that we can see the goodness of a person in this rather direct way. She may simply exude a "glow" of nobility or fineness of character, or as I have occasionally seen in a longtime member of a contemplative religious order, there may be an inner peace that can be perceived to be good directly, not simply because it can be explained on the theoretical level as a component of *eudaimonia*. If we then attempt to find out what it is about such a person that makes him good, we may be able to identify that goodness as involving certain feelings or motivations such as feelings of compassion or of self-respect or of respect for others, or motives of benevolence, sympathy, or love, all of which are components of virtues. In each case we would not determine that his love, compassion, or benevolence is good because of its relation to anything independently identified as good. We would simply see that these feelings or motivations are the states whose goodness we see in him. Alternatively, we may focus our attention directly on the motivation itself and see that it is good, and again, we might be able to see this independently of any evaluative judgment about the acts or consequences to which the motivation gives rise. These considerations, of course, are not adequate as a defense of this type of theory, but they do indicate that our range of options among virtue theories may be wider than is sometimes thought.

It is useful to have some idea of how the territory of the virtues can function in a theory in advance of the presentation of the nature of a virtue. This gives us some sense of the potential power of the concept of virtue. But I believe it is also wise not to be too hasty in casting our lot with one particular theory or even type of theory in advance of examining the concept we are investigating. In the next two sections I will develop the concept of a virtue, first in general and then with particular attention to the intellectual virtues and their relation to the virtues traditionally called "moral." We will only turn to a question that forces a choice between one form of virtue theory over another in section 4 when we look at the explanation for the goodness of intellectual virtues.

2 THE NATURE OF A VIRTUE

2.1 *The many notions of virtue*

The first thing that can be said about a virtue is that it is an excellence, although not every excellence is a virtue. Curiously, the concept of excellence is clearer than is the concept of virtue, although the latter has always had more theoretical importance. Some writers on virtue have observed that *"arete"* in ancient Greek was broader in scope than *"virtus"* in medieval Latin and that both terms were broader than "virtue" in modern English, referring to excellences of many more kinds than are usually considered virtues today, and the concept was not limited to human excellences (von Wright 1963, p. 137). Aristotle's list of virtues included excellences of the speculative intellect, as well as social graces such as wit and conversational ability, practical abilities such as the proper management of money, and aesthetic qualities such as those exhibited by the "great-souled" man. It is not clear, however, that the concept of virtue in modern English

84

has any one sense at all. Hume's English might be considered modern, and yet his use of the term "virtue" is one of the broadest in the history of philosophy. Among those qualities he endorses as virtues are the following: justice, fidelity, honor, allegiance, chastity, humanity, generosity, charity, affability, lenity, mercy, moderation, public spirit, discretion, caution, enterprise, industry, assiduity, frugality, economy, good sense, prudence, discernment, temperance, sobriety, patience, constancy, perseverance, forethought, considerateness, secrecy, order, insinuation, address, presence of mind, quickness of conception, facility of expression (*An Enquiry concerning the Principles of Morals,* sec. VI, pt. 1). This list is dazzling in its scope and it certainly suggests that the English word "virtue" can be applied very broadly. But on the other hand, the popular sense of virtue in Victorian England was limited to chastity, and today the word "virtue" has an archaic ring to some ears and has dropped out of use entirely in many quarters. Although there has been a resurgence of interest in virtue in professional ethics during the last three decades, this literature has been devoted almost exclusively to moral virtue, and some writers seem to assume that virtue *means* moral virtue. The sense of virtue used in most of this literature is broader than the Victorian sense of virtue but narrower than either the Humean or the Aristotelian notions.

The central idea that virtue is an excellence has never been seriously questioned, and that gives the notion of virtue a degree of univocity that we found wanting in the notion of justification in Part I. A second almost universal claim about virtue is that it is a state of the soul, or to use terminology with less loaded philosophical associations, it is a property that we attribute to the person in a deep and important sense. We think of a person's virtues as closely associated with her very identity, although not every such state is a virtue or the contrary of a virtue. The purpose of this section will be to identify what it is about virtue that sets it apart from other excellences and other states of the soul.

The concept of a virtue has both theoretical and practical significance. Its practical importance lies in the fact that we can use it in making decisions and in evaluating others. Being able to recognize courage, loyalty, and honesty, as well as courageous, loyal, and honest acts, is an important part of moral education, and as we saw in Part I, Anscombe (1958) and Mayo (1958) have argued that evaluation in terms of such concepts is easier and more natural than it is in terms of the purely formalistic concepts of right and wrong. And even if Anscombe and Mayo are mistaken in thinking that virtue concepts have an advantage in this respect, it is clear that the importance of virtue concepts is partly tied to their practical usefulness.

In addition to the practical importance of the concept of a virtue, it is a prominent concept in theoretical ethics. As mentioned in section 1, most moral theories find it useful to explicate the nature of a virtue and to relate it to other concepts that are important in theoretical ethics, particularly the concepts of the good and the right. One of the constraints in the account that follows, then, will be to explain the nature of a virtue in a way that permits us to give an account of the relations among virtue, the good, and the right while at the same time preserving as much as possible an idea of virtue that is close enough to common sense to permit it a practical function in moral decision making.

To think of virtue is almost immediately to think of examples of particular traits such as courage, generosity, compassion, justice, honesty, wisdom, temperance, and self-respect. This suggests that the fact that most of these qualities are virtues is part of the pretheoretical notion of virtue, and it places a constraint on any acceptable account. This constraint cannot be rigid, of course, but if a given account has the consequence that several of these traits are not virtues, that definitely counts against it. On the other hand, traits such as honor, thrift, humility, obedience, gratitude, and the Christian virtues of faith, hope, and charity are more weakly connected with the pretheoretical notion because they have not appeared on as many different lists of virtues in different cultures and in different eras of history. It would therefore count against an account to a lesser degree if it did not make one of these qualities a virtue.

John Locke stresses the diverse conceptions of virtue in different times and places but claims that everywhere what is called a virtue is what is judged to be praiseworthy and what is called a vice is what is judged to be blameworthy:

Virtue and Vice are names pretended and supposed everywhere to stand for actions in their own nature right and wrong:
and as far as they really are so applied, they so far are coinci-
dent with the divine law above mentioned. But yet, whatever is
pretended, this is visible, that these names, virtue and vice, in
the particular instances of their application, through the several
nations and societies of men in the world, are constantly attributed only to such actions as in each country and society are
in reputation or discredit. Nor is it to be thought strange, that
men everywhere should give the name of virtue to those actions, which amongst them are judged praiseworthy; and call
that vice, which they account blameable; since otherwise they
would condemn themselves, if they should think anything
right, to which they allowed not commendation, anything
wrong, which they let pass without blame. Thus the measure of
what is everywhere called and esteemed virtue and vice is this
approbation or dislike, praise or blame, which by a secret and
tacit consent, establishes itself in the several societies, tribes,
and clubs of men in the world; whereby several actions come to
find credit or disgrace amongst them, according to the judge-
ment, maxims, or fashions of that place. (*Essay* II.28)

Locke notes, however, that in spite of these variations, there is
also a great degree of uniformity in the notions of what is virtuous
and vicious, and he rejects a conventionalist conclusion:

And though perhaps by the different temper, education, fashion, maxims, or interests of different sorts of men, it fell out,
that what was thought praiseworthy in one place, escaped not
censure in another; and so in different societies, virtues and
vices were changed: yet, as to the main, they for the most part
kept the same everywhere. For, since nothing can be more natural than to encourage with esteem and reputation that wherein
every one finds his advantage, and to blame and discounte-
nance the contrary; it is no wonder that esteem and discredit,
virtue and vice, should, in a great measure, everywhere correspond with the unchangeable rule of right and wrong, which
the law of God hath established; there being nothing that so
directly and visibly secures and advances the general good of

mankind in this world, as obedience to the laws he has set them, and nothing that breeds such mischiefs and confusion, as the neglect of them. (*Essay* II.28)

In contemporary philosophy Alasdair MacIntyre has also called attention to the way the lists of virtues have changed over time and place, even within Western cultures, and also rejects a conventionalist conclusion. MacIntyre traces the historical development of the idea of virtue from Homer through Aristotle and the Christian virtues, to the virtues treated in Jane Austen's novels, to the utilitarian virtues of Benjamin Franklin, and on to the dearth of virtues recognized today (1984, chap. 14). MacIntyre argues that in spite of these differences and with one or two exceptions, there is a common core concept of virtue, a concept that we will look at presently. As we have seen, the fact that virtue is an excellence is uncontroversial, and to that extent there is at least a minimal core concept of virtue. More controversial and more interesting is the question of whether there is a substantive concept at the core of the idea of a virtue. In this regard some writers have noted the many similarities among the lists of the particular virtues in different cultures,[4] whereas others find the differences more salient. Occasionally a trait that appears as a virtue on one list actually appears as a vice on another. It has frequently been pointed out, for example, that Aristotle would have thought of humility as a vice, and some feminists say that such masculine, militaristic virtues as honor and civic pride are covertly traits that involve the subjugation of women and other powerless groups. Furthermore, even when the same virtue concept appears to be common to very different cultures, there may be great differences in the patterns of behavior to which it leads. Clearly, the courage of a samurai warrior would have been exhibited quite differently from the courage of an American woman historian in the later twentieth century. Nonetheless, it is possible that the American woman and the samurai would have little trouble in recognizing each other as persons of courage. In other respects, however, they might not admire each other. This sug-

---

[4] E.g., Carroll Kearley n.d.

gests that we should not be too hasty to conclude either that there is no commonality among the virtues recognized throughout history or that the commonality is extensive enough to render the exceptions insignificant. The evidence is neither overwhelmingly in favor of a common substantive concept nor overwhelmingly against it. However, the fact that writers on virtue almost always begin by identifying a list of typical virtues suggests that the pretheoretical notion of virtue includes the idea that certain particular traits are among the virtues. An analysis of virtue is hopeless, I believe, unless we can assume that most of a selected list of traits count as virtues and do so in a way that is not strictly culture bound.

The foregoing considerations lead me to propose that an account of virtue should contain the following features: Virtue is an excellence; virtue is a deep trait of a person; those qualities that have appeared on the greatest number of lists of the virtues in different places and at different times in history are, in fact, virtues. These qualities would probably include such traits as wisdom, courage, benevolence, justice, honesty, loyalty, integrity, and generosity. Some virtues are intellectual, others are moral, and some may be neither intellectual nor moral. In any case, there is nothing in either the most common lists of virtues or in the theoretical treatment of virtue that requires us to think of the word "moral" in "moral virtue" as redundant. Finally, the account of a virtue should aim for a high degree of theoretical significance combined with practical usefulness. This would include attentiveness to the way the concept of virtue is used in the history of philosophy, as well as the way it is used in contemporary virtue ethics. In what follows I will attempt an account of virtue that is faithful to these constraints.

2.2 *Virtue and the good*

Virtue is an excellence of the person and so it is connected directly with the idea of good, but this raises a number of questions about the sense in which virtue is good. For one thing, when we call a virtue good, we may mean that it makes a person good, or we may mean it is good *for* its possessor. In the former sense of good, a virtue is *admirable* in its possessor; in the latter sense, it is *desirable*. These senses of good are not equivalent, as can be seen from the fact that wealth is good in the latter sense but not the former, and although benevolence is good in the former sense, it is at least open to question whether it is good in the latter sense. Second, we may ask whether a virtue is also connected with good as a property of something other than the agent, such as the good of the world as a whole. In addition, as we saw in section 1 on the different forms of virtue theory, theories can be distinguished on the question of which is conceptually and ontologically prior, the good or virtue. In this subsection I will concentrate on the different ways in which virtue is connected with the goodness *of* the agent, with what is good *for* the agent, with what is good for the world, and with the related question of whether a virtue can lead to wrongful behavior.

Let us begin with a question in the metaphysics of value. As a property, a virtue may be considered an abstract object. Is that abstract object good in itself or do we *call* it good only because it makes its possessor good? The question is posed by Aquinas as follows:

> For virtue is man's goodness, since it is virtue that makes its subject good. But goodness does not seem to be good, as neither is whiteness white. It is therefore unsuitable to describe virtue as a "good quality." (*ST* I-II, q. 55, a. 4, obj. 1)

In reply he says:

> We must, however, observe that as accidents and non-subsistent forms are called beings, not as if they themselves had being, but because things are by them, so also are they called good or one, not by some distinct goodness or one-ness, but because by them something is good or one. So also virtue is called good, because by it something is good.

Here Aquinas seems to be unwilling to call good a property of a property, so good is not a property of virtue itself. A virtue is properly *called* good, not because good is a property of *it*, but because it makes its possessor good. I will not dwell on the ontological point even though it is a fascinating one, but want to call attention to the fact that Thomas's position in this passage stresses the idea that what is good about virtue is that it makes *its possessor* good. This is interesting because it is not only inner directed but is clearly a claim about the way in which a virtue contributes to the admirability of its possessor. In addition, however, Aquinas thought that virtue is connected with external good: "the Philosopher says: 'Virtue is that which makes its possessor good, and his work good likewise'" (*ST* I-II, q. 55, a. 3). Aquinas explicitly says that one cannot make bad use of virtue, and he quotes approvingly what he calls "the definition usually given of virtue as 'a good quality of the mind, by which we live rightly, of which no one can make bad use, which God works in us, without us'" (*ST* I-II, q. 55, a. 4).[5] Virtue is, then, both a good-making quality of a person and a quality that cannot lead to bad use. Presumably "bad use" means wrongful behavior. This could reasonably be taken to imply that virtue is good *for* the world. So Aquinas's position in this passage seems to be that virtue makes its possessor good and is good *for* the world, although he takes no position on whether virtue is good *for* its possessor.

Both claims are controversial and deserve some attention.[6] Let us begin with the question of whether virtue is always a good-making quality of a person (i.e., it makes its possessor admirable) and then turn to the question of whether it is always good for the rest of the world.

On the face of it the courage of a Nazi soldier makes him worse overall than if he were cowardly. Gregory Trianosky (1987) invents a compassionate but biased judge whose compassion for

---

5 In the translation by the Dominican Fathers it is noted here that this definition is close to that of Peter Lombard, *Sent.* II, d. 27, chap. 5, but the form of the definition seems to come from Peter of Poitiers, *Sent.* III, chap. 1 (*PL* 211, 1041). Aquinas qualifies the claim that one cannot make bad use of a virtue in the reply to objection 5. There he says that one can make bad use of a virtue taken as an object, as when we have an evil attitude toward virtue, but "one cannot make bad use of virtue as principle of action, so that an act of virtue be evil."

6 Rorty (1988, pp. 314–29) denies that a person is always made better by virtue.

the victims of crime makes him even more unfair than he would have been without the compassion and, presumably, worse over-all because of it. The idea in each case is that all other things being equal, the addition of courage to the Nazi's character and the addition of compassion to the judge's character result in each of them becoming morally worse.

One response to these cases is to say that the traits exhibited by the Nazi and the judge are not courage and compassion respectively. Another is to say that these traits are courage and compassion, but courage and compassion are not always virtues. A third is to say that the Nazi and the judge do have the traits of courage and compassion, and these traits in these cases are virtues, but virtues are not good making in every instance. A fourth response is to say that the traits exhibited by the Nazi and the judge are courage and compassion and that courage and compassion are always virtues and are always good to have, but the good-making properties of virtues and the bad-making properties of vices do not always add up arithmetically to yield a rating of the agent's overall goodness. I will defend the fourth response.

I have nothing to say against those who take the first response. If the traits of the Nazi and the judge are not courage and compassion respectively, then these cases are no challenge to the position that virtues like courage and compassion always make their possessors good. The second response is more interesting since it is a challenge to the claim that certain specific traits always make their possessors good, though not a challenge to the claim that *virtues* always make their possessors good. Philippa Foot implies a position of this kind when she suggests that courage does not always act as a virtue (1978, p. 15). This position seems to me to raise some serious difficulties about the identity of traits. If the virtuous trait of courage is distinct from the nonvirtuous trait of courage, this difference can have nothing to do with motivations, beliefs, attitudes, or dispositions to act. Instead, a trait would need to be identified by the way acting on such a trait interacts with acting on certain *other* traits. Alternatively, if the virtuous trait of courage is the same trait as the nonvirtuous trait of courage, it follows that whether a trait is a virtue or a vice is an accidental feature of it. I find these two alternatives undesirable but will not attempt to refute this response.[7]

Gregory Trianosky's (1987) assessment of the two cases is closest to the third response. He says that although we would not praise the Nazi for his courage, prize the presence of compassion in the biased judge, or encourage the development of these virtues in those persons in whom the virtues would make them worse, these traits are still virtues in these cases (p. 132). Our inclinations to praise, prize, and encourage a certain trait are only the typical external signs of the presence of virtue; they do not constitute the essence of virtue. This leads Trianosky to postulate that a virtue is a certain kind of potentiality. "A virtue is a state, disposition, relation, or quality with a certain power. Being a virtue is like being an explosive. The gunpowder in a certain keg may still *be* an explosive even if due to its dampened condition it cannot now *operate as* an explosive" (p. 132). A bit farther on he says, "The power that a trait always has insofar as it remains a virtue is a *normative power:* the potential for contributing to the overall moral worth of the life of its possessor" (p. 133). Trianosky's position, then, differs from that of Aquinas in that the latter says virtue is a good-making quality of a person, whereas the former says it is only potentially so.

I agree with Trianosky (1987, p. 132) that the traits of the Nazi and the judge are courage and compassion if suitably described, that these traits are virtues, and that in these cases a virtue can make a person worse overall. Nevertheless, I think Aquinas is right to consider a virtue good in itself in every instance, not just potentially good, and Trianosky's account does not fully explain this. My position is that *a virtue is worth having even in those cases in which it makes a person worse overall.* The reason for this, in brief, is that without it a person would have more moral work to do to attain a high level of moral worth. Although the compassionate but unfair judge may be worse overall than he would be if he

---

[7] See Watson 1984, n. 6, for an argument that a virtue and a fault can be the same trait. Watson admits he begs some questions about trait identity in that argument.

were less compassionate, his compassion is a good thing in itself and it is worth having even *for him* because with it he only has to overcome unfairness; without it, he would have to overcome both unfairness and lack of compassion. A person with a virtue is closer to becoming a person with a high level of moral worth than he would be if he lacked the virtue, and this is the case even when the virtue makes him morally worse. So if we compare compassionate but unfair judge *A* and uncompassionate and unfair judge *B* to a truly virtuous judge *C*, I would maintain that *A* is closer to being like judge *C* than is *B*, even though *B* is now better than *A*, and even though judge *A* does more wrong things than judge *B* because of the combination of his compassion and his bias.[8]

An analogy can be made with the learning of an art that involves a large number of distinct skills such as playing the cello. An intermediate-level cellist may play quite well but have a defect in bowing technique. As he concentrates on perfecting his bowing, he may notice that for a while he plays the cello worse than he did before because the improved technique makes his intonation somewhat worse, or perhaps it makes his playing less expressive. His learning of the technique is an advance, however, because it puts him closer to being a fine cellist than he was without it. Without it, in fact, he can never attain a high level of excellence at playing the instrument, and his teacher would be right to encourage him to acquire it. Similarly, as the unfair judge becomes compassionate, his compassion may for a time make him worse because more unfair. But he is actually closer to being a virtuous person with compassion, and he cannot be a virtuous person without compassion. This may be part of the reason that

---

[8] The argument that courage makes the Nazi worse and that compassion makes the judge worse may be examples of what Shelly Kagan (1988) calls contrast arguments that commit "the additive fallacy." The moral is that we should not expect to be able to identify the separate and independent contributions of individual factors in, say, the evaluation of a person's character by contrasting cases that differ in a single factor. Such factors may make their contribution as clusters or in some other way. So even if the courageous Nazi is worse overall than the cowardly Nazi, we cannot infer from that that it is *courage* that made the Nazi worse. I thank Charles Young for calling my attention to Kagan's article.

sometimes when a person who is courageous, persevering, and loyal but is also committed to an evil cause is converted and embraces a good end, he excels morally in a very short time. Presumably this is because his courage, perseverance, and loyalty are qualities that make him learn virtuous living more quickly. He may even go from a paradigm of evil to a moral hero very rapidly. Perhaps Saint Augustine is an example of such a person; another is Saint Francis of Assisi. Francis's generosity amounted to profligacy before his conversion, arguably making him a worse person than he would have been without it; at least, his handling of money was irresponsible. After his conversion his generous impulses were transferred from the entertainment of his friends to supplying the needs of the poor. If he had not had the virtue of generosity all along, he would not have been able to rise to such a high level of moral worth in such a short time.

I would therefore elucidate the sense in which virtue makes its possessor good as follows: Anyone who has it is closer to reaching a high level of excellence than one who lacks it, other things being equal, and it usually results in an actual increase in a person's overall moral worth. The possession of a virtue does not necessarily lead to an increase in the quantity of right acts, because there are certain combinations of a virtue and a vice that tend to produce more wrongful acts than would be produced by the vice alone. This should lead us to be wary of any attempt to postulate a strict correspondence between the possession of virtue and the performance of right acts, but this is not to deny that virtue is the more fundamental concept. The way in which virtue is related to right will be addressed in 6.1.

The way in which virtue makes its possessor good also applies to intellectual virtues. A person is a better person for being open-minded, careful, and thorough in evaluating evidence, intellectually courageous, and able to recognize and to rely on trustworthy authorities. This claim anticipates some things we will discuss later about the relation between intellectual goods and other human goods, but the point about the intellectual virtues that is parallel to the one just made about the moral virtues is that there are putative cases in which the possession of an intellectual virtue makes a person worse overall than he would be without it. So

Francis Bacon says, "In fact, as is clear, the more active and faster a man is, the further astray he will go when he is running on the wrong road" (*Novum Organum,* trans. and ed. Urbach and Gibson, I.61). A person who is intellectually courageous but lacks open-mindedness may be led further astray from the truth by his courage than he would have been without this virtue. Just as the biased but compassionate judge is led to perform more wrongful acts because of the combination of his unfairness and compassion than he would have if he had not been compassionate, so too a person might be led into more false beliefs by the combination of her closed-mindedness and intellectual courage than she would have been if she had not had the courage.

My position on the epistemic case is parallel to my position on the case of the judge. It is better for a person to be intellectually courageous even when her courage leads her to maintain beliefs in the face of adversity that ought to be given up because they were formed out of narrow-mindedness. She is wrong in her beliefs, and even more wrong than she would have been if she had not been intellectually courageous. Still, I propose that she is closer to a high level of epistemic status with the courage than without it.

Although a virtue is always a good thing for a person to have, then, there is a complication in that equal degrees of a virtuous trait are not always associated with equal degrees of internal good in the agent. There are individual differences in the degree to which a virtue makes an agent good. This point was noticed by Aristotle in his discussion of the sense in which virtue is a mean when he says that the mean is relative to a person (*NE* II.6.1106b). So what counts as the mean between foolhardiness and cowardice will differ from one person to another, just as what counts as the right amount of food to eat differs from person to person. When we look at the intellectual virtues, we see the same phenomenon. Some persons are intellectually successful by careful plodding, whereas others do their best work when they indulge in exuberant intellectual impetuousness. These individual differences seem to strain the distinction between virtue and vice since the mean relative to a particular individual may lean very far in the direction of one vice or its contrary. Still, it is fair to say that human thinkers should be neither too impetuous nor too slow and plodding, neither too steadfast in their views nor too open to accepting the views of others, neither too reliant on authority nor too intellectually independent, etc. There is such a thing as too thorough, too careful, too attentive to detail. But what counts as too much or too little may vary from person to person, as well as from one intellectual context or discipline to another. This suggests that although a virtue is always good-making, there is no determinate degree and kind of activity exhibited by a virtuous person that is uniformly good-making, and similar remarks apply to vice. An exception may be the virtue of *phronesis*, or practical wisdom, which I will argue in section 5 is a higher-order virtue.

We may think of a virtue as good-making in the sense of being an *admirable* trait, but it does not automatically follow that a virtue is good *for* its possessor in the sense of benefiting her or being desirable. In *The Gay Science*, Nietzsche maintained that people believe the former but not the latter:

> A man's virtues are called *good* depending on their probable consequences not for him but for us and society: the praise of virtues has always been far from "selfless," far from "unegois-tic." Otherwise one would have had to notice that virtues (like industriousness, obedience, chastity, filial piety, and justice) are usually harmful for those who possess them, being instincts that dominate them too violently and covetously and resist the efforts of reason to keep them in balance with their other instincts. When you have a virtue, a real, whole virtue (and not merely a mini-instinct for some virtue), you are its *victim*. But your neighbor praises your virtue precisely on that account. (1974, p. 92)

I have not argued that virtues are good for their possessors in the sense intended by Nietzsche, but it is worth considering whether they are. Plato, of course, thought so, and in contemporary philosophy Alasdair MacIntyre's well-known account of virtue makes the benefit of a virtue to its possessor intrinsic to its definition. MacIntyre defines virtue as "an acquired quality the possession and exercise of which tends to enable us to achieve those goods which are internal to practices and the lack of which effectively prevents us from achieving any such goods" (1984, p. 178). Like almost all other virtue theorists, MacIntyre is thinking only of moral virtues in this definition, but I see no reason why it cannot apply to intellectual virtues as well. Such intellectual virtues as intellectual carefulness, thoroughness, reliance on trustworthy authority, courage, and perseverance are traits that are ways of exercising the motivation for knowledge, and since most practices involve to one degree or another the need to acquire true beliefs related to the practice, the full possession of the goods internal to practices relies on the possession of intellectual virtues. Some practices are wholly intellectual, such as the practice of philosophy, and the way in which intellectual virtues are needed to enjoy the internal goods of philosophy is much deeper and more extensive than the way intellectual virtues are needed to enjoy the internal goods of, say, farming. Still, even among the traditional moral virtues some are more directly related to the enjoyment of the internal goods of certain practices than are others. The virtues of cooperation are less important for the enjoyment of chess than for the enjoyment of team sports, for instance.[9] So the fact that the intellectual virtues are more important for some practices than for others does not prevent their satisfying the core concept of virtue identified by MacIntyre.

Let us now turn to the question of the relation between a virtue and external good. This issue has already been addressed in part

---

[9] Philosophers may disagree about the extent to which philosophy is a cooperative practice, and so there will be disagreement about the extent to which the virtues related to cooperation and social interaction are necessary for the enjoyment of the goods internal to philosophy. In my experience philosophy is far from a solitary endeavor. In fact, I would argue that oral philosophy is the purest form of philosophy, and since it takes at least two persons to engage in oral philosophy, the virtues governing the proper interaction between two or more persons would be necessary to get the full benefit of philosophy in its purest form. This is not to say that philosophers lacking these social virtues cannot be brilliant philosophers whose discoveries are discussed for centuries. But I do mean to say that those same philosophers would have gained more of the internal goods of philosophy had they possessed such virtues. In fact, they would have been better philosophers.

in our discussion of the relation between virtue and the perfor-mance of right or wrong acts since presumably, there is some connection between the performance of right/wrong acts and benefit/harm to the world as a whole. But let us consider in particular whether virtue always has good external conse-quences. The history of the concept of virtue clearly supports the view that it is a feature of the concept that its exercise normally has good external consequences, and we may consider this fea-ture a component of the pretheoretical notion. Aristotle seemed to think that although the business of morality is personal flourish-ing, the relationship between the individual and the community makes the good of the latter closely associated with *eudaimonia*. Modern moral philosophers have been considerably more skepti-cal than were the ancient Greeks about the close association be-tween the flourishing of the individual and that of the com-munity.[10] Michael Slote (1992b) divides the virtues into self-regarding and other-regarding and assumes that the virtues in these two classes are prima facie antagonistic. For this reason the question of the extent to which virtue benefits others as well as ourselves is more pressing in the contemporary philosophical milieu. Note that nothing in this feature requires us to say that a virtue is good even in part *because* of the goodness of its conse-quences. Pure virtue theorists deny that virtue is an excellence because it is a means to some external good, but that does not commit them to denying that virtue always brings about good to others. It is clear that virtuous persons acting out of virtue have certain aims, and we generally think that it is not sufficient to merely *have* the aims in order to be virtuous, but that a virtuous person reliably produces the ends of the virtue in question. So compassionate persons are reliably successful in alleviating suf-fering; fair persons are reliably successful in producing fair states of affairs; generous persons are reliably successful in giving to those who are in need, and so on.

There are a number of ways a virtue theory can explain our concern about success in a virtue, and as we will see in section 4, stronger and weaker virtue theories explain this differently. But it

---

[10] See Wong 1991, pp. 445–6, for a similar point.

does seem to me to be a plain fact about the way we ordinarily think of virtue that a virtuous person is someone who not only has a good heart but is successful in making the world the sort of place people with a good heart want it to be. The concept of a virtue, then, combines our commonsense moral interest in good motivations with our commonsense moral interest in moral success.[11] So "virtue," I will say, is a success term.

With perhaps the exception of a few virtues that do not seem to have much to do with anybody other than the agent,[12] we would normally say that if the world as a whole were not better off for the presence of a given trait in individual persons in typical cases, we would simply not consider such a trait a virtue.[13] We may assume, then, that nothing is a virtue unless it benefits both the possessor and others in the typical case. But this raises a question analogous to the one just considered on whether a virtue always makes its possessor good. Would we consider a trait a virtue in the *particular* case if it were not beneficial to others or externally good-making in that case? Presumably the main reasons it is problematic to call the courage of the Nazi and the compassion of the unfair judge virtues are not only that these qualities seem to make their possessors worse but also that these same qualities are bad for the world.

My answer to this second problem is the same as to the first.

---

[11] Michael Slote suggested to me that the dual interest of common sense in the feelings of the heart and external success was behind the debate over nuclear deterrence. Those opposed to it usually relied on a negative moral judgment about the quality of the motivations or intentions needed to implement such a policy. On the other hand, the fact that it was successful in preventing a nuclear war was reason enough for other people to consider it morally justified. So we are morally concerned about the quality of people's intentions, but we also care about preventing grave harm. The nuclear deterrence example shows that these two concerns of morality may conflict, but the fact that we care about both gives us reason to analyze virtue in a way that includes both concerns.

[12] Wisdom may be an example, but Dewey Hoitenga has pointed out to me that it was Solomon's wisdom that enabled him to determine the true mother when two women were fighting over the same infant. If so, even wisdom may not be solely self-regarding.

[13] Amelie Rorty makes this point in 1988, pp. 299–313.

Even though the world is worse off as a whole because the unfair judge is compassionate than it would be if he lacked compassion, compassion is still a virtue in this case and is still an excellence because the world is closer to a state of well-being if he is compassionate than if he is not. His compassion makes his own character closer to an admirable one and the world itself closer to a desirable one than either would be without the compassion. To consider this problem more closely, consider a world full of persons like the unfair but compassionate judge, and compare it with a world full of persons who are both unfair and uncompassionate. Which world is closer to the world in which persons who are both fair and compassionate predominate? There are, of course, different ways to measure closeness. If the normative differential of these worlds is measured solely in terms of the rightness/wrongness of the acts of the judges and their external effects, then the second world would be rated closer to the ideal for the reasons Trianosky gives. But if the normative differential is measured in terms of how much a world has to be *changed* to turn it into an ideally desirable world, then the first world would be rated closer to the ideal and, hence, higher in value. That is because in the first world judges only need to learn how to be fair; in the second world, judges need to learn *both* fairness and compassion, and that is a much bigger project. I conclude, then, that virtue is related to good, not by invariably increasing the goodness of its possessor and goodness for the world, but by invariably making its possessor closer to a high level of admirability and the world closer to a high level of desirability.

To summarize 2.2, virtue is related to good in a number of ways. First, a person is good through the possession of virtues. Because a person has a virtue, both the possessor of the virtue and the world are closer to a state of goodness than either would be otherwise. A virtue usually results in an actual increase in the possessor's moral worth, and it usually results in an actual increase in the good for the world. That virtues are excellences that are both praiseworthy in their possessors and beneficial to others is an aspect of the idea of virtue that ought to count as a constraint on any acceptable account. The question of the conceptual and ontological priority of good and virtue is a different matter, however, and will be deferred until section 4, when we look at the varieties of virtue theories.

2.3 *Virtues distinguished from natural capacities*

Virtue, we have said, is an excellence, but not every excellence is a virtue. We also said that virtue is a property of the soul, and this is consistent with the normal practice of excluding physical excellences from the category of virtues, although it may not be wholly misguided to speak of "physical virtues." In any case, this inquiry will be limited to virtues of the soul.

The next question we will address is whether virtues are natural or acquired excellences. Few philosophers have doubted that virtues are distinct from natural faculties, although it is more common to confuse faculties with the intellectual virtues than with the moral virtues. As we saw in Part I, Ernest Sosa (1985) states that intellectual virtues are faculties, and John Greco (1993) gives as examples of intellectual virtues such faculties as sight, hearing, and memory. Now in one sense of virtue, Sosa and Greco are right. Sometimes we call any human excellence a virtue, in which case the virtues would include not only good faculties such as good eyesight but also properly functioning natural cognitive processes such as valid deductive reasoning, natural capacities such as native intelligence, good qualities of temperament such as an affable disposition, and skills such as keyboard skills, in addition to such traits as courage and wisdom. On the narrower concept of virtue, a virtue is an *acquired* human excellence. Aristotle takes this position, and it has been one of the less contentious claims about virtue in the history of the concept.[14] Admittedly,

---

[14] At the beginning of Book II of the *Nicomachean Ethics* Aristotle says that the intellectual virtues owe their birth and growth to teaching, which implies that they are acquired traits, but when he goes on to say that none of the *moral* virtues arise in us by nature, we may wonder why he did not say none of the virtues of either sort arise by nature. His lack of perspicuity on this point leads to a further confusion in Book VI, which is devoted to the intellectual virtues. There his examples include such things as being good at geometry, a trait that is much closer to having a natural origin than the moral virtues.

the distinction between natural and acquired is somewhat vague since even natural qualities can often improve with training and practice, but there is an important philosophical motivation for calling attention to the category of acquired excellence, and that is the interest in focusing on those excellences for which we are responsible. Being acquired is not sufficient for being a quality for which we are responsible, but it is certainly necessary. The virtues ought, then, to be found among the acquired traits. But before accepting this conclusion, let us look at both Aristotelian and contemporary defenses of it.

Aristotle says: "Again, we have the faculties by nature, but we are not made good or bad by nature" (*NE* II.5.1106a8–9). The reason we are not good or bad by nature was given at the beginning of Book II:

> [I]t is plain that none of the moral virtues arises in us by nature; for nothing that exists by nature can form a habit contrary to its nature. For instance, the stone which by nature moves downwards cannot be habituated to move upwards, not even if one tries to train it by throwing it up ten thousand times; nor can fire be habituated to move downwards, nor can anything else that by nature behaves in one way be trained to behave in another. Neither by nature, then, nor contrary to nature do the virtues arise in us; rather we are adapted by nature to receive them, and are made perfect by habit. (*NE* II.1.1103a19–25)

I find this argument convincing if incomplete. An animal acting on instinct alone does not have virtue, even if the instinct is a good one, and the same goes for the human. But we ought to be alert to the possibility that some of our natural tendencies may be plastic enough to change with education, and if so, it might be quite appropriate to call the resulting quality a virtue. But we do not praise the natural faculty or capacity itself and blame the natural defect, and one reason for this is that these qualities are wholly involuntary. Of course, we have already seen that the problem of moral luck makes it a mistake to think that moral praise or blame is *proportional* to voluntary control; nevertheless, the completely involuntary is outside the moral realm. But the concentration on the voluntary/involuntary distinction blurs a more important distinction that is the critical one in the elimination of natural capacities from the category of moral virtues, and that is the distinction between the personal and the subpersonal. A virtue is a deep quality of a person, closely identified with her selfhood, whereas natural faculties are only the raw materials for the self. The Aristotelian way to put it is that they are merely potentialities. Natural faculties, capacities, and talents may be praised in the same way we praise natural beauty or strength, but we do not blame the lack of them. Virtues are qualities that deserve praise for their presence and blame for their absence. Even greater blame is due to a person who has the contrary of a virtue, namely, a vice, but we do not blame a person for having the contrary of intelligence or good looks.

Some contemporary writers on the virtues give stronger criteria for virtue possession that eliminate natural traits from the domain of the virtues. Philippa Foot (1978) says that nothing is a virtue unless it involves the will and resistance to contrary temptation, and G. H. von Wright (1963, p. 149) says that although temptation is no longer operable in the virtuous person, it must have been at one time. This implies not only that a virtue is not a natural trait but also that a tendency to the contrary trait is natural. But surely this is too strong. Virtues such as temperance may be directed primarily toward avoiding the bad, but as long as virtues primarily involve motivations to the good, there need not be anything in the motivations themselves that requires resistance to contrary tendencies.[15] Otherwise it would be impossible for a person who is tempted neither one way nor the other to gradually develop a virtuous trait out of such positive motivations. I would imagine that some persons become benevolent, generous, or loyal in this way. If so, there need be no natural disposition either

---

[15] Charles Young has suggested to me that there are two very different ways of conceiving of the virtues that may be behind my disagreement with Foot and von Wright. On one conception, a positive one, the virtues are ways of going right; on the other, a negative conception, the virtues are ways of avoiding going wrong. The same virtue will look quite different on a negative conception than it does on a positive one. See Young 1988 and 1994 for the way this point relates to the accounts of temperance and liberality respectively.

toward a virtue or toward the contrary vice.[16] This suggests one of the differences between the way virtue is praised and the way a natural talent or capacity is praised. At some time in a person's development there must be a realistic possibility that she will develop a certain vice rather than the associated virtue. This is not to say, of course, that there is an equal probability either way, but only that it is compatible with the nature of the person that she develop in the way that leads to vice rather than the way that leads to virtue. This means that both virtues and vices are compatible with human nature and, indeed, with the nature of any particular human being. The nature of virtue must reflect the fact that vice is in the same category, only the latter is blameworthy while the former is praiseworthy. The particular kind of praiseworthiness that applies to virtue, then, reflects the fact that the virtuous person might have been vicious instead. It is the fact that the person could have gone either way that distinguishes virtue from certain other excellences, particularly all those that are natural or inborn.

It is important for the nature of virtue that it have a corresponding vice (or two corresponding vices, if we accept the Aristotelian doctrine of the mean). For the same reason we do not think of a deficiency or weakness as a vice if it does not have a corresponding virtue. Claustrophobia is not a vice, and not only because claustrophobia is involuntary, as Foot says. It is not a vice because there is no corresponding virtue that the claustrophobic person could have developed instead.[17]

Aristotle is right, then, in saying that virtues are not faculties or natural capacities. He concludes the discussion of the genus of

---

[16] Hilary Kornblith has suggested to me that it is better to treat the question of whether there is a natural tendency toward virtue or vice as an empirical matter. This seems reasonable.

[17] Aristotle believes every virtue has two vices corresponding to it, where the former is praiseworthy and the latter are blameworthy, but he also considers a state more horrible than vice, namely brutishness, which is an essentially subhuman state. One is blameworthy for being in such a state, but there is no praiseworthy virtue corresponding to it. At the other extreme there is superhuman virtue. Such virtue is praiseworthy, but there is no blameworthy vice corresponding to it (*NE* VII.1145.15–26). I thank Charles Young for calling my attention to this feature of Aristotelian virtue and vice.

virtue as follows: "If, then, the virtues are neither passions nor faculties, all that remains is that they should be states of character [*hexis*]" (*NE* V.2.1106a10–11). We can add from the foregoing discussion that they are states of excellence that develop over time in a person, who could have developed the contrary state. This suggests that intrinsic to the nature of virtue is the way in which it is acquired. It also suggests that a virtue may be something like a skill. A discussion of these points will be taken up in 2.4 and 2.5.

2.4 Virtues distinguished from skills

More controversial than the question of whether a virtue is a natural faculty, process, capacity, or quality of temperament is the question of whether a virtue is a skill, since skills, like virtues, are acquired excellences. I will argue that virtues are distinct from skills.

One of the problems in discussing the differences between skills and virtues is that the common vocabulary is very misleading. Sometimes the same term can apply to both a virtue and a range of skills, as probably is the case with "fairness," "prudence," "discretion," and "self-control." On the other hand, sometimes the same term is used to apply to a particular emotion and to the virtue that governs that emotion, without any necessary reference to overt behavior, as in the case of "compassion" or "sincerity." For this reason compassion and sincerity are probably not very often confused with skills. The reaction of Gregory Trianosky to this situation is to say that the virtues are not all of the same type (1987, p. 124). Trianosky may be right; however, this might show instead that common *terms* for the virtues do not consistently designate virtues rather than feelings or emotions, on the one hand, or skills, on the other.

Although Aristotle distinguishes virtues from both natural qualities and skills, some of his examples of virtues, such as excellence in deliberation, are easy to confuse with these other categories. Von Wright (1963, p. 137) says that Aristotle was misled by the Greek language into thinking that virtues are more like abilities and skills than they actually are. Regardless of the reason,

Aristotle's lack of care in distinguishing virtues and skills has led to much subsequent mischief. Since the failure to make the distinction is more common with the intellectual virtues than with the moral virtues, it has led to one of the alleged grounds for distinguishing the two kinds of virtue. There are several arguments for distinguishing virtues and skills that I find persuasive. I will mention several from Aristotle and the recent literature and will propose some of my own.

One ground for distinguishing skills and virtues has been proposed by Philippa Foot, who points out that skills are only capacities (1978, p. 9).[18] Making essentially the same point, Gilbert Meilaender (1984) says that a skill need not be exercised, but a virtue does not exist unless it is exercised on the appropriate occasions. So a person could have the skills of a hockey player or of a speaker of Japanese but, for reasons of his own, choose not to exercise them when called for. He might, in fact, even make mistakes characteristic of an unskilled player or speaker on purpose, but that would not demonstrate his lack of full possession of such skills. On the other hand, the fact that he does not act justly or courageously on the occasions calling for such behavior does demonstrate that he does not fully possess the virtues of justice and courage respectively.[19] Of course, there is a difficulty in knowing what counts as the occasions calling for such behavior in the case of virtues, but the principle Meilaender uses here seems to me to be right.

Let us next look at several arguments by James Wallace and Sarah Broadie. In the first place, Wallace argues that virtues are not skills because some skills are not worth having, but all virtues are worth having (1978, p. 43). This argument does not support the conclusion that virtues are not skills, however, but only that the class of virtues is not coextensive with the class of skills. On

---

18 Here Foot relies on the point discussed earlier that virtues are in a different category than capacities.

19 Having made the distinction between virtues and skills, Meilaender does go on to say that virtues are nonetheless skills that suit us for life generally. I find this an unhelpful extension of the concept of a skill. The differences between virtues and skills mentioned in this section are too numerous to permit the collapse of the two concepts.

Wallace's reasoning it might be the case that every virtue is a skill, although not every skill is a virtue.

A better argument is Wallace's contention that skills are or are closely associated with techniques, whereas virtues are not. A technique is a sort of action that is inherently difficult in a way peculiar to itself – technically difficult – and a skill is the mastery of such a technique, Wallace says. Virtues, on the other hand, are not masteries of techniques. Although some virtues involve being able to do difficult things, the difficulties involved are due to contrary inclinations (past or present), not to technical difficulties in the actions themselves (1978, p. 46). Wallace intends this distinction to apply only to the moral virtues, however, saying that the difference between intellectual and moral virtues corresponds "in a way" to the distinction between virtues and skills (p. 44).

I find this argument persuasive as applied to moral virtues, but unlike Wallace, I believe it applies equally to intellectual virtues. Intellectual care, thoroughness, perseverance, fairness, and courage are not technically difficult. Their difficulties arise primarily from a lack of sufficient passion for the truth or from a desire to appear right in one's own eyes or in the eys of others or, perhaps, from just plain laziness. As I will point out later, there *are* intellectual skills that involve technical difficulties, but these are not what I am calling intellectual virtues.[20]

A third difference mentioned by Wallace is that a person can forget a skill but not a virtue (1978, p. 46). This does not mean one cannot lose a virtue such as courage, Wallace says, but one does not do so by forgetting how to be courageous. Wallace says he got the idea from Gilbert Ryle, but it is also suggested by Aristotle's statement at *NE* I.10.1100b11–17:

[20] Robert Roberts (1984, p. 129) argues that a certain class of virtues, those of self-control, may involve technical abilities. These virtues include courage, temperance, and patience. But since Roberts also argues that the virtues in this class are skills, it is not surprising that he maintains that they invoke techniques. I claim, in contrast, that the skills of self-control are not themselves virtues, although persons may acquire these skills in the process of acquiring the virtue. A person who has the *virtue* of patience or courage, I would say, has gone beyond the need for the technical skills a person who has trouble maintaining his patience or his courage requires.

For no function of man has so much permanence as virtuous activities (these are thought to be more durable even than knowledge of the sciences), and of these themselves the most valuable are more durable because those who are happy spend their life most readily and most continuously in these; *for this seems to be the reason why we do not forget them.* (Emphasis added)

If this point is right about moral virtues, it ought to apply to intellectual virtues as well. One can lose the quality of intellectual fairness or caution in roughly the same way one can lose moral fairness or caution; in neither case is it lost by forgetting how to be fair or cautious. Intellectual virtues that do not have moral analogues, such as insightfulness or the ability to think up explanations, can also be lost, but again it is not accurate to describe the process as "forgetting how" to do such things.

Robert Roberts (1984) finds Wallace's argument questionable both on the grounds that many skills also have the feature of being unforgettable and on the grounds that at least some of the virtues can be forgotten:

In general, it is only more complicated skills that are forgettable, and even here it is unlikely that a skill, well-learned, will be completely forgotten. Someone who has played the piano well, and then lets twenty years elapse without practicing, will get rusty indeed. But that she has not lost all her skill will be evident from how quickly it comes back with practice. (P. 240)

Furthermore, Roberts argues that certain of the virtues can be partially forgotten in the same way as a skill:

It seems to me that courage, etc., cannot be flat forgotten; but if we allow that getting "rusty" is a sort of forgetting or partial forgetting, it is not so obvious that one cannot forget courage. See the autobiography of Gordon Liddy, who in prison felt it necessary to exercise himself in withstanding pain, to make sure that he hadn't gone "soft." (P. 240)

It is not clear to me that it is the virtue of courage that Liddy was exercising in prison, but let us concede the point that a person may undergo a type of forgetting of certain virtues and that certain skills are not wholly forgotten once mastered. The passage just quoted from Aristotle suggests a somewhat different way of distinguishing skills and virtues that seems to me to have more force. Sarah Broadie interprets Aristotle in this passage as distinguishing a virtue from a skill on the grounds that it is incompatible with the possession of the former that one would voluntarily let it go, although it does not count against the possession of a skill that one voluntarily gives it up (1991, p. 89). So even though a skill may be *worth* keeping, it is not incompatible with the possession of the skill to give it up voluntarily. In contrast, it is partly constitutive of virtue that the possessor never voluntarily lets it go. Whether or not this point represents Aristotle's intent in the above passage, it seems to me that Broadie has correctly identified a difference between virtues and skills.

The fourth difference between skills and virtues given by Wallace is that it is possible for a person who does not possess a virtue to act in a way fully characteristic of that virtue, whereas this is not so with skills (1978, p. 53). Wallace takes this point from Aristotle, who makes it in the course of distinguishing moral virtues from "arts" (*techne*). Aristotle formulates the problem this way:

> The question might be asked, what we mean by saying that we must become just by doing just acts, and temperate by doing temperate acts; for if men do just and temperate acts, they are already just and temperate, exactly as, if they do what is in accordance with the laws of grammar and of music, they are grammarians and musicians. (*NE* II.4.1105a17–21)

Aristotle responds as follows:

> Or is this true even of the arts? It is possible to do something that is in accordance with the laws of grammar, either by chance or at the suggestion of another. A man will be a grammarian, then, only when he has both done something grammatical and done it grammatically; and this means doing it in accordance with the grammatical knowledge in himself.

Again, the case of the arts and that of the virtues are not similar; for the products of the arts have their goodness in themselves, so that it is enough that they should have a certain character, but if the acts that are in accordance with the virtues have themselves a certain character it does not follow that they are done justly or temperately. The agent also must be in a certain condition when he does them; in the first place he must have knowledge, secondly he must choose the acts, and choose them for their own sakes, and thirdly his action must proceed from a firm and unchangeable character. These are not reckoned as conditions of the possession of the arts, except the bare knowledge; but as a condition of the possession of the virtues knowledge has little or no weight, while the other conditions count not for a little but for everything, i.e., the very conditions that result from often doing just and temperate acts. (II.4.1105a22–35)

Both Wallace (1978) and Broadie (1991, pp. 82–6) interpret Aristotle's use of the term "*techne*," translated as "art," as meaning skill. Wallace sees Aristotle as claiming that skills and virtues are dissimilar in that it is enough that an act meet certain standards of proficiency and that it be done with knowledge in order to exhibit a skill, but that is not enough to exhibit a virtue. The conditions for possessing a virtue include additional qualities of the agent's will and enduring character.

Broadie extracts two additional grounds for the distinction between skills and virtues from this passage. Take first her translation of 1105a20–8:

It is possible to do something grammatical either by chance or under the guidance of another. A man will be proficient in grammar, then, only when he has both done something grammatical and done it grammatically; and this means doing it in accordance with the grammatical knowledge in himself. Again the case of the arts and that of the excellences are not similar; for the products of the arts have their goodness in themselves, so that it is enough that they should have a certain character once they have been produced.

111

Commenting, Broadie says:

> This last point is odd if it means that the product's being in the
> right condition is sufficient evidence of skill in the (immediate)
> producer, since Aristotle has just said that the product could be
> correct through chance or someone's instruction. Instead he
> must mean that we are satisfied with things which are normally
> produced by art or skill provided they are up to standard, even
> when they were produced by someone without skill. If we
> assess what such a doer has done by *what he has made,* we can
> say that what he has done is good. The lack of skill implies no
> defect in what he has done on this occasion, and it might rea-
> sonably be claimed that the skill is of value only because who-
> ever possesses it is more likely to produce acceptable articles.
> Aristotle's point is that it is not like this with virtue and right
> actions (hence, he implies, virtue is too different from skill for
> one to be justified in drawing conclusions about virtue from
> premises about skill). (1991, p. 83)

Later, in discussing Aristotle's third condition for virtuous action, namely, that the agent must act from "a firm and unchangeable character," Broadie says: "The third condition also
distinguishes moral qualities from skills. . . . it says nothing
against a person's skill if he fails to exercise it in the face of
distractions or with someone begging him not to" (1991, p. 89). It
does count against a person's virtue, however, if distractions or
persuasions lead him to fail to exercise it.

I have thought of two other considerations supporting the distinction between virtues and skills that I have not encountered in
the literature. First, on all accounts, a vice is the contrary of a
virtue, not its contradictory, but a skill has no contrary. The only
candidate for the contrary of a skill is the lack of the skill, but
surely, a vice is not simply the lack of a virtue.[21] This is because
vice, like virtue, is acquired by habituation. Children and people
who are childlike in their lack of experience are neither virtuous

---

[21] In selected cases there may exist something like the contrary of a skill – an
antiskill. Perhaps playing a musical instrument very badly is an example.

nor vicious. If, as Aristotle says, each virtue has two contrary vices, the point is even stronger since clearly a skill does not have two contraries.[22]

Second, the behavior consisting in the exercise of a skill is not essentially connected to anything valuable, whereas it is in the case of a virtue. If a skill has value, that is because of features of the situations in which it is used extrinsic to the skill itself. On the other hand, a virtue is intrinsically valuable.

Finally, let me illustrate the distinction by example. If we compare lists of virtues and skills, I think we can see that there are both moral virtues and moral skills, and intellectual virtues and intellectual skills. Skills serve virtues by allowing a person who is virtuously motivated to be effective in action. Consider first the relation between moral virtues and moral skills. Some examples of moral virtues that have accompanying skills are compassion, moral wisdom, fairness, self-improvement, generosity, and courage. Examples of skills that a person with each of these virtues might have are as follows:

Compassion skills: knowing what to say to the bereaved
Moral wisdom skills: being able to talk a young person into staying in school or getting out of a street gang
Fairness skills: knowing how to fairly evaluate student papers or papers submitted to a professional journal
Skills of self-improvement: knowing how to develop a certain talent
Skills of generosity: being effective in giving to others (e.g., in a way that does not embarrass them)
Skills of courage: knowing how to stand up to a tormentor

Typically, moral virtues have many skills associated with them, although there may be moral virtues that have no corresponding skills. Perhaps humility and sincerity are in this category, as well as the Christian virtues of faith and hope. Some moral skills may

---

22 The closest view to the one I have just given is Wallace's point that "[n]ot all excellences have opposite action-states that are bad, however, and this is true of skills" (1978, p. 50). Aristotle's point about a virtue as a mean between two contrary vices is meant to apply only to moral virtues, not to intellectual virtues. I will argue later that many intellectual virtues typically have two contrary vices as well.

not correlate with a particular virtue. For example, tact is a skill that aids numerous virtues, including some that are nonmoral. When we speak of self-control, we may mean either the virtue of temperance or a set of skills used by a self-controlled person.

The distinction between moral virtues and skills just described applies to intellectual virtues and skills as well. Let us begin with some examples of intellectual virtues and follow them with examples of intellectual skills.

Intellectual virtues
- the ability to recognize the salient facts; sensitivity to detail
- open-mindedness in collecting and appraising evidence
- fairness in evaluating the arguments of others
- intellectual humility
- intellectual perseverance, diligence, care, and thoroughness
- adaptability of intellect
- the detective's virtues: thinking of coherent explanations of the facts
- being able to recognize reliable authority
- insight into persons, problems, theories
- the teaching virtues: the social virtues of being communicative, including intellectual candor and knowing your audience and how they respond

Intellectual skills
- verbal skills: skills of speaking and writing
- perceptual acuity skills, e.g., fact-finding skills; these are the skills of the detective or the journalist
- logical skills: skills of performing deductive and inductive reasoning, the ability to think up counterexamples
- explanatory skills, e.g., the ability to think up insightful analogies
- mathematical skills and skills of quantitative reasoning
- spatial reasoning skills, e.g., skills at working puzzles
- mechanical skills, e.g., knowing how to operate and manipulate machines and other physical objects

Many of the intellectual skills listed here are not closely associated with specific intellectual virtues, but some are. Perceptual acuity skills, for example, probably are connected with the virtue of sensitivity to detail and with intellectual care and thoroughness. Verbal and logical skills are very important concomitants of what I have called the virtues of being a good communicator, as well as of many others. Spatial reasoning skills, mathematical skills, and mechanical skills are important for effectiveness in many of life's roles, and the person who is virtuous in such roles would be ineffective without the associated skills. Being a virtuous parent probably involves a host of skills, including many of those listed above. There are intellectual skills connected with moral virtues and moral skills connected with intellectual virtues. For example, the moral virtues of honesty and truthfulness involve skills of communication – not misleading others – but these are intellectual skills. On the other hand, the virtue of intellectual perseverance might involve the skill of knowing how to resist harassment or browbeating. There are undoubtedly many other such examples.

The conclusion to be drawn from this discussion is that virtues and skills have numerous connections, but virtues are psychically prior to skills. I propose that this is because the motivational component of a virtue defines it more than external effectiveness does, whereas it is the reverse in the case of skills. Virtues have a broader range of application than do skills, at least typically, whereas skills tend to be more subject specific, context specific, and role specific. The more direct connection of skills with external behavior makes them more easily taught than virtues, although this is not to say that virtues cannot be taught. As von Wright has argued, skills are tied to *specific* activities, but there is no essential tie between a specific virtue and a specific activity (1963, p. 139). Since skills *are* connected with actions of a certain specifiable sort, it follows that effectiveness in action requires skills, and to the extent that a virtuous person is motivated to produce external consequences desirable from the point of view of the virtue, he would also be motivated to acquire the skills that are associated with such effectiveness in action. So, for example, a courageous person in certain roles would be motivated to acquire the skills of effective combat. A fair person who is a teacher would be motivated to learn procedures for fair grading, and if she does not learn such procedures, we would probably have some doubts about the extent to which she possesses the virtue of fairness.

Intellectual virtues, like moral virtues, are psychically prior to skills and include a motivational component, whereas intellectual skills are more like techniques needed for effectiveness in the pursuit of knowledge.

I conclude that virtues are distinct from skills. Many virtues have correlative skills that allow the virtuous person to be effective in action, and thus, we would normally expect a person with a virtue to develop the associated skills. Still, it is possible for her to have a virtue and to lack the corresponding skills. Virtues are prior to skills and are strongly connected to motivational structure, whereas skills are more connected to effectiveness in action.[23]

2.5 *Virtue and habit: the transformation machine*

A virtue is an acquired excellence and a vice is an acquired defect. It takes time to develop virtues and vices, and this feature is connected with the fact that we hold persons responsible for these traits. Once a virtue or vice develops, it becomes entrenched in a person's character and becomes a kind of second nature. The fact that a trait is among the more permanent of a person's qualities means that she bears a fuller responsibility for it than she does for qualities that are more fleeting. So a person's responsibility for her virtues and vices is connected with the fact that they are gradually acquired and are relatively permanent, and these two properties of permanence and gradual acquisition are not independent. Virtues and vices form part of what makes a person the person that she is. The features of gradual acquisition and entrenchment suggest that a virtue is a kind of habit, and that is what Aristotle maintained. But it would be too hasty to conclude

---

[23] A dramatic example of this difference is in the area of economic and social justice. The possession of such virtues as compassion and justice are independent of the skills needed to produce material goods and such nonmaterial goods as freedom for as many people as possible. It is not uncommon for people to have the virtues just mentioned but to support social programs that are opposed to their own ends. Much social and economic controversy is over means and not ends, so even when the requisite virtues are possessed, the necessary skills may still be beyond our reach.

that a virtue is *identical* with a habit if, as Gilbert Ryle has argued (1949, pp. 42–4), habits are only one sort of "second nature," and higher-grade dispositions such as skills and virtues are not purely automatic but exhibit intelligence in their operation. Both pure reflex habits and virtues are acquired through a process of repetition over time, and it should be useful to consider whether it is intrinsic to the nature of a virtue that it be acquired in this way, or whether the fact that a virtue requires training and develops over time is just an accidental feature of it. Can we imagine acquiring a virtue by some other process than by the training Aristotle describes?

One way to test the importance of the acquisition process for the nature of virtue is via Robert Nozick's imaginary transformation machine. This tantalizing machine is not as well known as Nozick's experience machine, but like the latter, Nozick proposes it in order to help us determine what really matters to us. If the thought experiment works, it can also help us determine what it is about the way a virtue is acquired that makes it a virtue.

> We learn that something matters to us in addition to experience by imagining an experience machine and then realizing that we would not use it. We can continue to imagine a sequence of machines each designed to fill lacks suggested for the earlier machines. For example, since the experience machine doesn't meet our desire *to be* a certain way, imagine a transformation machine which transforms us into whatever sort of person we'd like to be (compatible with our staying us). Surely one would not use the transformation machine to become as one would wish, and therefore plug into the experience machine! (1974, p. 44)

Here Nozick continues in a footnote:

> Some wouldn't use the transformation machine at all; it seems like cheating. But the one-time use of the transformation machine would not remove all challenges; there would still be obstacles for the new us to overcome, a new plateau from which to strive even higher. And is this plateau any the less earned or deserved than that provided by genetic endowment

117

and early childhood environment? But if the transformation machine could be used indefinitely often, so that we could accomplish anything by pushing a button to transform ourselves into someone who could do it easily, there would remain no limits we *need* to strain against or try to transcend. Would there be anything left *to do*? (P. 44)

Nozick continues by postulating one more machine:

> So something matters in addition to one's experiences *and* what one is like. Nor is the reason merely that one's experiences are unconnected with what one is like. For the experience machine might be limited to provide only experiences possible to the sort of person plugged in. Is it that we want to make a difference in the world? Consider then the result machine, which produces in the world any result you would produce and injects your vector input into any joint activity. We shall not pursue here the fascinating details of these or other machines. What is most disturbing about them is their living our lives for us. (P. 44)

Nozick's machines call attention to some of the things that matter to us, he says, and that is why we would not want to use them. This is undoubtedly true, but it is not my main concern here. I think there is something especially wrong with the transformation machine that bears examination. Unlike the experience machine and the result machine, it is not clear to me that such a machine is even possible.

Nozick gives no account of the kind of qualities the transformation machine could produce, but in the passage quoted above he implies that what he has in mind is primarily a matter of motivation or "willpower." We imagine that by pushing a button we could transform ourselves into someone who can do easily what would otherwise be difficult, but which we were already motivated to do. The machine gives us a motivational shot, so to speak, an idea that bears a resemblance to the traditional Catholic doctrine of actual grace. This suggests that before connecting to the machine, the subject has the higher-order motivation to have the motivation to perform certain acts but, when the time comes, finds himself unable to bring himself to do it. Such a person would be like a writer with writer's block or an addict motivated to give up his addiction. In each case he is motivated to have a motivation he does not have sufficiently for the needed action. A friend of mine went to a hypnotist in an effort to overcome his writer's block. Unfortunately, the hypnosis did not work, but if it had, it would have been similar to the transformation machine, although presumably even the most effective hypnosis does not work as quickly.

The examples of hypnosis for writer's block and the Catholic doctrine of actual grace surely do describe perfectly possible mechanisms, and for this reason there does not appear to be anything impossible about the transformation machine. The question, though, is whether a *virtue* could be produced in this way. Nozick's description suggests that he thinks of the transformation machine as a device for overcoming moral weakness, or *akrasia*, and it does seem logically possible for a machine to give a person a dose of motivational power, which is primarily what is lacking in the akratic person.[24] That also seems to be the point of hypnosis and actual grace. The transformation machine could then make such a person morally strong. It is clear in Aristotle, however, that moral strength (continence) is not the same as virtue (*NE* VII.1), and this distinction seems correct on the face of it. One difference between the virtuous person and the morally strong person is that the latter is simply able to overcome temptation in those cases in which she knows the right thing to do and is generally motivated to do the right thing, whereas the former has acquired a habit of *feeling* as well as acting, a habit of being motivated in a certain way, and she is just not subject to the temptations of the morally strong individual. A more important difference for the present point, however, is that the virtuous person has a superior form of moral knowledge. She is able to know the right thing to do in a way that cannot be predicted in advance. Aristotle claims that moral virtue is logically connected with *phronesis*, and *phronesis* involves an insight into particulars that may not be fully captured by any general rule. This means

---

[24] I thank David Blake for this point.

that *phronesis* is logically connected with experience, at least for humans, so it is logically impossible for humans to obtain virtue without experience. The machine cannot give a person courage, but it can make her less susceptible to fear; it cannot give her temperance, but it can make her less susceptible to the desire for pleasure and aversion to pain; it cannot give her generosity, but it can move her to feel more caring about others' needs. It is logically possible, then, for the machine to strengthen preexisting motivations, thereby permitting a person to overcome temptations, and the machine could even give a person certain feelings such as compassion. But Nozick's transformation machine cannot give a person virtue as his experience machine can give a person experience and as his result machine can bring about desired consequences. When Nozick observes that the transformation and experience machines are not enough, he says that something must matter to us in addition to experiences *and* what one is like, and so he postulates the result machine. But the insufficiency of the transformation machine does not show in the first instance that something matters to us in addition to what one is like; it shows primarily the insufficiency of the transformation machine to make us a person who is *like* a person with an admirable character.

A human person's moral identity is intrinsically connected with a series of experiences of interaction with the world around her. It is possible, of course, that the relationship between beings similar to us and their environment is different. There might even be actual intelligent beings of a different species in some other part of the universe whose character does not develop gradually with a series of interactions with their environment, as ours does. So it is possible that there are creatures whose virtues are not connected with habits. But it is still the case that the virtues of human beings in the ordinary human environment are acquired at least in part through the acquisition of certain habits of feeling and acting. This means that Nozick's transformation machine, unlike his experience machine and his result machine, is not even conceptually possible if it is intended to produce human virtues. The reason is that a virtue is not a *human* virtue if it is acquired at the flip of a switch. The problem is not simply that the will is not involved in the transformation machine, since on Nozick's description its use could be chosen by the subject herself. The problem is that the subject has contributed nothing *but* a single act of will to the acquisition of the desired trait. But a single act of will does not a virtue make, and the reason for this is not primarily because, given the facts of human nature, a single act of will is causally insufficient to transform oneself. Rather, a single act of will is logically insufficient to transform oneself into a person whose resulting quality is something we would praise in the sense we praise a virtue.

Robert Roberts gives a similar argument in "Will Power and the Virtues" (1984). There he argues that the class of virtues of willpower are needed for the development of the agent's agent-hood and thus must be the result of struggle:

> We can guess that it will never be possible to give a person a moral "identity" – a tough and abiding passion for justice or a stable and focused desire to relieve suffering – by injecting him with a drug or giving him a brain operation or fiddling with his genes. But the impossibility of giving somebody moral charac-ter in this way seems to be more than psychological. For even if we could in this way produce a being who was indistinguish-able, in terms of his present dispositions, from a saint, still I think we would have no inclination whatsoever to canonize him. For the praise of his saintliness, and thus for his deeds, would not be due *him*. If it were due anyone, the pharmacolo-gist or brain surgeon would seem more likely candidates. So the idea of somebody acquiring moral character without strug-gle seems not only psychologically, but logically, amiss. (P. 235)[25]

David Brown (1985) uses intuitions similar to the ones I have been developing here to argue that it is impossible for a person to be suddenly transformed at death from an ordinary good but imperfect person to the state of moral perfection in which a per-

---

[25] A related discussion of this point appears in William Mann's paper "Hope" (1993, pp. 274–5), in which he says that undergoing gene therapy cannot produce a virtue, but it can allow a fledgling virtue to grow.

son allegedly finds himself in heaven. He concludes that if there is a heaven, there must be a purgatory. The application of the problem of sudden transformation to an afterlife is beyond the scope of this book, but one of Brown's arguments is both interesting and directly relevant to the transformation machine problem. Brown calls it the argument from identity:

> The general point of the argument is best seen by indulging in a thought experiment. Imagine someone looking like you and having your present "memories" waking up tomorrow in your bed, but with at least one significant difference; he is morally perfect. It is very doubtful whether he would regard himself as the same person as you. He is much more likely to see himself as a different person who has, somewhat strangely, been substituted into your body. The reason for supposing this is the lack of significant connexions between his character and yours. He would be unable to understand how he has become the type of person he now is. Thus, for example, through his "memory" he would know of previously existing strong desires, but be totally unable to account for their present absence. . . .
>
> But the difficulties are not confined to the disappearance of what were once conscious temptations. This new individual will also see as wrong what he will have no "memory" of having regarded as wrong at the time. All those self-deceptions you once indulged in he will view with disdain, for example, the times when you thought you were right to be angry when deep down you were just being spiteful. Thus it is not just the individual's orientation towards the future which will be totally different. He will also have a transformed attitude towards your past. Attitudes which your memories tell him he endorsed at the time he will wish totally to reject and yet be unable to account for what has brought about the transformation.
>
> The most natural reaction for an individual in this situation would surely be to experience at the very least a profound identity crisis, the most natural resolution of which would be for him to refuse to identify with the foregoing "memories" that he finds so alien to his present character. (Pp. 451–2)

It is part of the ability to have a concept of the self that changes in character can be understood by the agent herself. She must be able to tell herself a story in which she has no trouble identifying with the person she remembers being at each stage of the process of change. I think Brown is right that this rules out sudden, radical change in character. It is, of course, possible to perform a morally praiseworthy act that is out of character but may be the beginning of an improvement in character. What Brown's point makes problematic is a certain way of evaluating persons who experience sudden conversion, such as Saul of Tarsus or Ebenezer Scrooge. It is perfectly consistent with our view of ourselves that we have a sudden insight or an abrupt change of mind. What I have ruled out is an account of such conversion according to which what changes instantly is a person's character. Conversion does not produce an instant virtue.

The idea that a virtue is acquired by gradual habituation is one of the more plausible parts of the Aristotelian legacy. There is a class of virtues that do not seem to be acquired by habit at all, however, and these are the virtues of originality and creativity. Not only do these excellences not require habituation, but they seem to flourish only in the absence of it. It is difficult to see how the ability to produce original ideas in the sciences or the arts could have been fostered by the gradual acquisition of habitual responses. For example, Ernest Dimnet tells us that Balzac "was a man who, between his twentieth and twenty-ninth year, consistently wrote trash, and, after that, produced nothing but masterpieces" (1928, p. 35).[26] Geniuses in other fields are also known to

---

[26] Ernest Dimnet was a French abbé who wrote in English and lectured in English at major universities in the United States where he was extremely popular with American audiences in the thirties. Besides *The Art of Thinking*, his most popular books were the sequel, *What We Live By*, and a two-volume autobiography, *My Old World* and *My New World*. Earlier Dimnet had become embroiled in the modernist dispute, and after one of his books was placed on the Index of forbidden books by the Catholic Church, he gave up writing on theological matters. A major theme of *The Art of Thinking* is the importance of originality and the stifling effect of habit and repetition: "Life, including such – apparently – helpful influences as education and literature, destroys this ten-

have made a sudden break with past habits of thought and action, and it is precisely their genius that permitted the break. Perhaps moral conversion can be understood equivalently as a type of creative genius in the moral life. If so, this might permit us to resolve the problem just addressed of how to evaluate the character of persons who undergo sudden conversions or suddenly perform acts that are stupendously good and also seemingly out of character. I said earlier that the concept of a virtue and of moral character will not permit cases of the instantaneous development of a virtue or of an instantaneous change in character. But if there are moral virtues that are the analogues of artistic creativity or originality, it might be that even before the conversion, the moral convert possessed a virtue that gave him a cast of mind that made him ripe for insights and able to embrace them with enthusiasm.

The existence of the virtues of creativity is a problem for the thesis that virtue must be acquired by habituation, but I will go farther and offer the conjecture that the ability to resist habit *in general* may actually be a distinguishing mark of creative people. This exacerbates the problem that these virtues pose for the habituation thesis since they are not simply an exception to the thesis; their existence indicates a difficulty in the analysis of the *other* virtues. I am suggesting that it is possible that there is something different about even the justice, compassion, generosity, and courage of highly original and creative persons than these same traits in other individuals. It is possible, of course, that a person is original only in his art or profession, but I believe that there are people who are original in almost everything they do. It follows that there is a strain in virtue, at least as it is exemplified in some persons, that resists the Aristotelian account of virtue acquisition.

One response to this problem, of course, is to exclude the qualities of originality and creativity from the class of virtues, but in spite of the greater theoretical economy of such a response, I

dency [originality], as April frost kills blossoms, and imitation, ignoble conformism, takes the place of originality. Mankind is like Herculaneum—covered over with a hard crust under which the remains of real life lie forgotten. Poets and philosophers never lose their way to some of the subterraneum chambers in which childhood once lived happy without knowing it. But the millions know nothing except the thick lava of habit and repetition" (p. 88).

tend to think it exhibits a failure to appreciate some of the most praiseworthy of all human traits – traits that express the highest reaches of the human personality and character. They ought not to be ignored in a full account of virtue. As far as I can see, the only reason to exclude them is that they seem to be closer to natural talents or strokes of luck than to acquired excellences, and so we may be ambivalent about holding their possessors responsible for them. A person struck by repeated insights often feels as if they came into her mind from without, as if it were a gift from the gods. So she would not feel responsible; she would just feel fortunate. If so, these traits would be outside the realm of virtue as we have been treating it here. But the virtues of originality cannot be so easily dismissed if I am right that virtues are traits that are vitally connected with a person's identity. Not only might such traits be among the most prominent of a person's excellences, but they might be claimed by the person herself as those that are most deeply constitutive of herself. This makes the set of virtues that include originality, creativity, inventiveness, and, perhaps, some forms of insightfulness somewhere in between virtue as it has traditionally been handled by moral philosophers and natural faculties and talents. I believe these traits can be handled by a virtue theory, but they will lie somewhat outside the range of the central cases of moral evaluation. I will suggest in 3.1 that they are most plausibly explained in a way that is analogous to the treatment of the supererogatory in duty ethics.

I conclude that it is part of the nature of a virtue in the standard case that it be an entrenched quality that is the result of moral work on the part of the human agent, and that it be acquired by a process of habituation. I will not treat this feature of virtue as without exception, but the way in which virtue is acquired is related to the way in which we go about evaluating moral agents. Differences in manner of acquisition result in differences in degree or kind of responsibility. For the most part, the kind of responsibility we think of as distinctively moral and the praise and blame that accompanies it are associated with traits that are acquired gradually in the course of forming habits. The class of traits that includes originality and creativity may be an interesting exception.

2.6 Virtues, feelings, and motivations

We have seen that a virtue is a state of the soul, that it is acquired, and that it is (at least usually) the result of habituation. We have also seen that virtues are connected with motivations and that this is one of the ways they are distinguished from skills, which are more closely related to external effectiveness. In this section we will look more closely at the way motivations are related to virtues, but to do that, we will need to compare virtues and feelings. Aristotle makes a point of distinguishing virtues from *pathe*,[27] which, like virtues, are states or properties of the soul. We begin with Aristotle's grounds for making the distinction between virtues and feelings.

Aristotle says he means by passions (*pathe*): "appetite, anger, fear, confidence, envy, joy, friendly feeling, hatred, longing, emulation, pity, and in general the feelings that are accompanied by pleasure or pain" (*NE* II.5.1105b21–2). He offers two reasons for thinking that virtue cannot be in this category. One is that we are not praised or blamed simply for the fact that we have certain passions, "for the man who feels fear or anger is not praised, nor is the man who simply feels anger blamed, but the man who feels it in a certain way" (*NE* II.5.1105b 32–3). The other is that "virtues are modes of choice or involve choice," whereas we feel passions without choice. Neither reason is very convincing, although as we will see, the first is better than the second.

Aristotle is right that we usually blame a person, not for the fact that she has a feeling, but for the way in which she feels it, the degree to which she feels it, or the circumstances in which she feels it. This certainly is the case with fear and anger. However, other feelings are themselves the objects of praise and blame, not just for the circumstances or way in which they are felt. Hatred, bitterness, and envy are feelings for which people are blamed, and such blame does not depend upon circumstances, or, at least, not principally upon circumstances. Similarly, love and sympathy are passions for which people are praised, and again, the praise

---

[27] *Pathe* is variously translated "feelings," "passions," or "affects." I will usually refer to them as feelings but will occasionally use an alternate translation.

does not depend principally upon circumstances. This suggests that some feelings in themselves reflect positively or negatively on their possessor, whereas other feelings reflect positively or negatively only in certain circumstances. This would lead to the conclusion that virtue cannot be *wholly* analyzed as a feeling, but not because we never praise or blame a person for her feelings.

Aristotle's second reason for excluding virtues from the class of passions is even less convincing. It is far too strong to claim that virtues are modes of choice. In whatever sense it is true to say that anger and fear are not modes of choice, neither are patience, compassion, kindness, or bravery. Of course, a series of choices can be a partial cause of the development of a virtue or vice in the long term, but the same can be said about instances of feeling. I may not choose to be afraid *now*, but my present fear may be partly the result of previous choices. In fact, if my present fear is partly a function of my cowardice and my cowardice is partly a function of previous choices, my present fear is partly a function of my previous choices. So neither feelings nor virtues are the direct result of choice, although both are indirectly affected by choice. A virtue may also involve choice indirectly in the sense that it disposes its possessor to make certain choices in certain sorts of situations, but then, this is not a very convincing way to distinguish virtues from passions, because the latter may also dispose a person to make certain choices while in their grip.

In spite of the fact that Aristotle puts too much emphasis on the connection of virtues with choice, I claimed in Part I that it is reasonable to classify them as voluntary, and to see the sense in which a virtue is voluntary is to see a deeper distinction between virtues and feelings. Feelings, like acts, occur at identifiable moments of time and have a continuous duration in time, generally lasting from a few seconds to no more than several hours. Because the occurrence of a feeling is identifiable in time, the test of its voluntariness is closer to the test of act voluntariness, usually expressed in the form of a counterfactual: An act *A* performed at time *t* is voluntary just in case the agent could have refrained from performing *A* at *t*. On this criterion a feeling would normally fail the test of voluntariness, whereas an act done out of habit would pass it. When I flip the switch on the coffeemaker in the morning,

I do not choose to do so and may have little consciousness of my act at all, but the act is voluntary because I could have refrained. The habit itself is voluntary derivatively because it is the result of a series of acts, many of which are voluntary. When we turn to the case of a virtue, its voluntariness is not like the voluntariness of flipping the switch on the coffeemaker, because a virtue is not an act, but it is like the voluntariness of the *habit* of turning on the coffeemaker. As we have seen, virtues have many of the features of habits in that they develop over a long period of time, and there are many acts in the causal process leading to the development of a virtue that the agent could have refrained from performing had she so chosen. A virtue, then, is voluntary in the same sense as the habit of turning on the coffeemaker in the morning is voluntary. Both are the result of a series of acts that pass the criterion for voluntariness given above.

So although the voluntariness of virtues and habits differs from the voluntariness of feelings, the difference is certainly less than Aristotle thought. Past chosen and otherwise voluntary acts form part of the causal history of my feeling angry at this time. Similarly, past chosen and otherwise voluntary acts form part of the causal history of the development of a virtue. There may typically be a difference in the degree of the voluntariness of feelings and virtues, but it is probably not a difference of kind.

I conclude that Aristotle is right that virtues are not feelings, but neither of the reasons he gives supports that position. The primary reason virtues are not feelings is that feelings, like acts, occur at particular moments of time but normally do not pass the test for act voluntariness, whereas virtues are habits that are the result of the performance of acts, many of which are voluntary. In addition, we have seen that although there are cases in which feelings are the objects of praise or blame, we do not think of them first and foremost as excellences or defects, whereas virtues are always excellences.

Virtues are not themselves feelings, but almost every writer on the moral virtues has connected them with feelings. Aristotle claimed that virtues regulate the feelings and involve the proper handling of pleasure and pain. Both Hobbes and Spinoza draw up lists of the moral virtues from their enumeration of the passions. Von Wright says the virtues are all forms of self-control; the role of a virtue is to counteract, eliminate, rule out the obscuring effects that emotion may have on our practical judgment (1963, p. 147). It is interesting to note that this assumes that the effects of emotion are negative. One gets the impression that if a person had no emotions at all, there would be no problem with her practical judgment. In the case of every specific virtue, there is some specific passion that the possessor of that virtue has learned to master, and that is why the various virtues are so many forms of self-control. According to von Wright, then, the goodness of the virtues resides in their capacity to protect us from harm, not in their capacity to supply us with some good.

Foot's position is similar to that of von Wright in that she says that virtues are corrective, standing at a point at which there is some temptation to be resisted or deficiency of motive to be made good,[28] and for this reason she does not include self-love as a virtue since self-love, she says, is automatic (1978, p. 8). But leaving aside the negative attitude toward emotion, Foot's connection of virtue with motive seems to me to be right. Motives are important for our study of virtue because they typically are forms of emotion and are action-guiding. Both features have been identified by traditional writers on the virtues as important components of virtue. I suggest that the concept of a motive is the place at which we can see the true connection between virtues and emotions or feelings.

A motive is a force acting within us to initiate and direct action. Motives are not only activating and directional but also tend to be persistent (see Petri 1991, pp. 3–5). These characteristics are features that we have already associated with traits of character. The nature of the motive force itself, however, seems to admit of some variation. On one extreme, there are motives that are often regarded as almost completely physiological, such as hunger, thirst, and fatigue. These motives are feelings, although they are not emotions. On the other extreme, there is the alleged pure motive of duty, which may not have a "feel" to it at all. The motives in the

---

[28] McDowell says this is continence, not virtue. I am inclined to agree.

large area in between are emotions of various sorts. These are the motives that I think are the most interesting for ethics and that are closely connected with virtues. I will not get involved here in debating whether all motives are forms of emotion or whether only most of them are. The ones I will use in my examples of virtues are all emotions. This does not mean that we have names for all of them; in fact, we do not. In many of my examples, I begin with the preanalytic notion of a particular virtue – say, benevolence – and then claim that it has a motivational component that is a type of action-directing emotion. I have no position on the question of whether emotions are states whose phenomenological content is essential. Although it is generally true that there is something that it is *like* to have a certain emotion, it is possible, even likely, that we do not always *feel* our emotions. We learn to identify our emotions partly by their feels and partly by their associated circumstances. So since I will often be unable to identify a name for the emotion itself, I may have to refer to it indirectly as, for example, benevolent feelings or the emotion that is characteristic of acts of courage. I will assume that when the reader imagines such cases, she imagines being in certain emotional states and is able to do so even if she and I are unable to identify the emotion by name.

I realize that sometimes the term "motive" is used merely to call attention to a desired end without any specification of an emotion or emotion disposition underlying it, as when we say that someone's motive in writing a book was to get tenure. This way of speaking calls our attention to the fact that a motive aims to produce a state of affairs with a certain character. Identifying a motive with the mere aim to produce some state of affairs is inadequate, however, for we generally feel that we have not understood what a person's motive is just by understanding at what he aims. I may know that Booth aimed at the death of Lincoln without knowing his motive in assassinating the president. For the same reason, it is problematic to identify a motive with a desire, since I do not know any more about Booth's motive if I know only that he *desires* Lincoln's death. So my desire for a lighter teaching load is sufficiently identified by identifying what it is I want, but my motive in trying to lighten my teaching load must refer to something else besides the aim of my motive. Nor is it enough to simply refer to *another* desire, such as the desire to have more time for writing, since to understand that I desire *A* and that *B* is a means to *A* is not enough to understand my motive in trying to bring about *B*. A motive does have an aspect of desire, but it includes something about *why* a state of affairs is desired, and that includes something about the way my emotions are tied to my aim. I will not offer an analysis of feeling or emotion in this work, although I will assume that emotions are frequently felt but differ from mere sensations.

A "motive" in the sense relevant to an inquiry into virtue is an **emotion or feeling that initiates and directs action towards an end.** Motives are connected with virtues in that virtuous persons tend to have certain emotions that then lead them to want to change the world or themselves in certain ways. Virtuous persons have motives associated with the particular virtue. A courageous person is motivated out of emotions characteristic of the virtue of courage[29] to face danger when something of importance is at stake. The courage, then, includes both an element of emotion and the aim to protect something of value. It has, then, an intentional element. A fair person is motivated out of emotions that make him like to see others treated equitably, and this leads him to want to produce a state of affairs in which the relations among people have this characteristic. In the same way, an open-minded person is motivated out of delight in discovering new truths, a delight that is strong enough to outweigh the attachment to old beliefs and to lead to the investigation of previously neglected possibilities. In doing so, she is drawn by the desire to form more true beliefs or, at least, to get closer to the truth than she was previously.

Motives are emotions, but many of them are almost continually operative and do most of their work at moderate or even weak

---

[29] I have said that there are cases in which we do not seem to have a word for a given feeling or emotion that is a component of a virtue, and this is one of them. I propose that there are feelings characteristic of courageous persons when they are acting courageously that cannot simply be described negatively (i.e., not being afraid). And I believe the same can be said for the other virtues, although I do not pretend to have an argument for this yet.

levels of intensity. Consider how the motive of thirst ordinarily leads to drinking adequate quantities of liquid without getting below a certain minimum level of intake, and a person motivated by thirst generally gives it no more than a passing thought. Similarly, emotions motivate us, for the most part, without getting to a level of intensity that forces our consciousness to focus on them for an appreciable length of time. Persistent, low-level emotions such as pride in one's work, delight in one's family, aesthetic enjoyment, or the dull sense of anxiety that drives people daily to get done what has to be done are among the more important motives because they drive most of our behavior.[30] The emotional components of kindness, justice, and fair-mindedness also operate for extended periods of time without the agent's having much, if any, awareness of them. The fact that our attention is drawn to them in extreme circumstances does not indicate that they operate only or even mostly in such circumstances.

We generally speak of a motive as an occurrence used to explain a particular act. In such usages a motive is understood as occurring at a particular moment of time or span of time, although I have also said that motives tend to be persistent. It is useful, then, to have a concept for a motive in the dispositional sense. I suggest that we use the term "motivation" in this way. Let us define a **motivation** as **a persistent tendency to be moved by a motive of a certain kind.** I propose that a virtue has a component of motivation that is specific to the virtue in question. So the virtue of benevolence involves the tendency to be moved by benevolent motives, which is to say, it involves a disposition to have characteristic emotions that direct action in a particular direction, probably the well-being of others. A benevolent motivation is,

---

[30] See Leeper 1970, pp. 152–5, for the view that emotions are motives and that they usually operate at persistent, low levels of intensity. Leeper writes, "At such low levels, emotions do most of their work without the individual's having any notable thought of being motivated, because the emotional processes tend to be experienced as objectified or projected as perceptions of the situation. They are usually not experienced as something special within oneself" (p. 152). Leeper also says that excessive attention to the stronger, flashier emotions has distorted the picture of how emotion affects our behavior (pp. 155–6).

therefore, a disposition to have a benevolent motive. A motive is an action-directing emotion. Even if an emotion can be had without being felt, a person who is disposed to have an emotion does feel it from time to time, and when it acts as a motive, it aims to produce a certain end. That end may be an external one, as in the case of benevolence or fairness, or it may be internal, as in the case of self-respect or open-mindedness. Some virtues may have no end at all, such as wisdom, but such virtues are not typical.[31]

A virtuous motivation makes the agent want to act effectively, and this has both general and particular consequences. The former include the desire to gain knowledge appropriate to the area of life that is the focus of the virtue and to develop the skills associated with virtuous effectiveness in that area of life. Particular consequences include the desire to find out the relevant nonmoral facts about the particular circumstances encountered by the agent in which action on the virtuous motive may be called for.

The motivation to gain knowledge of a certain sort and to act in a certain way does not reliably lead to success, although it reliably leads the agent to do as much as is in her power to be successful. The connection between motivation and success may differ from virtue to virtue. For example, the motivation to be persevering may reliably lead to acting with perseverance; the motivation to treat others fairly (in argument or in other areas) may reliably lead to acting fairly. If so, some virtues already have a weak reliability component built into the nature of the virtue that is entailed by the motivational component alone. But it is doubtful that this is true of all virtues. It is not too difficult for a woman with a dependent personality to be motivated to become autonomous, but it is much harder for her to *be* autonomous. The motivations to integrity, open-mindedness, courage, compassion, and generosity are probably far more common than their successful achievement, and the same can be said in varying degrees of most other virtues. I conclude that the "success" feature of virtue is a component

---

[31] Stanley Godlovitch (1981) has pointed out that wisdom has very little, if anything, to do with practical action and its consequences. This does not deny that the presence of wisdom makes the world better as a whole, but it does deny that the *point* of wisdom is some external end, even in part. (See Sommers and Sommers 1985, p. 300.)

distinct from the motivation component. Virtue possession requires reliable success in attaining the ends of the motivational component of the virtue. This means that the agent must be reasonably successful in the skills and cognitive activities associated with the application of the virtue in her circumstances. A person of virtue, among other things, understands some aspect of the world very well. A courageous person is good at understanding how to evaluate the level of danger in a situation, understands the consequences of various courses of action, and knows which dangers are worth facing in a certain manner and which are not. A just person understands what justice demands and is good at perceiving the details of a particular situation that are relevant to the application of rights and duties. A compassionate person understands the level of need of persons around him and can predict the effects of various forms of expressing compassion on persons with different personalities. Virtue, in short, involves knowledge and understanding of the world in the applicable area, both in general and in the particular case. This is not to say that virtue is incompatible with any false beliefs about a situation, but a virtuous person cannot be systematically wrong in her judgments about the world as they apply to her feelings and choices.

To conclude, a virtue is related to feelings or emotions in the following sense. A virtue has a component of motivation, which is a disposition or tendency to have a certain motive. A motive is an action-initiating and directing emotion. It is, therefore, an intentional state; it is directed toward a certain end. A motive, then, includes an element of desire. The desire to produce an end of a certain kind leads the agent to find out the nonmoral facts relevant to effectively producing such an end and to develop the skills associated with the virtue. Reliable success in reaching the internal or external end of a virtuous motivation is a component of virtue.

2.7 General account of a virtue

A serious problem in any attempt to give a general account of the nature of virtue is that our language does not contain a sufficient number of names that convey the full unified reality of each virtue. Some names pick out reactive feelings (empathy), some pick out desires (curiosity), some pick out motivations to act (benevolence), whereas others pick out patterns of acting that appear to be independent of feeling and motive (fairness). For this reason it is easy to confuse a virtue with a feeling in some cases (empathy, compassion), and with a skill in others (fairness). The result is that it is very difficult to give a unitary account of virtues using common virtue language. MacIntyre (1984) blames the problem on a defect in our culture, but this cannot be an adequate explanation since Aristotle's list was no better in this respect than ours. When we examine Aristotle's virtues and vices we see that he had difficulty in finding names for some of them, and a few of his names seem forced, such as his term *"anaisthesia,"* which he coins for the trait of insensibility to pleasure. As already mentioned, Gregory Trianosky's response to this situation is to say that virtues are not all traits of the same general type (1987, p. 124). Robert Roberts (1989) also concludes that there are several distinct kinds of virtue. This response is understandable and it is possible that we will eventually be forced into it, but I believe it should only be taken as a last resort, and I see no reason to take it yet. It is more plausible that the problem derives from a defect in our virtue language rather than a division in the nature of virtue itself.

Let us begin by reviewing the features of virtue we have already identified. First, a virtue is an acquired excellence of the soul, or to use more modern terminology, it is an acquired excellence of the person in a deep and lasting sense. A vice is the contrary quality; it is an acquired defect of the soul. One way to express the depth required for a trait to be a virtue or a vice is to think of it as a quality we would ascribe to a person if asked to describe her after her death. Perhaps no quality is really permanent, or, at least, no interesting quality, but virtues and vices are in the category of the more enduring of a person's qualities, and they come closer to defining who the person is than any other category of qualities.

Second, a virtue is acquired by a process that involves a certain amount of time and work on the part of the agent. This is not to suggest that a person controls the acquisition of a virtue entirely; that is plainly false. Nevertheless, the time and effort required partly account for a virtue's deep and lasting quality, one that in part defines a person's identity and that leads us to think of her as responsible for it. This means that typically a virtue is acquired through a process of habituation, although the virtues of creativity may be an exception.

Third, a virtue is not simply a skill. Skills have many of the same features as virtues in their manner of acquisition and in their area of application, and virtuous persons are expected to have the correlative skills in order to be effective in action, but skills do not have the intrinsic value of virtues. Other differences have been enumerated in 2.4.

Fourth, a virtue has a component of motivation. A motivation is a disposition to have a certain motive, and a motive is an emotion that initiates and directs action to produce an end with certain desired features. Motivations can become deep parts of a person's character and provide her with a set of orientations toward the world that emerge into action given the appropriate circumstances. A motivation is best defined, not as a way of acting in circumstances specifiable in advance, but in terms of the end at which it aims and the emotion that underlies it. The easiest way to identify a motivation is by reference to the end at which it aims, but it also involves an emotion disposition, and that is harder to identify by name.

This brings us to another important feature of virtue: "Virtue" is a success term. The motivational component of a virtue means that it has an end, whether internal or external. A person does not have a virtue unless she is reliable at bringing about the end that is the aim of the motivational component of the virtue. For example, a fair person acts in a way that successfully produces a state of affairs that has the features fair persons desire. A kind, compassionate, generous, courageous, or just person aims at making the world a certain way, and reliable success in making it that way is a condition for having the virtue in question. For this reason virtue requires knowledge, or at least awareness, of certain nonmoral facts about the world. The nature of morality involves, not only wanting certain things, but being reliable agents for bringing those things about. The understanding that a virtue involves is necessary for success in bringing about the aim of its motivational component. This means that virtue involves a component of understanding that is implied by the success component.

A virtue therefore has two main elements: a motivational element, and an element of reliable success in bringing about the end (internal or external) of the motivational element. These elements express the two distinct aims of the moral project that we find in commonsense moral thinking. On the one hand, ordinary ways of thinking about morality tell us that morality is largely a matter of the heart, and we evaluate persons for the quality of their motivations. But morality is also in part a project of making the world a certain kind of place – a better place, we might say, or the kind of place good people want it to be. Because of the latter interest, we are impressed with moral success, not to the exclusion of an interest in people's cares and efforts, but in addition to it.

A **virtue,** then, can be defined as **a deep and enduring acquired excellence of a person, involving a characteristic motivation to produce a certain desired end and reliable success in bringing about that end.** What I mean by a motivation is a disposition to have a motive; a motive is an action-guiding emotion with a certain end, either internal or external.

This definition is broad enough to include the intellectual as well as the traditional moral virtues. It may also be broad enough to include virtues other than the moral or intellectual, such as aesthetic, religious, or perhaps even physical virtues, but I will not consider virtues in these other categories in this work. The definition may not apply to higher-order virtues such as integrity and practical wisdom, however. The latter will be examined in section 5, but an account of the former will be reserved for a future project. Next we will turn to a discussion of the categories of the intellectual and the moral virtues.

3 INTELLECTUAL AND MORAL VIRTUES

3.1 *Aristotle's distinction between intellectual and moral virtues*

It is a commonplace of Western philosophy to regard human cognitive and feeling processes as distinct and relatively autonomous. At least it is usually thought that the former is capable of operating independently of the latter and that it ought to do so in the rational person, whether or not the latter is independent of the former. This part of our philosophical heritage is so strong that philosophers have maintained what Michael Stocker (1980) calls a "purified view of the intellect" long after it was given up by cognitive psychologists and in spite of the fact that a few philosophers like Hume and James called attention to the close connection between believing and feeling (discussed in Pt. I, sec. 3). Related to the alleged independence of the cognitive and feeling processes is the alleged distinctness of the intellectual and the moral virtues, a position we owe to Aristotle. Although it is no longer usual to draw the distinction in precisely Aristotle's fashion, few philosophers have doubted that the division is deep and important. At any rate, few philosophers have opposed Aristotle's claim that such virtues as courage and temperance differ in nature from such qualities as wisdom and understanding. An exception was Spinoza, who connected both the passions and virtue with adequate ideas of God's nature, and he made understanding, an intellectual virtue, the key to all the virtues. Perhaps no other philosopher has unified the moral and intellectual virtues as solidly as Spinoza, who has the following to say about understanding:

> Again, since this effort of the mind, by which the mind, in so far as it reasons endeavors to preserve its being, is nothing but the effort to understand.. it follows.. that this effort to understand is the primary and sole foundation of virtue, and that . . . we do not endeavor to understand things for the sake of any end, but, on the contrary, the mind, in so far as it reasons, can conceive nothing as being good for itself except that which conduces to understanding. (*Ethics*, Pt. IV, prop. 26; parenthetical references removed)

Another apparent exception was David Hume. Hume insists that the distinction between the intellectual and the moral virtues is merely verbal, and that such qualities of intellect as wisdom, a capacious memory, keenness of insight, eloquence, prudence, penetration, discernment, and discretion should count as among a person's "moral" virtues since they are as much objects of praise as his honesty and courage (*Enquiry concerning the Principles of Morals,* App. 4). But since Hume also says it is merely a verbal matter whether the class of virtues includes all the human talents and the class of vices all the human defects, it is clear that he is using a much broader notion of virtue than that which dominated philosophy both before and after (App. 4, para. 1). Hume's inclusion of intellectual virtues within the class of moral virtues therefore loses most of its drama.

In 2.3 I argued that the Aristotelian division between a virtue (*arete*) and other states of the soul such as skills and natural abilities is an important one. In this section I will argue that the Aristotelian division between the two *kinds* of virtue, intellectual and moral, is not. The characteristics that allegedly distinguish the two kinds of virtue do not divide up the spectrum in anywhere near the desired fashion, and intellectual virtues ought to be treated as a subset of the moral virtues in the Aristotelian sense of the latter. Although there are some rough differences in the degree to which these two kinds of virtue involve strong feelings and desires, I will argue that an intellectual virtue does not differ from certain moral virtues any more than one moral virtue differs from another, that the processes related to the two kinds of virtue do not function independently, and that it greatly distorts the nature of both to attempt to analyze them in separate branches of philosophy. Intellectual virtues are best viewed as forms of moral virtue.

Plato's enumeration of the virtues in the *Republic* includes wisdom alongside temperance, courage, and justice, and Plato shows no interest in separating intellectual from moral virtue. In fact, Julius Moravcsik (1992) has recently argued that Plato makes no sharp distinction between moral and nonmoral virtues, whether in terms of the source of virtue or of its function (p. 300). Aristotle, however, does make such a division. What's more, he makes a further division within the intellectual virtues between those that aim at speculative insight or theoretical knowledge and those that pertain to practical thinking aiming at the production of artifacts or the performance of acts. These virtues are art (*techne*) and practical wisdom (*phronesis*) respectively.

It is obvious that there is *some* difference between such states as thinking, doubting, understanding, judging, affirming, denying, or drawing an inference, on the one hand, and hoping, fearing, desiring, loving, being sympathetic, angry, excited, joyful, or sorrowful, on the other. We would normally call the former thinking states or states of the intellect, while the latter are considered states of feeling or emotion. The former are often thought to be more active and the latter more passive, which is why the general category of feeling and desiring has traditionally been called the category of the passions. It follows, then, that if there are virtues that pertain to the former as well as to the latter, there is automatically *something* different about the two classes. We may question, though, how deep and important this difference is.

When we consider how entrenched the distinction between moral and intellectual virtue is in Western philosophy, it is remarkable that Aristotle's grounds for distinguishing them are so unpersuasive. He identifies several characteristics that allegedly separate the intellectual from the moral virtues, all of which ultimately rest on his view that the two kinds of virtue govern different parts of the soul. In both the *Nicomachean Ethics* and the *Eudemian Ethics* Aristotle refers to a rational and to a nonrational or partly rational part of the soul as the basis for the two classes of virtue introduced in the passages immediately following. In the *Eudemian Ethics* he says:

> As it is human virtue that is the object of our inquiry, let us assume that there are two parts of a soul that share in reason, but that they do not both share in reason in the same way; one's nature is to prescribe, the other to obey and listen; if there is something that is non-rational in a different way from this, let us disregard that part. It makes no difference if the soul is divided into parts or lacks parts, as it certainly has distinct capacities, including the ones mentioned – just as in a curve the concave and convex are inseparable, and the white and the

straight may be, though the straight is not white, except incidentally, and it is not essentially the same. (II.1.1219b27–36)

In this passage we are cautioned not to take the claim about the soul's parts as a strong ontological claim, which, he says, is irrelevant to his concerns. Nonetheless, Aristotle's division of the soul into a thinking (rational) and a feeling (nonrational or partly rational) part amounts to more than merely observing that thinking is one thing, feeling another.[32] In fact, as we will see, Aristotle's

---

[32] In Michael Woods's commentary on this passage, he says the following: "Aristotle here dismisses the question whether the soul has parts in a strong sense of 'part,' as irrelevant to his present concerns. This is in line with the methodological doctrine that ethics should concern itself with metaphysical questions only in so far as they are relevant. (Compare 1214a12–14.) This passage is only partly parallel to the comparable passage in E.N. The two examples given here seem to be different from each other, and the second seems more apt for Aristotle's purposes. What Aristotle seems to be contrasting with the case of two physically separate parts is the case when there are two things distinguishable only in thought. If so, Aristotle, in speaking of the rational or desiring part of the soul, ought to regard himself as committed only to the existence of certain capacities. In fact, however, when Aristotle speaks of parts of the soul, here and in the psychological works, the structure is represented as *explaining* the various capacities that are to be found, and thus as not simply reducible to them. Here when he postulates that the soul has two parts he seems to mean more than that the soul may be considered as a source of both rational and non-rational behavior" (*Eudemian Ethics* [hereafter abbreviated EE], trans. Woods, pp. 102–3).

Aquinas's commentary on the related passage in the *Nicomachean Ethics* stresses the division of the parts of the soul here discussed as based on a difference in two kinds of rationality, one by nature, the other by participation: "Then at 'Virtue is divided,' he [Aristotle] divides virtue according to this difference in the parts of the soul. . . . Since human virtue perfects the work of man which is done according to reason, human virtue must consist in something reasonable. Since the reasonable is of two kinds, by nature and by participation, it follows that there are two kinds of human virtue. One of these is placed in what is rational by nature and is called intellectual. The other is placed in what is rational by participation, that is, in the appetitive part of the soul, and is called moral. Therefore, he says, we call some of the virtues intellectual and some moral" (trans. Ross, I.L.XX.C243).

In *De Anima* Aristotle rejects the view that the soul has parts in a quantitative sense of "part." The whole soul is present in all bodily parts: "all the same,

---

various discussions of thinking and feeling indicate that he believes thinking and feeling are structurally very different, and that this difference can explain the difference between the intellectual and the moral virtues.

Aristotle ties the difference between the intellectual and the moral virtues to the difference between the soul's parts in the passage immediately following the one just quoted:

> Virtue is of two forms, virtue of character, and intellectual virtue. For we praise not only the just, but also the intelligent and the wise. For virtue, or its function, was assumed to be commended, but those things are not actualizations, though there exist actualizations of them. The intellectual virtues, having, as they do, a rational principle, such virtues belong to the part that has reason and prescribes to the soul in so far as it possesses reason, whereas the virtues of character belong to the part that is non-rational, but whose nature is to follow the rational part; for we do not say what a man's character is like when we say that he is wise or clever, but when we say that he is gentle or daring. (*EE* II.1.1220a5–13)

The distinction between the intellectual and the moral virtues is therefore linked to the difference between the two parts of the

in each of the bodily parts there are present all parts of the soul, and the souls so present are homogeneous with one another and with the whole; this means that the several parts of the soul are indisseverable from one another, although the whole soul is divisible" (*De Anima*, trans. Smith, 411b26–7).

In his commentary on this passage, Aquinas says that Aristotle "states and then rejects a view of certain philosophers that the activities in question [sensing, rational judgment, desiring, deliberating, etc.] spring severally from the soul's parts, not from the soul in general; that the soul is so divided into parts that it understands with one, desires with another, just as some people hold that the sensitive part is in the brain and the vital part is in the heart, and so on.

"Now this is partly true and partly false. If you take it to mean that the soul has different parts potentially, it is quite true that its parts and powers are distinct and that one of them understands and another senses. The soul is a whole in the sense that it has a total capacity with partial capacities subordinate to the whole. But if you take it quantitatively, as though the soul were of a certain size with parts of certain sizes, then this opinion is false. And this was how the philosophers in question thought of the soul – even to the extent that they made out the soul's different powers to be different souls" (I.V. 204–5).

soul, and that is based on a functional difference: the thinking part commands, and the feeling part obeys. This is merely stated without argument in the passage just quoted from the *Eudemian Ethics,* but in the *Nicomachean Ethics* Aristotle defends the division by the experience of internal moral conflict, which, he says, indicates that our reason is engaged in a struggle with another element of the soul.[33] But certainly conflict *per se* is insufficient to indicate a division of parts. After all, one desire can conflict with another desire, yet Aristotle does not take that as evidence that the conflicting desires reside in different parts of the soul.[34]

In the *Eudemian Ethics,* Aristotle uses another difference between the parts of the soul to account for the difference in the two kinds of virtue. There he defines the general category of the affections in terms of pleasure and pain: "By affections [*pathe*] I mean such things as anger, fear, shame, desire – in general anything which, as such, gives rise usually to perceptual pleasure and pain" (*EE* II.2.1220b12–14). A similar passage appears in the *Nicomachean Ethics:* "Feelings are appetite, anger, fear, confidence, envy, joy, love, hate, longing, emulation, pity, and in general those things which are accompanied by pleasure and pain" (*NE* II.5.1105b21–3). This feature can then be used to distinguish the virtues of this part of the soul from the intellectual virtues, and he says it is evident that "virtue of character has to do with pleasant and unpleasant things" (*EE* II.2.1220a36). In a later passage he gives another argument that the virtues of the feeling part of the soul involve the proper handling of pleasure and pain:

> Capacities and states are defined by the affections, and affections are differentiated by pleasure and pain; so it follows both from these considerations and from the things that have been asserted before, that every virtue of character has to do with

---

[33] See Hutchinson 1986, p. 74, for an analysis of this argument. The conflict criterion for psychic partition goes back to *Republic* IV.

[34] Charles Young has pointed out to me that Aristotle actually denies that a desire can conflict with a desire, although he allows that one can have incompatible desires, that is, desires not both of which can be satisfied. In discussing the nature of choice Aristotle says, "Desire is contrary to choice, not desire to desire" (*NE* 3.2.1111b15–16).

pleasure and pain. For, with any state of the soul, those things whose nature it is to make it better or worse are the things to which the nature of the state relates and with which it is concerned. It is on account of pleasures and pains that we call men bad, for pursuing or avoiding them as they should not, or those they should not. That is why everyone actually defines virtues in an off-hand manner as being insusceptibility and lack of disturbance in the sphere of pleasures and pains, vices in opposite terms. (*EE* II.4.1221b36–1222a5)

We now have a second reason for thinking of the intellectual and the moral virtues as importantly different. But can we divide the class of virtues into those that "have to do" with pleasure and pain and those that do not? And if so, would the former look like the class of moral virtues in either Aristotle's sense or ours? This is very doubtful. Most feelings are experienced as pleasant or painful, but it is not evident that they all are; curiosity may be one that is not.[35] More important, the virtues that handle those that *are* pleasant or painful often do not relate to their pleasantness or painfulness in any significant sense. Aristotle seems to have thought that feelings are in need of discipline by the virtues because of their pleasantness or painfulness, but while the feelings involved in generosity or kindness, for example, may have aspects of mild pleasantness or painfulness, it probably is not the case that it is the pleasantness or painfulness itself that is in need of discipline by these virtues, and it is doubtful whether the sense in which generosity or kindness "has to do" with pleasantness or painfulness plays any significant role in distinguishing these virtues from the virtues that govern intellectual states.

Perhaps Aristotle is making the weaker claim that we distinguish feeling states from cognitive states on the basis that pleasure and pain accompany the former and not the latter, so we can identify virtues of character by their indirect relation to pleasure and pain, whereas the intellectual virtues have no such relation. But even this claim is false, for states of intellect such as

[35] "Curiosity" may not be the name of a feeling, but a feeling does typically accompany the state of curiosity. It is this feeling that I claim is probably neither pleasant nor painful.

understanding, confusion, joy at the confirmation of a hypothesis, and the opposing state, intellectual surprise,[36] can be experienced as pleasant and painful as much as can feeling states and desires. So the virtues that pertain to the one do not necessarily have more to do with pleasure and pain than the virtues that pertain to the other. Some intellectual states, in fact, can be accompanied by even stronger sensations of pleasure than, say, feelings of gratitude or respect. Indeed, Aristotle was aware of that since he says in Book X of the *Nicomachean Ethics* that each activity is perfected by its proper pleasure, that it is disputable whether the activity is not the same as the pleasure (*NE* X.5.1175b33), and that the pleasures of thought are superior (1176a2).[37] So although it may be true that many feeling states are accompanied by strong sensations of pleasure or pain, and this is not usually the case with states of the intellect, this is hardly enough to justify distinguishing two kinds of virtue on the basis of a relation to pleasure and pain.

There is one more possibility. When Aristotle says that pleasure and pain "attend" the affections, he may mean that pleasure or pain are mentioned in the *definitions* of the affections.[38] So in the *Rhetoric* he defines anger as a desire accompanied by pain (II.2) and fear as a pain or disturbance due to a mental picture of some future evil (II.5), and so on. If this is what Aristotle had in mind, and if he is right that definitions of emotional states refer to pleasure or pain, whereas definitions of intellectual states do not, all this gets us is a way of distinguishing between states of thinking and feeling, and I have not claimed that there is no such difference. In spite of everything we have said, there is a plain intuitive difference between thinking states and feeling states, so if we ignore the problems in Aristotle's claims about the parts of the soul and their connection to pleasure and pain, perhaps we

---

[36] See Scheffler 1982 for an interesting discussion of the cognitive emotions of joy at confirmation and surprise at an unexpected consequence.

[37] Plato had already argued the same way in Book IX of the *Republic* where he says that each part of the soul has its own proper pleasure and that the pleasures of the intellective part are the highest. I thank Michael Stocker for reminding me of this.

[38] I thank Charles Young for suggesting this interpretation to me.

can simply distinguish the moral from the intellectual virtues on the grounds that the former but not the latter involve the proper handling of feelings, whereas the latter but not the former involve the proper direction of cognitive activities. But even this claim will not work. It is true that many moral virtues, such as temperance, courage, and the virtues opposed to envy, jealousy, vengeance, and spite, are more directly related to the handling of strong feelings than are intellectual virtues, but this does not divide the class of virtues into two distinct categories. The moral virtue that many theorists consider central, namely, justice, has only a peripheral relationship with feelings, as do such virtues as honesty, sincerity, candor, and trustworthiness. On the other hand, intellectual virtues involve the proper use of the passion for truth, which, at least in some people, can be very strong indeed.

It is interesting that we think of the virtues as related to feelings and desires primarily when those feelings tend to be excessively strong and often lead to harm of oneself or others. Although there definitely is a desire for truth which sometimes can be strong enough to amount to a passion, we would not think of this desire right off as something in need of taming, the way we think of sexual desire or fear in the presence of danger. Rather than to err in the direction of overdoing it, people are more likely to err in the direction of insufficiency. But, of course, the same can be said for many of the feelings managed by moral virtues. Compassion is a virtue that manages the feeling by the same name, and this feeling is usually one that needs to be promoted rather than restrained. The same can be said for most of the feelings involved in benevolence, mercy, forgiveness, trust, and hope. This suggests that the management of the desire for truth is different from the management of very strong passions and is instead more like the management of the desire for good, which needs to be promoted rather than restrained. Nevertheless, there *are* feelings and desires that need to be restrained by the intellectual virtues. One of the strongest feelings people must overcome in their quest for knowledge in any field is the desire that some particular belief be true. The feelings that accompany prejudices can be strong; the desire to hold on to old beliefs can be strong; the desire that one's previously published views not be proven wrong can be strong. In each case there are desires or feelings that need to be restrained or redirected.

Pascal saw the passion of self-love as weakening the love of truth and leading to self-deception, the deception of others, and hypocrisy, vices that are, at least in part, intellectual:

> It is no doubt an evil to be full of faults, but it is a still greater evil to be full of them and to be unwilling to recognize them, since this entails the further evil of deliberate self-delusion. We do not want others to deceive us; we do not think it right for them to want us to esteem them more than they deserve; it is therefore not right either that we should deceive them and want them to esteem us more than we deserve . . .

> This aversion for the truth exists in differing degrees, but it may be said that it exists in everyone to some degree, because it is inseparable from self-love. It is this false delicacy which makes those who have to correct others choose so many devious ways and qualifications to avoid giving offence. They must minimize our faults, pretend to excuse them, and combine this with praise and marks of affection and esteem. Even then such medicine still tastes bitter to self-love, which takes as little of it as possible, always with disgust and often with secret resentment against those administering it.

> The result is that anyone who has an interest in winning our affection avoids rendering us a service which he knows to be unwelcome; we are treated as we want to be treated; we hate the truth and it is kept from us; we desire to be flattered and we are flattered; we like being deceived and we are deceived. (*Pensées*, fragments not found in the Copy, p. 348)

Plato recognized the need for natural feeling and moral rectitude in the apprehension of truth, particularly in moral matters, and gave a dramatic argument for their power in a letter:

> To sum it all up in one word, natural intelligence and a good memory are equally powerless to aid the man who has not an inborn affinity with the subject. Without such endowments there is of course not the slightest possibility. Hence all who have no natural aptitude for and affinity with justice and all the

other noble ideals, though in the study of other matters they may be both intelligent and retentive – all those too who have affinity but are stupid and unretentive – such will never any of them attain to an understanding of the most complete truth in regard to moral concepts. The study of virtue and vice must be accompanied by an inquiry into what is false and true of existence in general and must be carried on by constant practice throughout a long period, as I said in the beginning. Hardly after practicing detailed comparisons of names and definitions and visual and other sense perceptions, after scrutinizing them in benevolent disputation by the use of question and answer without jealousy, at last in a flash understanding of each blazes up, and the mind, as it exerts all its powers to the limit of human capacity, is flooded with light. (Letter VII.344a-b, trans. Post)

One final problem with dividing the moral from the intellectual virtues on the grounds that the former handle feeling states and the latter handle thinking states is that there are states that are actually blends of thought and feeling. Curiosity, doubt, wonder, and awe are states of this kind, each of which can either aid or impede the desire for truth. Curiosity is interesting because both Augustine and Aquinas call curiosity a vice, whereas it would be much more common these days to think of curiosity as valuable.

Feelings are involved in intellectual virtues, and intellectual virtues are involved in handling feelings, but their operation shows how blurry the distinction between intellectual and moral virtues really is. Intellectual prejudice, for example, is an intellectual vice, and the virtue that is its contrary is fair-mindedness, but clearly we think of prejudice as a moral failing and fair-mindedness as a morally good quality. It is possible that the intellectual form of prejudice and the moral form are the same vice, and the same point could apply to other cases in which an intellectual trait has the same name as a moral trait, such as humility, autonomy, integrity, perseverance, courage, and trustworthiness. William James has said in "The Sentiment of Rationality" (1937) that faith is the same virtue in the intellectual realm as courage is in the moral realm: "Faith is the readiness to act in a cause the prosperous issue of which is not certified to us in advance. It is in fact the same moral quality which we call courage in practical affairs; and there will be a very widespread tendency in men of vigorous nature to enjoy a certain amount of uncertainty in their philosophic creed, just as risk lends a zest to worldly activity" (p. 90). I will not take a stand here on whether a moral and an intellectual virtue can be the very same virtue. In any case, if there is a distinction between intellectual and moral virtue/vice, it cannot be on the grounds that the latter handles feelings and the former does not.

Not only is the proper handling of feelings involved in intellectual as well as moral virtues, but almost all moral virtues include an aspect of proper perceptual and cognitive activity. As I argued in 2.2, virtue is a success concept. No one has the virtue of fairness or courage or compassion or generosity without generally being in cognitive contact with the aspect of reality handled by the respective virtue. Otherwise, one could not be reliably successful. We may make allowances for *some* mistakes in beliefs or perceptions in the possession of a moral virtue, but no one who regularly misperceives the situation or has mistaken beliefs about what should or should not be done in such cases can be said to possess the moral virtue that governs cases of that type. For example, a person who regularly acts in a way that causes suffering to others can hardly be said to possess the virtue of compassion, no matter what his intentions and motivation. Similarly, a person who adopts policies in grading that clearly favor male over female students or vice versa cannot be said to possess the virtue of fairness, no matter how these policies look from his point of view. Being reasonably intelligent within a certain area of life is part of having almost any moral virtue.

In the *Nicomachean Ethics* Aristotle gives a different reason for distinguishing the intellectual and the moral virtues. He claims there that they are learned or acquired in different ways. Intellectual virtues are qualities that can be taught, whereas moral virtues are habits that are acquired by practice and training (*NE* II.1.1103a14–20). Wallace accepts this distinction and connects it with the distinction between skills and virtues (1978, pp. 44–5).

I have already explained why I think it is a mistake to identify

149

intellectual virtues with skills. I suggest that Aristotle's distinction between qualities that can be taught and those that are acquired by imitation and practice is closer to distinguishing skills and virtues, not intellectual and moral virtues. We saw in 2.4 that there are both moral and intellectual skills and moral and intellectual virtues. What can be taught are skills such as the codified part of logic. Moral skills, such as procedures for grading fairly or processes for aiding famine-ridden countries that will have the desired effect can also be taught. What cannot be taught, or, at least, cannot be taught so easily, are intellectual virtues such as open-mindedness, the ability to think up an explanation for a complex set of data, or the ability to recognize reliable authority. These qualities are no more teachable than generosity or courage.

I propose that the stages of learning the intellectual virtues are exactly parallel to the stages of learning the moral virtues as described by Aristotle. They begin with the imitation of virtuous persons, require practice which develops certain habits of feeling and acting, and usually include an in-between stage of intellectual self-control (overcoming intellectual *akrasia*) parallel to the stage of moral self-control in the acquisition of a moral virtue. In both cases the imitation is of a person who has *phronesis*. If moral behavior is not strictly rule governed, there is no set of directions sufficient to lead one to act morally in every case. But as we saw in Part I, intellectual behavior is no more rule governed than moral behavior. No set of rules is sufficient to tell us when to place intellectual trust in the reliability of another, or what a person with intellectual courage, perseverance, or discretion would do, and so on. For this reason imitation of the person with *phronesis* is important for acquiring both intellectual and moral virtues, a topic to which we will return in section 5.

Courage is often used as a paradigm case of a virtue. One acquires courage by imitating a courageous person. Such imitation involves training the feelings as well as learning how to identify those situations in which it is morally valuable, perhaps even compulsory, to face danger, and those in which it is not. Normally a stage follows in which the person knows what to do but lacks the ability to do it. Aristotle says such a person suffers from *akrasia*, or weakness of will. Gradually he learns to overcome weakness and in more and more circumstances is able to act courageously even when the temptation not to do so is strong. At this stage he is a morally self-controlled person. It is only when courage becomes relatively easy for him and it is not necessary to fight strong contrary temptations that he can be correctly said to possess the virtue of courage. When he has been courageous for a long time, he may not even have to face contrary temptations at all and will eventually find courageous activity pleasant.[39]

One learns how to *believe* the way she should rather than the way she wants in a way parallel to her learning how to *act* the way she should rather than the way she wants. And just as ultimately she learns to want to act the way she should, ultimately she learns to want to believe the way she should. She learns such intellectual virtues as open-mindedness, the ability to recognize reliable authority, and the ability to think up good explanations for a complex set of data by imitating persons who have these qualities to an exemplary degree. In many cases she has to overcome contrary inclinations, or what might be called intellectual *akrasia*, and will have to go through a stage of developing intellectual self-control before she masters the virtue. In most cases the acquisition of an intellectual virtue involves training the feelings. For example, the ability to recognize reliable authority partly involves having trained feelings that permit one to be a reliable judge of the intellectual trustworthiness of another. The affective responses involved in the judgment that certain people are reliable or trustworthy are both a partial cause and a partial reason for the judgment of their reliability. Ultimately, she finds herself *wanting* to trust a person whom she knows she should trust and not wanting to trust the untrustworthy or unreliable.

A young person has neither intellectual virtues nor intellectual vices, just as she has neither moral virtues nor moral vices. She does not begin with a vice and work up to the virtue. But it is helpful to begin an account of the path to acquiring intellectual

---

[39] Aristotle says: "The man who does not rejoice in noble actions is not even good; since no one would call a man just who did not enjoy acting justly, nor any man liberal who did not enjoy liberal actions; and similarly in all other cases" (*NE* I.8.1099a16–19).

virtues by mentioning some intellectual vices, since in many cases the learning of a virtue involves overcoming temptations that exemplify the contrary vice. In any case, if we start with the vice, we can see the range of differences in intellectual character and how they correspond to the range of differences in moral character.

Some examples of intellectual vices are as follows: intellectual pride, negligence, idleness, cowardice, conformity, carelessness, rigidity, prejudice, wishful thinking, closed-mindedness, insensitivity to detail, obtuseness,[40] and lack of thoroughness. There is probably also a vice contrary to intellectual perseverance, which involves giving up too soon and may be a form of intellectual laziness or proneness to discouragement. Some forms of self-deception may be a vice, but other forms may instead be a form of intellectual *akrasia*.

A person who has intellectual vices may be unaware that she exhibits these vices on the occasions in which she does so. She may even mistake a vice for a virtue, just as in the case of moral vices. Aristotle thought that part of the process of acquiring virtue is learning where the mean is between two extremes. Some of the intellectual vices mentioned above may have contrary vices, where one is an excess and the other a deficiency, and the virtue is a mean between them. For example, there may be such a thing as intellectual rashness, the contrary of intellectual cowardice. In addition, it may be possible to be overly thorough, overly sensitive to detail, overly cautious, etc. Lorraine Code (1987, p. 59) remarks, "One hesitates to attribute intellectual virtue to a voracious collector of facts, such as Sartre's self-taught man, or to an information gatherer of encyclopedic mind." These cases also

---

[40] Obtuseness in the moral sense is the inability to recognize the moral relevance of certain details in a situation in which moral decision is required. Moral theorists who put very strong emphasis on moral principle and little emphasis on the relevance of variations in circumstances have sometimes been accused of overlooking this vice. As I see it, the point can be extended to other forms of obtuseness. A person who fails to see the relevance of details in the weighing of evidence for a hypothesis or in the judgment of the reliability of an authority would also be guilty of obtuseness, but her obtuseness is intellectual rather than moral.

show an intellectual excess of sorts, but they are probably not so much vices as a waste of intellectual energy that could be put to better use.

The extremes between which an intellectual virtue is a mean need not necessarily be vices but may be pathological states. William James, in *The Principles of Psychology,* volume 2, describes how the virtue governing doubt and inquiry can be pathologically exalted, as well as its opposite, the tendency to believe without inquiry. The first quality he calls the questioning mania. This trait is "the inability to rest in any conception, and the need of having it confirmed and explained" (chap. 21, sec. "Belief"). As an example James quotes from T. S. Clouston, *Clinical Lectures on Mental Diseases* (1883):

> To one whose mind is healthy thoughts come and go unnoticed; with me they have to be faced, thought about in a peculiar fashion, and then disposed of as finished, and this often when I am utterly wearied and would be at peace; but the call is imperative. This goes on to the hindrance of all natural action. If I were told that the staircase was on fire, that I had only a minute to escape, and that thought arose – "Have they sent for fire-engines? Is it probable that the man who has the key is on hand? Is the man a careful sort of person? Will the key be hanging on a peg? Am I thinking rightly? Perhaps they don't lock the depot" – My foot would be lifted to go down; I should be conscious to excitement that I was losing my chance; but I should be unable to stir until all these absurdities were entertained and disposed of. In the most critical moments of my life, when I ought to have been so engrossed as to leave no room for secondary thoughts, I have been oppressed by the inability to be at peace. And in the most ordinary circumstances it is all the same. (James 1981, vol. 2, pp. 914–15, n. 3)

James says that the contrary psychological state, the state of mental rest, can also be pathologically exalted:

> One of the charms of drunkenness unquestionably lies in the deepening of the sense of reality and truth which is gained therein. In whatever light things may then appear to us, they

seem more utterly what they are, more "utterly utter" than when we are sober. This goes to a fully unutterable extreme in the nitrous oxide intoxication, in which a man's very soul will sweat with conviction, and he be all the while unable to tell what he is convinced of at all. ("Belief," para. 3)

It follows from James's examples that there is a proper degree of doubt and the urge to inquire further. One must be neither too sanguine in one's convictions nor too obsessed with the desire to inquire further before reaching the state of settled belief. One must, in short, know when to stop, but also when to start and when to continue. The virtue that is the mean between the questioning mania and unjustified conviction has no simple name, as far as I know, but it is something like being both properly inquiring and properly doubtful. The learning of virtue consists in part of learning the extent of proper doubt and proper inquiry.

Once she becomes aware that she has a vice and acquires the ability to tell how she should behave intellectually on the proper occasion and, moreover, acquires the desire to be intellectually virtuous, but without doing so, she is in the state of intellectual *akrasia*, a state higher than vice. Cases of intellectual *akrasia* include the varieties of believing what you want to believe but know you shouldn't. These cases are forms of self-deception. Just as in acting it makes sense to say, "I know this is wrong, but I can't help doing it," in believing it makes sense to say, "I know this belief is not justified, but I can't help believing it." Intellectual *akrasia* involves self-deception more than does moral *akrasia* because there is probably a stronger link between believing and believing justified than between doing and believing right. Of course, very often when a person believes, she does not believe one way or the other whether the belief is justified. Similarly, very often when a person acts, she does not believe one way or the other whether the act is right. This is not *akrasia*, although it may be a fault.

Amelie Rorty (1983, p. 178) mentions a case of intellectual *akrasia* in which a person lapses into ways of thinking or talking that she knows to be intellectually lax. Similarly, a person may

catch herself lapsing into intellectual attitudes of which she disapproves, such as unfairness to the ideas of others.

Another example of intellectual *akrasia* would be knowing that
the word of a certain person cannot be trusted but believing on
his authority something that supports your own position. It frequently happens that people read newspaper articles that support their own political position but ignore the articles of those
who may be more dependable and whom, furthermore, they
know to be more dependable, or *would* know, if they were paying
attention.

The stage after *akrasia* is intellectual self-control. At this stage a
person has to stop herself from accepting inadequate evidence or
poor testimony or lapsing into ways of speaking or reasoning of
which she disapproves. But, unlike the previous stage, she does it
successfully. Still, she lacks the virtue because she finds it difficult
to weigh evidence properly or judge authority reliably or reason
with care and according to the rules. Her behavior may be correct,
but it is not grounded in a "firm and unchangeable character," as
Aristotle characterizes the person who truly possesses virtue.

The final stage is the intellectual virtue. Examples include intellectual carefulness, perseverance, humility, vigor, flexibility,
courage, and thoroughness, as well as open-mindedness, fair-
mindedness, insightfulness, and the virtues opposed to wishful
thinking, obtuseness, and conformity. One of the most important
virtues, I believe, is intellectual integrity.

Is there something analogous to the supererogatory in cognitive activity? Lorraine Code mentions the Soviet scientist who,
through exceptional diligence, is able to obtain work generally
unavailable in his country in order to test his own theories. Such a
person exhibits intellectual virtues in a degree far beyond what
could be expected in his circumstances (pp. 61–2). We also put a
special premium on the virtue of originality. Just as we value an
original work of art much more highly than a good copy, we value
intellectual originality and inventiveness more than knowledge
learned from others. Since intellectual originality goes beyond
what is expected of an intellectually virtuous person, it might also
qualify as analogous to supererogatory moral traits.

Before concluding 3.1, I want to mention one other argument I have encountered in discussion for classifying intellectual and moral virtues into distinct kinds. It is based on the observation that the possession of the intellectual virtues seems to be independent of the possession of the moral virtues. It is not difficult to find individuals who have numerous intellectual virtues but are radically immoral, it is said. Similarly, it is not difficult to find people who are morally virtuous but who are deficient in the intellectual virtues. The conclusion is that the empirical evidence justifies the conclusion that the moral and the intellectual virtues are different *kinds* of virtue.

Since intellectual virtues are more frequently confused with skills than are moral virtues, there is not even an appearance of a difficulty here unless it is clear that we are comparing the presence or absence of moral virtue with intellectual *virtue*, not simply with intellectual skills. With this proviso we can ask whether it often happens that the moral and the intellectual virtues are possessed independently, and if so, whether this indicates a difference in the nature of these two classes of virtue.

The question of the unity of the virtues is a thorny one, and it is difficult to know precisely what counts as evidence that a person possesses one virtue and not another. Let us suppose, first, that our standards for virtue possession are not too severe, that is, that we do not insist that a person with virtue X exhibits X behavior in *every* circumstance in which it is appropriate. As McDowell (1979) says, to have a virtue it is not necessary that one be perfect. It is sufficient if one is reliably virtuous in sensitivity and behavior. Since it does not seem difficult to get empirical evidence that a person is reliably kind but not reliably courageous, or reliably just but not reliably temperate, a view of the virtues that does not demand perfection, combined with the empirical evidence, would then support the claim that a person can have one moral virtue and not another. That being the case, it should not be surprising that there is also empirical evidence that a person can have an intellectual virtue such as intellectual honesty, care, or perseverance but lack a moral virtue such as compassion or generosity. The standards of virtue possession that support the position that there is a degree of independence between the possession of the intellectual virtues and the possession of the moral virtues also support the position that there is a degree of independence between the possession of one moral virtue and another. In fact, for any given person, we could divide up the class of moral virtues into the ones she possesses and the ones she does not. But when we do so, does anyone take this to be a good reason to think that the one class of moral virtues pertains to a different part of her soul or is fundamentally different in kind from the other? Surely not. And by parity of reasoning, even if a person has the whole class of intellectual virtues and not the moral, or conversely, that should not lead us to think that the two classes of virtue have a different nature or reside in different parts of her soul. If, however, it could be shown that there is a much higher degree of independence between the possession of the intellectual virtues and the possession of the moral virtues than there is between the possession of one moral virtue and another, that might indicate an interesting difference in kind between the two classes of virtue, but, to my knowledge, no such evidence exists.

Suppose, on the other hand, that our criteria for the full possession of a virtue are as severe as Aristotle's. Aristotle thought that no one possesses one moral virtue fully without possessing them all, and such a position requires that we be somewhat skeptical about the empirical evidence that purports to show the independent possession of one virtue and another. With Aristotle's criteria it is much more difficult to support the objector's claim that there are persons who fully possess the intellectual virtues and not the moral virtues. In 3.2 we will look at some of the logical and causal connections among the members of these two classes of virtue. It may turn out, then, that the considerations that led Aristotle to assert a unity of the moral virtues would apply as well to the intellectual virtues. In any case, I do not see that we should expect a different answer to the question of whether the moral and intellectual virtues are unified than to the question of whether the moral virtues alone are unified.

To conclude, intellectual virtues do not differ from moral virtues in the way in which they are acquired. Both require training through the imitation of virtuous persons and practice in acting virtuously. Both also involve handling certain feelings and acquiring the ability to *like* acting virtuously. Both also have stages in between vice and virtue consisting of *akrasia* and self-control. Some of the traditional moral virtues have more of a taming function than most of the traditional intellectual virtues, and that may explain why moral *akrasia* looms larger in our vocabulary of character than intellectual *akrasia*. Still, we have not yet seen any reason for dividing moral and intellectual virtues into distinct kinds.

3.2 Some connections between intellectual and moral virtues

So far I have argued that no one has offered adequate reason to think the moral and intellectual virtues differ any more than one moral virtue differs from another. Both moral and intellectual virtues involve a combination of understanding some aspect of the world and training of the feelings, and both are learned by a process described by Aristotle in his account of the moral virtues. In addition, as we saw in Part I, both are in the realm of the voluntary. Although some virtues may be more voluntary than others and some involve strong feelings more than others, this does not divide up the spectrum into moral and intellectual. So the two types of virtue are very similar in their nature and the manner of their acquisition. In this section I wish to show how intimately the moral and the intellectual virtues are connected in their operation.

There are both logical and causal connections between moral and intellectual virtues that are just as extensive and profound as the connections among the various moral virtues. For example, honesty is on all accounts a moral virtue. It is a virtue that requires that one tell the truth. But it is not sufficient for honesty that a person tell whatever she happens to believe is the truth. An honest person is *careful* with the truth. She respects it and does her best to find it out, to preserve it, and to communicate it in a way that permits the hearer to believe the truth justifiably and with understanding. But this in turn requires that she have intellectual virtues that give her as high a degree of justification and understanding as possible. She must be attentive, take the trouble to be thorough and careful in weighing evidence, be intellectually and perceptually acute, especially in important matters, and so on, for all the intellectual virtues. The moral virtue of honesty, then, logically entails having intellectual virtues.

The causal connections among intellectual and moral virtues are numerous. Envy, pride, and the urge to reinforce prejudices can easily inhibit the acquisition of intellectual virtues. A person without sufficient self-respect and an inordinate need to be liked by others may tend to intellectual conformity. An egoistic person will want to get his way, and this includes wanting to be right. He will therefore resist any demonstration of a mistake in his beliefs. If his belief is about a topic of contemporary debate, his egoism may lead him to read only those articles that support his own position and to discuss politics only with like-minded individuals. Or if he is a philosopher, he may invite debate but will not fairly evaluate criticisms of his position and will invest most of his intellectual energy in winning the argument. He has, then, intellectual failings resulting from a moral vice.

Furthermore, many moral virtues such as patience, perseverance, and courage are causally necessary for having intellectual virtues. In addition, there are virtues that apply both to the moral and to the intellectual realm, and we have seen examples in which the same word serves for both. Perseverance is a moral virtue and there is undoubtedly a close causal connection between moral perseverance and intellectual perseverance, and we have said that it is possible that they are in fact the same virtue. The same point holds for such virtues as courage, humility, and discretion, all of which have both moral and intellectual forms. Vices such as laziness, prejudice, and obtuseness have both moral and intellectual forms. A lack of imagination is probably causally connected to both intellectual and moral vices, although I am doubtful whether to identify a lack of imagination as either an intellectual or a moral vice in itself.

John Benson defines autonomy in a way that makes it both a moral and an intellectual virtue: "The virtue of autonomy is a mean state of character with regard to reliance on one's own powers in acting, choosing, and forming opinions" (1987, p. 205).

He argues that "autonomous moral thinking is closely parallel to autonomous theoretical thinking, the one being concerned with what should be done, the other with what is the case. . . . Autonomy is a proper degree and kind of reliance on others, what is proper being determined by the end of the activity in which one is engaging" (pp. 208–9). This virtue, Benson says, is closely allied to courage, as well as to humility, and it shows the connection between cognitive and volitional processes: "To be autonomous in one's thinking calls for intellectual skills, including the ability to judge when someone else knows better than yourself. But it calls also for the ability to control the emotions that prevent those skills from being properly exercised" (p. 213).

Related to autonomy is trust, another virtue that has both a moral and an intellectual form. Trust – knowing when to rely on others – might be considered the reverse side of autonomy, although trust in oneself is also a form of this virtue. Trust is a mean between gullibility and suspiciousness and it operates in both the intellectual and the practical spheres.

Trust in the sense of reliance is necessary at all stages of belief formation. First, there is trust in our senses. William Alston (1986a) has defended Thomas Reid's argument (1941) that we must trust some of our faculties without noncircular reasons for their reliability. Such trust is not vicious since it is entailed by the human condition. Belief formation also involves trust in one's memory, one's intellectual skills, and, in fact, in one's other virtues, such as intellectual care and thoroughness. In addition, we need to trust other people, past and present, since very little of our knowledge comes to us directly. Finally, we have to trust the world to cooperate with our faculties, for example, that the world does not change so much from moment to moment that we cannot rely on inductive inferences.

The examples just given are of trust in only the minimal sense of rational reliance. Trust as an intellectual virtue involves trusting those persons, faculties, and processes that are reliable in giving us the truth, whereas trust as a moral virtue involves trusting those who are reliable in their relationship to ourselves. But trust as a moral virtue involves more than simple reliance, as

Annette Baier has pointed out. Trust is a narrower concept than reliance since we can still rely where we can no longer trust:

> What is the difference between trusting others and merely relying on them? It seems to be reliance on their good will toward one, as distinct from their dependable habits, or only on their dependably exhibited fear, anger, or other motives compatible with ill will toward one, or on motives not directed on one at all. We may rely on our fellows' fear of the newly appointed security guards in shops to deter them from injecting poison into the food on the shelves, once we have ceased to trust them. We may rely on the shopkeeper's concern for his profits to motivate him to take effective precautions against poisoners and also trust him to *want* his customers not to be harmed by his products, at least as long as this want can be satisfied without frustrating his wish to increase his profits. (Baier 1993, p. 349)

Although Baier does not examine intellectual trust in her discussion, her distinction between genuine trust and mere reliance applies as much to trust as an intellectual trait as to trust as a moral trait. Baier analyzes trust as a three-place predicate of the form *A* trusts *B* with valued thing *C*, and she says that trust implies that *B* has the capability of harming *C*. In the case of intellectual trust the valued thing would be our possession of the truth. The person or persons in whom we place our trust are in a position to deceive us, but we trust that they will not because of their goodwill toward us. Just as in the moral case, we may continue to rely on them when we can no longer trust them, say, when we know that their fear of retaliation will motivate them to continue to tell us the truth. So when we depend upon the expertise of others for knowledge, we can rely on them to give us the truth in a way that does not necessarily include any expectation of goodwill on their part, just as we rely on the public not to poison the food in the market when it is obvious that poisoning could only be accomplished at great personal risk to potential poisoners. The similarities in the cases is striking enough that this may be one of the cases in which there is really only a single virtue that operates in both the moral and the intellectual spheres.

The virtue of integrity is one of the most important of all virtues and is also one of the least often discussed. Integrity in one of its senses involves wholeness or a unity of the self. As we saw earlier (Part I, sec. 1.2), integrity is a higher-order virtue, and it shows more than any other example the need for an account of the virtues that recognizes the functional unity of the person. Moral integrity includes having a positive moral evaluation by the self of one's own moral traits, as well as a positive evaluation of the extent to which one has been morally successful. Analogously, intellectual integrity involves a positive epistemic evaluation of one's own intellectual traits, as well as a positive evaluation of the results of one's cognitive efforts in the knowledge one has obtained. But there must be a connection between moral and intellectual integrity, for integrity is above all the virtue of being true to oneself, and assuming that the self is singular, it is incoherent to be true to your moral self but not to your intellectual self or conversely. Integrity requires, then, a functional unity not only between moral and intellectual integrity but between moral and intellectual virtues in general. It is beyond the scope of this book to attempt to argue against those philosophers who have thought that the self is divided, but it is worth remarking that a rejection of that view leads one to reject as well any clear separation in the operation of the moral and the intellectual virtues.

Hypocrisy is one of the few vices sought out and roundly condemned in contemporary Western society. This vice also combines intellectual and moral failings, at least in one of its forms. If the hypocrite is someone who merely pretends to have moral beliefs that he does not uphold in his own behavior, then he is simply a deceitful cynic. But in the more interesting form, the hypocrite's deceit becomes self-deceit. He manages to convince himself that he believes what he says he believes, although his behavior expresses a deeper way in which he does not really believe what he claims. His moral failing leads to an intellectual failing in knowing himself. Such a person suffers a psychic split that is opposed to integrity in the sense of self-unity. The hypocrite should be distinguished from the person who sincerely believes certain forms of behavior are morally unacceptable and counsels others to refrain while knowingly engaging in it himself. This is moral weakness, not hypocrisy.

Naïveté is an interesting trait because it seems to combine a lack of good practical judgment – an intellectual deficiency – with such morally admirable qualities as general innocence and a lack of deviousness. It is possible that there are even causal connections between the intellectual failing and the morally good aspects of the trait. If so, naïveté creates some problems for the idea of the unity of the virtues, but not for the position that there are causal connections between intellectual and moral virtues.

Let us conclude this discussion of the connections between moral and intellectual virtues with selections from two of the few important philosophers in the history of philosophy who discuss intellectual vice: Francis Bacon and John Locke. Both of them associate intellectual failings with the passions and the moral vices.

In the first book of the *Novum Organum* Francis Bacon classifies the major sources of intellectual error. Notice how closely he associates these problems with the inappropriate influence of the emotions.

> The human understanding is not a dry light, but is infused by desire and emotion, which give rise to "wishful science." For man prefers to believe what he wants to be true. He therefore rejects difficulties, being impatient of inquiry; sober things, because they restrict his hope; deeper parts of Nature because of his superstition; the light of experience, because of his arrogance and pride, lest his mind should seem to concern itself with things mean and transitory; things that are strange and contrary to all expectation, because of common opinion. In short, emotion in numerous, often imperceptible ways pervades and infects the understanding. (Bk. I, aphorism 49)

Bacon then enumerates four types of error in belief formation arising from different sources. He calls them "idols," suggesting that they are spectral forms, alluring the mind into false paths.

1. *Idols of the Tribe.* These have their roots in human nature generally, "or from its attachment to preconceived ideas, or from its narrowness, or its restlessness, or from an infusion of emotions, or from the inadequacy of the senses, or from the mode of impression" (aphorism 52). "The human understanding is like an uneven mirror that cannot reflect truly the rays from objects, but distorts and corrupts the nature of things by mingling its own nature with it" (aphorism 41).

2. *Idols of the Cave.* These arise from the individual's particular nature, of both mind and body, and come also from education, habits, and by chance (aphorisms 42, 53–8).

3. *Idols of the Marketplace.* These have crept into the understanding through the alliance of words and names. "For while men believe their reason governs words, in fact, words turn back and reflect their power upon the understanding, and so render philosophy and science sophistical and inactive" (aphorisms 43, 59–60).

4. *Idols of the Theater.* These have their source in the fashion of the day, including theological and philosophical fashion. They "are not innate, nor are they secretly insinuated into the understanding, but are imposed and received entirely from the fictitious tales in theories, and from wrong-headed laws of demonstration" (aphorisms 44, 61–2).

Locke's catalogue of the ways thought can go wrong is derived from his classifications of the different kinds of men and coincides with some of Bacon's categories:

(a) The first is of those who seldom reason at all, but do and think according to the example of others, whether parents, neighbors, ministers, or whom else they are pleased to make choice of to have an implicit faith in, for the saving of themselves the pains and troubles of thinking and examining for themselves.

(b) This kind is of those who put passion in the place of reason, and being resolved that shall govern their actions and arguments, neither use their own, nor hearken to other people's reason, any farther than it suits their humor, interest, or party. . . .

(c) This third sort is of those who readily and sincerely follow reason, but for want of having that which one may call
large, sound, roundabout sense, have not a full view of all that
relates to the question. . . . They converse but with one sort of
men, they read but one sort of books, they will not come in the
hearing but of one sort of notions. (*Of the Conduct of the Understanding*, sec. 3, pp. 208–9; similar ideas are expressed in
Locke's *Essay* IV.20)

Both Bacon and Locke emphasize the connections between
moral and intellectual character in their enumerations of the ways
things can go astray in human thinking. An appreciation of this
connection is important for an understanding of both moral and
intellectual character. I will have reason to return to their examples when we criticize some contemporary theories of knowledge
in Part III.

4 THE TWO COMPONENTS OF INTELLECTUAL VIRTUES

We saw in section 2 that a virtue has a motivational component
and a component of reliability in attaining the aims of the motivational component. Notice that this means that each virtue is defin-
able in terms of a particular motivation. For example, benevolence is the virtue according to which a person is
characteristically motivated to bring about the well-being of others and is reliably successful in doing so. Courage is the virtue
according to which a person is characteristically motivated to risk
danger to himself when something of greater value is at stake and
is reliably successful in doing it. Justice is the virtue according to
which a person is characteristically motivated to respect others as
persons and is reliably successful in treating them that way. These
definitions may not be wholly accurate, but I believe they are
accurate enough to illustrate the pattern according to which each
virtue can be defined. I have already noted that there are some
exceptional virtues that may not fit this pattern, such as wisdom
and integrity, but the only form of wisdom I will discuss in any

detail is practical wisdom, the topic of section 5,[41] and I will leave for a later project the task of giving an account of the higher-order virtue of integrity.

In 4.1 I will show how the intellectual virtues can be defined in terms of derivatives from the motivation for knowledge and reliable success in attaining the ends of these motivations. In 4.2 I explain the value of the components of intellectual virtues according to two forms of pure virtue theory. If we were to pursue a happiness-based theory, then the goodness of both components of each virtue would be explained teleologically. A virtuous motivation and reliable success in achieving its aims would be good because of their relation to the good of human flourishing or happiness. On the other hand, if we were to pursue the type of theory I call motivation-based, we would assign intrinsic and independent value to the motivational components of virtues and derive the goodness of the reliability component from the goodness of the motivational component. I will argue that either one of these approaches can offer a promising way to explain the nature and value of intellectual virtues, but I find the motivation-based theory especially exciting, perhaps because of its novelty.

4.1 *The motivation for knowledge and reliable success*

In this subsection I will argue that the individual intellectual virtues can be defined in terms of motivations arising from the general motivation for knowledge and reliability in attaining the aims of these motives. Since all of the intellectual virtues have the same foundational motivation and since all of the other moral virtues have different foundational motivations, this means that a distinction between an intellectual and a moral virtue can be made on the basis of the motivational component of the virtue. I maintain that this is the only theoretically relevant difference be-

---

[41] Aristotle makes contemplation the highest achievement of the intellect, and a full account of intellectual virtue ought to investigate it. In the present work, however, I am aiming to present an account of virtue that is principally concerned with the concepts and issues of greatest interest to contemporary epistemology and ethics. Once that is accomplished, I hope that others will join me in investigating the more rarified, but more valuable, intellectual virtues.

tween intellectual virtues and the other moral virtues, and so there are good grounds for continuing to call these virtues "intellectual," even though I have argued that they are best treated as a subset of the moral virtues. It may be that at the deepest level the moral and intellectual virtues arise from the same motivation, perhaps a love of being in general.[42] If so, such a motivation would serve to unify all the virtues, but I will not analyze the relations among the virtuous motivations in this work.

The simplest way to describe the motivational basis of the intellectual virtues is to say that they are all based in the motivation for knowledge. They are all forms of the motivation to have cognitive contact with reality, where this includes more than what is usually expressed by saying that people desire truth. As we saw in Part I, understanding is also a form of cognitive contact with reality, one that has been considered a component of the knowing state in some periods of philosophical history. I will not give an account of understanding in this work, but I have already indicated that it is a state that includes the comprehension of abstract structures of reality apart from the propositional. I will assume that it either is a form of knowledge or enhances the quality of knowledge. Although all intellectual virtues have a motivational component that aims at cognitive contact with reality, some of them may aim more at understanding, or perhaps at other epistemic states that enhance the quality of the knowing state, such as certainty, than at the possession of truth per se. A few stellar virtues such as intellectual originality or inventiveness are related, not simply to the motivation for the *agent* to possess knowledge, but to the motivation to advance knowledge for the human race. We will also look at how the motivation to know leads to following rules and belief-forming procedures known by the epistemic community to be truth conducive, and we will see how the individual intellectual virtues are knowledge conducive.

The task of defining virtues immediately raises the question of how virtues are individuated and whether they are unified at

---

[42] In *Reason and the Heart,* Chap. 2 (1996), William Wainwright discusses the love of being in general as an epistemic virtue recognized by Jonathan Edwards.

some deeper level. I will not go very far into this matter, although it is an interesting one and ought to be pursued in a full theory of virtue. I have already said in section 3 that I have no position on the question of whether intellectual virtues that share a name with certain moral virtues are two different virtues or one. Even within the class of intellectual virtues it is difficult to demarcate the boundaries of the individual virtues if I am right that they all arise out of the motivation for knowledge since that implies that all intellectual virtues are unified by one general motivation. But, of course, the same thing can be said about all the other moral virtues since they also can be unified by one general motivation for good, and knowledge is a form of good.

Let me address one more point before beginning. The definition of intellectual virtue in terms of the motivation for knowledge is circular if we then go on to define knowledge in terms of intellectual virtue, as I intend to do in Part III. For the purposes of my entire project, then, the thesis of 4.1 must be formulated less succinctly but without circularity as the thesis that the individual intellectual virtues can be defined in terms of derivatives of the motivations for truth or cognitive contact with reality, where the motivation for understanding is assumed to be a form of the motivation for cognitive contact with reality. In this subsection I am formulating the position in terms of the motivation for knowledge because I think that that is closer to the way people actually think of their own motives and the way those motives are described by others, but I am not wedded to this view. The formulation in terms of knowledge motivation is simpler, and, of course, it is only circular when the theory of virtue is combined with the theory of knowledge; it is not a problem for the theory of Part II, which can stand alone. When the theory of virtue and vice presented in Part II is placed together with the account of knowledge in Part III, the motivational basis for intellectual virtue needs to be described as the motivation for truth or cognitive contact with reality, where that is understood to include contact that is high-quality and nonpropositional.

4.1.1 *The motivation for knowledge* Intellectual virtues have been neglected in the history of philosophy, but there were discussions of them in the early modern period as part of the general critical examination of human perceptual and cognitive faculties that dominated that era. Both Hobbes and Spinoza connected the intellectual as well as the moral virtues with the passions, and both traced the source of these virtues to a single human motivation, the motivation for self-preservation or power. In the early part of this century John Dewey stressed the place of the intellectual virtues in what he called "reflective thinking," arising from the desire to attain the goals of effective interaction with the world. We will look first at some remarks by Hobbes and Dewey, and then I will turn to the contemporary treatment of the intellectual virtues by James Montmarquet in the course of giving my own argument for the derivation of the motivational components of intellectual virtues from the motivation to know.

Let us begin with the lively discussion of the causes of intellectual virtue and vice in Hobbes's *Leviathan:*

> The causes of this difference of wits are in the passions, and the difference of passions proceeded partly from the different constitution of the body and partly from different education. For if the difference proceeds from the temper of the brain and the organs of sense, either exterior or interior, there would be no less difference of men in their sight, hearing, or other sense than in their fancies and discretions.[43] It proceeds, therefore, from the passions, which are different not only from the difference of men's complexions, but also from their difference of customs and education.
>
> The passions that most of all cause the difference of wit are principally the more or less desire of power, of riches, of knowledge, and of honor. All which may be reduced to the first – that is, desire of power. For riches, knowledge and honor are but several sorts of power.

---

[43] Hobbes implies here that people do not differ as much in their sensory faculties as in their virtues and vices. He also says that part of what leads us to call a quality a virtue is that it is uncommon. The Hobbesian approach would hesitate, then, in attributing anything virtuous to cases of simple perceptual beliefs that are produced by normally functioning faculties.

And therefore a man who has no great passion for any of these things but is, as men term it, indifferent, though he may be so far a good man as to be free from giving offense, yet he cannot possibly have either a great fancy or much judgment. For the thoughts are to the desires as scouts and spies, to range abroad and find the way to the things desired, all steadiness of the mind's motion, and all quickness of the same, proceeding from thence; for as to have no desire is to be dead, so to have weak passions is dullness; and to have passions indifferently for everything, GIDDINESS and *distraction;* and to have stronger and more vehement passions for anything than is ordinarily seen in others is that which men call MADNESS. (Pt. 1, chap. 8, pp. 68–9)

A couple of points in this passage are of interest to our present concern. First, the motivation for knowledge is not a basic motive but is a form of the motivation for power, according to Hobbes. Second, Hobbes's cognitively ideal person is not passionless, but cognitive defects can be traced to an excessively strong, excessively weak, or misplaced desire for power. I will not question the first point. I think Hobbes is probably wrong in his reduction of the desire for knowledge to the desire for power, but I will not dispute it here since even if he is right, the effect is simply to add another motivational layer beneath the one I am proposing in this book, and so it is no threat to the structure of the theory I am proposing. But I want to call attention to Hobbes's second point, which I find insightful. Hobbes says that cognitive virtues and vices arise from differences in a motivation, and that motivation is a passion that admits of excess, deficiency, and distortion of various sorts, and this seems to me to be generally right. I differ with Hobbes mainly in that I identify this motivation with the motivation for knowledge, whereas Hobbes includes several other forms of the motivation for power along with the motivation for knowledge.

If the human drive for knowledge naturally and inexorably led to success, there would be no need for intellectual virtues. But this motivation can be deficient or distorted in many ways, leading to intellectual vices. Deficiency is presumably one of the most common problems, and Ralph Waldo Emerson expresses a pessimistic view of the human drive for knowledge that illustrates how a natural human motivation can be affected by lethargy:

> God offers to every mind its choice between truth and repose. Take which you please, – you can never have both. Between these, as a pendulum, man oscillates. He in whom the love of repose predominates will accept the first creed, the first philosophy, the first political party he meets, – most likely his father's. He gets rest, commodity, and reputation; but he shuts the door to truth. He in whom the love of truth predominates will keep himself aloof from all moorings, and afloat. He will abstain from dogmatism, and recognize all the opposite negations between which, as walls, his being is swung. He submits to the inconvenience of suspense and imperfect opinion, but he is a candidate for truth, as the other is not, and respects the highest law of his being. ("Intellect," Essay 11)

In this passage Emerson describes how a deficiency in the desire for truth leads to such cognitive vices as lack of autonomy, closed-mindedness, and dogmatism. This may lead us to wonder whether an excess of the motivation for knowledge can also lead to intellectual vices, as Hobbes implies in the passage quoted above. This is parallel to the question of whether a person can be a moral fanatic: excessively motivated by a desire to do or to produce good. Since it is problematic whether this is possible, we will not examine it yet but will take up a discussion of a putative case of an excessive motivation to know at the end of this subsection.

Few philosophers have given positive directions on how to think that are intended to circumvent the pitfalls in forming beliefs. The stress has generally been on the mistakes. A well-known exception is Descartes in *Rules for the Direction of the Mind*, and another is John Dewey in *How We Think*. I will not discuss the former since it has been exhaustively examined many times, but I find Dewey intriguing if rather nonspecific. Although he does not discuss the motivation for knowledge directly, he does discuss the motivations to reach our goals in action and to make systematic preparations for the future and the desire to be free from the control of nature, all of which are closely connected with knowledge (1933, chap. 2, sec. 1). These values require the practice of what Dewey calls "reflective thinking," which he outlines in some detail:

> No one can tell another person in any definite way how he *should* think, any more than how he ought to breathe or to have his blood circulate. But the various ways in which we *do* think can be told and can be described in their general features. Some of these ways are better than others; the reasons why they are better can be set forth. The person who understands what the better ways of thinking are and why they are better can, if he will, change his own personal ways until they become more effective; until, that is to say, they do better the work that thinking can do and that other mental operations cannot do so well. The better way of thinking that is to be considered in this book is called reflective thinking. (1933, p. 3)

The disclaimer in the first sentence of the above passage is surely too strong, but the rest of the paragraph is reasonable. Dewey goes on to say that reflective thinking requires not only certain skills, but also certain "attitudes":

> Because of the importance of attitudes, ability to train thought is not achieved merely by knowledge of the best forms of thought. Possession of this information is no guarantee for ability to think well. Moreover, there are no set exercises in correct thinking whose repeated performance will cause one to be a good thinker. The information and the exercises are both of value. But no individual realizes their value except as he is personally animated by certain dominant attitudes *in his own character* [emphasis added]. It was once almost universally believed that the mind had faculties, like memory and attention, that could be developed by repeated exercise, as gymnastic exercises are supposed to develop the muscles. This belief is now generally discredited in the large sense in which it was once held. . . .
>
> What can be done, however, is to cultivate those *attitudes* that are favorable to the use of the best methods of inquiry and testing. Knowledge of the methods alone will not suffice; there

must be the desire, the will, to employ them. This desire is an affair of personal disposition. But on the other hand the disposition alone will not suffice. There must also be understanding of the forms and techniques that are the channels through which these attitudes operate to the best advantage. (Pp. 29–30)

In this passage Dewey places special importance on the desire to employ better ways of thinking, claiming that knowledge of methods is not sufficient. He thus traces a path from our motivation to believe truly and to act effectively to the formation of "attitudes" or intellectual virtues that lead us to employ certain methods of thinking and forming beliefs. For my purposes, the salient point is that the foundation of these virtues is a motivation: the motivation to think more effectively.

The "attitudes" Dewey says one needs to cultivate are the following:

Open-mindedness. "This attitude may be defined as freedom from prejudice, partisanship, and such other habits as close the mind and make it unwilling to consider new problems and entertain new ideas" (1933, p. 30)

Wholeheartedness. "When a person is absorbed, the subject carries him on. Questions occur to him spontaneously; a flood of suggestions pour in on him; further inquiries and readings are indicated and followed; instead of having to use his energy to hold his mind to the subject . . . the material holds and buoys his mind up and gives an onward impetus to thinking. A genuine enthusiasm is an attitude that operates as an intellectual force. A teacher who arouses such an enthusiasm in his pupils has done something that no amount of formalized method, no matter how correct, can accomplish" (pp. 31–2)

Responsibility. "Like sincerity or wholeheartedness, responsibility is usually conceived as a moral trait rather than as an intellectual resource. But it is an attitude that is necessary to win the adequate support of desire for new points of view and new ideas and of enthusiasm for and capacity for absorption in subject matter. These gifts may run wild, or at least they may lead the mind to spread out too far. They do not of themselves insure that centralization, that unity, which is essential to good thinking. To be intellectually responsible is to consider the consequences of a projected step; it means to be willing to adopt these consequences when they follow reasonably from any position already taken. Intellectual responsibility secures integrity; that is to say, consistency and harmony in belief" (p. 32).

In the contemporary literature Laurence BonJour (1980) and Hilary Kornblith (1983) introduced a motivational element into the discussion of epistemic normativity in the notion of epistemic responsibility, defined by Kornblith as follows: "An *epistemically responsible agent* desires to have true beliefs, and thus desires to have his beliefs produced by processes which lead to true beliefs; his actions are guided by these desires" (p. 34). Although Kornblith does not specifically discuss intellectual virtues, he implies that a motivation or desire is at the root of the evaluation of epistemic agents, and that seems to me to be right. A more extensive treatment of epistemic virtue and its connection with motivation has been given by James Montmarquet (1986a, 1992, and 1993, chap. 2), who connects a large set of intellectual virtues with the desire for truth, claiming that these virtues are qualities a person who wants the truth would want to acquire. However, it is not Montmarquet's intention to define intellectual virtues the way I am proposing here or to derive them all from the motivation for truth or from the motivation for knowledge. Still, Montmarquet's work has an obvious affinity with the theory I am proposing. I want to give it close attention.

Recall Montmarquet's classification of the epistemic virtues (Part I, sec. 1.1). Briefly, they are the virtues of impartiality, or openness to the ideas of others; the virtues of intellectual sobriety, or the virtues of the careful inquirer who accepts only what is warranted by the evidence, and the virtues of intellectual courage, which include perseverance and determination. Notice that there is quite a bit of overlap between these sets of virtues and Dewey's. The major differences are in Dewey's virtue of wholeheartedness and Montmarquet's virtues of courage.

Montmarquet calls the desire for truth "epistemic conscientiousness" and argues that *some* intellectual virtues arise out of this desire.

> The first point to be made . . . is that such qualities as open-mindedness are widely regarded as truth-conducive. In contrast to the highly controversial claims of various theories, the truth-conduciveness of qualities such as openness and intellectual sobriety is widely acknowledged to be a fact, not only by the expert (if there are "experts" on any such matter as this), but also by the average nonexpert individual (at least if he or she is suitably queried). Take openness. Unless one starts from the unlikely presumption that one has found the truth already and that the contrary advice and indications of others is liable, therefore, only to lead one astray, one can hardly possess a sincere love of truth, but no concern about one's own openness. Or take intellectual sobriety. Here, too, unless one starts from the unlikely presumption that one's immediate reactions and unchecked inferences are so highly reliable as not to be improved by any tendency to withhold full assent until they are further investigated, the virtue of sobriety will have to be acknowledged. Or, finally, take intellectual courage. Again, unless one makes an initially unappealing assumption that one's own ideas – true as they may seem to oneself – are so liable to be mistaken as to require not only deference to the opinions of others, but also a deep sense that these are opinions more liable to be correct than one's own (even when one cannot see how or why) [, unless] one makes such an initial assumption, one will have to acknowledge intellectual courage as a virtue. (1993, pp. 27–8)

The reader should not be misled into thinking that this is an argument that these virtues are truth conducive; in fact, Montmarquet questions the truth conduciveness of openness and courage, as we will see. It is, instead, an argument that they are traits persons who *desire* the truth would want to have. I take this to mean that such persons would be *motivated* to act the way open-minded, intellectually sober, cautious, courageous, and persevering people act in their belief-forming processes. So if a person is motivated to get the truth, she would be motivated to consider the ideas of others openly and fairly, to consider the evidence with care, not to back down too quickly when criticized, and all the rest. This seems to me to be correct. It means that the motivation for knowledge gives rise to the motivation to act in ways that are distinctive of the various intellectual virtues Montmarquet mentions. Undoubtedly it also leads to the motivation to acquire Dewey's trait of intellectual responsibility; in fact, the motivation to be able to accurately predict consequences is a form of the motivation to know. The trait that Dewey calls "wholeheartedness," the attitude of enthusiasm, which moves us onward in thinking, is also a form of the motivation to know, in fact, an intensification of it. It is reasonable to conclude, then, that a wide range of intellectual virtues arise out of the same *general* motivation, the motivation for knowledge, and have the same general aim, knowledge.

4.1.2 *The success component of the intellectual virtues* Intellectually virtuous motivations lead the agent to guide her belief-forming processes in certain ways. They make her receptive to processes known to her epistemic community to be truth conducive and motivate her to use them, even if it means overcoming contrary inclinations. As Dewey tells us, it is not enough to be aware that a process is reliable; a person will not reliably *use* such a process without certain virtues. At least this is the case with reliable processes that are not unconscious or automatic. Contemporary research in epistemology has focused extensively on the concept of a truth-conducive belief-forming process, as well as on many specific examples of these processes. I have no intention of duplicating or replacing this work here. My purpose is to point out that the motivation for knowledge leads a person to follow rules and belief-forming processes that are truth conducive and whose truth conduciveness she is able to discover and use by the possession of intellectual virtue.

Intellectually virtuous motivations not only lead to following reliable procedures but also lead to the development of particular skills suited to the acquisition of knowledge in a certain area. As we saw in 2.4, skills are more closely connected to effectiveness in a particular area of life or knowledge than are virtues, which are psychically prior and provide the motivations to develop skills. Intellectual skills are sets of truth-conducive procedures that are acquired through habitual practice and have application to a certain area of truth acquisition. Since the path to knowledge varies with the context, the subject matter, and the way a community makes a division of intellectual labor, people with the same intellectual virtues will not all need to have the same skills, at least not to the same degree. Clearly the importance of fact-finding skills, skills of spatial reasoning, and skills in the subtler branches of logic are not equally important for all areas of the pursuit of knowledge. But all of these skills could arise in different people from the same intellectual virtues – for example, carefulness, thoroughness, and autonomy.

We have already seen that virtue is more than a motivation. Of course, we would expect many virtuous motivations to lead to success in carrying out the aims of the motive. So, for example, the motive to be careful or persevering probably leads somewhat reliably to success in being careful or persevering, but the correlation with success is probably much less in the case of such virtuous motives as the motive to be autonomous, the motive to be courageous, and perhaps even the motive to be open-minded. The weak connection between motive and success is also noticeable in Dewey's virtue of wholeheartedness (if it is a virtue), since it is surely naïve to think that the motivation to be enthusiastic reliably leads to being enthusiastic. But even when the motivational component of a virtue is *generally* related to success, we do not call a person virtuous who is not reliably successful herself, whether or not most people who have the trait are successful in carrying out the aims of the virtue in question. So if she is truly open-minded, she must actually be receptive to new ideas, examining them in an evenhanded way and not ruling them out because they are not her own; merely being motivated to act in these ways is not sufficient. Similarly, if she is intellectually courageous, she must, in actual fact, refrain from operating from an assumption that the views of others are more likely to be true than her own and must be willing to withstand attack when she has good reason to think she is right, but not otherwise. Parallel remarks apply to the other intellectual virtues. It follows that each of these intellectual virtues has a motivational component arising out of the motivation to know and a component of reliable success in achieving the aim of the motivational component.

We saw in 2.5 that most virtues are acquired by habituation and we only consider them virtues when they are entrenched in the agent's character. Entrenchment is a necessary feature of virtues because they are often needed the most when they encounter resistance. For example, the tendency to be motivated by compassion does not signify the existence of the *virtue* of compassion in a person who loses this motivation in the presence of physically unattractive persons in need, even if these circumstances do not arise very often. Similarly, the tendency to be motivated to fairly evaluate the arguments of others does not signify the existence of the virtue of intellectual fairness in a person who loses this motivation when confronted with arguments for unappealing conclusions, even if she is lucky enough not to encounter such arguments very often. So the motivational component of a virtue must be inculcated sufficiently to reliably withstand the influence of contrary motivations when those motivations do not themselves arise from virtues. The more that virtuous motivations and the resulting behavior become fixed habits, the more they are able to reliably achieve the ends of the virtue in those cases in which there are contrary tendencies to be overcome.

One way to distinguish among the truth-conducive qualities those that are virtues and those that are not is by the difference in the value we place on the entrenchment of these traits. Montmarquet (1993, pp. 26–7) mentions that we would not want the desire to uphold behaviorist psychology to be an entrenched trait even if it is truth conducive, unlike the desire for the truth itself or, I would add, the desire to be open-minded, careful in evaluating evidence, autonomous, etc. The latter traits, when entrenched, lead to the truth partly *because* of their entrenchment, whereas the desire to uphold behaviorism is less likely to lead to the truth if it is entrenched than if it is not. The intellectual virtues are a subset of truth-conducive traits that are entrenched and whose entrench-

ment aids their truth conduciveness.[44] The value of the entrenchment of a trait would, of course, depend partly on the environment in which it is entrenched.[45] Most of the qualities I have been
calling intellectual virtues – traits such as open-mindedness,
carefulness, and perseverance – are to a great extent environment
neutral, but this does not mean that there are not other intellectual
virtues that are more context sensitive.

Many intellectual virtues, including those mentioned by
Dewey, not only arise from and serve the motivation to know the
truth, but are also crucial in such activities as the arts, crafts, and
games. The ultimate aim of these activities is not knowledge but
something practical: creating an artistically superior sonnet, making a fine violin, winning a chess game.[46] These ends cannot be
successfully achieved without knowledge in one of its senses, but
probably not the kind of knowledge whose object is true propositions. At least, that sort of knowledge is not the one most fundamentally connected to success in these activities, which is more a
matter of knowing-how rather than knowing-that. Still, some of
the same virtues that arise out of the desire for knowledge and aid
its successful achievement can also aid the achievement of these
practical ends and, in some people, may arise more out of a desire
for the practical end than out of a desire for knowledge. I do not
claim, then, that intellectual virtues arise only from the motivation to know, much less do I claim they arise only from the motivation to have propositional knowledge, and I certainly do not

---

[44] Charles Young has suggested to me that a problematic case is the desire that
the interesting be true, a quality whose entrenchment might have value, he
suggests, independently of its capacity to reliably lead to the truth. There is a
passage in the *Meno* (81de) in which Socrates seems to be saying that even if
we have no rational grounds for preferring the religious story of 81ad to the
eristic story of 80d, we are better off believing the former: it makes us energetic
seekers, whereas the eristic story makes us lazy. I have noticed in myself and
others the tendency to go for the more metaphysically exciting position on
such issues as the nature of time or the existence of abstract objects, quite apart
from a consideration of the weight of the argumentative evidence. Such a
tendency is clearly dangerous, but it is not obviously a bad thing. There might
even be value in its entrenchment.

[45] I thank Hilary Kornblith for drawing my attention to this point.

[46] I thank Charles Young for this point.

claim that their exercise is properly directed only at knowledge. The value of intellectual virtues extends beyond their epistemic use. So not only is the distinction between intellectual and moral virtues highly artificial, as I argued in section 3, but the distinction between intellectual virtues and the practical virtues needed for doing such things as creating sonnets, making violins, or winning chess games is artificial as well. Again, I will not discuss the problem of virtue individuation. There may be *some* difference between, say, the kind of openness displayed in writing a Shakespeare sonnet and the kind of openness displayed in pure scientific investigation. This difference may amount to a distinction in the virtues themselves if virtue identity is determined by the ultimate end of the virtue. The point is that even if this is the case, there are practical and intellectual virtues so similar to each other that they are very difficult to distinguish, and this means that it is highly implausible to maintain that intellectual virtues are fundamentally different in kind from the virtues needed for the kinds of practical activities just named.

Amelie Rorty (1994, p. 12) points out that while the utility and success of intellectual virtues depend on their becoming habits that lead to action without prior deliberation, habits can become pathological or idiotic. They become pathological, she says, when they become so habitual that their exercise extends to situations that no longer concern their internal aims. So generosity is pathological when it debilitates its recipients. The capacity to generate what Rorty calls "bravura virtuoso thought experiments" becomes pathological when it applies only to a very rare, narrow range of circumstances (p. 13). A virtuous habit becomes idiotic when its exercise resists a reasonable redirection of its aims, a redirection that is appropriate to changing circumstances. Rorty gives the example of courage when one is unable to make the transition from its military use to its use in political negotiation. In the intellectual sphere, the virtue of properly arguing from authority becomes idiotic when it is used to block the investigation of the legitimacy of the authority itself (p. 14). Some of these problems can be addressed by the function of the virtue of *phronesis*, to which we will turn in section 5, but we do need to be reminded of the potential negative effects of habit, already noted in 2.5. Nevertheless, these considerations do not falsify the claim that there is an element of habit in virtue. So far, then, our analysis of the components of intellectual virtue has identified a component of habitual motivation arising from the motive to know and a component of reliable success in achieving the aims of the virtue in question.

I have said that the primary motivation underlying the intellectual virtues is the motivation for knowledge. Such a motivation clearly includes the desire to have true beliefs and to avoid false ones, and we have looked at how such a motivation leads a person to follow rules or procedures of belief formation that are known to her epistemic community to be truth conducive. The motivation for knowledge also leads its possessor to acquire the motivational components distinctive of the individual intellectual virtues: open-mindedness, fair-mindedness, intellectual flexibility, and so on. And the motivation to be, say, open-minded, will lead to acquiring patterns of behavior characteristic of the open-minded; the motivation to be fair-minded will lead to acquiring patterns of behavior characteristic of the intellectually fair; and so on. It is doubtful that such patterns of behavior are fully describable in terms of following rules or procedures. It is clear, then, that the following of truth-conducive procedures is not all that a knowledge-motivated person does, both because the motivation for truth leads to behavior that is not fully describable as the following of procedures, and because the motivation for knowledge includes more than the motivation for truth. The motivation for knowledge leads us to be aware of the reliability of certain belief-forming processes and the unreliability of others, but it also leads us to be aware that there are reliable belief-forming mechanisms whose reliability is not yet known. And similarly, there are unreliable belief-forming mechanisms whose unreliabilility is not yet known. This is something we cannot ignore; otherwise, knowledge about knowledge would not progress. This means that intellectual virtues such as flexibility, open-mindedness, and even boldness are highly important. It also suggests that there is more than one sense in which a virtue can be truth conducive. In the sense most commonly discussed by reliabilists, truth conduciveness is a function of the *number* of true beliefs and the *proportion* of true to false beliefs generated by a process. There is another sense of truth conduciveness, however, which is important at the frontiers of knowledge and in areas, like philosophy, that generate very few true beliefs, no matter how they are formed. I suggest that we may legitimately call a trait or procedure truth conducive if it is a necessary condition for advancing knowledge in some area even though it generates very few true beliefs and even if a high percentage of the beliefs formed as the result of this trait or procedure are false. For example, the discovery of new reliable procedures may arise out of intellectual traits that lead a person to hit on falsehood many times before hitting on the truth. As long as these traits (in combination with other intellectual virtues) are self-correcting, they will eventually advance human knowledge, but many false beliefs may have to be discarded along the way. A person motivated to know would be motivated to act cognitively in a manner that is truth conducive in this sense, I would argue, in addition to acting in a way that is truth conducive in the more common sense.

The virtues of originality, creativity, and inventiveness are truth conducive in the sense just described. Clearly, their truth conduciveness in the sense of producing a high proportion of true beliefs is much lower than that of the ordinary virtues of careful and sober inquiry, but they are truth conducive in the sense that they are necessary for the advancement of human knowledge. If only 5 percent of a creative thinker's original ideas turn out to be true, her creativity is certainly truth conducive because the stock of knowledge of the human race has increased through her creativity. The way in which these virtues are truth conducive is probably circuitous and unpredictable, and for this reason it is doubtful that they give rise to a set of rules, and, in fact, they may even defy those rules already established. Often creative people simply operate on intuition, which is usually what we call an ability when it works and we don't know how it works. Ernest Dimnet relates the story that Pasteur was constantly visited by intuitions that he was afterward at great pains to check by the ordinary canons of science (1928, p. 187). Presumably, following the canons in the absence of his bold and original ideas would not have gotten him (or us) nearly as far. Dimnet tells another anecdote about the creative process in novelists. Apparently, when Sir Walter Scott hit upon the idea for a new novel, he would read volume after volume that had no reference to his subject, merely because reading intensified the working of his mind. Dimnet comments that this process did for Scott's power of invention what the crowds in the city did for Dickens's (p. 7). Of course, novelists are not aiming for truth in the sense that is the major focus of this book, but the same point could apply to creative work in philosophy, history, mathematics, and the sciences. The knowledge-motivated person will want to have the virtues of creativity to the extent that she is able, and that gives us another reason why the motive to know includes more than the motive to follow procedures known to be reliable. The division of epistemic labor probably limits the number of people who are strongly motivated in this way, but their existence is important for the knowledge of the whole community.[47]

In "The Doctrine of Chances," C. S. Peirce (1992) expressed the opinion that even the scientific method is truth conducive only in a sense similar to the one I have just described. Peirce says that the scientist must be unselfish because he is not likely to arrive at the truth for himself in the short run. Instead, his procedures are likely to lead the scientific community to better theories and more comprehensive truths in the long run.[48] If Peirce is right, the sense in which the virtues of originality and creativity are truth conducive is not clearly different from the way in which the virtues of careful scientific inquiry are truth conducive.

---

[47] A careful study of the psychology of creativity would probably show that motivation operates in a different way in the virtues of creativity and originality than it does in the other intellectual virtues. The motivation to be creative does not lead to being creative in the way the motivation to be careful leads to being careful. I imagine that creative people begin by being creative involuntarily and find it pleasant, exciting, even thrilling. These feelings give them the impetus to permit their creativity a certain latitude, which may lead them to ignore the established canons, at least temporarily. This means that the motivational component in creativity does not so much lead its possessors to *acquire* the trait as allow them to give it free rein, and this may lead to ignoring the dictates of certain other virtues.

[48] Christopher Hookway 1993 has an interesting discussion of this position of Peirce and related views.

Another reason the motivation to know is not fully expressed by following well-known reliable belief-forming processes is that, as already remarked, the motivation to know includes the motivation for understanding. Knowledge has been associated with certainty and understanding for long periods of its history, but generally not with both at the same time.[49] The virtues that lead to the kind of knowledge that gives the possessor certainty may be different from the virtues that lead to understanding, and the following of belief-forming processes known to the epistemic community to be reliable may be insufficient for either one. For one thing, to aim at certainty is not just to aim at truth but to aim to have an awareness of truth that has a certain quality. To get an awareness with that quality it may not be enough to use processes known or truly believed by one's epistemic community to be reliable. One may need to be aware of how and why one's belief-forming process is justified, or at least how and why it is reliable and the degree of its reliability. The virtues that enable one to see how one's belief can stand up to attack contribute to certainty. Virtues that lead to clarity in one's grasp of a matter may also contribute to certainty. Aiming at understanding is even farther removed from using procedures known to be reliable, because as we saw in Part I, understanding is not a property whose object is a single proposition. Those virtues that enable the agent to see connections among her beliefs – introspective attentiveness and insight in its various forms – are understanding conducive. All of these virtues deserve careful attention, and although I will not stop to investigate them individually, I hope that others will do so.

4.1.3 *Montmarquet on the virtues and truth conduciveness* So far we have seen that intellectual virtues arise out of the motivation for knowledge and lead to the use of reliable belief-forming procedures, among other things. It is now time to look squarely at the question of whether the intellectual virtues are, in fact, knowledge conducive. I will give a brief intuitive argument for an affir-

---

[49] See Tiles and Tiles 1993 and Everson 1990 for historical discussions of the difference between the values of certainty and understanding in different periods of epistemological history.

mative answer to this question first, followed by an examination of a series of objections to my thesis, mostly taken from James Montmarquet.

The motivation to know leads to the motivation to act in intellectually virtuous ways. These motivations arise because of the general belief that success in achieving the aims of these motives is knowledge conducive. I have already suggested that some intellectually virtuous motivations aim at something that enhances the quality of knowledge, such as understanding and certainty, but even these motivations are connected with the motive for cognitive contact with reality, and almost all the virtues we have named so far are acquired because of the general belief in their truth conduciveness. Of course, the prevailing *belief* in the truth conduciveness of, for example, open-mindedness, intellectual courage, and intellectual sobriety (carefulness, attentiveness, thoroughness) is not a demonstration that these virtues *are* truth conducive, but is it not the case that we only consider these traits virtues *because* we take them to be truth conducive, or knowledge conducive in some other way? So if it turned out that we were wrong about the truth conduciveness of one of these traits, that trait would cease to be considered an intellectual virtue. What we would not do is to continue to treat it as an intellectual virtue and then go on to declare that intellectual virtues are not necessarily truth conducive. I suggest, then, that any evidence of an intellectual virtue that is not truth conducive (or knowledge conducive) is more reasonably interpreted as evidence that such a trait is not a virtue than as evidence that some intellectual virtues are not truth conducive. Thus, not only is an open-minded person motivated to consider the ideas of others without prejudice, including those that conflict with her own, and is reliably successful in doing so, but her reliable success in being open-minded is truth conducive. Therefore, the beliefs she forms out of open-mindedness are truth conducive. A comparable account can be given for each of the other intellectual virtues.

At this point we must make another theoretical judgment parallel to the judgment we made about building a reliability component into the definition of a virtue. I said earlier (sec. 2.6) that it is not enough that in general the possession of a virtuous motivation is reliably connected with success in acting virtuously. A particular person does not have the virtue unless he himself not only has the virtuous motivation but is reliably successful in achieving his virtuous end. The same question arises with respect to reliability in reaching the truth. Let us suppose that open-minded behavior is generally truth conducive, so as long as Joe's behavior is reliably open-minded, it is truth conducive in the weak sense that behavior of this sort usually leads to the truth. But perhaps *Joe's* open-mindedness is not truth conducive due to simple bad luck or perhaps because his open-mindedness exacerbates the effects of his inability to recognize trustworthy authority, the way the courage of the Nazi described in 2.2 exacerbates the effects of his cruelty. Just as the courage of the Nazi may lead him to act even worse than he would have without courage, Joe's open-mindedness may lead him farther away from the truth than he would have been without it.

I have argued that the trait of the Nazi may be courage and is worth having even for him since it brings him closer to a state of moral excellence than he would be without it, and I said that the same thing holds for the intellectual virtues. Even if Joe's open-mindedness is not truth conducive *for him*, it is still a virtue and it is still a good thing for Joe to have that trait. We would not advise Joe to think in a closed-minded way even if for a time it meant that his belief-forming processes were more reliable in attaining the truth. Notice that I said "for a time" his belief-forming processes would be more reliable if he were closed-minded rather than open-minded. I suggest that as long as we look at a large number of Joe's beliefs formed over time, open-mindedness will be ultimately truth conducive, even for him. I conclude that it is true that an agent does not possess an intellectual virtue unless the trait *as possessed by him* is truth conducive in the long run, but there may be a period of time during which it is not truth conducive. This raises the so-called generality problem in explicating the sense in which a virtue is reliable. It indicates that we ought to take a very large class of instances of the virtue as the set of cases against which reliability is measured. We will have occasion to turn to the generality problem again.

Montmarquet raises several objections to the position that intellectual virtues are truth conducive and intellectual vices are not: (1) Some intellectual virtues may not be truth conducive even though they would be desired by persons who love the truth. Montmarquet says open-mindedness is such a virtue. (2) Some intellectual virtues not only seem to fail to lead to the truth but do not seem to even be associated with the *desire* for truth. He cites intellectual creativity and inventiveness as examples. (3) If we look at intellectual giants in the history of ideas, they do not seem to differ significantly in intellectual virtue, yet they do differ significantly in the truth of their beliefs and systems of belief. While not an objection to the above thesis, Montmarquet also maintains that (4) some vices (e.g., dogmatism and cowardice) may arise out of a desire for knowledge, even if they are not truth conducive. In addition to these objections, I will consider one other: (5) Some intellectual vices appear to be truth conducive. I will answer each of these objections in turn.

First, let us look at Montmarquet's argument that some intellectual virtues may not be truth conducive even though they would be desired by lovers of truth. He says open-mindedness is such a virtue:

The open-minded person must tend to see others' ideas as having at least a certain initial plausibility. He or she must be more than open, relative to what strikes them as initially plausible; they must have at least some initial tendency to see others' ideas *as* plausible.

But if this quality is not to degenerate into mere gullibility, does not a kind of objective reliability have to be built into this characterization of open-mindedness? Must not, in other words, this tendency somehow be keyed to the *actual* plausibility of others' ideas?

I have basically two problems with any such suggestion. First, it is not clear that "plausibility" itself is an objective commodity, like, say, truth. We *find* certain things plausible, but relative to our own background beliefs. Still, it might be insisted that the open-minded person's reactions are keyed not to some mysterious notion of "objective plausibility," but to the plausibility judgment of some broader epistemic community (i.e., to "our" judgments as to what is plausible). Even this, however, seems unpromising. Surely, an open-minded person – for instance, one coming from some different "epistemic community" – might not share our judgments. Second, let us suppose that "plausibility" did denote some purely objective likelihood to be true (however that is to be understood). The mere tendency to have one's reactions, as it were, track such objective likelihoods is not, on reflection, open-mindedness at all. It is *sagacity* perhaps . . . open-mindedness must involve at least some resistance to one's own immediate reactions of unfamiliarity and even implausibility. To this it might be countered that perhaps one's overriding reaction might track objective plausibility even if one's initial reactions did not. But that would, I'm afraid, still miss the point of what open-mindedness is: it is the tendency, for example, to resist initial dismissals based on unfamiliarity that partially constitutes open-mindedness. Whether it turns out that this resistance tracks, or nearly tracks, objective truth will certainly be of epistemological interest. But it is not part of open-mindedness. (1993, pp. 24–5)[50]

We have already seen that Montmarquet says that the virtue of open-mindedness arises out of the *desire* for truth, so his point here is that truth conduciveness is not built into the concept of open-mindedness, and that it is in fact an open question whether this virtue is truth conducive. Now I have already given a general argument to the effect that we consider intellectual traits virtues only if they are thought to be knowledge conducive. If queried on the reasons for admiring open-mindedness, most people would undoubtedly mention the fact that closed-minded people tend to be stuck, not in truth, but in falsehood, and even in those cases in which the closed-minded person is lucky enough to have the truth, his closed-mindedness generally prevents him from having knowledge, even if he has true beliefs. This is because closed-

---

50 Montmarquet seems to use the term "truth tracking" as synonymous with "truth conducive" or "reliable," but this is confusing since the concept of truth tracking was introduced by Nozick (1981) for a process that would produce true beliefs in suitably described counterfactual circumstances. In that usage the terms are not synonymous.

mindedness tends to prevent a person from going through the process that would justify his beliefs or would give him a high-quality grasp of the truth if justifiedness is not the appropriate concept. Still, Montmarquet makes some specific points in the above passage that require response.

Montmarquet objects that open-mindedness is defined in terms of the concept of plausibility but that plausibility is not an objective notion like truth; it is relative to the background beliefs of the believer. But, of course, the same can be said for justifiability on many accounts, and that is not usually taken to be a reason to think that justifiability is not related to truth. This brings up the problem of the internal/external split in the notion of rationality that Richard Foley (1993) says is the post-Cartesian situation. We can do the best we can by our own subjective lights and still not be guaranteed truth. But the problem here, as Foley recognizes, is the skeptical hypotheses. Leaving these hypotheses aside, there is no reason not to expect a reliable connection between the subjective notions of rationality, justifiability, and plausibility and the objective notion of knowledge and its component of truth. Of course, the extent to which any egocentric concept is reliably connected to an objective quality is a large question, and that question can be raised about rationality and justifiability as well as about plausibility. But the fact that that question can be raised does not, by itself, give us reason to reject the claim that plausibility in general is correlated with truth, any more than it gives us reason to reject the claim that rationality or justifiability is generally correlated with truth.

Montmarquet has another point. He says that if plausibility can be defined in a way that answers his first objection, it would then not be open-mindedness at all, but some other trait: "The mere tendency to have one's reactions, as it were, track such objective likelihoods is not, on reflection, open-mindedness at all." But the point is not that open-mindedness is the *mere* tendency to lead to the truth; rather, the point is that open-mindedess as Montmarquet defines it does reliably lead to truth. The passage concludes with his remark that it would be of epistemological interest to find out whether open-mindedness is truth conducive, but that doing so is not part of open-mindedness. And I agree with

Montmarquet that it is not part of the *concept* of open-mindedness that it is truth conducive. What I have claimed is that we would not consider it a *virtue* if it were not truth conducive. So far we have no objection to this thesis.

A harder problem according to Montmarquet is the existence of intellectual virtues that not only do not seem to be truth conducive, but do not even seem to be connected with the desire for truth. Creativity and originality are examples, he says (1993, chap 2, sec. 4). I find Montmarquet's argument here puzzling. He connects the intellectual virtues he discusses up to this point in the chapter with the desire to attain truth and to avoid error, and then says that these desires are not rich enough to be epistemically virtuous because the epistemically virtuous have such other goals as the possession of a deep explanatory understanding of the world. And as we would anticipate, Montmarquet infers that the intellectually virtuous person's desires are broader than the desire for truth (p. 33). But then he unexpectedly concludes (p. 34) that such traits as innovativeness and creativity are not epistemic virtues. I do not see the sense of this. Surely the conclusion is that these traits are intellectual virtues that are connected with something other than the desire for truth. I have already argued that the actual motivation of the intellectually virtuous is for knowledge, not merely truth, and so the motivation to possess the components of knowledge in addition to true belief are motivations of the intellectually virtuous. If, as we have already seen (Part I, sec. 2.2), Plato was right that knowledge includes understanding, Montmarquet's example of the epistemically virtuous desire for understanding is not a counterexample to the position for which I have been arguing. But more important, as we have seen, there is a plausible sense in which such traits as creativity and inventiveness *are* truth conducive. They operate on the borders of knowledge and lead to the discovery of new truths for the human race. Their truth conduciveness is not a matter of generating a high proportion of true to false beliefs but in being necessary for the extension of human knowledge in certain areas of inquiry.

This leads to an answer to the third objection. Montmarquet reminds us that such giants in the history of thought as Aristotle, Ptolemy, Albertus Magnus, Galileo, Newton, and Einstein probably did not differ significantly in intellectual virtue, even though they undoubtedly did differ in the truth of their ideas or the truth conduciveness of their methods (1993, pp. 32–3). Without going into the particularities of Montmarquet's choice of examples, I will agree that these thinkers are equal in intellectual virtue, and that being the case, their traits are all truth conducive in the sense I have mentioned. I also agree that their beliefs are not equally true or their methods equally truth conducive in the sense of leading to a high proportion of true to false beliefs. But here I think we can use an insight of Thomas Nagel in "Moral Luck" (1979a). In the last note of the paper (n. 11), Nagel says that there is epistemic luck analogous to moral luck in the sense he has vividly described in that paper. Nagel points out that the Nobel Prize is not given to individuals who make mistakes, no matter how brilliant they are – and presumably, he would add, no matter how intellectually virtuous they are. But surely this is not a problem for the thesis that intellectual virtue is knowledge conducive. It is merely a humble reminder that at the boundaries of knowledge intellectual virtue is not enough. We need luck as well.

The fourth problem is that there are intellectual vices that arise out of the motivation for knowledge but are not truth conducive or otherwise knowledge conducive. Montmarquet's examples are the lack of autonomy and dogmatism:

> Some persons . . . may shun possible sources of contrary ideas to their own, not so much fearing that these ideas are true, as fearing that they lack the wherewithal to avoid being *misled* into thinking them true. Such persons betray a degree of intellectual cowardice but not necessarily any lack of desire for truth. . . . By contrast, the conscientious dogmatist (or "enthusiast") displays an opposite vice: fundamentally he is *overconfident* of his intellectual powers, thus unable or unwilling to suspend his doxastic commitments to see whether his certitude is truly warranted. . . . Unregulated by these, bare conscientiousness . . . may degenerate into some form of intellectual dogmatism, enthusiasm, cowardice, or related evil. That is, bare conscientiousness by no means guarantees a proper orientation towards one's own or others' beliefs, and this is why the

qualities we have been enumerating seem so necessary to intellectual inquiry (and integral to our notion of a virtuous inquirer). (1993, pp. 25–6)

These cases do not pose an objection to the thesis that intellectual virtues are truth conducive and intellectual vices are not, nor to the thesis that intellectual virtue arises out of the motivation for knowledge, since I have not claimed that every trait that arises out of that motivation is an intellectual virtue. Still, they pose problems to the extent that we expect the motive to know to give rise to virtues rather than vices in typical cases. To my mind the more interesting case here is the closed-minded, nonautonomous person who is afraid of being misled into falsehood because of his lack of confidence in his own intellectual powers. Of course, there is always the possibility that such a person has made an accurate assessment of his own abilities, in which case his lack of investigation of contrary views may not exhibit a vice. But let us suppose that he has genuinely underestimated his ability, and his lack of intellectual autonomy is motivated by a fear of being led away from truth. Such a person is similar to the individual who attempts to maintain moral innocence by avoiding persons and situations that might tempt him away from his moral values. In a sense both of these persons display a kind of integrity, but their excessive cautiousness (what Montmarquet probably correctly considers cowardice) prevents them from growing in knowledge in the first case and moral awareness in the other. If we looked more deeply into the psychology of these individuals, I suspect that we would find that the dominant motive is not a love of knowledge or of the good but is something like inflexibility or fear of the unknown. Nevertheless, Montmarquet may be right that this is a case in which an intellectual vice arises in part from a love of knowledge.

Dogmatism is an easier case to manage. It is very unlikely that such a trait arises out of the desire for knowledge since dogmatic individuals are more like Emerson's lover of repose than honest inquirers after truth: "He in whom the love of truth predominates will keep himself aloof from all moorings, and afloat. He will abstain from dogmatism, and recognize all the opposite negations between which, as walls, his being is swung" ("Intellect," Essay 11). But even if Emerson is wrong and the dogmatic individual does love truth, surely he does not love knowledge, because his dogmatism does not permit him to penetrate the grounds for justifying or warranting his beliefs, and his love does not embrace the value of understanding.

The fifth objection is that intellectual vices can be truth conducive. It is even possible that the dogmatist just mentioned has a truth-conducive trait, whether or not Montmarquet is wrong about such a person's desire for knowledge. The alleged truth conduciveness of vices is another case in which the generality problem about reliability emerges. Surely dogmatism is not truth conducive for most people most of the time. When intellectual vices are truth conducive, they are only truth conducive relative to a narrow range of belief-forming practices, usually of a single individual and usually only within the scope of a particular area of knowledge or belief. So, for example, people who would say that the dogmatism of a particular person in her religious beliefs is truth conducive would no doubt deny that her dogmatism about matters of health is truth conducive, much less that dogmatism is a truth-conducive trait for most people most of the time. But the entrenchment feature of virtues and vices can tell us something about the generality problem and can explain why dogmatism is a vice. As a trait becomes habitual, it is naturally generalized in certain ways and not others. Psychological investigation ought to be able to tell us whether a person who is dogmatic about one subject area is also likely to be dogmatic in other areas and, if so, how far her dogmatism is likely to spread. If a person's tendency to dogmatism naturally spreads beyond a limited subject area, the evidence that her dogmatism within such a limited area is truth conducive is no objection to the claim that dogmatism is not a truth conducive trait, even for her. Her dogmatism is not truth conducive if its use is naturally extended to areas in which it is not truth conducive, even if it happens to be truth conducive when she is pronouncing on matters of religion. It is possible, of course, that a person is dogmatic only within a very limited area, one that he knows extremely well and one in which his dogmatism is truth conducive. And it may even be possible that such a person has no tendency to dogmatism in areas in which it is not truth conducive. If this can happen, I am willing to say that his trait is not a vice. It probably is not even dogmatism.

4.1.4 *Motivation in excess* I wish to conclude this subsection on the intellectual virtues and the motivation to know by asking whether the motivation for knowledge can be excessive. In the passage quoted early in this subsection, Hobbes claims that the motivation for power in its various forms, including the motivation for knowledge, can be excessive, and he calls it madness. The excess is no doubt less common than deficiency, but it shows how anything can become obsessive. My favorite example is a delightful passage from Lawrence Sterne's *The Life and Opinions of Tristram Shandy:*

> When my uncle Toby got his map of Namur to his mind, he began immediately to apply himself, and with the utmost diligence, to the study of it; for nothing being of more importance to him than his recovery, and his recovery depending, as you have read, upon the passions and affection of his mind, it behoved him to take the nicest care to make himself so far master of his subject, as to be able to talk upon it without emotion.
>
> In a fortnight's close and painful application, which, by the bye, did my uncle Toby's wound, upon his groin, no good, – he was enabled, by the help of some marginal documents at the feet of the elephant, together with Gobesius's military architecture and pyroballogy, translated from the Flemish, to form his discourse with passable perspicuity; and before he was two full months gone, – he was right eloquent upon it, and could make not only the attack of the advanced counterscarp with great order; – but having, by that time, gone much deeper into the art, than what his first motive made necessary, my uncle Toby was able to cross the Maes and Sambre; make diversions as far as Vauban's line, the abbey of Salsines, etc., and give his visitors as distinct a history of each of their attacks, as of that of the gate of St. Nicholas, where he had the honour to receive his wound.

But desire of knowledge, like the thirst of riches, increases ever with the acquisition of it. The more my uncle Toby pored over his map, the more he took a liking to it! – by the same process and electrical assimilation, as I told you, through which I ween the souls of connoisseurs themselves, by long friction and incumbition, have the happiness, at length, to get all be-virtued – be-pictured, – be-butterflied, and be-fiddled.

The more my uncle Toby drank of this sweet fountain of science, the greater was the heat and impatience of his thirst, so that before the first year of his confinement had well gone round, there was scarce a fortified town in Italy or Flanders, of which, by one means or other, he had not procured a plan, reading over as he got them, and carefully collating therewith the histories of their sieges, their demolitions, their improvements, and new works, all which he would read with that intense application and delight, that he would forget himself, his wound, his confinement, his dinner.

In the second year my uncle Toby purchased Ramelli and Cataneo, translated from Italian; – likewise Stevinus, Moralis, the Chevalier de Ville, Lorini, Cochorn, Sheeter, the Count de Pagan, the Marshal Vauban, Mons. Blondel, with almost as many more books of military architecture, as Don Quixote was found to have of chivalry, when the curate and barber invaded his library.

Towards the beginning of the third year, which was in August, ninety-nine, my uncle Toby found it necessary to understand a little of projectiles: – and having judged it best to draw his knowledge from the fountainhead, he began with N. Tartaglia, who it seems was the first man who detected the imposition of a cannon-ball's doing all that mischief under the notion of a right line – This N. Tartaglia proved to my uncle Toby to be an impossible thing.

— Endless is the search of Truth.

No sooner was my uncle Toby satisfied which road the cannon-ball did not go, but he was insensibly led on, and resolved in his mind to enquire and find out which road the ball did go: For which purpose he was obliged to set off afresh with old Maltus, and studied him devoutly. – He proceeded next to Galileo and Torricellius, wherein, by certain Geometrical rules, infallibly laid down, he found the precise part to be a Parabola – or else an Hyperbola, – and that the parameter, or latus rectum, of the conic section of the said path, was to the quantity and amplitude in a direct ratio, as the whole line to the sine of double the angle of incidence, formed by the breech upon an horizontal plane; – and that the semi-parameter, – stop! my dear uncle Toby – stop! – go not one foot farther into this thorny and bewildered track, – intricate are the steps! intricate are the mazes of this labyrinth! intricate are the troubles which the pursuit of this bewitching phantom Knowledge will bring upon thee. – O my uncle; – fly – fly, fly from it as from a serpent. – Is it fit – good-natured man! thou should'st sit up, with the wound upon thy groin, whole nights baking thy blood with hectic watchings? – Alas! 'twill exasperate thy symptoms, – check thy perspirations – evaporate thy spirits – waste thy animal strength, – dry up thy radical moisture, bring thee into a costive habit of body, – impair thy health, – and hasten all the infirmities of thy old age. – O my uncle! my uncle Toby. (Bk. II, chap. 3)

If Uncle Toby has intellectual vices, they are the vices of excess: excessive attentiveness, thoroughness, diligence, perseverance. Such traits have sometimes been called, with irony, "virtues in excess."[51] Recall Lorraine Code's remark that one hesitates to attribute intellectual virtue to "a voracious collector of facts" (1987, p. 59). But interestingly, these traits do not seem to detract from the goal of knowledge in Uncle Toby's case, and his motivation itself does not seem to be out of line, unless we think that the proper motivation for knowledge resists the extreme specialization of Uncle Toby's endeavors. But that seems unlikely. It is more probable that any defects arising from an overabundance of the desire to know are not specifically intellectual but involve the agent's general well-being, as Tristram Shandy believes to be the case about Uncle Toby. This is not to deny that there can be vices of excessive attentiveness, thoroughness, and perseverance that detract from the goal of knowledge. My conjecture is that it is not

---

[51] See Watson 1984 for an interesting discussion of puzzles involving the idea of virtue in excess.

an excess of the motivation to know that gives rise to such vices, and an extreme degree of the motivation to know does not necessarily give rise to vices. So the extreme degree of the motivation to know is either not a defect at all, or it is a defect only in the very broad sense that it detracts from having a morally balanced character, in which case it may lead to a lack of integrity in one sense of that notion. Happiness-based theories might explain the defect here, if there is one, by its failure to contribute to *eudaimonia*.

4.2 *The value of the components of intellectual virtues*

In this subsection we will look at how the value of intellectual virtues as defined earlier can be explained by each of the two forms of pure virtue theory we are considering. I will discuss the components of intellectual virtue, first, as they would be viewed by a happiness-based theory and, then, according to a motivation-based theory. I will argue that either theory can offer a plausible explanation of the value of intellectual virtues and their components as described in the account I have given earlier, although I find the motivation-based theory especially fascinating. Since this theory is a form of the nonteleological, agent-based approach, it is an interesting alternative to current ethical theories. In giving the motivation-based account we will look at how followers or violators of epistemic rules are commended or criticized primarily because of the epistemic motivations such behavior exemplifies. The conclusion is that the value of both epistemic rules and the reliability component of intellectual virtues rests on the value of motivations arising from the desire for knowledge. If the value of the latter can be explained in a way that does not refer to any other value, it follows that the value of both the virtues and the rules is motivation-based.

4.2.1 *The value of intellectual virtue in a happiness-based theory* Let us begin with the more familiar happiness-based theory. An ethical theory based on the idea of human flourishing would explain the value of virtues of all kinds in terms of their contribution to the life of *eudaimonia*. Each of the virtues is a constituent of the flourishing life, and that means, on the account I have given, that a person leading a flourishing life has the motivational component of each virtue and is reliable in bringing about the aims of these motivations. So she is characteristically motivated by compassion for the suffering of others and is reliably successful in alleviating their suffering, she is motivated to evaluate the opinions and arguments of others with an open mind and is reliably successful in doing so, and so on for all the virtues. An alternative happiness-based account would say that virtues are means to bringing about a flourishing life. This approach would not define human flourishing in such a way that the possession of virtues is an intrinsic part of it, but it would argue that the possession of virtues is a causal condition for flourishing. So a person who is characteristically motivated by compassion for the suffering of others and who is reliably successful in alleviating their suffering is more apt to flourish than she would be otherwise. Similarly, a person who is characteristically motivated to be open-minded in evaluating the opinions and arguments of others and is reliably successful in doing so is also more apt to flourish than she would be otherwise, etc. I will not pursue this variant of happiness-based ethics further, since it seems to reduce virtue theory to a version of consequentialism, but I mention it because philosophers attracted to reliabilism might find an ethical theory of this type suitable to combine with their own epistemic theory.

The Aristotelian position that the moral virtues are all constituents of a life of *eudaimonia* is well known and I will not rehearse it here. More interesting for the present discussion is the idea that the intellectual virtues also are components of *eudaimonia*. Although it is uncommon to find this view expressed today, lofty claims were made about the connection between epistemic goods and *eudaimonia* in both classical Greek and medieval philosophy. The classical idea was that *eudaimonia* involves the fulfillment of human nature, and knowledge is at least part of such a fulfillment, perhaps the most important part. In Book X of the *Nicomachean Ethics* Aristotle characterizes *eudaimonia* as a life of contemplation; Aquinas describes the ultimate end of human life as the Beatific Vision, a state that is simultaneously the enjoyment of perfect happiness and a perfect revelation of truth. The medieval doctrine of the convertibility of the Good and the True gave a metaphysical basis to the close association between the ends of the moral virtues and the ends of the intellectual virtues, although most of this sounds foreign to the modern mind.[52] Today it is unusual to think of the human ends of happiness and truth as so closely connected. It is not that philosophers have given up on the notion of human flourishing or some modern equivalent of *eudaimonia*, but few have been bold enough to describe in any detail, much less defend, the nature of such a state.

An interesting example of a theory of the intellectual virtues in the contemporary literature that attempts to link them with the good life is that of Jane Braeton (1990). Braeton argues that the intellectual virtues as a set constitute a kind of social ability whose value lies in their promotion of the end of living in a community in which all have the opportunity to live well.[53] She identifies six intellectual virtues:

1) The first is an imaginative ability: the ability to represent alternative subjective points of view, not merely of a perceptual character, but also of an ideological character; 2) The second is an ability to reason hypothetically about the likely responses of others to given courses of events, given their various subjective points of view; 3) The third is an abstractive ability, namely the ability to recognize social norms and values as socially constructed, rather than as *a priori* truths. This ability is necessary for transforming existing social arrangements. 4) The fourth is the creative imaginative ability to postulate what the social world would be like if it were based upon alternative social norms; 5) The fifth is an inductive ability to hypothesize about the sources of discord and well-being both in personal and interpersonal affairs. 6) The sixth, which involves each of the above abilities, is the ability to rechart intellectual virtue itself. (P. 6)

---

[52] See MacDonald 1991 for a collection of essays on the medieval identification of being with goodness.

[53] Braeton says she prefers the concept of intellectual virtue to that of intelligence because it is more honest. Intelligence also is evaluative, but less obviously so.

Braeton's teleological view of the intellectual virtues relates them to the flourishing of the community rather than to individual flourishing, and her list of virtues reflects modern feminist sensibilities. It would be interesting to see the development of a connection between these virtues and an account of knowledge, on the one hand, and an account of human flourishing, on the other, although I will not pursue such an account myself.

One reason contemporary thinkers have a difficult time linking the value of knowledge with human flourishing is that we are so sensitized to cases of value conflict, cases in which knowing the truth is not only valueless but is positively evil. That may be the case in Ibsen's play *The Wild Duck*, where the wrong knowledge at the wrong time leads to suicide and grief. Henry James's novel *Wings of the Dove* is another instance in which a significant piece of knowledge leads to death, in this case the death of the heroine. We may be reminded of a line from Ecclesiastes: "He that increaseth knowledge increaseth sorrow" (1.18). Of course, it may be that what makes these important works of literature so powerful is that they give us a message that most of the time is false, but they do call attention to the possibility of conflict among the goods of life. The ancients were certainly aware of such conflicts, but they were much less inclined than we are to see human living as a matter of juggling competing values.[54] This makes the task of describing the life of human flourishing a daunting task for us, but perhaps not an impossible one.

A defense of a happiness-based approach to explaining the value of intellectual virtues as I have defined them would require an account of human happiness or flourishing, and I am not prepared to do that. I imagine that it can be done, however, and if so, I see no reason to think that the relation between flourishing and the intellectual virtues will be any weaker than the relation between flourishing and the moral virtues. At least to the extent that a happiness-based pure virtue theory is a plausible way of

---

[54] See, e.g., Nagel 1979b for an argument that value is not and cannot be made to be unitary. Nussbaum argues (1986) that unlike Plato, Aristotle maintained that the attempt to harmonize the goods of a rich human life can lead to tragedy.

accounting for the traditional moral virtues, I think it is also reasonable to expect that such a theory can produce an explanation of the value of the intellectual virtues. In fact, the connection between the virtues that arise from the motivation for knowledge and that reliably lead to it are easier to associate with the life of *eudaimonia* than are many of the other-regarding moral virtues such as benevolence, mercy, and generosity. Knowledge is primarily a self-regarding good, even though the search for it usually requires the cooperation of others. Since the primary aim of the motivation to know is to possess something for oneself and only indirectly for others, its contribution to the flourishing of its possessor is straightforward, even if there are exceptions, as already noted. In the case of the other-regarding moral virtues, their place in the flourishing life is not credible without a more extensive story.[55] Of course, any problems in explaining the place of these other-regarding virtues in the life of *eudaimonia* also detract from the attempt to make *eudaimonia* the ground of the value of the intellectual virtues because the happiness-based approach is appealing largely due to its potential power as a complete ethical theory.

If an account of human flourishing can be given that is capable of grounding the value of both moral and intellectual virtues, such a theory would have certain advantages. The virtues are many and virtue theorists have always looked for a unifying principle for both theoretical and practical reasons. Theoretically a principle of unification would give the theory the advantage of simplicity. We have seen many reasons for thinking that the moral and the intellectual virtues are not independent, and a reasonable explanation for this phenomenon might be a teleological theory that bases all the virtues, including the intellectual, on flourishing or happiness. In practical life a happiness-based theory holds out the hope of resolving cases of apparent virtue conflict. Of course, if the hope is merely theoretical, it is not of much use, so the major

---

[55] As Dewey Hoitenga has suggested to me, the essence of the story would go something like this. A person is dependent for her happiness on the reciprocating virtue of others, and that will be more forthcoming if she is virtuous also. This intimates something like the Golden Rule.

201

job in making such a theory work would be in the detailed description and defense of the connection between the various virtues and a single recognizable state of *eudaimonia*. Hopefully, ethicists attracted to this approach will find some of the ideas in this part of the book helpful. But many contemporary philosophers are suspicious of the whole idea of flourishing, sometimes because they associate it with Aristotle's teleological metaphysics, which most philosophers nowadays reject. Other philosophers have attacked the concept of flourishing directly (e.g., Harman 1983; Conly 1988). This may make a nonteleological virtue theory preferable. Let us now turn to such an account of the value of intellectual virtues.

4.2.2 *The value of intellectual virtue in a motivation-based theory* In an agent-based ethical theory, the goodness of virtues is not explained by their relation to something else that is the primary good, in contrast with happiness-based or other theories based on an independent conception of the good. The form of agent-based ethics I have proposed here is what I call motivation-based. Let us look at how such a theory would account for the value of a virtue. Take the example of benevolence. On my account of the components of a virtue, benevolence is the virtue according to which a person is characteristically motivated to bring about the well-being of others and is reliably successful in doing so. Now to use the term "well-being" is to construe the states of affairs at which the benevolent person aims as a good thing, but this makes the relation between the goodness of the motive and the goodness of well-being ambiguous. According to a motivation-based theory there is something intrinsically good about the motive of benevolence that is independent of any consideration of the goodness of well-being. In other words, the motive of benevolence does not derive its goodness from the goodness of that at which it aims. In a strong form of the theory it can even be maintained that the goodness of the states of affairs we call "well-being" is itself derivative from the goodness of the motive of benevolence. So the goodness of a benevolent motive is more fundamental than the goodness of the state of affairs the benevolent motive aims to produce. I suggested in section 1 that we may have experiential support for this view.

Now it is reasonable to say that reliable success in bringing about the aim of a good motive, whatever that aim may be, is also good. It follows that reliable success in bringing about human well-being is good. It is good because the *motive* of benevolence is good. The goodness of the virtue of benevolence can therefore be explained in a motivation-based theory as the combination of a set of motivations that are good in a motivation-based way and reliable success, which is good in a way that derives from the good of the motivations. Hence, the good of the virtue is based in the goodness of the agent's motivations.

To explain the value of the components of intellectual virtues in a motivation-based theory, we begin with an argument for the intrinsic and primary value of the motivation for knowledge. I will argue that the goodness of the motivation for knowledge is not derived from its connection with any other good, not even the good of knowledge. Since we have already seen that the motivational components of the various intellectual virtues arise out of the motivation for knowledge and are specifications of it, it follows that the value of the motivational components of the intellectual virtues are also independent of any good outside the agent.

The primacy of the value of the motivation to know is partly indicated by its universality and the fact that it seems fatuous to question it. It is difficult to see how we could prove the universality of the motivation, but it is not difficult to get evidence for the *belief* in its universality. As all philosophers are aware, Aristotle begins the *Metaphysics* with the declaration, "All men by nature desire to know." If this is more an expression of ingenuous hope than a statement of plain fact, it is true enough to describe a good many of our race. Aristotle continues:

> An indication of this is the delight we take in our senses; for even apart from their usefulness they are loved for themselves; and above all others the sense of sight. For not only with a view to action, but even when we are not going to do anything, we prefer seeing (one might say) to everything else. The reason is

that this, most of all the senses, makes us know and brings to light many differences between things. (Trans. Ross)

John Locke also mentions the universal attraction to knowledge in a way that is markedly similar to Aristotle's, if not as sweeping:

> There is nobody, I think, so senseless as to deny that there is pleasure in knowledge: and for the pleasures of sense, they have too many followers to let it be questioned whether men are taken with them or no. (*Essay* II.21, para. 44)

But even if the desire for knowledge were universal, that would not be sufficient to demonstrate its value. The kind of knowledge Locke is really interested in requires some exertion of the mind, an effort that is accompanied by even greater pleasure. And Locke makes it clear that the value of the drive to know is not dependent upon its successful attainment. Let us look again at a passage quoted in a footnote in Part I with its continuation:

> He that hawks at larks and sparrows has no less sport, though a much less considerable quarry, than he that flies at nobler game: and he is little acquainted with the subject of this treatise – the UNDERSTANDING – who does not know that, as it is the most elevated faculty of the soul, so it is employed with a greater and more constant delight than any of the other. Its searches after truth are a sort of hawking and hunting, wherein the very pursuit makes a great part of the pleasure. Every step the mind takes in its progress towards Knowledge makes some discovery, which is not only new, but the best too, for the time at least.
>
> For the understanding, like the eye, judging of objects only by its own sight, cannot but be pleased with what it discovers, having less regret for what has escaped it, because it is unknown. Thus he who has raised himself above the almsbasket, and, not content to live lazily on scraps of begged opinions, sets his own thoughts on work, to find and follow truth, will (whatever he lights on) not miss the hunter's satisfaction; every moment of his pursuit will reward his pains with some delight;

and he will have reason to think his time not ill spent, even when he cannot much boast of any great acquisition. (*Essay,* "Epistle to the Reader," beginning)

Notice Locke's musing at the end of this passage on the value of the *attempt* to get knowledge even when the attempt fails. Locke must think that the motivation for knowledge is valuable apart from the value of knowledge itself.

To prevent the misconception that only a philosopher would proclaim the value of the motivation to know with such enthusiasm, consider a charming anecdote from Boswell's *Life of Samuel Johnson:*

> On Saturday, July 30 [1763], Dr. Johnson and I took a sculler at the Temple-stairs, and set out for Greenwich. I asked him if he really thought a knowledge of the Greek and Latin languages an essential requisite to a good education. JOHNSON. "Most certainly, Sir; for those who know them have a very great advantage over those who do not. Nay, Sir, it is wonderful what a difference learning makes upon people even in the common intercourse of life, which does not appear to be much connected with it." "And yet, (said I) people go through the world very well, and carry on the business of life to good advantage, without learning." JOHNSON. "Why, Sir, that may be true in cases where learning cannot possibly be of any use; for instance, this boy rows us as well without learning, as if he could sing the song of Orpheus to the Argonauts, who were the first sailors." He then called to the boy, "What would you give, my lad, to know about the Argonauts?" "Sir, (said the boy,) I would give what I have." Johnson was much pleased with his answer, and we gave him a double fare. Dr. Johnson then turning to me, "Sir, (said he) a desire of knowledge is the natural feeling of mankind; and every human being, whose mind is not debauched, will be willing to give all that he has to get knowledge." (Boswell 1934, pp. 457–8)

Those of us with considerable teaching experience may be less optimistic than Aristotle or Johnson, but it is likely that the more negative experiences of a university professor indicate a lack of

205

the student's interest in a certain *type* of knowledge rather than a lack of interest in knowledge altogether. Without going so far as to declare unequivocally that every human being desires knowledge to a noticeable degree, we can safely say that the desire for knowledge is a widespread and important motive of human persons, one that is restricted neither to certain cultures nor to certain eras of history, nor is it restricted to certain social classes. And, in fact, the extent to which it is *not* precisely universal only serves to demonstrate its value because if it were possessed by everyone and to an equal degree, we probably would not give it much notice. There is something about its near universality combined with its variations in intensity that calls our attention to its value.

Here we must be cautious. I am not arguing that we value knowledge and in so valuing we are motivated to try to get knowledge, which leads us to value the motivation itself. The claim I am making is the Lockean one that the motivation for knowledge is an intrinsic good that is not derivative from the value of the possession of knowledge. Let me defend this claim another way. What is involved in the motive for knowledge, and what is it about the behavior of those with this motive that makes us value it?

First of all, it is not merely the motive to have many true beliefs. There are numerous ways to see this, but we might begin with a case of a true belief that nobody considers knowledge but which is often used to illuminate the way we make epistemic evaluations. The example is that of the lucky guess. If by picking a number out of the air I believe that there are 564 cars in the parking lot, and it just so happens there *are* 564, it is obvious that I do not *know* there are. What's more, I *should not* have guessed, even though I hit upon the truth. And I myself, upon reflection, would agree that I should not have guessed, assuming I am motivated by a desire for knowledge rather than, say, the opportunity to win a large cash prize if I guess correctly. The guess that by luck is true is comparable in value to the act of recklessly shooting a gun in the air, accidentally hitting and maiming a tyrant, and thereby preventing him from signing an unjust proclamation. I have brought about a good, but I hardly get any credit for it, in part because I have not succeeded in achieving what *I* set out to do. But it is not simply that I do not deserve credit. In fact, I deserve blame. Why?

Probably the first reason that comes to mind is that my guessing permits too great a risk of falsehood, and that is incompatible with the motive for knowledge, which we have already said includes both the negative motive of avoiding falsehood and the positive motive of attaining truth. My belief comes from an intellectual procedure that does not reliably lead to truth. In fact, a guess hardly qualifies as a procedure at all. More significant, I *ought to know* that guessing is an unreliable procedure, and so I can be criticized for forming a belief based on a guess because we expect people to know that guessing is unreliable. As we saw in 4.1, the motivation to know leads persons to follow procedures known to be reliable and not to follow procedures known to be unreliable. If I guess, that indicates a defect in my motivation for knowledge, a defect I myself would recognize if I were sufficiently self-critical.[56]

This has the important implication that the main reason we criticize the guesser is that his guessing reflects poorly on his motivation, and the same thing would apply to other unreliable belief-forming procedures that are widely known to be unreliable. For example, a person whose beliefs are uncritically picked up from those around him is criticizable even if a large percentage of his beliefs are true. It is probably also true that his belief-forming process is not a reliable way of getting to the truth, but that is not the fundamental reason we criticize him. He is subject to criticism because he should have known better than to form his beliefs in such a way. His belief-forming procedure shows a lack of motivation for knowledge. The same remarks apply to people who are dogmatic, closed-minded, unfair in evaluating the opinions of others, insufficiently attentive or thorough, subject to wishful thinking, untrusting of authorities in specialized fields or, at the other extreme, unable to reason autonomously, and so on.

---

56 Hilary Kornblith has suggested to me that the guesser is culpably ignorant in a way similar to that of a person who allegedly cares about not hurting people's feelings but does not bother to find out what *does* hurt their feelings. Similarly, the guesser allegedly cares about the truth but does not bother to find out what does and does not lead to truth.

In each case we fault the person because her attitude and be-havior betrays a defect in her motivation for knowledge. Using an unreliable belief-forming process is an unfortunate thing, but what is truly bad is to have an insufficiently strong motivation for knowledge, and what is wrong is to use procedures that a person ought to know are unreliable in leading to the end of that motiva-tion. It is also bad to fail to have knowledge, but the badness of a bad motivation is not derivative from the badness of the failure to have knowledge.

There is another reason I am deserving of criticism if I believe as the result of guessing. If I once form a belief according to a procedure that I should know to be unreliable, it will be easier for me to do so again, and I may eventually acquire an unreliable intellectual habit, one I should have known better than to let myself acquire. Beliefs are produced by a limited number of pro-cesses, and I tend to use the same ones over and over, so these processes become habits. Another reason we think of the belief formed by guessing as defective, then, is that guessing in one case may lead to guessing in other cases and may eventually lead to a bad intellectual habit – an intellectual vice. Once a believer has such a vice, his problem becomes a social one since believers form a community, and his unreliability means that others in the com-munity cannot trust his cooperation in their own pursuit of knowledge, nor can he trust himself in forming beliefs in the future. Guessing, then, shows a defect not only in the guesser's motivation to get knowledge for himself but in his motivation to aid his epistemic community in its knowledge acquisition. The people in his community will blame him because he does not care enough about knowledge, either for himself or for others. From motivation-based perspective, all of these problems in violating proper epistemic procedures can be traced back to a fundamental motivational defect.

The vice of being a chronic guesser has no name and that is undoubtedly because it is so rare. But we can imagine such a person, and the way we would evaluate him draws attention to some of the things we expect out of persons who are epistemically blameless, and if we follow this through, it leads us to the primary object of blame. First, we are responsible to be aware of the difference between reliable and unreliable processes in general, at least as far as these processes are knowable to the epistemic community of which we are a part. Obviously this has limits, and the boundaries are vague, but it indicates that we are blameworthy for failing to be aware of and to use reliable procedures up to a point. Second, we are responsible for our own habits of forming beliefs by either reliable or unreliable processes insofar as they fall within the boundaries just mentioned. Third, the considerations on guessing show the connection between knowably reliable procedures and the motivation for knowledge. The use of unreliable procedures in cases in which the person should have been aware of the unreliability indicates a defect in motivation. The primary object of criticism, then, is the motivation itself. I conclude that epistemic criticism of beliefs includes as an important part criticism of belief-forming processes whose reliability or lack of reliability is accessible to the believer. Such criticism is directly explainable in a motivation-based theory.

We are now in a position to explain the goodness of intellectual virtue in a motivation-based fashion, parallel to the motivation-based explanation we gave for the goodness of benevolence. I have argued that (1) the motive for knowledge is an intrinsic good that is not dependent for its goodness upon its relations to other goods, not even to the good of the possession of knowledge, and (2) the motivational component of each of the intellectual virtues is derived from this motive (sec. 4.1). Since it is a reasonable maxim that (3) reliable success in achieving the aim of a good motive is itself a good thing, it follows that (4) the goodness of the reliability component of an intellectual virtue derives from the goodness of the motivational component. Therefore, (5) the goodness of both components of intellectual virtues is agent-based. So the goodness of intellectual virtues is intrinsic and independent of any good not based in the agent's motivations. The goodness of all of these virtues arises directly from the goodness of the motivation for knowledge, an internal property of human agents. Assuming that parallel claims about the moral virtues can be defended, that is, the goodness of the moral virtues arises out of the intrinsic goodness of the motivational components of the moral virtues, we have the foundations of a motivation-based theory that is broad enough to handle epistemic evaluation as well as traditional moral evaluation. The way to derive the deontic concepts of right act, justified belief, and (moral or epistemic) duty from the motivation-based concept of a virtue will be given in section 6.

We have looked at how the value of a virtue and each of its components can be explained by two forms of pure virtue theory. Each theory has its own set of theoretical advantages and disadvantages. Theoretical support for motivation-basing comes partly from the fact that it unifies moral phenomena in a way that is difficult for act-based theories, and partly from the recognition of the difficulty in making happiness-based teleology work. In motivation-based ethics all moral judgments – those about motives, virtues, acts, and the impersonal good – are derived from the goodness of the motivational component of virtue. This is an important advantage in a theory. Even act utilitarianism, a theory that does well in giving a unitary account of moral judgments, does so at the cost of an improbable account of the evaluation of motives. Contemporary utilitarians judge the moral value of such motives as benevolence, love, and caring solely in terms of the consequences of these motives, a view that conflicts with the commonsense idea that what is praiseworthy or blameworthy about motives is largely a matter of the condition of the heart. Deontological theories also have a hard time explaining the value of motives and either ignore them or make them subservient to the motive of duty, leading to well-known objections to this class of theories. Virtue theories have the advantage over act-based theories in their handling of motives, but a drawback of a happiness-based virtue theory, the principal competitor to a motivation-based theory, is that its teleological structure is unwelcome to many contemporary thinkers. On the other hand, a happiness-based theory has some advantages over a motivation-based theory. Perhaps the most significant one is that it unifies moral phenomena in a deeper way than does the motivation-based approach. I have said nothing about the number of motives that would count as fundamentally good on such a theory, but since we have already discussed at least two – the motive for knowledge and the motive of benevolence, – there are presumably a plurality of motives, and I have given no argument that their goodness is connected in any significant way, unless the motive for good is an identifiable motive. If so, there are a plurality of goods at the foundation of such a theory. In contrast, a happiness-based theory places happiness or human flourishing at the foundation, and so the goodness of all virtues and their motivational constituents is unified in the concept of happiness. In addition, a happiness-based theory has the advantage of tradition behind it, whereas a motivation-based (or agent-based) theory is new.[57] The novelty of a theory may count either for it or against it, but I believe a motivation-based theory is interesting enough to tempt readers to consider it both for the purposes of ethics and for the purposes of epistemology.

5 THE IMPORTANCE OF *PHRONESIS*

5.1 Aristotle and Aquinas on practical wisdom

Central to Aristotle's ethics is the virtue of *phronesis,* or practical wisdom, defined as "a truth-attaining intellectual quality concerned with doing and with the things that are good for human beings" (*NE* VI.5.1140b21).[58] Aristotle classified *phronesis* as an intellectual virtue, yet it is so intimately connected with the moral virtues that it is mentioned in the definition he gives of moral virtue in Book II (*NE* 1106b36–1107a20), and he says that no one can have the moral virtues without *phronesis* and anyone with *phronesis* has the moral virtues: "It is plain, then, after what has been said, that it is not possible without practical wisdom to be really good morally, nor without moral excellence to be practically wise" (*NE* VI.13.1144b30–1). So a virtue that resides in the

---

[57] Michael Slote says that he knows of only one clear instance of an agent-based theory in the history of philosophy, and that is the theory of the nineteenth century philosopher James Martineau, who is discussed by Sidgwick. I think Josiah Royce's philosophy of loyalty is also agent based, although not everything Royce says is compatible with this interpretation. I believe I have also found forms of an agent-based theory (more specifically, a motivation-based theory) in Confucius and Mencius.

[58] I have used for this passage only the translation from Greenwood, *Aristotle's Nicomachean Ethics Book VI* (New York: Arno Press, 1973).

intellect is both a necessary and a sufficient condition for the possession of the virtues that reside in the appetitive part of the soul, and the very concept of moral virtue refers to the person with *phronesis*. Furthermore, Aristotle says this in spite of the fact that he has gone to the trouble of maintaining the relative autonomy of the parts of the soul, as we have already seen. That subsequent commentators have been willing to walk an explanatory tightrope to account for this view of practical wisdom is testimony to the patience of philosophers and their reverence for Aristotle. I will try to show in 5.1 and 5.2, however, that *phronesis* is much simpler to explain and accounts for a much broader range of the data of experience if we understand its connection to the moral and the intellectual virtues differently from the way Aristotle did.

Aquinas's definition of *prudentia* is very close to Aristotle's definition of *phronesis,* and Aquinas takes himself to be discussing the same virtue: "Prudence is of good counsel about matters regarding man's entire life, and the end of human life" (*ST* I-II, q. 57, a. 4, reply obj. 3). Like Aristotle, Aquinas considers *prudentia* an intellectual virtue, and like Aristotle the possession of *prudentia* is a necessary and sufficient condition for the possession of the moral virtues: "[T]here can be no moral virtue without prudence" (*ST* I-II, q. 58, a. 4); without the moral virtues there is no prudence (*ST* I-II, q. 58, a. 5).

The intimate connection between the possession of *phronesis* and all of the moral virtues is the key to the Aristotelian doctrine of the unity of the virtues:

> But in this way we may also refute the dialectical argument whereby it might be contended that the virtues exist in separation from each other. . . . This is possible in respect of those of which a man is called without qualification good; for with the presence of the one quality, practical wisdom, will be given all the virtues." (*NE* VI.13.1144b32–1145a5)

Similarly, although Aquinas denies that the intellectual virtues are connected, he argues that all of the moral virtues are connected through prudence:

[N]o moral virtue can be without prudence; since it is proper to moral virtue to make a right choice, for it is an elective habit. Now right choice requires not only the inclination to a due end, which inclination is the direct outcome of moral virtue, but also correct choice of things conducive to the end, which choice is made by prudence, that counsels, judges, and commands in those things that are directed to the end. In like manner one cannot have prudence unless one has the moral virtues: since prudence is "right reason about things to be done," and the starting point of reason is the end of the thing to be done, to which end man is rightly disposed by moral virtue. Hence, just as we cannot have speculative science unless we have the understanding of the principles, so neither can we have prudence without the moral virtues. (*ST* I-II, q. 65, a. 1, corpus)

We have already seen how Aristotle divides the soul into two parts. In Book VI he follows this up with a division within the rational part itself:

We said before that there are two parts of the soul: rational and irrational. Now we will speak of the rational part in the same way. Let us suppose two parts of the rational soul: one by which we consider the kind of things whose principles cannot be otherwise; the other by which we consider contingent things. (*NE* VI.1.1139a 4–9)

The former is called the speculative intellect; the latter is the practical intellect. The virtues of the speculative intellect include speculative wisdom (*sophia*), intuitive reason (*nous*), and knowledge (*episteme*). These virtues pertain to that part of the intellect directed toward the necessary. The virtues of the practical intellect are art (*techne*) and practical wisdom (*phronesis*). These virtues are directed toward the contingent, the former pertaining to things to be made, the latter pertaining to things to be done.

Aquinas follows Aristotle in dividing the intellect into two parts:

[T]ruth is not the same for the practical as for the speculative intellect. Because the truth of the speculative intellect depends on conformity between the intellect and the thing. And since the intellect cannot be infallibly in conformity with things in contingent matters, but only in necessary matters, therefore no speculative habit about contingent things is an intellectual virtue, but only such as is about necessary things. On the other hand, the truth of the practical intellect depends on conformity with right appetite. This conformity has no place in necessary matters, which are not affected by the human will; but only in contingent matters which can be effected by us, whether they be matters of interior action, or the products of external work. Hence it is only about contingent matters that an intellectual virtue is assigned to the practical intellect, viz. art, as regards things to be made, and prudence, as regards things to be done. (*ST* I-II, q. 57, a. 5, reply obj. 3)[59]

Given the Aristotelian–Thomistic assumption that the virtues of the speculative intellect have as their object the grasp of the necessary, it is not surprising that Aquinas sees little connection between the possession of the intellectual virtues other than *prudentia* and the moral virtues: "Other intellectual virtues can, but prudence cannot, be without moral virtues"(*ST* I-II, q. 59, a. 4).

The distinction between the speculative and the practical intellect is decidedly not the modern distinction between using the intellect to find out what is the case and using the intellect to decide what to do, because as we have seen, both Aristotle and Aquinas define the speculative intellect as aiming at the necessary, whereas the practical intellect aims at deciding what to make or to do in contingent matters. What is so striking about this distinction to the contemporary mind is that it leaves out one of the most common uses of the intellect – grasping the contingent. Most of the virtues I have called intellectual virtues govern precisely the employment of the intellect that Aquinas and Aristotle overlook. These virtues regulate intellectual inquiry and the voluntary aspects of perceptual processes, as well as those emotions that influence belief formation. Some of these virtues may ultimately lead the believer to necessary truths, but that would not be

---

[59] See Nelson 1992, chap. 3, for a discussion of this and related passages from Aquinas.

typical; in any case, it is not part of their definition. I am not even denying the possibility that there are intellectual virtues that are uniquely equipped to lead their possessors to necessary truths. I am merely claiming that not all of the ones that do not lead to making or acting are in that category. Granted, to Aristotle and Aquinas the range of the necessary was considerably broader than it is to us, having included virtually all of the natural sciences, but even so, the lack of a set of virtues dealing with belief about contingent matters is a serious omission from the point of view of a contemporary investigation into the nature of intellectual virtue.

In his discussion of the importance of the virtue of prudence in Aquinas, Daniel Mark Nelson (1992) argues that for Thomas an important difference between speculative and practical reason is that knowledge of ends in practical reason takes the place of knowledge of principles in speculative reason. One of his pieces of evidence is the following passage:

> [P]erfection and rightness of reasoning in speculative matters depends upon the principles from which the reasoning proceeds, for, as we have said [q. 57, a. 2], science depends upon understanding, which is the habit of principles, and science presupposes such understanding. Now in human acts, ends stand in the same relation as principles do in speculative matters. Consequently, for prudence, which is right reasoning about what is to be done, it is required that man be well disposed in regard to ends, and this depends on right appetite. (q. 57, a. 4, corpus; quoted by Nelson 1992, pp. 95–6)

Since prudence has the same relation to ends as the virtues of the speculative intellect have to principles, Aquinas must think of ends as the ground or material upon which prudence operates. The reasoning side of *phronesis* does not dictate the ends; that is given by the appetitive side – desiring what is worthy of desire in the appropriate manner. Aquinas and Aristotle do recognize, of course, the place of ends in speculative reasoning (science) in that such reasoning aims at necessary truth, and without desire for truth there would be no reasoning, but apparently they did not think desires disrupt the speculative use of reason as they disrupt the practical use.

> This is why we call temperance [*sophrosyne*] by this name; we imply that it preserves one's practical wisdom [*sodsousa ten phronesin*]. Now what it preserves is a judgement of the kind we have described. For it is not any and every judgement that pleasant and painful objects destroy and pervert, e.g., the judgement that the triangle has or has not its angles equal to two right angles, but only judgements about what is to be done. For the originating causes of the things that are done consist in the end at which they are aimed; but the man who has been ruined by pleasure or pain forthwith fails to see any such originating cause – to see that for the sake of this or because of this he ought to choose and do whatever he chooses and does; for vice is destructive of the originating cause of action. (*NE* VI.5.1140b12–20)

In this passage Aristotle considers only two classes of opinions: those concerning necessary truths, such as that the angles of a triangle equal two right angles, and those concerning what is to be done. He claims that opinions in the first category are unaffected by desires and feelings and that it is only opinions in the second category that are so affected. One thing that is surprising about this passage is that he has ignored opinions about contingent matters other than those concerning what is to be done. But in addition, anyone familiar with the practice of the natural sciences will probably be amazed at Aristotle's claim that opinions about the subject matter of mathematics and the natural sciences (what *he* considers the necessary) are undistorted by desires and emotions.

The source of these and other problems in the Aristotelian–Thomistic analysis of practical wisdom is the Aristotelian division of the soul. On the one hand, Aristotle recognized the need for a cognitive element in moral goodness since no one acts without thought. In addition, there needs to be something that acts as coordinator and director in moral action. Otherwise, it is unclear how the numerous distinct moral virtues are united in a single self. Such a unifying or coordinating force must combine both reasoning and desiring, Aristotle figured, and so he called it the virtue of rational desire (*orexis dianoetike*) or desiring reason (*orektikos nous*), and this is how Aristotle identified *phronesis*. At this point one would think that Aristotle would draw the conclusion that there must be something wrong with his distinction between intellectual virtues, which handle reason, and moral virtues, which handle desire. Instead, Aristotle placed *phronesis* in the category of the intellectual virtues, but given the fact that *phronesis* is obviously practical in its ends, it is noticeably different from the use of the intellect to grasp necessary truths. This left him with only one recourse – to rely on a division of the intellect as well. But that move creates difficulties of its own since it ignores one of the most common uses of the intellect, namely, to find out what the world is like, and that requires certain *practical* abilities, abilities that are neither speculative in his sense nor practical in his sense of leading to overt action.

In spite of the objections I have given to Aristotle and Aquinas, both of them have things to say that are congenial to the approach I favor. To take Aristotle first, consider the interesting remark at the conclusion of Book VI. There Aristotle talks about the relation between *sophia* and *phronesis*:

> But again it [practical wisdom] is not *supreme* over philosophical wisdom, i.e. over the superior part of us, any more than the art of medicine is over health; for it does not use it but provides for its coming into being; it issues orders, then, for its sake, but not to it. Further, to maintain its supremacy would be like saying that the art of politics rules the gods because it issues orders about all the affairs of the state. (*NE* VI.13.1145a 6–11)[60]

Aristotle might be interpreted in this passage as giving *phronesis* the commanding function even in those areas that provide the content of *sophia*, and in spite of the fact that *sophia* is higher and the commands are given for the sake of *sophia*.

---

[60] See Anthony Kenny 1992, pp. 98–9, for an interesting commentary on this passage. Note that Kenny translates "*phronesis*" as "wisdom" and "*sophia*" as "understanding" throughout the book.

Finally, consider one of Thomas's most interesting remarks on prudence:

> Ambrose, and Tully also, take the word prudence in a broad sense for any human knowledge, whether speculative or practical. And yet it may also be replied that the act itself of the speculative reason, in so far as it is voluntary, is a matter of choice and counsel as to its exercise; and consequently comes under the direction of prudence. On the other hand, as regards its specification in relation to its object which is the "necessary truth," it comes under neither counsel nor prudence. (*ST* II-II, q. 47, a. 2 reply obj. 2)

This passage is the closest I can find in Aquinas to the view I will propose in 5.2.

The distinction between the speculative and the practical intellect and the accompanying distinction between speculative wisdom (*sophia*) and practical wisdom (*phronesis*) were not always made in Aristotle's way in Hellenistic and medieval philosophy. Occasionally there were moves to bring *sophia* and *phronesis* closer together, moves that could be interpreted either as emphasizing the practical aspect of speculative wisdom or as emphasizing the theoretical aspect of practical wisdom. The former move is more Platonic, but the latter is closer to the view I find most promising. There is evidence that the Stoics in particular extended the domain of the practical intellect in the way I wish to promote in this book. Harry Wolfson (1970) mentions the Stoic idea of assent (*sunkatathesis*), which apparently was a term proposed by the Stoics to refer to judgments of truth as well as to judgments of goodness, but which both arise from the practical intellect:

> In the literature which records the teachings of the Stoics, only one definition of faith is to be found. It is said of them that they define faith as "a strong assumption . . . confirming that which is assumed." Now this is nothing but a reproduction of Aristotle's statement that faith is a "vehement assumption," which . . . refers to faith as a special kind of knowledge by the side of sensation, opinion, and scientific knowledge. Of the use of faith in the sense of a judgment of the truth of all the kinds of

knowledge, such as we have found in Aristotle, the Stoics do not speak. They do speak, however, of assent . . . as being such a judgment. In Aristotle . . . the term assent, as a verb, is used with reference to the judgment of the practical intellect as to whether a thing is desirable and good. What the Stoic seems to have done here, therefore, is to extend the meaning of that term so as to include also the meaning of Aristotle's term faith and thus to use it as a judgment of the truth of a thing as well as a judgment of the goodness of a thing. (Pp. 116–17)

In section 3 I argued that intellectual virtues are forms of moral virtue. If a judgment of truth requires intellectual virtues, it follows that such a judgment requires moral virtues. Intellectual virtues are actually certain practical abilities in the formation of beliefs and, in general, in the activities of intellectual inquiry. This should lead us to suspect that if Aristotle and Aquinas are right that practical wisdom is a necessary and sufficient condition for moral virtues, then practical wisdom is also a necessary and sufficient condition for the intellectual virtues I have discussed. It may be that it is not quite right to consider the relationship between *phronesis* and moral and intellectual virtues exactly as Aristotle and Aquinas describe the relationship between *phronesis* and the moral virtues, but we can conclude at this point that whatever that relationship is, *phronesis* does not relate to the intellectual virtues any differently than it relates to the traditional moral virtues. In 5.2 we turn to a close examination of the nature of that relationship.

5.2 A proposal on the function of phronesis

Although Aristotle's account of the position of *phronesis* in our psychic structure is problematic, his explanation of how *phronesis* operates is illuminating. The need for such a virtue is set up early in the *Nicomachean Ethics* when Aristotle remarks that ethics is not a precise science and that we ought not to expect more precision out of a science than it is capable of giving (I.3.1094b11–14). Although we are told in Book II that virtue is a mean between extremes, Aristotle is careful to warn us that this observation is insufficient as a guide to practical choice because the location of the mean is "as a man of practical wisdom would determine it" (II.6.1107a1–2). Good judgment cannot always be reduced to the following of a decision procedure specifiable in advance of the situation in which action occurs. But I maintain that to the extent that this is true for overt action, it is also true for cognitive activity. As we saw in section 4, intellectual virtues have the same relation to rules as do moral virtues. Some rules arise out of the motivation for knowledge and the motivational components of intellectual virtues, but the motivational elements of intellectual virtues lead their possessors to do much more than to follow rules. We will need to look more carefully at the paths leading from particular virtues or vices, whether moral or intellectual, to the actual formation of a belief or performance of an act since I think we will find that there is a need for a virtue like *phronesis* in the paths of both kinds.

Let us start by examining the principal reasons why a virtue like *phronesis* is theoretically necessary to make sense of both morally right action and justified belief in a virtue theory. We will then turn to common moral experience and the inquiries of previous philosophers for support for its existence.

One theoretical need for *phronesis* is to determine the mean at the time of action when the governing virtues are Aristotelian means between extremes. I have argued that intellectual virtues are forms of moral virtue and that some of them are means between extremes in Aristotle's sense. This is easy to see in the case of virtues for which the same word serves to identify both an intellectual virtue and a moral virtue in the traditional sense of the latter, such as intellectual courage, carefulness, autonomy, perseverance, and humility.[61] We saw in section 2 that these virtues are means between an extreme of excess and an extreme of deficiency, just like their moral counterparts. If so, practical wisdom would be necessary to find the mean for these virtues. For

---

[61] Of course, we have already taken note of the fact that humility is not an Aristotelian virtue. But if humility is the virtue whereby a person is disposed to make an accurate appraisal of her own competence, intellectual humility could reasonably be interpreted as a mean between the tendency to grandiosity and the tendency to a diminished sense of her own ability.

example, in the case of intellectual carefulness, it takes *practical* wisdom, not speculative wisdom or some other virtue, to tell how much evidence is enough to support a belief; clearly, it will differ from case to case. The same point goes for perseverance, courage, and autonomy. We need to make choices in intellectual inquiry, just as much as in deliberation leading to action, and the extent to which we should persevere in a line of inquiry or face and answer attacks from others is a matter of judgment. We need the same kind of judgment to strike the proper balance between relying on the authority of others and relying on our own intellectual powers. Furthermore, the mean is probably different for different people. Some people can get away with impetuosity, in the intellectual realm or otherwise, to a far greater extent than others, and some may actually thrive on it. Variations in intellectual talents will make it appropriate for one person to go the route of meticulous thoroughness much more than one with a wider intellectual scope but less talent for detail. It is debatable whether the ability to make a judgment of the mean in each of these cases can be explained or replaced by following a rule or principle. Aristotelians typically say that the answer is no, but that is not my point here. Whether or not the practically wise person's behavior can be explained as the implicit following of a rule, it is clear that moral behavior requires the ability to do *something* that Aristotle identifies as acting out of the virtue of *phronesis.* It takes *phronesis* to know *how persevering* one should be to be persevering, *how careful* one should be to be careful, *how self-sufficient* one should be to be autonomous, and so on. The first theoretical need served by *phronesis*, then, is to determine the mean between extremes in those cases in which the virtue is a mean.

Second, the individual virtues apply to areas of life that overlap in numerous ways. Following Aristotle, moral virtues are typically named by calling attention to a certain feeling (fear, sexual desire, covetousness) or some area of human activity (giving and receiving goods, responding to other persons in need), and we define the virtue as that quality which properly handles the feeling or human activity in question. But, of course, a single set of circumstances can easily be an instance of more than one such feeling or activity, and in such cases more than one virtue applies. The features of a situation that are relevant for one virtue may not be for another. So what concerns the virtue of courage is the nature and extent of some danger and the value and effectiveness of facing it in various ways. But in a situation of danger, many other features of the situation may concern other virtues, such as generosity, fairness, or humility. Sometimes the courageous thing to do is not the humble or generous or fair thing to do. Suppose there are salient features of the situation that pertain both to courage and to humility. It might be that in *this* case humility is more important than courage. That is to say, it may be more important to act in a humble manner than to do what courage would have dictated in the absence of considerations of humility. Or it might be that humility is not so important in this case, although this is not to say that humility is *usually* less important than courage. The person who knows how to act (and feel) in these cases does not simply act from a combination of humility and courage and the knowledge of the proper function of these virtues. If we are to avoid an excessive and unworkable fragmentation of value, there needs to be some virtue that permits a person to sift through all the salient features of the situation – that is, all those features that are pertinent to *any* of the virtues – and to make a judgment that is not simply the judgment of a person qua courageous, qua generous, or qua humble but is the judgment of a *virtuous* person.[62] Therefore, the ability to mediate between and among the individual moral virtues must itself be a virtue. *Phronesis* is defined in part as the virtue that has this function.[63]

The mediation between individual virtues is necessary between and among the various intellectual virtues as well as the

---

[62] I do not mean to imply that there will always be a unique right choice in every case of virtue conflict but only that some ways of resolving conflicts are better than others. I will discuss the possibility of moral dilemmas in 6.1.

[63] Gary Watson (1984, p. 65) argues that some of these cases of apparent virtue conflict are cases in which neither response is wrong but neither response can *express* both of the virtues in conflict. So one response may express kindness while the other may express honesty. Watson offers the conjecture that it is in such indeterminate cases that persons reveal their moral individuality. The same point could be made about the ways in which persons reveal their intellectual individuality.

various moral virtues. Mediation between intellectual courage and intellectual humility or fairness is necessary just as much as mediation between moral courage and humility or fairness. A person needs to know at what point to make an intellectual commitment just as much as she needs to know when to make a moral or a personal commitment. But intellectual commitment can run up against the virtues of intellectual caution, thoroughness, or fairness to the views of others. Knowing what to do in these cases is not a simple matter of having a combination of the virtues in question.[64] A virtue is needed that permits a person to see the big picture, and this will be a virtue that balances such virtues as carefulness, thoroughness, and fairness with perseverance and commitment. Intellectual virtues, then, need a mediating virtue just as much as do the traditional moral virtues.

This is not yet to say that the virtue that mediates between the intellectual virtues must be the same virtue as that which mediates between the moral virtues (i.e., *phronesis*). To see that, consider the fact that there also must be a virtue that mediates between moral and intellectual virtues. An example of the need for such mediation is the case in which the moral virtue of self-confidence or courage requires having beliefs that are at odds with such intellectual virtues as strict fairness in the evaluation of evidence, thoroughness, or reliance on the most knowledgeable members of one's community. One may jump to conclusions in trusting oneself and yet be the better for it. One may ignore contrary evidence when one has to perform a courageous act, and *everyone* is the better for it. Neither individual moral virtues nor individual intellectual virtues dictate definitively what is to be done in such situations. Therefore, there has to be a virtue for which all the features relevant to *any* virtue are relevant. As far as I can tell, the only candidate for such a virtue in the philosophical tradition is *phronesis*. We have, then, a second theoretical reason why *phronesis* is necessary in a virtue theory: namely, as a media-

---

[64] Montmarquet (1993, p. 28) mentions the problem of knowing how far one should go to be intellectually courageous without being "headstrong" and how far one should go in being open to the views of others without being intellectually cowardly. Montmarquet does not mention *phronesis* as a way to solve these conflicts, however.

tor between and among the individual moral and intellectual virtues.

A third theoretical need for *phronesis* is to coordinate the various virtues into a single line of action or line of thought leading up to an act, in the first case, or a belief, in the second. The problem here is that virtuous procedures underdetermine action and belief in the particular case even when there is no conflict among the relevant virtues and even when finding the mean is not the salient issue. The weighing of evidence rarely leads to a decisive answer either for or against a belief. In fact, even when we list all the known procedures used by a virtuous person, there is still an indeterminacy with respect to most beliefs. The majority of the beliefs of virtually all educated adults greatly exceeds that which they could infer from evidence, the procedural rules of deductive or inductive logic, the weighing of testimony from others, and other procedures of belief formation known to be reliable. This is to say, not that most persons are irrational, but rather that rationality is underdetermined by procedures. When we glance through a newspaper, we find that we are asked to assent to numerous propositions, few of which satisfy any acceptable rule of belief formation, even taking into account the cumulative effect of all the evidence we have ever heard or read. On a typical day we encounter propositions about such matters as the consequences of various fiscal policies, the guilt or innocence of an accused murderer, the trustworthiness of particular politicians, the greenhouse effect, the weather forecast. To be honest we must admit that there is no adequate evidence for most positions on these matters. And even when we turn to the more sophisticated beliefs of the professional historian, the situation is hardly better if we can accept anything close to the view of Charles Beard, who has said that all recorded history is essentially an "act of faith" – what the purported historian thinks of what someone else thought, saw, heard, or believed. Philosophers often make intellectual caution a matter of professional pride, but in my experience, the beliefs of philosophers on philosophical issues exceed that which they can justify to others or even to themselves on the basis of following commonly accepted epistemic procedures. This could be taken as evidence that philosophers are as irrational as everyone else,[65] but it seems to me more likely that there is an element that can be vaguely described as "good judgment" in belief formation, even when the subject matter is philosophy. This was noted by John Henry Newman (1979) in what he called the "illative sense," a cognitive ability he explicitly linked to Aristotle's concept of *phronesis*.[66] It is possible that judgment of this kind supervenes rules or procedures not yet discovered, but even if that is the case, it is no argument against the existence of the kind of judgment to which I am referring, and it is certainly not an argument against our relying on this judgment until these procedures are discovered.

We do have the option, of course, of withholding belief about all these matters, but in many cases belief is forced because decisions have to be made that will not wait. In "The Will to Believe" William James has a well-known discussion of the decision to believe in cases of forced belief. And even if belief is not literally forced, there are often practical advantages in having opinions on important issues since others will listen to a person who actually believes more than one who merely conjectures. I am suggesting that both the Jamesian forced-belief situations and the desirable-belief situations are quite common. When these cases arise, only a portion of the grounds for the belief is determined by procedures known to be epistemically reliable. We saw in 4.1 that the motivation for knowledge leads to behavior that goes beyond known rules, the most obvious examples being behavior arising from the virtues of boldness, creativity, inventiveness, and insight. This means that it is a mistake for epistemologists to spend all their time on procedures, rules, and so on. The third reason why *phronesis* is needed, then, is that many human activities, whether of the overt kind traditionally handled by ethics or the internal activities of thinking and forming beliefs, can be neither fully described nor evaluated in terms of the following of a set of known procedures or rules. Good judgment is required in all

---

65 On the prejudices of philosophers, see Nietzsche at the beginning of *Beyond Good and Evil*.

66 I have looked at the connection between Newman's illative sense and *phronesis* and applied it to the methodology of theology in Zagzebski 1995.

areas of human activity, including the cognitive. Persons with practical wisdom learn how and when to trust certain feelings, and they develop habits of attitude and feeling that enable them to reliably make good judgments without being aware of following a procedure. There is a very strong element of inclination in most beliefs, even in the beliefs of those persons most intellectually practiced and aware. The difficult part is to train the inclinations themselves to reliably produce the desired end – in the case of intellectual activity, knowledge.

If the evidence proposed so far is not yet convincing, consider the way a good detective solves a mystery in the classic detective story. He will exhibit such virtues as the ability to recognize the salient facts, insightfulness, and the ability to think up explanations of complex sets of data. These virtues are probably not means between extremes, and so *phronesis* is not necessary to determine a mean. Nonetheless, these virtues are no more rule governed than our previous examples. No specifiable procedures tell a person how to recognize the salient facts, how to get insight, or how to think up good explanations, much less how to use all three to get to a single end. All of these virtues operate together in the good detective. In the classic detective novel many other characters in the novel, as well as the reader, have access to the same data as the detective. They may also have good memories and have very good reasoning skills insofar as such skills can be taught. That is to say, they know the right procedures for valid deductive reasoning and may even know such things as the probability calculus and the looser rules of inductive logic. We may also suppose that they do not commit any of the so-called informal fallacies either. But they do not all have the ability to figure out the murderer's identity. A good detective story will explain how the detective came to his conclusion and should do so in a way that shows the reader that she could have figured it out herself if she had had the requisite intellectual traits. In some stories the detective claims that it is a matter of putting the evidence together in a certain order that permits him to "see" a pattern that points to a certain culprit, analogous to seeing where to put a piece of a jigsaw puzzle. Others stress the idea that solving a murder mystery is primarily a matter of psychological insight into human nature and the motives that lead people to murder. Still others stress the simplest explanation of the facts. In all these cases the detective's ability is something that is clearly not the following of a set of rules, at least not insofar as they can be known and taught. Of course, a person might be able to learn how to be a good detective by frequent and intense exposure to good detectives. The point is that they do not learn it by learning how to follow a procedure.

In spite of the theoretical need for *phronesis* in a virtue theory, it is doubtful that anyone would be convinced of its existence if it were not supported by our moral experience. Ultimately we must ask whether we are reasonably confident that we know individuals with *phronesis* or know *of* such people. If not, we can simply respond to the examples I have given by refusing to admit that they show any special quality in the detective, the historian, the philosopher, or the ordinary newspaper reader. We could say that the detective is simply lucky or is a plodder; if he works on a case long enough, eventually he will hit on the truth. The brilliant flash of discovery so deftly described in mystery novels is only fiction. The historian and the philosopher have no business actually *believing* what they write since they have insufficient evidence for their claims, and it would be better if they admitted their work is historical fiction and philosophy fiction respectively, only not so clever as the detective novel. As for the newspaper reader, perhaps his defects are too evident to require comment. The most intellectually respectable thing to do is to follow the rules of reasoning and evidence and refrain from forming beliefs beyond their boundaries. Or, at least, it can be argued.

Aristotle thought that we see *phronesis* in some of the persons in our community, and the contemporary experience of it has been well described by John Casey (1990):

> We all have the idea of a sensible man – the man of good judgement, who seems to get all sorts of things right, and not just things of which he has already had experience, or of which he has specialized knowledge. We are not surprised at the range of such a man's practical understanding. It will be revealed in his principles of conduct, and in his moral assessment

of particular situations. It can be shown in financial dealings, in qualities of "leadership," in appreciation of public affairs, in assessment of character. Such a man may also have various practical skills. Indeed, one would be surprised if a person of practical intelligence in large matters showed himself to be helpless in smaller ones. And the intelligence and good sense he shows seems to be the same sort of thing in all these different areas; it strikes us as just the sort of practical intelligence *he* would have. One can only appeal to common experience that such people do exist. If they do, they are men of practical wisdom. (P. 147)

In giving examples of the wide range of abilities of the practically wise man, Casey mentions several that are highly cognitive, such as good judgment in financial dealings and the ability to accurately assess the character of others. The practically wise person gets "all sorts of things right." If there are persons of this sort, I suggest that we would expect them to get their belief forming right as well.

One of the most important aspects of *phronesis*, both in its manner of acquisition and in its manner of operation, is its social basis. Aristotle makes it clear that virtue is learned by imitation and it depends upon the presence of persons with *phronesis* in the community, and *phronesis* itself is never found in the young (*NE* VI.8.1142a12–21). If I am right that the intellectual virtues have the same relation to *phronesis* as do the moral virtues, it follows that good thinking is socially based as well. We acquire intellectual virtues, just as we acquire moral virtues, by imitating those who are practically wise. We learn from others how to believe rationally, just as we learn from them how to act morally. The social basis of belief formation is in some ways even more striking than the social basis of acting since we are probably even more dependent upon other people for the rationality or justifiability of our beliefs than for the rightness of our acts. This means that the intellectual healthiness of the whole community is vitally important for the justifiability of our own beliefs. When I am in a position of trying to find out whether or not to believe something, it is important for me to connect to the social network of beliefs in the proper way. I must know where to look – what books to read, which people to consult. So I need to be in a position to know who has the best judgment on these matters, just as I need to know who has the best judgment in matters of moral choice. Both situations require practical wisdom, whether the end is a cognitive state or an overt act.

Perhaps it is true that to the extent to which we cannot recognize persons with practical wisdom, we cannot define intellectual virtue and the related concept of rationality precisely. It is probable that the quality of intellectual virtue is not something one either has or does not have. It comes in degrees, just as kindness, justice, and humility come in degrees. In an especially rigorous age, great demands are made on the process by which one acquires a true belief before it is thought to be worthy of being called justified, rational, or epistemically virtuous. In a more lax age, weaker standards apply. Since the Enlightenment, very high, perhaps unreasonably high, standards have been claimed to be necessary for a belief to be appraised positively. We still have not completely emerged from the age of skepticism, and there are elements in our philosophical culture that pull us in more than one direction on the question of rigor. The same point, of course, applies to rigorism in moral evaluation. An advantage of a virtue approach is that it is flexible enough to adapt to either highly rigorous or more lenient standards of evaluation.

I have been arguing that we ought to consider the virtue of *phronesis,* or practical wisdom, as a higher-order virtue that governs the entire range of moral and intellectual virtues. It is no more an intellectual virtue than a moral one, nor does it have a special relation to the traditional moral virtues, a relation that it does not have to the intellectual virtues. If I am right in this, there are some problems in the way Aristotle and Aquinas think of practical wisdom, and most of these problems can be traced to their insistence on dividing the soul into intellectual and appetitive parts. On the other hand, both Aristotle and Aquinas at times describe practical wisdom in such a way that if we take them at face value, it would be surprising if *phronesis* did *not* function in roughly the way I have defended. Consider Aristotle's definition of *phronesis* quoted at the beginning of 5.1. He defines *phronesis* as "a truth-attaining intellectual quality concerned with doing and with the things that are good for human beings." Surely such a definition permits an interpretation of this capacity that is broader than that subsequently applied by Aristotle. Assuming that knowledge is one of the human goods, *phronesis* would govern the capacity to act with regard to knowledge. But one acts with regard to knowledge by perceptual and cognitive activities, some of which are organized into structured intellectual inquiries and some of which are much more informal.

The same point applies to what Aquinas says about *prudentia:* "Prudence is of good counsel about matters regarding man's entire life, and the end of human life" (*ST* I-II, q. 57, a. 4, reply obj. 3). This definition is somewhat narrower than Aristotle's since deliberation is a narrower category than acting. Still, on Aquinas's own account the ultimate end of human life is a form of knowledge (the Beatific Vision), and lesser forms of knowledge are part of the natural end of human living, so it follows that whatever deliberation serves these ends should be governed by the virtue of prudence. Although this does not appear to be Aquinas's own interpretation of prudence, I suggest that it is the most reasonable one.

I conclude that the proper way for us to conduct ourselves cognitively is exactly the same as the proper way for us to conduct ourselves in more overt forms of behavior, namely, by acting the way a person with practical wisdom would act. We can learn what to do in specific situations in one of the two ways described by Aristotle: we can acquire practical wisdom ourselves, or until we are able to do that, we can imitate persons who have practical wisdom. If I am right about the function of *phronesis,* it is as important for epistemologists to analyze as for moral philosophers. Good judgment applies not only to what to do and how to do it but also to what to believe and how to go about believing it. This position requires looking at the cognitive activities leading up to forming and holding a belief as forms of acting. Unfortunately, we have inherited a long tradition that insists that we keep these activities separate. "First you think, then you act," is almost a truism. Of course, it does sometimes happen (although not as often as one would be led to believe from the philosophical literature) that we first do a certain kind of thinking, namely, deliberating, before we act. And even when we do not deliberate but act impulsively, habitually, or carelessly, we usually do a form of thinking first, at least to the extent of processing sensory information. So it is undoubtedly true that thinking precedes acting. What I have been suggesting is that the kind of thinking that precedes acting is only one of many kinds of thinking and that the acting that follows thinking is only one of many kinds of acting. Thinking is itself a form of acting. Some of it may be too passive to deserve the name "acting," but then some of our more overt behavior is too passive to deserve to be called acting either. Thinking can be acting and thinking can precede acting. Furthermore, acting can precede thinking. We may act in a directed and self-conscious manner, as when we actively search for information, but we often act first even in those cases in which we do nothing intentionally or even consciously before we think. Anybody experienced enough in the art of thinking to be reading this book knows that ideas generate ideas, but some ideas are generated by acts, both intentional and unintentional. I intentionally read a paper on epistemology or virtue in the hope that it will give me ideas; I unintentionally sit next to a person on an airplane who says something illuminating, I intentionally watch a film or read a novel but unintentionally think of a way in which it relates to my theory on intellectual virtue. There is no special order between thinking and acting. We do both most of the time. It takes tremendous philosophical ingenuity to devise a theory that separates these activities enough to permit a division in normative theory between ethics and normative epistemology. It is my position that this ingenuity is misplaced.

A crucial task for any pure virtue theory is the derivation of deontic concepts such as that of a duty and of a right act from the concept of a virtue. Because the theory I am proposing assimilates beliefs as well as acts into the domain of moral evaluation, we will need to make the parallel derivation of a justified belief and of an epistemic duty from an intellectual virtue. Let us turn to this matter next.

6 THE DEFINITION OF DEONTIC CONCEPTS

In this section we investigate the relationship between virtues and vices, on the one hand, and the moral properties of acts and beliefs, on the other. Acts and beliefs arise from moral and intellectual traits, and the moral properties of the former can be defined in terms of the latter. In this section I will demonstrate the way this can be done. The concepts to be defined include that of a right act, a justified belief, a moral duty, an epistemic duty, and an act of virtue. An important feature of my account of these concepts is that it is indeterminate with respect to either a pure virtue theory or the weak form of virtue theory Slote calls agent focused (see sec. 1). According to a merely agent-focused theory, the behavior of virtuous persons does not make an act right but is simply the best way to determine rightness, whereas a pure virtue theory treats the rightness of an act as strictly dependent upon virtue. In a pure virtue theory, an act is right *because* it is the sort of act a virtuous person might do, whereas in an agent-focused theory, what is done by a virtuous person is just the best *criterion* of rightness. So the definitions of deontic concepts to be proposed in this section are compatible with almost any form of virtue theory, and I take that to be an advantage, but they need to be read differently if placed within a weak virtue theory – a merely agent-focused theory – than if placed within a pure virtue theory. It is only within the latter that they are actually definitions. Both forms of pure virtue theory define the normative properties of acts and beliefs in terms of virtues and vices, although they differ in the way they handle the relationship of virtues to the good. However, in a weak (merely agent-focused) virtue theory, what these "definitions" do is help us fix the properties of right and wrong to their proper objects, but they do not tell us what makes right right and wrong wrong. Occasionally I will say something in this section that shows a preference for a form of pure virtue theory, and when that happens, those readers who are willing to accept only the weaker theory will need to make the necessary modifications of my points to fit their theory. I will not do this explicitly myself because it would be tedious, but I hope it is clear that it can be done rather easily.

6.1 *Right acts, justified beliefs*

In a virtue theory a right act is, roughly, what a virtuous person would or might do in a certain situation. Such a definition immediately runs up against an important asymmetry between the aretaic concepts of virtue and vice and the deontic concepts of right and wrong. In modern ethical discourse "right" usually means "not wrong" or "permissible." To do what is right is not the same as to do what is praiseworthy or commendable; it is merely to escape blame. Act-based ethicists have invented the category of the supererogatory to handle acts that are better than what duty requires, but this category gets little attention, and its analysis is generally peripheral to the heart of the theory. In contrast, an act that is not only something a virtuous person might do but expresses the agent's virtue is morally praiseworthy, not simply free from blame, and is the central concept in virtue ethics. So aretaic concepts differ from deontic concepts in that the focus of the former is on the conditions for both blameworthiness and praiseworthiness, whereas the focus of the latter is on the conditions for blameworthiness and lack of blameworthiness. This makes it easier to use aretaic concepts to define deontic concepts by beginning with the definition of wrong. In brief, a wrong act is an act a virtuous person would not do in a certain situation. A right act is an act which is such that it is not the case that a virtuous person would not do it. We can put it less awkwardly, using the Lewis rule for defining "might" in terms of "would" (Lewis 1973, pp. 21–4)[67] as follows: A right act is an act that a virtuous person might do in certain circumstances.[68]

The rightness of cognitive activity can be defined in a parallel fashion. Right cognitive acts are, roughly, what persons with the intellectual virtues would or might do in certain circumstances.

---

[67] But see DeRose forthcoming for a contrary view on the relation between these conditionals.

[68] Note that this way of defining the morally permissible (right) is not Aristotelian. According to Aristotle, what is merely permissible is what is outside the scope of all the virtues. Since each virtue controls a specific sphere of human activity, any action within that sphere is either virtuous or vicious; there is no third alternative. I thank Charles Young for pointing this out to me.

Beliefs are not acts but cognitive states that also result from the operation of the character traits of intellectual virtues and vices. We saw in Part I that beliefs cover a range of voluntariness but are sufficiently voluntary to be evaluated in a sense similar to the moral, and we have seen in section 3 of this part that the intellectual virtues are forms of moral virtues. This means that if the central evaluative property of beliefs derives from intellectual virtues, that property derives from *moral* virtues. It follows that such a property is, not just analogous to the rightness of acts, but very much like rightness in its moral import. The most common term for this property of beliefs is "justified," and I will use that term here, even though we looked at the confusion surrounding the notion of justification in Part I, and I said there that it is at least arguable that Alston is right in claiming that there is no target concept that is the object of the prevailing disputes over justification. But it is clear that *some* normative property of beliefs functions in epistemic evaluation in a way that is very similar to the property of rightness as ascribed to acts. If justification (or justifiedness) is not that property, I will be happy to drop it in favor of something else, but I doubt that there is any other candidate with as good a claim to being the desired property as justification.

I have tied the rightness of an act to the hypothetical behavior of virtuous persons. It is no doubt obvious that a person can perform a right (permissible) act who is not actually virtuous, but the act must mimic the behavior of virtuous persons in certain respects. A virtuous person's behavior arises out of virtuous motives and is reliably successful in achieving virtuous ends. What makes the virtuous person reliably successful in addition to her motive is her understanding of the moral and nonmoral facts about the situations she encounters. The level of understanding a virtuous person has, then, is whatever is sufficient to make her reliably successful in producing the ends of the virtue. It follows that to do what a virtuous person does is to do what a person would do who has virtuous motives and such a level of understanding. If to perform a right act is to do what virtuous persons might do, the conclusion is that a right act is what a virtuously motivated person might do in certain circumstances, given the understanding of the facts of the particular case we would expect her to have because of her reliability in bringing about the ends of her virtuous motivation.

We are now ready to define three deontic concepts in terms of the concept of virtue:

A *right act* is what a person who is virtuously motivated, and who has the understanding of the particular situation that a virtuous person would have, might do in like circumstances.

A *wrong act* is what a person who is virtuously motivated, and who has the understanding of the particular situation that a virtuous person would have, would not do in like circumstances.

A *moral duty* is what a person who is virtuously motivated, and who has the understanding of the particular situation that a virtuous person would have, would do in like circumstances. That is to say, something is a duty if and only if it is wrong not to do it.

Let us look more closely at the hypothetical form of the definitions just given. I have defined the concepts of right act, wrong act, and moral duty in such a way that internal states of the agent do not matter. But, of course, we do think such states matter morally, and this will lead us to formulate definitions of more concepts here and in the next subsection.

First, we will need to distinguish between the evaluation of the act or belief and the evaluation of a person *for* doing an act or having a belief. Such a distinction might seem peculiar on some ways of looking at the psychology of action, but ethicists often have no trouble speaking of an act in abstraction from the agent of the act. So if a person does the just thing out of a motive of gain, a common response is to say that the act itself is right, but the agent is not praiseworthy for doing it; he gets no moral credit for it. Similarly, a person might form a belief that an intellectually virtuous person is apt to form in the same circumstances but be motivated out of a desire to appear important or sophisticated. The distinction made by some epistemologists between the justification of a belief and the justification of a person for having the belief is appropriate here and is exactly analogous to the distinction in moral evaluation just made. Even when the belief itself is justified, the believer may not be praiseworthy for having the belief.

We now run up against the problem of slippage between the concepts of what a virtuous person *might* do and what a virtuous person *would* do. What a virtuous person might do includes acts completely outside the moral realm, such as reading a book, as well as acts within the moral realm that are simply within the range of activity of virtuous persons even when they are not expressing their virtue.[69] So, for example, a virtuous person who has the virtue of generosity does not express generosity on each and every occasion in which it is possible to act generously. To forgo an opportunity to act generously is not a wrong act and, hence, is a right (permissible) act, assuming that the act does not violate some other moral duty. But it would be going too far to say a person has merited praise for acting rightly in reading a book or forgoing an opportunity to express generosity. And it would be going too far in the other direction to say that we praise persons only for doing their moral duty, as already remarked. In fact, we praise them even more for expressing virtue in situations in which it is not required. Since virtuous persons are much more strongly inclined to act in ways that express virtue than are the nonvirtuous, we can identify the situations in which the agent is praiseworthy for an act in terms of what virtuous persons would probably do in such situations. This has the advantage of permitting a conceptual link among the definitions of right act, moral duty, and praiseworthiness for doing an act.

We may, therefore, retain the definition of rightness/ justification for acts/beliefs given above but define another evaluative concept, one that applies to the agent of the act and that is stronger:

A person *A* is praiseworthy (justified) for doing an act (having a belief) *S* just in case *A* does what a virtuous person would (probably) do (believes what a virtuous person would [probably] believe) in the same circumstances and is motivated by virtuous motives.

Allowing for the differences between the motivational component of one virtue and another, a more precise definition would distinguish among these motivations and would require that the

---

[69] I thank Charles Young for pointing out this distinction in this context.

agent be motivated by the motive that goes with the virtue in question. So *A* is praiseworthy (justified) in doing an act *S* courageously (believing a belief *B* courageously) only if his motive in doing *S* (believing *B*) is the motive that is the component of the virtue of courage. Parallel definitions can be given for the praiseworthiness of an agent for doing an act or having a belief that is humble, discreet, open-minded, fair, and so on. Other refinements of the evaluative concepts that apply to acts and beliefs or to persons for such acts and beliefs may become necessary depending upon the way virtues are individuated.

What is the function of the understanding of the particular situation that a virtuous person has? One thing this understanding does is lead her to follow appropriate rules or methods, and we have already seen examples of ways in which virtuous motivations lead a person to follow rules or procedures that reliably lead to the desired end (4.2). So intellectually virtuous persons follow procedures that are known to be truth conducive, fair persons follow procedures that are known to result in a fair state of affairs, etc. This is the place in which skills become important because skills are closely connected with procedures for producing the desired end, whether it be getting to the truth, comforting the bereaved, or grading students fairly. So virtue theory need not ignore the place of rules in theoretical ethics or in actual decision making. As we have seen, virtues are distinguished from skills and procedures, but my position is that the motivational components of the former lead to the acquisition of the latter.

A few comments on the function of rules as the link between virtues and acts is in order. We saw in Part I that one consideration that has pushed some moral theorists in the direction of virtue ethics is the idea that morality is not strictly rule governed. This concern should not be overstated. To say a set of rules (or one big rule) is not sufficient for us to understand morality and to make the right moral decisions is not to say that we ought to drop rules altogether. Rules have a place in the practical task of making a moral decision, and their justification therefore needs to be explained theoretically. To see how rules enter into the thinking of the moral agent, notice that the definition just given of a right act includes both a motivational component and a component of understanding of the relevant facts of the situation, including nonmoral facts. A right act is a morally successful act.[70] An important question of moral psychology is how these two components elicit a particular act. Moral particularists are inclined to reject the use of a rule as an intermediary between the agent's particular states of motivation and understanding and her ensuing act, but a virtue theorist, even a pure virtue theorist, need not take this position. We have already seen that a pure virtue theory does not, or need not, eliminate the concept of a right act, but rather, it makes the right act derivative from aretaic concepts. For the same reason, a pure virtue theory need not eliminate moral rules, duties, or other deontic notions from the theory, but rather, it makes them derivative from the underlying aretaic concepts. So a pure virtue theory can have as many rules as you like as long as they are understood as grounded in the virtuous motivations and understanding of the nonmoral facts that virtuous agents possess.

One alleged problem in making the virtuous agent more fundamental than the moral rule is the converse of the complaint by some virtue theorists that morality is not strictly rule governed. The objection is that there *are* some moral rules or principles that admit of no exceptions, and their exceptionless quality is allegedly undermined by the idea that their justification is grounded in the aretaic concepts of the virtuous and the vicious. But Michael Slote has shown that this worry is groundless because there are virtue-theoretic parallels to both perfect and imperfect duties: "to say that there is a virtue-theoretic equivalent of the perfect duty not to lie is to say (very roughly) that it is, in every instance of the right kind, deplorable (of one) to lie.."

---

[70] Michael Slote has said in correspondence that the motivation of a virtuous person would lead her to find out the relevant facts of the matter before making a decision, and so it could be claimed that the understanding component is included in the motivation component. But although I agree that the motivation component would lead the agent to make the right *efforts* to understand the nonmoral facts relevant to the decision, and although I also agree that if we reject skepticism, we can assume that moral efforts are not systematically unsuccessful, the concept of a right act depends crucially on what is *actually* going on, not just on what a virtuously motivated person would *believe* is going on, because a right act is morally successful.

(1992b, p. 166). The possibility of such a definition shows that there is nothing in the idea of grounding moral rightness in what virtuous persons do that precludes the possibility that virtuous persons never act in a certain way in situations of a certain kind, and that is sufficient to give rise to a perfect duty. So the inner states of virtuous agents can give rise to rules. If a rule is exceptionless, the *reason* it is exceptionless is traceable to the motivations and understanding of virtuous agents. So the claim that a rule is exceptionless is logically independent of the claim that it is a bottom-level moral principle. Pure virtue theorists deny the latter but are not committed to denying the former.

Unfortunately, some virtue theorists are partly responsible for encouraging the idea that there are no exceptionless rules. One of the things that is gained by a virtue theory is not the elimination of rules or the elimination of exceptionless rules but the addition of a feature to morality that grounds moral judgment in those cases in which the rules do have exceptions. This additional feature is often identified with the virtue of *phronesis*, as we have seen. *Phronesis* is necessary if the rules are not enough, but this is not to deny that there may be plenty of cases in which the rules *are* enough.

We have already seen that on my conception of *phronesis*, one of its functions is to mediate between individual moral or intellectual virtues when they produce a prima facie conflict. As long as there is more than one virtue (or rule or duty), it seems possible that the same act could be both right (permissible) and wrong (impermissible). For example, an act might satisfy the definition of a right act when judged by the standards of compassion but be a wrong act when judged by the standards of loyalty or integrity. The practically wise person is able to weigh the demands of all relevant virtues in a given situation and to decide on the course of action that is most virtuous, all things considered. The way the virtues are mediated in the virtue of *phronesis* leads to a simpler set of definitions of the concepts of act evaluation when all evaluatively relevant circumstances are taken into account:

A *right act, all things considered,* is what a person with *phronesis* might do in like circumstances. A *wrong act, all things considered,* is what a person with *phronesis* would not do in like

circumstances. A *moral duty, all things considered,* is what a person with *phronesis* would do in like circumstances.

Let us now look briefly at a serious problem for moral theory, not just for virtue ethics. This is the possibility of moral dilemmas, or cases in which no matter what a person does, she does the wrong thing. An act may be wrong when judged by the standards of one virtue when the only other alternative is wrong when judged by the standards of another virtue. This is very likely the situation of the character Sebastian Rodrigues in Shusaku Endo's haunting novel *Silence.*[71] This problem is a large one and deserves extended treatment if a theory is to have adequate practical import. All I can do here is to point in the direction that I think is the right one.

I have said that an important function of *phronesis* is to mediate the conflicting demands of the different virtues. If there are no situations in which morality demands conflicting acts, all things considered, then *phronesis* enables the agent to judge the right thing to do and to avoid doing the wrong thing. But if there are genuine moral dilemmas, cases in which no matter what the agent does, she does something wrong, *phronesis* may still be necessary to decide the least bad course of action, if there is one. That is, even in the case of a genuine moral trap, one in which every alternative is wrong, there may still be some choice that is morally preferable, all things considered. If so, *phronesis* would enable the agent to make such a judgment. But the worst possibility is that there are dilemmas in the strongest sense, namely, cases in which all alternatives are wrong and there is no morally preferable or less bad choice. If this can happen, it will be necessary to modify the definitions I have given of deontic concepts to handle such cases. I suggest that the definitions be modified in such a way that the standard of right and wrong is not what a virtuous

---

[71] A penetrating discussion of the moral dilemma vividly described in this novel has been given by Philip L. Quinn (1989). Quinn argues that Endo's novel depicts a case in which the two great commandments, to love God with all our heart and to love our neighbor as ourselves, conflict. In virtue discourse the conflict can be described as a conflict between loyalty to God and compassion for the suffering.

person would or might do but rather the *attitude* that a virtuous person would have toward an act. If a virtuous person can be in a situation in which all options are acts she would not do if it were not for the fact that she is in a trap and has to do *something,* she will feel very differently about her own act in such a situation than she does in nondilemma situations. Presumably, she will feel guilt and remorse comparable to what she feels when she does something virtuous persons do not do. Of course, even in non-dilemma cases of moral conflict, she will feel regret at having to do something she would otherwise not do, such as hurting a person with the truth, but her feelings and attitude will not be guilt or remorse in such cases. This may permit an alternative way of defining "right act" and "wrong act" within a pure virtue theory. Very roughly, a wrong act is an act that would make a virtuous person feel guilty, and a right act is an act that would not make a virtuous person feel guilty. I will not pursue this further, however, since I have no position on the possibility of dilemmas.

We now turn from the evaluation of acts to the evaluation of cognitive activity. The definition of a justified belief is exactly parallel to the definition of a right act.

A *justified belief* **is what a person who is motivated by intellectual virtue, and who has the understanding of his cognitive situation a virtuous person would have, might believe in like circumstances.**

An *unjustified belief* **is what a person who is motivated by intellectual virtue, and who has the understanding of his cognitive situation a virtuous person would have, would not believe in like circumstances.**

A belief of *epistemic duty* **is what a person who is motivated by intellectual virtue, and who has the understanding of his cognitive situation that a virtuous person would have, would believe in like circumstances.**

It is necessary to distinguish between two interpretations of the way in which an epistemic duty can be violated. Does a person violate her epistemic duty by failure to believe or only by actual disbelief? Here we need to consider the possibility of a disanalogy between acts and beliefs. Beliefs admit of three possibilities: belief, lack of belief, and disbelief. In the case of an act, it might appear that there are only two possibilities: Either you do the act or you do not. Is there anything in acting that is exactly comparable to disbelieving? I think the answer may be yes, and perhaps the first philosopher to notice the three-way split in acting was Duns Scotus. In the *Ordinatio* (I.1), Scotus distinguishes three states of the will: choosing to accept (*velle*), choosing to reject (*nolle*), and refraining from choice (*non velle*).[72] Truth telling is an example. When asked a question that I do not wish to answer, I may choose to tell the truth, choose to lie, or choose not to tell the truth but not to lie either, in which case I would simply refrain from saying anything. (The practical problems in carrying out this distinction are obvious; the conceptual distinction is not difficult.)

This three-way distinction permits us to distinguish between two senses of duty. Let us begin with the definition of a moral duty given earlier and its epistemic parallel. I said that an act is a moral duty in certain circumstances if and only if it is wrong not to do it. This is a very strong concept of duty. If we were to make the definition of an epistemic duty exactly parallel, we would say that **a belief is an epistemic duty (strong sense) in certain circumstances if and only if it is unjustified not to believe it.** This gives us a strong notion of a duty to have a belief.

The distinction between not believing and disbelieving permits us to formulate an alternative notion of epistemic duty that is weaker: **A belief is an epistemic duty (weak sense) in certain circumstances if and only if it is unjustified to disbelieve it.** That is to say, an intellectually virtuous person would not disbelieve it in like circumstances. On this definition, a person who does not believe what an intellectually virtuous person would believe in her circumstances but does not disbelieve it either would not be violating her epistemic duty, although she would according to the stronger definition.[73]

---

[72] Vatican ed., vol. 2, p. 100. See also *Ordinatio* IV, suppl. d. 49, qq. 9–10, in Wolter 1986. This distinction is examined in Ingham, 1996. I thank Sr. Mary Beth Ingham for a helpful discussion on this distinction.

[73] Perhaps a more perspicuous way of putting the idea of epistemic duty has been suggested to me by Philip Quinn. It is an epistemic duty to adopt whatever propositional attitude a virtuous person would have in the circum-

If Scotus is right that acting has a three-way division, this would permit us to distinguish a stronger and weaker sense of moral duty for acts that parallels the epistemic distinction. We can say that **an act is a moral duty (strong sense) in certain circumstances if and only if it is wrong not to do it. An act is a moral duty (weak sense) in certain circumstances if and only if it is wrong to choose to reject it (Scotus's *nolle*).** So there is a moral duty to tell the truth in the strong sense if and only if it is wrong to refrain from telling the truth. It is a moral duty to tell the truth in the weak sense if and only if it is wrong to lie. Presumably there is a moral duty to tell the truth only in the weak sense, but some of our other duties apply in the strong sense, for example, the duty of parents to care for their children. Parents have violated that duty if they fail to care for their children, even if they do not actually choose to reject their children's care.

The definitions I have given assume that the justified/ unjustified distinction is comparable to the right/wrong distinction. To say a belief is justified is to say it is not unjustified in the same way that to say an act is right is to say it is not wrong. This usage seems to me to be the most common in epistemology; in fact, epistemologists sometimes defend the justification of a belief on the grounds that to have it violates no epistemic duty or obligation, or exhibits any epistemic impropriety.[74] Again, the justifiedness of a belief parallels the rightness of an act, and it cannot be immediately inferred from the justifiability of the belief that the believer is to be praised or commended for having it, because that would require that he actually holds the justified belief in a virtuous manner – that is, from the right motive and with the right understanding. His belief is justified just in case it is a belief

---

stances. Thus, if a virtuous person would believe p, it is an epistemic duty to believe p; if a virtuous person would disbelieve p, it is an epistemic duty to disbelieve p; if a virtuous person would withhold belief in p, it is an epistemic duty to withhold belief in p. If there is no one propositional attitude that a virtuous person would adopt in the circumstances, there is no epistemic duty relative to p in such circumstances.

[74] Alvin Plantinga has argued this way in several places in his defense of the epistemic justification of religious belief.

a virtuous person might have in his circumstances, but that is not to say yet that *he* is to be evaluated positively for having it.

Let us compare the understanding element of the definition of justified belief and the same element in the definition of a right act. We saw in our account of a virtue that a virtuous person not only is motivated a certain way but is reliable in bringing about the ends of the motivation. This means that she has the awareness or understanding of relevant nonmoral facts about herself and her environment necessary for making it probable that she will be successful. In the particular case, she has the degree of understanding of the moral and nonmoral facts that a reliable person would have in that kind of case. A right act is what a person would or might do who not only is virtuously motivated but has the awareness of the facts relevant to the particular case that a virtuously reliable person would have. These facts contextualize the act, and the degree to which they are needed depends upon a prior position on the particularity of moral decision making, a dispute to which I will not contribute here. But it is clear that *some* degree of understanding of the facts, both moral and nonmoral, is required for adequate moral judgment.

Similarly, a justified belief is what a person would or might have who not only is virtuously motivated but also is aware of facts that contextualize the belief in question. Since an intellectually virtuous person is reliable in bringing about the aims of the virtue, which in this case are internal, this means that she is generally successful in acting open-mindedly or with intellectual autonomy, courage, carefulness, and so on. Take the case of open-mindedness. If she is reliable in acting open-mindedly, not only must she be appropriately motivated, but she must be reliably aware of the views of others that are worth considering. She must be generally successful in putting herself in a position to hear and reflect upon such views, which means she must be aware of facts about her epistemic situation that are not simply normative. In the particular case, she has the degree of understanding of these facts that a virtuously reliable person would have. So a justified belief is what a person would or might believe who not only is virtuously motivated but has the understanding that a virtuously reliable person would have concerning those aspects of her epistemic situation relevant to the belief.

Intellectual virtues can give rise to both perfect and imperfect epistemic duties in the same way that moral virtues can give rise to both perfect and imperfect moral duties. It is indisputable that some epistemic rules admit of no exceptions – the law of non-contradiction, for one. But as I argued above, the existence of exceptionless rules is no problem for a pure virtue theory. What is at issue is the grounding of the rules, not the extent of their application.

The problem of conflict between intellectual virtues can be handled the same way as conflict between moral virtues. The practically wise person is able to judge how to direct her cognitive activity and to form beliefs in cases in which, say, the intellectually courageous thing to do conflicts with the intellectually humble thing to do, or in which intellectual thoroughness conflicts with the following of insight. More profoundly difficult cases are those in which the intellectually virtuous thing to do conflicts with the morally virtuous course of action, as appears to be the case in Sinclair Lewis's novel *Arrowsmith*. In that novel, Dr. Martin Arrowsmith is a physician and medical researcher who believes he is on the brink of discovery of a vaccine against the plague virus. He goes to an island in the West Indies where there is a plague epidemic to test the vaccine, but is forced to face a conflict between his moral duty to prevent the death of those in his care and his intellectual duty to find out whether the vaccine is effective. In this case, of course, the intellectually virtuous course of action may have long-term morally beneficial consequences as well, so the conflict is between what is straightforwardly morally virtuous action and a course of action that is intellectually virtuous, as well as perhaps morally virtuous in another way. I propose that practical wisdom is necessary to handle such cases, but I will not conjecture on the correct resolution of Arrowsmith's problem.

Given the importance of *phronesis* for belief-forming activity as well as for activity in the broader sense, we can formulate a set of definitions of the evaluative properties of beliefs parallel to the ones given for the evaluative properties of acts: **A *justified belief, all things considered*, is what a person with *phronesis* might believe in like circumstances. An *unjustified belief, all things considered*, is what a person with *phronesis* would not believe in like circumstances. A belief is a *duty, all things considered*, just in case it is what a person with *phronesis* would believe in like circumstances.**

Notice that the definitions of the evaluative concepts of acts and of beliefs, all things considered, are identical. The mediating function of *phronesis* over the entire range of virtues, both moral and intellectual, has the important consequence that the justified-ness of a belief, all things considered, is the same as the rightness of an act, all things considered. That is, the property attributed to beliefs as justifiedness, all things considered, is the same as the property attributed to acts as rightness, all things considered.

Now that we have defined justified belief in terms of intellectual virtues, we have finally reached the point at which the theory I am presenting here connects with other contemporary theories that define the concept of justification in terms of intellectual virtue. Probably the most meticulous attempts to connect justification with intellectual virtue appear in the recent work of Alvin Goldman (1992) and Ernest Sosa (1991, 1993), to which I alluded in Part I. Goldman and Sosa do very little to investigate intellectual virtue itself, concentrating on the fact that an intellectual virtue is something that produces a "high ratio" of true beliefs, but once the connection is made, they both use considerable acumen to make it work out as a theory of justification. In other words, the target concept is justification; intellectual virtue is introduced as the most significant concept in the analysans, but most of the attention is focused on elements in the analysans other than intellectual virtue. I will not attempt in this book to work out the way my project can be linked up with Sosa's or Goldman's, but I see no reason to think it cannot be done.

6.2 *Acts of virtue*

Virtues motivate their possessors to bring about changes in themselves or the world. Since there is a weak association between

motivation and success in a benign universe, it follows that reliability in a very broad sense is implied by the motivational
component of many virtues, but probably not all. The motivations
to have autonomy and integrity, for example, do not carry a person very far. This was already noted in 2.6. And even when motivation is regularly associated with success in general, it may not
be in the case of a particular person. I have argued that "virtue" is
a success term in the sense that we do not say that a given person
possesses a given virtue unless she is reliably successful in bringing about the aim of the motivation specific to that virtue. But
beyond that, we are interested in success in an even more particular sense. We, and the agent herself, are morally concerned with
the success of the particular act that arises out of her virtuous
motive. No matter how reliable she is generally, she may fail in a
particular instance. So even if she fully exercises a virtue with a
high degree of understanding of herself and her environment, she
may still fail in her aim. Although we judge her motive the same
whether she succeeds or fails, we do not judge the failed act the
same way as the successful act. It is time to consider this
distinction.

The fact that we can be moral failures in particular instances
even when we are the right *sorts* of persons doing the best we can
under the circumstances is one of the sources of moral luck. It also
calls attention to the fact that there is yet another ambiguity in the
moral evaluation of acts. At the weakest level of evaluation, we
call an act morally right when it is the act that *would be expected* of
a person, or at least is one that would not be *un*expected. The
definition of a right act given in 6.1 captures this idea. Beyond
that, we expect persons to be virtuously motivated themselves,
and so a person may satisfy stronger conditions, those for being
praiseworthy for doing an act, also defined in 6.1. Beyond that,
we find persons even more praiseworthy who have fully acquired a virtue and who express it in their acts. But clearly, an
agent can satisfy any or all of these conditions even when, on
some particular occasion, she is unsuccessful in her moral aim.
When this happens, there is something morally praiseworthy
missing from her act.

We praise success in reaching the ends of virtue and withhold praise (in that sense) from the cases of failure, and the important thing to see is that such praise is nonetheless *moral* praise. What's more, it is not *mere* success that is praiseworthy but, rather, success that is explained by the fact that the act has the other morally desirable features we have identified. So accidental success is not good enough to merit the kind of moral praise I am describing. Since the evaluative judgment that is relevant here is a judgment about acts, it requires us to define another category of acts that arise from virtue or virtuous motives. I propose that it is desirable in theoretical ethics to have a concept for an act that gets everything right – in its motive, in the behavior to which it gives rise, and in its end – and that is successful in reaching its end because of these morally praiseworthy features of the act.

Let us call an act *an act of virtue A* if and only if it arises from the motivational component of *A*, it is something a person with virtue *A* would (probably) do in the circumstances, and it is successful in bringing about the end (if any) of virtue *A* because of these features of the act. Notice that this definition is an extension of two definitions given in 6.1: the definition of "right act" and the definition of "is praiseworthy for doing an act." The idea is that an act is an act of virtue *A* if and only if the agent is praiseworthy for doing the act and the act is successful in bringing about the end of the *A* motivation because of the features of it that make the agent praiseworthy for doing it.

Let us now consider some examples and applications of this concept. I suggest that we not call an act "an act of justice" if it does not lead to the production of a just state of affairs. For example, a judge or jury might reach a wildly mistaken verdict out of a motive of justice. Such a verdict is perfectly compatible with the judge or jury being just persons, with their acting out of the virtue of justice in their deliberations and findings, and with their making no errors in following proper judicial procedures. People who criticized the jury verdicts in the first Rodney King trial almost always based their judgment on the verdict itself, and in most cases the judgment was not intended to impugn either the motives or the character of the jury members. The fact that there was negligible evidence against the motives of the jury was typically not taken to be inconsistent with the judgment that the jury's verdict was not *an act of justice*. It was said to be a "miscarriage" of justice. So the jury was not praised *for* the verdict, even though individual jury members might have been praiseworthy for acting out of just motives.

Similarly, what I am calling "an act of compassion" successfully brings about the beneficent effect on the sufferings of another that the virtue of compassion aims to produce. The desired alleviation of suffering occurs because of those features of the act that make it compassionate (namely, its compassionate motive) and the fact that what the agent does is what a compassionate person with understanding of the situation would be inclined to do in such circumstances. When the compassionate person fails, she still has the virtue of compassion and may even express it through her act and be praiseworthy for doing so, and we may even say she acts compassionately, but the failure of the act to attain its end prevents it from having a significant morally desirable feature, and there is a distinctive sort of praise that the agent would not be given *for* performing the act. My suggestion is that we withhold the label "act of compassion" from such acts.

Let us consider two other examples: the Aristotelian virtues of liberality and temperance. Although Aristotle does not analyze the components of virtue in the way I have described, he does believe that the liberal person and the temperate person have certain aims. Liberality is one of the two virtues that involve the proper handling of wealth. It is concerned with the giving and receiving of wealth, and especially in giving it (*NE* IV.1.1119b25–6). A liberal person has acquired a disposition to use wealth in the proper way, and this includes giving to the right people (IV.1.1120a10–11). But suppose a person who has the virtue of liberality and is generally reliable in giving to the right people nonetheless gives to the wrong person on some particular occasion, perhaps to a person who is feigning need. He might be motivated by the virtue of liberality, and his act might even be something a liberal person would be inclined to do in such circumstances, but I suggest it would be inappropriate to call his act an act of liberality. The same point is applicable in the case of temperance.[75] Aristotle understands a temperate person as one who regulates appetites occasioned by physical needs. Presumably a temperate person not only is motivated to regulate his appetites in the proper way but is generally successful in doing so. Suppose, however, that in spite of the most virtuous motivations and a habit of reliable success, he is unsuccessful on some particular occasion. I think it would be odd to describe his act as an act of temperance; in any case, I suggest that we adopt a usage according to which an act of this kind would not count as an act of temperance.

I have also suggested that our usage require that in an act of virtue, success is achieved through the operation of the other praiseworthy features of the act. So a guilty verdict in a murder trial is an act of justice only if the defendant is in fact guilty and if the verdict of guilt was accomplished through the operation of just motives and procedures. Similarly, an act of compassion must be successful in alleviating the suffering of another because of the operation of the compassionate motive and act. An act of liberality must be successful in giving wealth to a person who truly deserves it, and success must be achieved through the operation of the motive and act of giving.[76]

---

[75] See Young 1988 for an account of Aristotle on the virtue of temperance and Young 1994 for an account of Aristotle on the virtue of liberality.

[76] A vagueness in my definition of an act of virtue ought to be resolved. What we ordinarily bring about by our acts in the sense relevant to the ends of a virtue is something that we bring about only partially. To return to the example of a jury verdict, a jury acting out of the virtue of justice is clearly not the sole factor in bringing about a just state of affairs even when their action would intuitively be regarded as the most salient causal factor in producing it. Even in the ideal case there is some element of luck in or cooperation of the external world with their just motives and intentions. So it is too facile to say that we call an act an act of justice only if *that act* brings about a just state of affairs because of the features of the act and agent that make the act right. The truth is that the act operates in conjunction with other factors in bringing about the desired end. This means that the idea of an act's bringing about a state of affairs that has the features at which the virtue aims because of the rightness of the act must be filled out more carefully. As an appoximation of such an account I suggest the following: **An act is *an act of virtue A* if and only if it arises from the motivational component of *A*, it is something a person with virtue *A* would be likely to do in the circumstances, it leads to a state of affairs that exhibits**

The importance of the aim may vary with the virtue. I have given examples of justice, compassion, and liberality, which are virtues with reasonably clear external ends, and temperance, which has a reasonably clear internal end. Intellectual virtues, as we have seen, also have internal ends. Some virtues, such as courage, may not have an end that is easily identifiable, and there may be virtues, such as wisdom, that have no end of any kind. My point is not that all virtues have easily identifiable ends, or even that all virtues have ends at all, but only that in those cases in which a virtue does include an end of bringing about some state of affairs, to that extent we should not call an act an act *of* the virtue in question unless that act is successful in its end.

As I have defined an "act of virtue," it is to some extent a term of art. I realize that a great number of people, including many who are highly reflective on these matters, use the expression "performing an act of courage" synonymously with "acting courageously"; and similarly for other virtue expressions. A person who goes down to defeat while risking his life for a greater good acts with courage; he acts courageously. Why not say his act is an act of courage? My response is to say (1) the distinction I am making is needed and important enough to be reflected in our form of speech, and (2) we make this distinction in a limited number of cases anyway. The latter would include some usages of "an act of justice," such as in the Rodney King verdict just cited. Discussions of judicial justice commonly distinguish between the following of correct judicial procedures, regardless of outcome, and finding the right person guilty. I suggest that the expression "acting justly" is compatible with an outcome whereby a murderer goes free, whereas the expression "an act of justice" is not. I am also urging the generalization of this difference to other virtues. The idea is that we really do make a moral distinction be-

the qualities that are the aim of virtue *A*, and *the best explanation* of the fact that the state of affairs has those qualities is that the act has these features. The idea for this expansion of the definition of an act of virtue comes from John Greco's definition of knowledge. As a way of handling Gettier problems, Greco (1994a) has proposed that in cases where *S* knows *p*, *S*'s believing *p* truly *is best explained* by the fact that *S*'s believing *p* is the result of a stable disposition toward reliable belief.

tween the successfully virtuous act and the unsuccessful one. To make the distinction in the forms of words I have suggested is clearly somewhat arbitrary, but I think it is not unreasonable and can be recognized as a viable usage once the considerations I have given here are appreciated. I recognize, then, that my definition of an "act of virtue" is partially stipulative. However, I would strongly object to the suggestion that it is wholly stipulative or artificial.

Virtues have both immediate ends that are distinctive of the individual virtue and ultimate ends that pertain to a whole range of virtues. To know the ultimate ends of virtues we need to look at the general motivations that give rise to the particular virtuous motivations. We have already seen that intellectual virtues all arise from the motivation for knowledge, but that each one has a particular motivational component that distinguishes it from other intellectual virtues. Although we have not explored very far the ways of classifying other sets of moral virtues, it may be that there is a group of virtues that cluster around the motivation for the well-being of others. So love, generosity, kindness, compassion, and benevolence may all arise from the same general motivation and have the same ultimate end. There may also be a group of virtues that cluster around respect for human dignity, and this group may include justice, fairness, honesty, integrity, and trust. In each case the ultimate end of each virtue would not simply be something unique to that virtue but would be a more general aim shared by a whole class of virtues. If the thesis of the unity of the virtues is correct, there may even be one ultimate end that pertains to the entire class of virtues, but it is not my purpose here to give a complete taxonomy of the virtues. What I wish to do is to point out that to the extent that the motivational component of a particular virtue can be traced to a deeper motivation, an act of virtue of that kind must be successful in bringing about the end of the deeper motivation, as well as of the particular one. What this means in practice is that an act of generosity is not only one that is successful in giving to others something they need in the particular sense of "need," but it must also be contributory to the general happiness or well-being of the recipient. At least that is the case if I am right in my conjecture that ultimately generosity aims at aiding the well-being of others. Similarly, since we have seen that intellectual virtues arise out of the motivation for knowledge, an act of open-mindedness must not only be success-ful in making the agent receptive to new ideas and arguments but must contribute in a significant way to the agent's acquisition of knowledge. A parallel point can be made for each of the other intellectual virtues.

An act of virtue is right in a very strong sense of right. It has all of the morally desirable features of an act, of the agent performing the act, of the relation between agent and act, and of the relation between act and end. We will return to the concept of an act of virtue in Part III when we define knowledge and take up the resolution of Gettier problems.

6.3 Beyond duty

It was pointed out in Part I that an important advantage of virtue ethics over act-based ethics is that gradations of moral evalution can be handled much better by the former than by the latter. As we have just seen, the primary evaluative division in act-based ethics is between the wrong and the not-wrong. The morally praiseworthy is relegated to the category of the supererogatory, generally as an afterthought. The reason for this is probably that it is taken for granted that our most important moral concern is to avoid wrongdoing. Moral excellence may be considered a laud-able goal, but perhaps a quixotic one in our cynical age. In any case, moral fervor is generally associated with the avoidance of evil rather than with the pursuit of good.

In contrast, Aristotelian virtue ethics understands the moral life in terms of aiming for the top rather than in avoiding the bottom. The character of a human being can be seen as lying along a scale that encompasses a number of different evaluative levels. As we saw in section 2, the morally strong occupies the level below the virtuous, and below which is the morally weak (akratic) person. The vicious person is worse in character than the morally weak individual but is not at the bottom of the scale. That distinction goes to the truly monstrous person who, Aristotle thought, is scarcely human (NE VII.5). Furthermore, even within the category of virtue or vice it is natural to make gradations, and our commonsense moral judgments reflect this. Even when a person satisfies the conditions for being courageous, patient, generous, or kind, it seems possible for her to reach greater heights of virtuousness that make her even more praiseworthy. And parallel remarks apply to the vices opposed to these virtues. The virtue of justice may be an exception, because it is common today to think of everything governed by justice as either a moral duty or a moral wrong, but there may still be some sense to the idea of a just person becoming more just if we think there can be growth in the understanding of the nonmoral facts that enable a just person to be more successful in implementing the aims of justice. In short, aretaic concepts permit a range of evaluative levels that do not appear in the concepts applied to act evaluation, at least not without difficulty.

Michael Slote has mentioned that there is a long tradition in philosophy that denies the possibility of rational, as opposed to moral, supererogation, and if accurate, that tradition would undermine my attempt to assimilate epistemic evaluation to moral virtue terms of evaluation. But Slote argues that practical rationality does admit of supererogatory degrees,[77] and it seems to me that the same can be said about rationality without the adjective "practical" attached. There may be objections to using the concept of the supererogatory per se, but not to the evaluation of persons as more or less rational. The intellectual virtues we have considered are, for the most part, as susceptible to levels of possession as are typical moral virtues. More important, there are good practical reasons for wanting to evaluate persons for their cognitive activity and belief-forming habits in a way that permits the nuances of such graded judgments. Religious beliefs and beliefs in scientific hypotheses or philosophical theses are just some of the cases in which we want to do much more than to merely avoid being epistemically blameworthy, beyond the pale, thrown out of the community of rational beings. Surely we want to reach a high grade of epistemic evaluation, not just to avoid a low grade. A

---

[77] This is a central point in *Beyond Optimizing* (Slote 1989). The idea is first introduced on p. 5.

well-developed virtue theory offers the best approach for making such fine distinctions in epistemic evaluation.

7 CONCLUSION TO PART II: THE SCOPE OF THE MORAL

The account of the virtues I have given in Part II subsumes the intellectual virtues under the general category of the moral virtues, or *aretai ethikai,* roughly as Aristotle understands the latter, and gives a theoretical structure for the evaluation of beliefs that is exactly parallel to the evaluation of acts in the sense of acts generally reserved to ethics. This might be thought to be a reductionist move of the sort criticized by Roderick Firth (1978), but this interpretation would be a mistake. My aim is to show that the concept of the moral is too narrow as commonly understood and that it ought to be extended to cover the normative aspects of cognitive activities. I think of this move as expansionist rather than reductionist since it would be more accurately described as expanding the range of ordinary moral evaluation to include epistemic evaluation, rather than as reducing the latter to the former. It has often been observed that the scope of the moral in classical Greek philosophy was more inclusive than it is today. If anything is surprising, it is that it was not even *more* inclusive, considering that it was intended to cover everything encompassed by human flourishing. Modern ethics, in contrast, generally considers morality much less a system for fulfilling human nature than a set of principles for dealing with individuals in conflict. This has narrowed the range of the moral considerably, usually covering only those activities that directly affect other persons, and, in consequence, the greatest emphasis is on the worst cases of human disharmony, expressed in the vocabulary of rights and duties. An important consequence of this approach to ethics is the disvaluing of those aspects of morality that involve primarily the self and only indirectly the community. Michael Slote (1992b) has pointed out the paradoxes that result from the insistence on the self/other asymmetry in ethics and has urged a more balanced view of the self-regarding and other-regarding virtues. Intellectual virtues are among the primarily self-regarding virtues. It is time to remedy their neglect by philosophers.

I have argued that when we make the primary object of moral evaluation traits of persons, as it is on a pure aretaic approach, considerations on the structure of these traits and their relation to acts, beliefs, and feelings make the separation of epistemic from moral evaluation anomalous. The aberration is magnified by the modern practice of separating the fields of epistemology and ethics to such an extent that epistemology is typically classified with metaphysics, and ethics is classified with political philosophy and aesthetics, and there is rarely any suggestion that the practitioners of the two fields have anything in common. If the evaluation of believing involves the evaluation of cognitive acts, and if cognitive acts are acts, we ought to expect a convergence of epistemic and moral evaluation at some point anyway. My position is that there is no reason at all to attempt to trace the convergence backward to the point at which moral and epistemic evaluation diverge. Epistemic evaluation just *is* a form of moral evaluation. I cannot offer anything that would qualify as an *account* of the moral to support this claim, but I am relying on the idea that there is no plausible a priori theory of the moral to start with, and so we may, and probably must, begin with a certain complex of concepts that noncontroversially belong to the sphere of the moral, and we may then argue that these concepts are most naturally understood as having a wider scope than previously accepted. As I see it, then, the scope of the moral expands from the inside out. For example, it expands from the concept of moral courage to the concept of intellectual courage, and from there to the concept of other intellectual virtues that do not have terminological equivalents in ethics: traits such as open-mindedness and intellectual thoroughness.

The ethics of character illuminates the unity between the morality of acting and the morality of believing. The ethics of duty may have the potential to do so also, but not as clearly; else, it would have done so already. This is not to deny that both traditions in ethics are often irritating in their philosophical psychology since both typically insist on dividing the psyche in a way that has persisted long after it was given up in psychology. In some circles today the dissociation between cognitive and feeling states is even more pronounced than it was in Aristotle's work, perhaps because of the dominance of the computer model of human information processing. But in spite of this glaring defect in its understanding of the structure of the human mind, the virtue tradition is brilliant in its understanding of the data of moral experience. Contemporary virtue theories have broadened this approach to include a sensitivity to the details of moral living as depicted in narrative literature. Literature is less likely to recognize those divisions among the goods of life that lead one group of philosophers to investigate the proper pursuit of knowledge and an entirely different group to investigate the proper pursuit of other goods, such as happiness. Whereas these connections are so often missing from the didactic literature, they can be displayed in narratives naturally and absorbingly.[78] This suggests that the use of literature might be fruitful for philosophers interested in epistemic evaluation as well as for ethicists.

There is evidence in recent philosophy of a desire for a broader understanding of the moral, and the interest in the relevance of literature to morality is one indication of such a desire. But clearly specifying the distinction between the moral and the nonmoral spheres of life and of inquiry has proven to be a remarkably difficult matter, and the difficulties are not purely theoretical. My argument that the range of our moral responsibility ought to include the area of cognitive activity might strike some readers as excessively moralistic. After all, the practice of blaming is vastly

[78] An example is John Casey's (1990) interesting discussion of Jane Austen's portrayal of Emma, in which he points out the connection between Emma's desire for truth and her moral qualities: "Moral goodness in Jane Austen is not something independent of active intelligence. Emma's desire for truth is frequently in danger of being undermined by egoism, just as it is supported by qualities such as sincerity, honesty, and directness. It is precisely this vision of the combination of knowledge and feeling as essential to moral goodness that makes sense of Jane Austen's valuing of the active and analytical as against passive feeling.

"In *Emma* the perception of truth is shown to depend upon moral qualities, and can be presented in terms of character" (p. 163).

overdone as it is,[79] and since it is easy to identify the concept of blame as the distinguishing mark of the moral, it is not surprising that Michael Slote (1992b) has urged that we drop the moral and *replace* it with an ethic of virtue in which evaluation has more in common with evaluation in aesthetics than in morality. I am in deep sympathy with the desire to tame the practice of blaming, but I do not think it is obvious that the concept of blame in the hard-hitting sense endemic to Western morality has a necessary connection to the concept of moral responsibility. If we lighten up the notion of blame, that may actually strengthen my argument for an extension of the range of moral responsibility. At least it may make it more palatable for some readers. In any case, my intent is surely not to "moralize" our whole lives in the usual sense of the term but to show that considerations from within morality itself give us reasons to significantly broaden it. If broadening it involves weakening it, I have no objections.

In Part II I have proposed a theory of virtue and vice that includes intellectual virtues as forms of moral virtue and have shown how the major concepts of act/belief evaluation can be defined in terms of the concept of a virtue, including that of a moral or an epistemic duty and of a right act or a justified belief. This shows that a pure virtue theory can provide the foundation of epistemic as well as moral evaluation. The unification of moral and epistemic evaluation is a welcome advantage. In Part III I will argue for the primacy of intellectual virtue in the state of knowledge, the analysis of which is another main concern of epistemology, probably the most important one. If I am right in these claims, it follows that normative epistemology is a branch of ethics.

[79] After writing these words I discovered that H. H. Price (1954) used this same worry to explain his reticence about attaching moral concepts to cognitive activity: "It seems to me that we are all far too much addicted to blaming people as it is. If we are to be allowed, or even encouraged, to blame them for the way they direct their thoughts, as well as for their actions, there will be a perfect orgy of moral indignation and condemnation, and charity will almost disappear from the world" (quoted in Dearden, Hirst, and Peters 1972, pp. 364–5).

Part III

The nature of knowledge

Part I surveyed the use of ethical theory in epistemology, showed the advantages of a pure virtue theory, and distinguished this approach from that typically used in contemporary epistemology and from other forms of "virtue epistemology." Part II developed a theory of virtue and vice broad enough to handle epistemic as well as moral evaluation and showed how the concepts of justified belief and epistemic duty can be defined within the theory. Now we turn to an investigation of the most critical concern of epistemology: the analysis of knowledge. We have already seen that the motivation to know is the most basic constituent of every intellectual virtue, and each intellectual virtue is constructed in such a way as to regularly lead to its end of attaining knowledge. Since intellectual virtues are forms of moral virtue, it follows that knowledge is intimately bound up with moral concepts, although it has not always been treated that way. In this, the final, part of the book, I begin by locating the concept of knowledge within the domain of ethics. I then propose a definition of knowledge and show how it is immune to Gettier problems. The theory is externalist according to the most common definition of externalism but has a stronger internalist aspect than the more common externalist theories. I then offer criticisms of two popular versions of so-called virtue epistemology – reliabilism and Plantinga's proper function theory – and answer anticipated objections to my theory. I conclude with a brief discussion of the connections among the disciplines of ethics, normative epistemology, and psychology.

1 KNOWLEDGE AND THE ETHICS OF BELIEF

The place of knowledge in normative epistemology is in an un-happy state of flux. On the one hand, knowledge is often in the background when the focus is on normative issues. These discussions typically involve such concepts as epistemic *responsibility,* epistemic *duty,* epistemic *virtue,* and the *justifiability* or *rationality* of beliefs. Of course, the concept of knowledge may be connected with these concepts, but it usually is not the first one to arise within a distinctively ethical discussion, and some epistemologists refuse to connect them at all.[1] On the other hand, knowledge has traditionally been the central concern of epistemology, even when its place was the negative one given to it by the fear of skepticism. In an attempt to avoid a split epistemology, I will approach the analysis of knowledge by looking first at its ethical dimension. I hope it is evident that a unitary theory of normative epistemology is desirable, and if such a theory is able to give knowledge a central place, that is all to the good.

A discussion of the ethics of knowledge is complicated by the fact that knowledge has more than one valuable aspect. Of course we value the truth, but the value we place on knowledge is more than the value of the truth we thereby acquire. If this were not the case, knowledge would have been infinitely easier to analyze than it has proven to be throughout the history of philosophy. Knowledge is valuable not only because it involves having a valuable possession – the truth – but because it involves a valuable relation between the knower and the truth. This relation is a credit to the knower, and (leaving skeptical worries aside) it is a

---

[1] Plantinga and Foley are both examples of this, but in different ways. Plantinga's main concern is knowledge, and he relegates the obviously moral concepts of justifiability and epistemic duty to a different and less important epistemological domain. Foley, on the other hand, prefers to focus on the egocentric concept of rationality and the ethical concepts associated with it. He is willing to accept the consequence that knowledge is less important than was previously thought in epistemological history.

relation at which we think we can realistically aim. This suggests that knowledge is not merely something that happens *to* us but is something to which we contribute through our own efforts and skills, and this leads us, at least in some moods, to think of ourselves as bearing responsibility for having or not having it.

It seems to me that the concept of the self is constituted as much by what we know as by what we do. A sense of responsibility for our own knowledge is as important for a sense of self-identity as a sense of responsibility for our own acts. We claim our putative knowing states as our own and take credit or discredit for them, just as we claim our acts as our own and take praise or blame for them. Of course, it is possible for someone under the guise of careful thinking to claim that it is not actually our knowing states that we consider our own but our states of justified belief. But this is not consistent with common practice. Winners of the Nobel Prize are given credit and take credit for being right,[2] not just for being justified. Perhaps it would be more honest to say that we want to take credit for our states of knowledge, but we do not want to take discredit for our states of justified belief that are not also states of knowledge. This, however, makes no sense, and it indicates that there may be some confusion surrounding the idea that knowledge is creditworthy or praiseworthy or something for which we are responsible. But one thing is certain. The greater the extent to which knowledge is a matter of luck, the more it becomes merely the object of empirical investigation, and the less interesting it is to us philosophically. I will comment on the links between the empirical side of epistemology and its normative side at the end of this book, but given that knowledge does have a normative dimension, we should attempt to link its analysis with the analysis of other normative concepts in epistemology. And as long as we think of knowledge as something for which we can realistically aim, we can expect that its normative dimension will not be too far removed from the set of ethical-epistemological notions we have been discussing. In what fol-

---

[2] See again the pertinent comment by Thomas Nagel in the last footnote of "Moral Luck" (1979a).

lows, I will propose that the concepts already developed in Part II are sufficient to enable us to define knowledge.

One difficulty in defining knowledge is the wide range of views on the rigor of its requirements. According to some theories, the conditions for being in a state of knowledge are narrow and strict, whereas according to others, they are broad and loose. The tradition leans to rigorism, although the contemporary trend is in the opposing direction. The lineage of rigorism is impressive, beginning with Plato. In the *Meno* Plato says true beliefs become knowledge when they have been tethered by an explanatory account (*aitias logismos*) (98a.3; see also *Phaedo* 76d and *Republic* 531e, 534b). Later commentators have hypothesized that a tethered belief is one that can withstand dialectical assault. Paul Woodruff suggests that a tethered belief is one that cannot be refuted (Everson 1990, p. 84). Since Plato, a long list of philosophers have embraced rigorist notions of knowledge, including such otherwise diverse thinkers as Augustine, al-Ghazali, Maimonides, Roger Bacon, Ockham, Francis Bacon, Descartes, Spinoza, Leibniz, Locke, Hume, and Prichard. Philosophers with looser requirements for knowledge have been decidedly the exception, with Thomas Reid leading the way in the eighteenth century in rejecting what he thought were the unreasonable demands of the rigorists. The contemporary effect of the rebellion against rigorism is widespread, and now it is commonly thought that as long as we can get past the skeptical challenge and have knowledge at all, it is not difficult to attain it, and the term "knowledge" is used to cover a multitude of states, from the simplest cases of ordinary perceptual contact with the physical world, requiring no cognitive effort or skill whatever, to the most impressive cognitive achievements. Indeed, one of the attractions of reliabilism is that it spreads the net of knowledge widely. Yet the contrast between reliabilism and the supreme rigorist theory, Plato's theory in the *Republic*, is so extreme, it is doubtful that philosophy has ever produced two more different theories about (allegedly) the same thing in its entire history.

Throughout this book I have referred to the fact that knowledge has always been considered valuable and important. I infer from that that a state gained too cheaply does not really deserve the accolade "knowledge," and this favors the idea that knowledge should be defined relatively strictly. It deserves quite a lot of effort, and presumably, effort is required. On the other hand, we need to consider the fact that if the requirements for knowledge are too strict, it loses its importance in another way. People automatically adjust their sights to the attainable. At least, if something is thought to be unattainable, it tends to lose importance. This is not to say that desirability and importance are proportional to attainability; they certainly are not. Nonetheless, it is probably the case that at some critical level of unattainability, the unattainable object loses its interest for us. Tiles and Tiles have proposed that this is precisely the reason why Hume abandoned the classical project of knowledge as a form of understanding and explanation in favor of the more attainable goal of discovering empirical regularities (1993, p. 114). Kant and the varieties of Idealism are further evidence that philosophers are not exempt from the very human trait of focusing interest on the attainable. If a cognitive grasp of the thing-in-itself is unattainable, that was reason enough for Kant to give an account of knowledge in which the object is not the thing-in-itself. Similarly, Idealists define truth in terms of the cognitively graspable. Redefining truth is one way to put knowledge within our grasp. The other way is to redefine the normative element of knowledge, making it easier to achieve. The latter is the favored approach today.

I said at the beginning of this book that although I allow contemporary concerns to dictate many of the questions I address in this work, I try to be faithful to the history of the concept of knowledge in my analysis. This leads me to conclude that knowledge ought to be defined in a way that is relatively rigorous, but it should still be something that is reasonably attainable. I am aware that the definition I will give is somewhat stricter than usual in contemporary philosophy, but it is also rather elastic. There are ways of interpreting it that ought to be acceptable to most of those who favor looser requirements, which is a desirable feature in the present philosophical climate. The definition is contemporary, but it has clear classical roots.

2 DEFINING KNOWLEDGE

2.1 The definition

We are now in a position to give a definition of the state of knowledge, but first I want to say something about the purpose of definitions in philosophy. My aim in defining knowledge is to give necessary and sufficient conditions for having knowledge that are both theoretically illuminating and practically useful. When I say that a definition should be theoretically illuminating, I mean that it should make sense of as much data as possible and put to rest as many unanswered questions as possible. The latter would have to include a resolution of Gettier cases since no definition of knowledge in the last thirty years can afford to ignore them. For that reason, I will give an account of Gettier problems and my response to them in section 3. But it should be admitted that some ways of handling these cases are theoretically illuminating and some are not. The definition of knowledge as "nonaccidentally true belief" is an example of one that is not. That definition may be accurate, but it does not tell us much. An obvious reason it does not tell us much is that it is so vague. A less obvious reason is that only philosophers who have thought about Gettier problems would have thought of it. Those who have not thought about these cases are left cold by such a definition, and that is not due wholly to their philosophical naïveté (although that may also be a factor). No, the fundamental problem with this definition is that there is something *missing* from it; it is negative where it should be positive. We need to investigate further to identify what is missing.

Contemporary epistemology has expended considerable effort in an attempt to make definitions of epistemic concepts immune to intuitive counterexamples, and the dialectical process of offering and responding to counterexamples often dictates the way in which definitions are formulated. This is true in many areas of philosophy, not just in epistemology. The effort is laudable in its intent, but there are problems with this approach. One problem is that the result can too easily be ad hoc. Definitions formulated in response to Gettier examples often have this problem. I propose

264

that a good definition ought to clarify and illuminate the nature of the definiendum, but its formulation should not function simply as a response to an attack. Even when definitions succeed in their aim of immunity to counterexamples, and this includes Gettier counterexamples, they may not tell us what we want to know about the thing defined. That is because the original question asked, "What is *x*?" was *not* a question that referred to counterexamples. This is one reason the definition "nonaccidentally true belief" is unsatisfactory. It is too obviously a response to problems in some *other* definition. Another problem is that it is negative where it should be positive. It tells us what knowledge is not rather than what it is. But the truth is, the definition "nonaccidentally true belief" is better than most. It at least has the virtue of succinctness. I propose that a good definition should be formulated in such a way that it does not contain features whose sole advantage is to answer counterexamples, one of the most common ways a definition can be ad hoc. The desirability of avoiding ad hoc definitions, then, leads me to aim for a definition of knowledge that would have been plausible even if no one had ever thought of Gettier cases.

Another problem with definitions driven by counterexamples is that the dialectical success of examples is no stronger than the strength of the intuitions supporting them. It can happen that the major effect of using examples and counterexamples is to highlight the differences in intuitions between the parties to a dispute rather than to advance the dispute or to resolve it. The example of people who can determine the sex of baby chicks without knowing how they do it or even if they do it correctly is probably a case of this sort. Philosophers with strong externalist intuitions about knowledge have no hesitation in saying that such persons *know* the sex of the chick and use this case as a counterexample to internalist theories.[3] But internalists are simply unpersuaded by the case. In the absence of general agreement about the case, then, it is not especially helpful to give a precise formulation of a defini-

---

[3] See Foley 1987, pp. 168–9, for a discussion of chicken sexers. Foley says that it is not implausible to suppose that the chicken sexer knows the sex of the baby chick, although his belief may not be epistemically rational.

tion that is inspired by a particular position on such a case. I infer from this another moral about definitions: We should beware of a false precision resting on vague or questionable intuitions about cases that lack independent support.

Objection by counterexample is the weakest sort of attack a theory can undergo. Even when the objection succeeds, it shows only that a theory fails to achieve complete accuracy. It does not distinguish among the various theories subjected to criticism by counterexample. Presumably some are much closer to the truth than others. John Rawls makes much the same point in *A Theory of Justice* (1971):

> Objections by way of counterexamples are to be made with care, since these may tell us only what we know already, namely, that our theory is wrong somewhere. The important thing is to find out how often and how far it is wrong. All theories are presumably mistaken in places. The real question at any given time is which of the views already proposed is the best approximation overall. To ascertain this some grasp of the structure of rival theories is surely necessary. (P. 52)

Although I believe that the method of argument by counterexample has been overused in philosophy, it is an easy way to engage discussion with rival viewpoints, and I will use it occasionally myself, both in criticizing some other theories and as a way of anticipating objections to the theory I am proposing here. Precision in a theory requires the assiduous use of cases against which to test the theory at some point in the theory's development. The definition of knowledge I will propose has not yet reached a level of precision that permits it to withstand all such attacks. However, I will begin such a test in this book, bearing in mind that precision is but one virtue of a definition, one that must be balanced against simplicity, elegance, conciseness, theoretical illumination, and practical usefulness.

Although I believe that definitions should not be obviously driven by counterexamples, I will give a definition that I believe is immune to Gettier problems. As I have already remarked, any account of knowledge proposed these days is hopeless if it cannot withstand these objections. But my primary aim is to define knowledge in a way that is theoretically illuminating and satisfies the other conditions I have described. In addition, I hope that it does not have obvious counterexamples, either of a Gettier style or otherwise.

Besides being theoretically illuminating, I have claimed that a valuable quality in a definition of knowledge is that it be practically useful. It may be too much to expect a single definition to serve both a theoretical and a practical purpose, but if one can be discovered that is successful at both purposes, so much the better. Given that we all have a strong personal interest in getting knowledge ourselves, it is desirable that a definition of knowledge be accompanied by an account of how to get it or, at least, an account of how to recognize when one has it and when one does not. This is not to say that any adequate definition of knowledge must provide that when a person knows, he knows that he knows. That would beg the question about one of the more important theoretical issues on the nature of the knowing state. However, the practical interest in getting knowledge ought to guide us in formulating our definition. In this respect defining knowledge is like defining happiness or a good life.

Let us review some of the features that ought to appear in the definition of knowledge and that have already been encountered in this book. Knowledge puts the knower in cognitive contact with reality or connects her cognitively to the truth, and it does so in a manner that could be called good, desirable, or important. We have also seen that there is some ambivalence about the degree to which we are responsible for our knowledge. The having or not having of knowledge responds to our effort, but it clearly is not solely a matter of effort or control on the part of the knower. We have also seen that the traditional way to define knowledge as "justified true belief" has been under attack for some time now, not only because of the Gettier counterexamples but because epistemologists have begun to worry about the status of the concept of justification, as we saw in Part I. A series of considerations arising from both ethics and epistemology led us to shift the focus of analysis away from the belief to the agent's traits, and this led to making justification secondary, derivative from intellectual virtue. This suggests that the concept of intellectual virtue does most of the normative work in the evaluation of cognitive processes and states, and so it is the first place to look for a way of understanding the nature of knowledge. We have also seen in this subsection that the definition should not be too vague, that it should not appear to be an ad hoc reaction to counterexamples, that it should not be more precise than general agreement warrants, and that it should be practically useful in guiding our search for knowledge.

With these constraints in mind, let us go back to where we left off in Part II when we defined epistemic justification. A key difference between knowledge and justifiedness is that the latter is a quality that even at its best only makes it *likely* that a belief is true. Justifiedness is a property that a belief has in virtue of being a member of a *set* of beliefs of a certain kind. Similarly, we call a *person* justified in having a belief because she has a property that (among other things) *tends* to lead her to true beliefs. Knowledge, in contrast, is not essentially a matter of a belief's being *like* anything else or *tending* toward anything, nor do we say that a person has knowledge because she has a property that tends toward anything. This is not to deny that there is a component of knowledge that is something like justification, but what is crucial in distinguishing knowing states from other good but lesser epistemic states is that the knowing state has a normative property that *that state* has in particular, not simply qua member of a set of states of a certain kind.

We might look at the difference between knowledge and justified belief as analogous to the difference between act and rule utilitarianism. In rule utilitarianism an act is right because it follows a rule the following of which tends to have good consequences. Similarly, a belief may be justified because it follows epistemic rules the following of which tends to lead to the truth or because it is an instance of a reliable belief-forming process (reliabilism) or on my account, because it is a belief that an intellectually virtuous person might have in the circumstances. That is to say, it is a member of the class of beliefs that a person who has virtuous motivations and is reliable in bringing about the end of those motivations might have in like circumstances. In the case of each theory of justified belief, success in reaching the truth is likely, or as likely as one can get in the circumstances, but is not guaranteed. In act utilitarianism, in contrast, an act is right because *that* act leads to good consequences, not because of some accidental, extraneous feature of the situation, but because of the properties of the act itself. Similarly, a state of knowledge is one in which the truth is reached, not accidentally, but because of certain properties of the belief itself. That particular belief must be successful in reaching the truth through those properties of it that make it epistemically valuable. An act of virtue was defined in Part II as an act that not only is virtuously motivated and reliable but is successful in the particular case in reaching the aim of the virtue through those features of the act. So an act of intellectual virtue not only is motivated by the particular virtue and expresses the agent's possession of the motivational component of the virtue but is successful in reaching both the immediate and the ultimate aim of that virtue, which is to say, it must lead to the truth because of the operation of the virtue.

We have seen that all intellectual virtues arise out of the motivation for knowledge and include an internal aim to operate cognitively in a way that is believed to be knowledge conducive, a way that is unique to each virtue. So the aim of open-mindedness is to be receptive to new ideas and arguments even when they conflict with one's own in order to ultimately get knowledge. The aim of intellectual thoroughness is to exhaustively investigate the evidence pertaining to a particular belief or a set of questions in order to ultimately get knowledge. The aim of intellectual courage is to defend one's belief or a line of inquiry when one has good reason to be confident that it is on the right track, and to fearlessly answer objections from others in order to ultimately get knowledge. Getting knowledge can be a matter either of reaching more truths or of gaining understanding of truths already believed. So it may be a way of increasing either the quality of true belief (cognitive contact with reality) or the quantity. So each intellectual virtue has an end that is unique to that virtue, but since every intellectual virtue arises out of the general motivation

269

for knowledge, an intellectual virtue also includes knowledge as its ultimate end.

The concept of an act of virtue combines all our moral aims in one concept. The agent has a virtuous motivation (disposition to have a virtuous motive), the act is motivated by such a motive, the agent acts in a way that a virtuous person would (probably) act in the same circumstances, the agent is successful in bringing about the state of affairs that a virtuous person desires, and the agent gets credit for bringing about such a state of affairs because it was brought about *through* the operation of her virtuous motive and activities.

I remarked in Part II that my account of intellectual virtue is satisfactory if the theory of that part stands alone, but since I wish to define knowledge in terms of intellectual virtue, intellectual virtue cannot be defined in the way I have just stated without circularity. Since the motivation for knowledge consists in the motivation for truth and other forms of the motivation for cognitive contact with reality, the definition of an act of intellectual virtue can be reformulated without using the concept of knowledge as follows: **An act of intellectual virtue A is an act that arises from the motivational component of A, is something a person with virtue A would (probably) do in the circumstances, is successful in achieving the end of the A motivation, and is such that the agent acquires a true belief (cognitive contact with reality) through these features of the act.**[4] I am interpreting cognitive contact with reality in a broad enough sense to include understanding and certainty.

I now propose that we define knowledge as follows:

Def 1: Knowledge is a state of cognitive contact with reality arising out of acts of intellectual virtue.

[4] We can modify the definition of an act of intellectual virtue parallel to the way suggested in Part II as follows: An act of intellectual virtue *A* is an act that arises from the motivational component of *A*, is something a person with virtue *A* would (probably) do in the circumstances, is successful in achieving the end of the *A* motivation, and is such that the best explanation for the agent's acquisition of true belief (cognitive contact with reality) is the fact that the belief arises out of an act that is motivated by *A* and is something persons with virtue *A* would (probably) do.

Alternatively,

Def 2: Knowledge is a state of true belief arising out of acts of intellectual virtue.

Since the fact that a belief arises out of acts of intellectual virtue entails that it is true, the second definition can be formulated without redundancy as follows:

Def 3: Knowledge is a state of belief arising out of acts of intellectual virtue.

The second definition follows the contemporary convention of defining knowledge as true belief plus something else, but its redundant element makes it misleading. The first definition may be preferable since it is noncommittal on such questions as the object of knowledge, the nature of truth, and the existence of propositions, which are not explored in this work. It also permits a broader interpretation of knowledge since knowledge may include cognitive contact with structures of reality other than the propositional.

Hilary Kornblith (1985) argues that Descartes has forced us to distinguish four distinct kinds of epistemic evaluation. We can evaluate either the nonvoluntary processes by which beliefs are formed or the voluntary acts that influence these processes, and then we can evaluate each of these from either an objective or a subjective perspective. Since the two questions asked from an objective perspective are not independent, Kornblith says we are left with three independent epistemic evaluations, and he proposes that an account of knowledge ought to incorporate all of them. "In particular, I want to suggest that knowledge requires: (1) belief which is arrived at in an objectively correct, that is, reliable, manner; (2) belief which is arrived at in a subjectively correct manner; and (3) belief which is the product of epistemically responsible action, that is, action regulated by a desire for true beliefs" (p. 273). The definition of knowledge proposed here satisfies Kornblith's three criteria.

In many places throughout this book we have looked at the ethical counterparts of concepts in normative epistemology and have found them in the aretaic concepts, the deontic concepts, and all the way up to the concept of an act of virtue. Here we find an exception because no concept in ethics is exactly comparable to the concept of knowledge. The closest analogue I can find is just the concept of an act of moral virtue itself, which we said in Part II is the concept of a right act in the strongest sense of right. An act of moral virtue has all the morally desirable features related to an act – in the act, in the agent, and in the relation between the agent and the act and its consequences. Similarly, an act of intellectual virtue has all the morally/epistemically desirable features an intellectual act can have, but our primary interest in the epistemic case is not in the act itself but in the state produced by the act. It may be true that to perform an act of intellectual virtue is to know, and if so, an act of moral virtue seems to be very close to an ethical counterpart to knowing. But knowledge is an enduring state, and so even though the concept of knowledge may be broad enough to encompass intellectual acts, it is certainly not limited to them. It is for this reason that I have defined knowledge as a state that *arises* from acts of intellectual virtue.

If there were an ethical counterpart to my definition of knowledge, it would satisfy the following schema: x **is a state of** y **arising out of acts of moral virtue.** As far as I can tell, there are no x and y that satisfy this schema.[5] In the definition of knowledge, what has the position of y is the ultimate aim of intellectual virtues, and knowledge is defined in part by the way we get there. Presumably, to find the moral counterpart we would look for an ultimate end of other groups of moral virtues to satisfy this definitional schema. We have seen that some moral virtues ultimately aim at such things as the well-being of others. But there does not seem to be any concept that is defined as the state of an agent when she brings about the well-being of others through acts of moral virtue.[6] One's own happiness, or *eudaimonia,* is probably also an ultimate end of (at least some) moral virtues, but the *concept* of *eudaimonia* does not seem to depend upon the way we get there in the way knowledge does. That is, we would not *deny*

---

[5] Dewey Hoitenga has suggested to me that this schema might be satisfied by the following: *Peace is a state of society arising out of acts of courage (as in war).*

[6] Brian Leftow has suggested to me that perhaps holiness is such a state.

that a woman is in a state of *eudaimonia* for the sole reason that she did not bring it about even in part through proper moral behavior, whereas we *do* deny that she has knowledge if she did not bring about that state through behavior that is proper according to the criteria of the particular theory.

It would be interesting to speculate on the significance, if any, of the fact that the structural similarity between normative epistemology and ethics breaks down at the concept of knowledge, but at this point I will return to an examination of the definition itself so that we can see how it can be tested and applied.

2.2 *High-grade and low-grade knowledge*

The definition of knowledge I have given is fairly rigorous. It requires the knower to have an intellectually virtuous motivation in the disposition to desire truth, and this disposition must give rise to conscious and voluntary acts in the process leading up to the acquisition of true belief (or cognitive contact with reality), and the knower must successfully reach the truth through the operation of this motivation and those acts. Such a definition has an advantage on the high end of knowledge, but a disadvantage on the low end. Let us look at both sides of the matter.

In Part I I identified a number of problems in contemporary epistemology, some of which favor a stricter definition of knowledge than that currently in vogue. Because the examples often used as paradigms of knowledge are on the low end of the scale, little effort is made to distinguish between, say, a person who has real understanding of her environment and one who merely knows that the room she is in has four walls. The neglect of the concept of understanding is one of the problems in contemporary epistemology that I believe a virtue approach can remedy. It is likely that understanding is the sort of state that cannot be reached merely through reliable truth-producing processes or properly functioning faculties, or doing one's epistemic duty or following epistemic rules. On the other hand, cultivating and exercising the intellectual virtues are the best we can do voluntarily to obtain understanding and, ultimately, wisdom. No doubt some virtues in particular are more critical than others in leading us to high-level states of knowledge that include understanding or wisdom, and I realize that I have not gone through enough instances of intellectual virtues and their applications to provide a good sense of the process whereby acts of virtue lead to these high-grade epistemic states. But given what we have said, it is reasonable to expect that the virtues of insightfulness and the various "synthetic" virtues – those that enable us to see patterns or simple structures in sets of data or items of experience – are more closely associated with producing understanding and wisdom than are the more commonplace virtues of intellectual attentiveness, carefulness, and perseverance. The quotation from Isaiah Berlin in Part I called our attention to a line from Archilochus: "The fox knows many things, but the hedgehog knows one big thing." To explain how knowing one big thing is produced by acts of intellectual virtue rather than by alternative belief-forming mechanisms would require a long and careful account, perhaps taking us through many examples of obvious high-grade knowledge gleaned from biographies of stellar thinkers or from literature. This is a valuable project, one to which I hope to turn at a later time, and one in which I hope others will be tempted to participate. So while my account of high-grade knowledge must be regarded as programmatic, I think it is sufficient to indicate that a virtue theory has an advantage over other theories in this respect.

The present obsession with justification and the neglect of understanding has resulted in a feature of epistemology already criticized by several epistemologists: its atomism. A true virtue epistemology permits a wider range of epistemic evaluation than that which focuses exclusively on properties of individual belief states. At the same time, we have seen that the most important of those properties of beliefs can be well handled within such a theory, so it is not necessary to forgo the standard concerns with defining justified belief and knowledge in a virtue theory. Plausible definitions of knowledge and justified belief can be generated, but without precluding the investigation of other evaluative concepts suggested by an analysis of intellectual character.

The definition of knowledge proposed in 2.1 has another advantage promised in Part I. In the section outlining the benefits of virtue theories (1.2) I discussed the higher-order virtue of cognitive integration. A person who is cognitively integrated has positive higher-order attitudes toward her own intellectual character and the quality of her epistemic states. Not only does she know, but she is in a position to know that she knows. In addition, her belief structure is coherent, and she is aware of its coherence. Further, she has a sense of the relative value of the different truths or aspects of reality to which she is related. She has, in short, a good intellectual character. My definition of knowledge is closely connected with having a good intellectual character. Although it does not require that to know p one knows that one knows p (an advantage), it nonetheless defines knowledge in such a way that the knower is in a good position to find out that she has knowledge when she has it, and that also is an advantage. What's more, a knower according to my definition is in a good position to evaluate her own belief structure for coherence, and as long as she has multiple intellectual virtues, including the virtue of *phronesis*, she is also in a good position to determine the relative value of her individual items of knowledge, as well as the status of her knowledge taken as a whole. All of these are advantages of a definition of knowledge based on intellectual virtue.

An objector might claim that the fact that belief-based theories of knowledge do not link it with understanding and wisdom, cognitive integration and coherence, and the knower's intellectual character is not a problem for these theories, because each of these epistemic values is distinct from the concept of knowledge. To this I answer that even though it would be too much to insist that a theory of knowledge include all of these other epistemic values, it is definitely an advantage of a theory if it can do so. It is an important theoretical aim to unify the phenomena to be explained in any given branch of theoretical inquiry. It is a virtue in a definition of knowledge, then, if it permits a natural extension to the definitions of understanding, wisdom, cognitive integration, and other higher-order epistemic values. The approach to defining knowledge I have used has such a theoretical advantage.

There is a very natural and obvious way to extend the definition of knowledge as I have proposed it to capture the essence of a higher epistemic state than mere knowledge. I have defined an act of intellectual virtue in such a way that to perform such an act it is not necessary that one actually possess the virtue in question. That is, it is not necessary that to perform an act of, say, intellectual courage one have the entrenched habit that courage requires. And the parallel point can be made for each of the other intellectual virtues. Acts of virtue *V* require the possession of the motivational component of *V* and that one act the way a person with *V* would or might act in the same circumstances, but the agent need not actually possess *V*. This is important because intellectual virtue probably requires some time to develop and mature in an agent, and yet it is likely that such agents can have knowledge long before they are fully virtuous. This naturally leads to the question of how to describe the state of an agent who not only satisfies the definition of knowledge in particular cases but has reached the point of actually possessing the various intellectual virtues. The full possession of intellectual virtue, as opposed to merely being capable from time to time of performing *acts* of intellectual virtue, is surely a superior epistemic state. What should we say about such a state?

Ancient Greek philosophy made more valuational distinctions among epistemic states than we do today. As noted in Part I, this causes some problems for us because it is difficult to know what the target concept is when we address the problem of knowledge. Is knowledge the highest epistemic state or just a very good and important state that is accessible to most people most of the time? The very strong presumption in the present era is that it is closer to the latter than to the former. If so, there may be a gap at the high end of epistemic value. Now I have no position on whether high-grade knowledge is the highest epistemic state, or whether that state ought to be honored by a different name. My point is that an epistemic state that satisfies my definition of knowledge and that also includes the condition that the agent is virtuous is a state that is clearly higher than that which minimally satisfies the definition of knowledge, and hence, it is either a state of high-grade knowledge or a state that deserves its own designation as an epistemic state higher than knowledge. The investigation of the nature of such a state ought to be useful, interesting, and perhaps important. I do not know whether we have a common name for it, but it is something towards which we ought to aspire. In fact, our aspiration to such a state follows automatically from the account of virtue I have given.

Knowledge as I have defined it fares well on the high end of the scale. But what should we say about the low end? In Part I I mentioned beliefs formed in a subpersonal way. This category would include perceptual beliefs and simple short-term memory beliefs. Our definition of knowledge may appear to eliminate beliefs in these categories from the category of knowledge, even when they are true and are formed in the usual way without any defects in the believer or glitches in the environment. Such beliefs not only are typically considered cases of knowledge but may even be offered as paradigm cases. Do these beliefs pose a problem for my theory?

We have already seen that the rigorist tradition in epistemology has been the dominant view. This was often attended by the position that there is no sense knowledge. A multitude of philosophers have thought that what we typically fancy to be objects of knowledge are really illusions, and a common object of attack was the objects of sense perception. A good example of this is the following remark by Aquinas, who not only excludes apprehension by the senses from the realm of knowledge but also claims that such apprehension is not governed by virtues:

> Nevertheless, even if there be habits in such powers [the senses], they cannot be called virtues. For virtue is a perfect habit, by which it never happens that anything but good is done; and so virtue must be in that power which brings the good act to completion. But the knowledge of truth is not consummated in the sensitive powers of apprehension, for such powers prepare the way to the intellectual knowledge. And therefore in these powers there are none of the virtues by which we know truth; these are rather in the intellect or reason. (*ST* I-II, q. 56, a. 5, obj. 3)

To take a completely different sort of philosopher, Francis Bacon warned of the illusions of the senses (Idols of the Tribe), as we saw in Part II (3.2). Bacon stressed the need for a subtle and disciplined use of the intellect in gaining knowledge and was suspicious of the facile derivation of beliefs from sense experience. This may be surprising to those who think of Bacon as not only the other father of modern philosophy, besides Descartes, but also the father of modern empiricism. Tiles and Tiles (1993) maintain that Bacon and Plato have different versions of the same claim about the illusions of the senses. This is not to say that contemporary philosophers are unaware of sensory illusion, but it is worth remarking that a long list of philosophers have been unwilling, or at least hesitant, to ascribe knowledge to states that engage the senses without significant contribution from the intellect. This is not to deny that there can be simple beliefs based on perception, such as "This is a white piece of paper," which are good enough to be states of knowing, but the dominant view in philosophical history has been that such states are states of knowledge only if they are based on *more* than sensory data.

It is important to see that worries about the relation between sense experience and knowledge need not be based on a *skepticism* about the senses. Even philosophers who are neither skeptical nor suspicious of the senses may withhold many perceptual beliefs from the category of knowledge, not because there is anything *wrong* with such beliefs, but because they simply are not good enough to qualify for the honor of being designated as knowledge. That is, there need not be an assumption that there is anything illusory or even misleading about the senses in the position that such beliefs do not qualify as knowledge. I alluded to this argument in Part I when I pointed out that sensory beliefs are subpersonal or even subhuman (4.2). Given that many such beliefs are formed in an unconscious manner without the agency of the agent, I argued that it is peculiar to think of them as paradigms of rationality or justifiability, as they are commonly treated these days. Rationality, after all, has traditionally been understood as that property which makes us most distinctively human. While there are no doubt other aspects of human nature that are also distinctive (e.g., human emotions), the ability to perceive white is not one of them. So if knowledge is associated with rationality and rationality with powers that are not shared with other animals, then the simpler the belief and the closer it is to bare perceptual data, the less likely it is to be a good candidate for knowledge – certainly not as a *paradigm* case of knowledge.[7]

In spite of the reservations arising from historical precedent, it is clear that the vast majority of contemporary philosophers do not hesitate to think of a multitude of perceptual beliefs as cases of knowledge. So even though I think it a mistake to consider such cases paradigms, it would nonetheless be a disadvantage of my theory if it had the consequence that such perceptual beliefs as "That is a white wall" were excluded from the category of knowledge. An obvious feature of these beliefs favoring their inclusion is that they fare well on the criterion of certainty. Compared to the high-grade beliefs in the sciences, philosophy, or the arts, the best perceptual beliefs are generally regarded as high on the scale of certainty, even if low on the scale of cognitive value. So I assume that we want an account of knowledge according to which true beliefs in normal circumstances based on unreflective perception, memory, or introspection qualify as knowledge. Does my definition include these cases?

The answer depends, of course, upon what it takes to perform an act of intellectual virtue. Recall that on my definition of an act of virtue, it is not necessary that the agent actually possess the virtue. But she must be virtuously motivated, she must act the way a virtuous person would characteristically act in the same circumstances, and she must be successful because of these features of her act. What she may lack is the entrenched habit that allows her to be generally reliable in bringing about the virtuous end. This definition permits those persons who do not yet fully possess a virtue but are virtuous-in-training to perform acts of the virtue in question.

How does a person of intellectual virtue act when it comes to forming beliefs based on sense experience or memory? Presumably, she is *sometimes* skeptical of her own senses, and she *sometimes* doubts her own memory, as in the case when it is weak and

---

[7] Compare the distinction between animal knowledge and reflective knowledge made by Ernest Sosa (forthcoming): "Animal knowledge requires only that the belief reflect the impact of its subject matter through the operation of a faculty or virtue. For reflective knowledge one not only must believe out of virtue. One must also be aware of doing so."

she has good contrary evidence. She probably does not doubt such introspective beliefs as that she is in pain, although we might expect her to consider from time to time if and why such introspection is trustworthy. But we would assume that most of the time she does not doubt or even reflectively consider her perceptual and memory beliefs. She does not because she maintains a presumption of truth in such cases until she is given reason to think otherwise. Such an attitude is itself an intellectually virtuous one; to act otherwise is to exhibit a form of intellectual paranoia. So this might give us reason to think that even young children can perform acts of intellectual virtue before they are old enough to acquire the intellectual virtues. As long as they are old enough to imitate the behavior of intellectually virtuous persons in their belief-forming processes, young children (and possibly animals) can have knowledge based on perception and memory. Their behavior is no different from that of the intellectually virtuous, and there may not even be any discernible difference in their motives.

We must admit that there is a difference in their behavior in counterfactual circumstances, however. Small children and animals do not doubt when it is not virtuous to do so, but they do not doubt when it *is* virtuous to do so either. This consideration would favor a compromise position on sense knowledge. True sensory beliefs count as knowledge in normal circumstances because intellectually virtuous persons who have these beliefs do what intellectually virtuous persons do in these cases, which does not require them to exert themselves, but they *would* exert themselves if the circumstances warranted it.[8] This gives us a view of perceptual and memory beliefs that sees them as low-grade knowledge as long as they satisfy certain conditions. Take the

---

[8] Ernest Sosa (forthcoming) expresses a similar view: "No human blessed with reason has *merely* animal knowledge. For even when perceptual belief derives as directly as it ever does from sensory stimuli, it is still relevant that one *lacks* contrary testimony. People automatically monitor their background information and sensory input for contrary evidence and normally opt for coherent hypotheses even when responding most directly to sensory stimuli. For even when response to stimuli is most direct, credible contrary testimony *would* change one's responses."

belief "This is a white piece of paper," which we will assume is formed under normal perceptual conditions and is true. To count as knowledge, this belief must arise in a way that imitates the way it arises in a person with intellectual virtue. The believer must have an intellectually virtuous motivation consisting of the disposition to desire truth, and the way in which the belief is formed must be the way it would be formed by an intellectually virtuous person in those circumstances. So the believer is not prejudiced, has no axe to grind, is not in the grip of wishful thinking (a great love of white paper?), etc. In addition, the believer's general attitude must be one that would lead her to reflectively consider the evidence should the evidence go against her natural urge to think she is seeing white paper. This approach broadens the concept of an act of intellectual virtue and it broadens the concept of knowledge accordingly. I assume this is an advantage. To other minds it may be a disadvantage because it makes knowledge inclusive of the mundane, the sort of thing Plato thought was unworthy of philosophical concern.

I have mentioned that there is historical precedent for preferring a rigorous notion of knowledge that is hesitant to include sensory beliefs and simple cases of memory beliefs in the category of knowledge. But I have also described a way to loosen the interpretation of my definition of knowledge in a way that allows many of these cases to be designated as knowledge, and this brings the theory in line with contemporary thinking. Let us conclude this section with some considerations on the way we might think about making a choice between these alternatives.

One important aspect of knowledge that I am not discussing in this book is the nature of the objects of knowledge. I mentioned in Part I that there are important issues here that need to be addressed in other works. Since this work is devoted to the examination of normative epistemic concepts, I have said very little about the nonnormative elements in the definition of knowledge. But clearly, the way we handle cases of memory and perception depends in part on the way we understand the objects of memory and perception. The theory of knowledge will look very different if the object of knowledge is a chunk of reality rather than a proposition, and again, it will look very different depending upon our understanding of the relationship between the human mind in particular and such objects. It is not at all obvious that the objects of knowledge, whether they be propositions or reality chunks, are the same for humans as for other animals, extraterrestrial creatures, or God. It is not even clear that the vast differences in conceptual understanding among humans do not lead them to actually perceive different things under identical perceptual circumstances. As William Blake said, "A fool sees not the same tree that a wise man sees."[9] And as for the differences among species, well-known work by Thomas Nagel (1986) has drawn our attention to the anthropomorphism inherent in our assumption that reality just is reality-as-perceived-by-humans.[10]

Therefore, we should not take for granted that beliefs arising from perception put us into cognitive contact with reality in a straightforward and uncontroversial sense. This is not to deny that the way in which the human mind is connected to reality is heavily dependent upon our sensory apparatus. It might even be true that all of our knowledge ultimately depends upon this apparatus, so that any defects in the apparatus are defects in our whole epistemic structure. And conversely, under the antiskeptical assumption that we are not too far off in our beliefs about reality, we must not be too far off in our use of the sensory apparatus that undergirds our belief structure. I have no quarrel with any of this. My point is that it should not be a pretheoretical constraint on a theory of knowledge that there is something privileged about the beliefs in this category, that they enjoy a special status in the pantheon of knowledge. The definition of knowledge I have proposed can be interpreted in a way that includes them, and it can be interpreted in a way that excludes them. The ultimate decision on the way to go on this matter should depend upon work outside the considerations examined in this book. In particular, it may be that perception in even ordinary situations is heavily concept laden, or it may be that empirical studies show

---

[9] William Blake, "Proverbs of Hell," from *The Marriage of Heaven and Hell* (1790–3).

[10] Of course, an important point of Nagel's is his claim that it is also a mistake to identify reality with reality-as-perceived-by-nobody-in-particular.

that adult human perception operates in interestingly different ways from the perceptual processes of children or animals. If so, that would favor a tightening of the concept of knowledge in the perceptual area. On the other hand, the theory of perception on either the empirical or the philosophical side may favor a broader and more generous interpretation of the conditions under which perceptual beliefs are formed virtuously. The approach I am proposing here is compatible with either one.

3 GETTIER PROBLEMS

3.1 The problem for JTB theories

Gettier problems arise when it is only by chance that a justified true belief (JTB) is true.[11] Since the belief might easily have been false in these cases, it is normally concluded that they are not instances of knowledge. The moral drawn in the years since Gettier published his famous paper (1963) is that either JTB is not sufficient for knowledge, in which case knowledge must have an "extra" component in addition to JTB, or else justification must be reconceived to *make it* sufficient for knowledge. In this subsection I will argue that given the common and reasonable assumption that the relation between justification and truth is close but not inviolable, it is not possible for either move to avoid Gettier counterexamples. What's more, it makes no difference if the component of knowledge in addition to true belief is identified as something other than justification, for example, warrant or well-foundedness. I conclude that Gettier problems are inescapable for virtually every analysis of knowledge which maintains that knowledge is true belief plus something else that does not entail truth.

Gettier problems arise for both internalist and externalist notions of justification. According to internalist theories, the grounds for justification are accessible to the consciousness of the believer, and Gettier problems arise when there is nothing wrong with the internally accessible aspects of the cognitive situation, but there is a mishap in something inaccessible to the believer.

[11] A previous version of this section has been published in Zagzebski 1994a.

Since justification does not guarantee truth, it is possible for there to be a break in the connection between justification and truth but for that connection to be regained by chance.

The original **Smith owns a Ford or Brown is in Barcelona** case is an example of this sort. Here we are to imagine that Smith comes to you talking about his new Ford, shows you the car and the bill of sale, and generally gives you lots of evidence that he owns a Ford. Based on the evidence you believe the proposition **Smith owns a Ford,** and from that you infer its disjunction with **Brown is in Barcelona,** where Brown is an acquaintance and you have no reason at all to think he is in Barcelona. It turns out that Smith is lying, owns no Ford, but Brown is by chance in Barcelona. Your belief **Smith owns a Ford or Brown is in Barcelona** is true and justified, but it is hardly the case that you know it.

In this instance the problem arises because in spite of the fact that you have done everything to reach the truth from your point of view and everything that anyone could expect of you, your efforts do not lead you to the truth. It is mere bad luck that you are the unwitting victim of Smith's lies, and only an accident that a procedure that usually leads you to the truth leads you to believe the falsehood: **Smith owns a Ford.** The fact that you end up with a true belief anyway is due to a second accidental feature of the situation – a feature that has nothing to do with your cognitive activity. What generates the problem is that an accident of bad luck is canceled out by an accident of good luck. The right goal is reached, but only by chance.

Internalist theories are not the only ones afflicted with Gettier problems, contrary to a recent claim made by Alvin Plantinga (1993b, p. 36). Consider how the problem arises for reliabilism. In this group of theories a believer is justified when her belief is formed in a reliable, or truth-conducive, manner, but there is no guarantee that justified beliefs are true, and a breakdown in the connection between a reliable belief-forming process and the truth is possible. When that happens, even if you manage to hit on the truth anyway, you do not have knowledge.

The well-known fake barn case can be described as an example of this sort. Here we are to imagine that you are driving through a region in which, unknown to you, the inhabitants have erected three barn facades for each real barn in an effort to make themselves look more prosperous. Your eyesight is normal and reliable enough in ordinary circumstances to spot a barn from the road. But in this case the fake barns are indistinguishable from the real barns at such a distance. As you look at a real barn you form the belief **That's a fine barn.** The belief is true and justified but is not knowledge.

In this case also the problem arises because of the combination of two accidental features of the cognitive situation. It is only an accident that visual faculties normally reliable in this sort of situation are not reliable in this particular situation; and it is another accident that you happened to be looking at a real barn and hit on the truth anyway. Again the problem arises because an accident of bad luck is canceled out by an accident of good luck.

Gettier problems cannot be avoided by Plantinga's recent theory either. Plantinga calls the property that in sufficient quantity converts true belief into knowledge "warrant" rather than "justification." On his proposal warrant is the property a belief B has for believer S when B is produced in S by S's faculties working properly in the appropriate environment, according to a design plan successfully aimed at truth (1993b, chap. 1).[12] But Plantinga does not maintain that every warranted belief is true any more than reliabilists maintain that every reliably formed belief is true or internalists maintain that every internally justified belief is true. This feature allows us to form a Gettier case for Plantinga's theory parallel to the other two cases we have considered. To do so we look for a situation in which a person's faculties are working the way they were designed in the appropriate environment, but she unluckily has a false belief. We can then add a second accident that makes the belief true after all.

Suppose that Mary has very good eyesight, but it is not perfect. It is good enough to allow her to identify her husband sitting in his usual chair in the living room from a distance of fifteen feet in somewhat dim light (the degree of dimness can easily be specified). She has made such an identification in these circumstances

---

[12] A very similar wording can be found in Plantinga 1988. In that paper he calls "positive epistemic status" what he now calls "warrant."

many times. Each time her faculties have been working properly and the environment has been appropriate for the faculties. There is nothing at all unusual about either her faculties or the environment in these cases. Of course, her faculties may not be functioning perfectly, but they are functioning well enough that if she goes on to form the belief **My husband is sitting in the living room,** that belief has enough warrant to constitute knowledge when true and we can assume that it is almost always true.

The belief is *almost* always true, we say. That is because warrant in the degree necessary for knowledge does not guarantee truth, according to Plantinga. If it *did* guarantee truth, of course, the component of truth in the analysis of knowledge would be superfluous; knowledge would simply be warranted belief. So it is possible for Mary to make a mistake even though her faculties are functioning properly enough for knowledge and the environment is normal for the faculties. Let us look at one such case.

Suppose Mary simply misidentifies the chair sitter, who is, we'll suppose, her husband's brother, who looks very much like him. Her faculties may be working as well as they normally do when the belief is true and when we do not hesitate to say it is warranted in a degree sufficient for knowledge. It is not a question of their suddenly becoming defective or, at any rate, more defective than usual, nor is there a mismatch between her faculties and the environment. No one is trying to surprise or fool her or anything like that. Her husband and his brother may not even know she is in the house, so the normal environment has not been doctored as it is in the fake barn case. Mary does exactly what she has done hundreds of times before. So her degree of warrant is as high as it usually is when she correctly identifies her husband because even in those cases it is true that she *might* have misidentified the chair sitter if it had been her husband's brother instead. Of course, she usually has no reason to suspect that it *is* her husband's brother, and we can imagine that she has no reason to suspect so in this case either. Although she knows that her brother-in-law looks a lot like her husband, we can suppose that she has no reason to believe that he is in the vicinity and that, in fact, she has strong reason to believe he has gone to Australia. So in the case we are considering, when Mary forms the false belief, her belief is as warranted as her beliefs normally are in these circumstances. In spite of well-functioning faculties and a benign environment, she just makes a mistake.[13]

Now, of course, *something* has gone wrong here, and that something is probably in Mary rather than in the environment. It may even be correct to say that there is a minor defect in her faculties; perhaps she is not perfectly attentive or she is a little too hasty in forming her belief. But she is no less attentive and no more hasty than she usually is in such cases, and usually it does not matter. People do not have to be perfectly attentive and perfectly cautious and have perfect vision to have beliefs sufficiently warranted for knowledge on Plantinga's theory. And this is not a *mistake* in Plantinga's theory. It would surely be unreasonable of him to expect perfectly functioning faculties in a perfectly attuned environment as his criteria for the warrant needed for knowledge. So Mary's defect need not be sufficient to bring her degree of warrant down below that needed for knowledge on Plantinga's account.

We can now easily amend the case as a Gettier example. Mary's husband could be sitting on the other side of the room, unseen by her. In that case her belief **My husband is sitting in the living room** is true and has sufficient warrant for knowledge on Plantinga's account, but she does not have knowledge.

In discussing Gettier problems Plantinga concludes: "What is essential to Gettier situations is the production of a true belief despite a relatively minor failure of the cognitive situation to match its design" (1988, p. 43). But this comment is problematic on his own account. As we have seen, Plantinga considers warrant a property that admits of degree, but it is clear that the degree of warrant sufficient for knowledge does not require faculties to be working perfectly in an environment perfectly matched to them. In Gettier-style cases such as the case of Mary, either the degree of warrant is sufficient for knowledge or it is not. If it is

---

13 This case has been slightly redescribed after correspondence with Alvin Plantinga showed me that the example had to be filled out more to be convincing. But Plantinga has said in conversation that he is not opposed to the position that warrant in the degree sufficient for knowledge entails truth. If so, his definition of knowledge contains a redundant element.

not, then a multitude of beliefs we normally think are warranted are not, and there is much less knowledge in the world than Plantinga's numerous examples suggest. On the other hand, if the degree of warrant *is* sufficient for knowledge, then Plantinga's theory faces Gettier problems structurally identical to those of the other theories. Furthermore, even if some aspect of the Mary example makes it unpersuasive, there must still be cases of warranted false belief on Plantinga's theory if the component of truth in knowledge is not redundant. With such a case in hand a Gettier example can be generated by adding a feature extraneous to the warrrant of the believer that makes the belief true after all. In such a case the degree of warrant is unchanged, but it is not knowledge, because the belief might just as well have been false.

It is not enough, then, to say that Gettier problems arise because of a minor mismatch between faculties and environment. What Plantinga should have said is that the problem is due to a relatively minor failure of the cognitive situation to connect to the truth. Adding the design feature does not solve the problem. As long as the property that putatively converts true belief into knowledge is analyzed in such a way that it is strongly linked with the truth but does not guarantee it, it will always be possible to devise cases in which the link between such a property and the truth is broken but regained by accident. Thus, Gettier counterexamples can always be generated.

The three examples we have considered suggest a general recipe for producing Gettier cases. It really does not matter how the *particular* element of knowledge in addition to true belief is analyzed. As long as there is a small degree of independence between this other element and the truth, we can construct Gettier cases by using the following procedure: Start with a case of justified (or warranted) false belief. Make the element of justification (warrant) strong enough for knowledge, but make the belief false. The falsity of the belief will not be due to any systematically describable element in the situation, for if it were, such a feature could be used in the analysis of the components of knowledge other than true belief, and then truth would be entailed by the other components of knowledge, contrary to the hypothesis. The falsity of the belief is therefore due to some element of luck. Now amend the case by adding another element of luck, only this time an element that makes the belief true after all. The second element must be independent of the element of warrant so that the degree of warrant is unchanged. The situation might be described as one element of luck counteracting another. We now have a case in which the belief is justified (warranted) in a sense strong enough for knowledge, the belief is true, but it is not knowledge. The conclusion is that as long as the concept of knowledge closely connects the justification component and the truth component but permits *some* degree of independence between them, JTB will never be sufficient for knowledge.

It is often observed that in typical Gettier cases the justified belief depends upon or otherwise "goes through" a false belief, so a way to handle these cases is to add what are commonly called "defeasibility conditions" to the analysis of knowledge. This move was especially popular during the sixties and seventies. It adds to the requirement that knowledge be JTB the restriction that the belief in question must also be justified in certain counterfactual situations. One way to define these conditions is in terms of the psychological effect on the subject, as in Steven Levy's definition of a defeasibility condition as "a requirement to the effect that for S to know that p there must be no other evidence against p strong enough to undermine S's belief that p, should this evidence come to S's attention" (1977, p. 115).

The three cases I have just described do have the feature that there is a false belief in the neighborhood of the belief in question that is such that should the subject discover its falsehood, it would undermine her belief in the proposition in question. So your belief that either Smith owns a Ford or Brown is in Barcelona is undermined if you discover that Smith does not own a Ford. Your belief that this is a barn is undermined if you discover that most objects that look like barns in this vicinity are not real barns. Mary's belief that her husband is sitting in the living room is undermined if she discovers that that man sitting over *there* in a particular chair is not her husband. In each case were the subject to be advised of the falsity of the underlying belief, she would retract the belief under discussion. The belief would be defeated by such new information.

Notice that this move puts a strain on the independence of the justification/defeasibility condition and the truth condition. If S's belief p is false, there will obviously be many other propositions that are logically or evidentially connected to p that are false also. Should S become aware of the falsity of any of these propositions, that would presumably undermine S's belief p, assuming S is rational. This means that the falsehood of p is incompatible with a strong defeasibility condition, contrary to the hypothesis that the justification and defeasibility components of knowledge do not entail the truth condition. This problem is even more apparent in statements of the defeasibility condition in terms of evidential support rather than a psychological requirement, as in Pappas and Swain's definition: "the evidence e must be sufficiently complete that no further additions to e would result in a loss of justification and hence a loss of knowledge" (1978, p. 27). Obviously, if the belief is *false*, further additions to e will result in a loss of justification, and hence a loss of knowledge. Undefeat*able* justified belief is immune to Gettier problems, but that is because undefeatability entails truth.

Strong defeasibility conditions, then, threaten the assumption of independence between the justification (warrant) condition and the truth condition for knowledge. But weaker defeasibility conditions are subject to Gettier-style counterexamples following the recipe described above. In each case we find an example of a false belief that satisfies the justification and defeasibility conditions and then make the belief true anyway due to features of the situation independent of the satisfaction of those conditions.

Suppose Dr. Jones, a physician, has very good inductive evidence that her patient, Smith, is suffering from virus X. Smith exhibits all of the symptoms of this virus, and a blood test has shown that his antibody levels against virus X are extremely high. In addition, let us suppose that the symptoms are not compatible with any other known virus, all of the evidence upon which Jones bases her diagnosis is true, and there is no evidence accessible to her that counts significantly against the conclusion. The proposition that Smith is suffering from virus X really is extremely probable on the evidence.

In this case there is nothing defective in the justification of Dr.

Jones's belief that Smith has virus X, and no false belief figures causally or evidentially into her justification, nor is there any false belief in the neighborhood. Furthermore, she would have believed that Smith had virus X in a wide range of counterfactual situations. Nonetheless, let us suppose that the belief is false. Smith's symptoms are due to a distinct and unknown virus Y, and the fact that he exhibits high antibody levels to virus X is due to idiosyncratic features of his biochemistry that cause him to maintain unusually high antibody levels long after a past infection. In this case Dr. Jones's belief that Smith is presently suffering from virus X is false, but it is both justified and undefeated. Of course, given that the belief is false, there must be *some* evidence against it accessible to her in some counterfactual circumstances, so if defeasibility conditions are strong enough, no false empirical belief passes the test. But as said above, that is to impose an unreasonably strong defeasibility condition, one that makes the justification/defeasibility condition entail truth. The most reasonable conclusion to draw in this case, then, is that Jones's belief is justified and undefeated but false.

Now to construct a Gettier-style example we simply add the feature that Smith has very recently contracted virus X, but so recently that he does not yet exhibit symptoms caused by X, nor has there been time for a change in the antibody levels due to this recent infection. So although the evidence upon which Dr. Jones bases her diagnosis does make it highly probable that Smith has X, the fact that Smith has X has nothing to do with that evidence. In this case, then, Dr. Jones's belief that Smith has virus X is true, justified, and undefeated, but it is not knowledge.[14]

It appears, then, that no account of knowledge as true belief plus something else can withstand Gettier objections as long as there is a small degree of independence between truth and the other conditions of knowledge. What are the alternatives? We have already seen that one way to solve the problem is to give up

---

[14] Charles Young has pointed out to me that Gettier cases can generate cases of moral luck. If Dr. Jones has the Gettier belief that Smith has virus X and he does, then if she gives the right treatment, she is just lucky in her success. And, of course, her treatment may have ethical implications. In general, if you act on a Gettier belief, you act rightly only as a matter of luck.

the independence between the justification condition and the truth condition. Justification would be defined in such a way that no false belief can satisfy it. Because Gettier cases are based on situations in which the belief is true but might just as well have been false, all such cases would be excluded from the class of justified (warranted) beliefs. On this approach the element of truth in the account of knowledge is superfluous, and knowledge is simply justified (warranted) belief. *S* **is justified in believing** *p* entails *p*. Not many philosophers have supported this view.[15]

So Gettier problems can be avoided if there is no degree of independence at all between truth and justification. A second way to avoid them is to go to the opposite extreme and to make the justification condition and the truth condition almost completely independent. It could still be the case that justification puts the subject in the best position available for getting the truth, but if the best position is not very good, most justified beliefs will be false. Perhaps most justified scientific hypotheses since the world began have been false. Perhaps Plato, Spinoza, Kant, and Hegel were justified in believing their metaphysical theories, but most of their theories (at least) were false. However, if one of them is true, some theorists might be willing to call it knowledge. On this approach the element of luck permitted in the state of knowledge is so great that alleged counterexamples based on luck do not count against it. From this viewpoint, Gettier cases would simply be accepted as cases of knowledge. You really *do* know that Smith owns a Ford or Brown is in Barcelona; you know that that is a fine barn; Mary knows that her husband is in the living room, etc. The idea here is that if knowledge is mostly luck anyway, there will be nothing bothersome about a case in which the

---

15 Robert Almeder (1992) argues that no belief sufficiently justified for knowledge can be false, but his reasons are completely different from the reasons I have given here. John Pollock (1986, pp. 183–90) defines what he calls "objective justification" in such a way that a belief is objectively justified only if it is ultimately undefeated, and no false belief can be ultimately undefeated. Similarly, Keith Lehrer (Clay and Lehrer 1989, p. 152) defines what he calls "undefeated justified acceptance" in such a way that it entails truth, and he goes on to define knowledge as undefeated justified acceptance. See also Trenton Merricks (1995).

truth is acquired by luck. And if so, Gettier cases are not puzzles. This response may not count as a solution to Gettier cases because it amounts to simply refusing to treat them as problems. I assume that this will not be a popular approach, and so I conclude that the moral of the story is that the truth condition for knowledge must be entailed by the other conditions.

Almost every contemporary theory of knowledge analyzes knowledge as true belief that is justified or warranted, and although justification or warrant puts the believer in the best position for getting the truth, the best position is assumed to be imperfect, for such is life. Properly functioning faculties need not be working perfectly, but only well enough; reliable belief-producing mechanisms need not be perfectly reliable, only reliable enough; evidence for a belief need not support it conclusively, but only well enough, and so on. And it is important to see that the fact that justification is not a perfect guarantor of truth is faithful to the preanalytic notion of justification. It is not, then, a *mistake* in the analysis of justification or warrant to leave open the possibility of a false justified/warranted belief. But given the fact that the argument of this subsection shows that the conditions for knowledge in addition to true belief must entail truth, it follows that JTB accounts of knowledge are in a bind. The definition of knowledge must make truth implied by the other component(s) of knowledge, but it must do so in a way that is plausible and is not ad hoc. In the next subsection we will look at how a virtue-based definition of knowledge can satisfy these requirements.

3.2 Resolving Gettier problems in a virtue theory

Let us now look at how our definition of knowledge in 2.1 handles Gettier problems. Many of the examples we considered in 3.1 could be described as instances in which believers have and exhibit intellectual virtue in the process of belief formation, their beliefs are justified by the definition I gave in Part II, and yet they hit upon the truth only by accident. Mary may have the intellectual virtues of carefulness and reasonable attentiveness. At least she does not seem to be especially careless or inattentive, nor are there any other intellectual vices that emerge from the description of her cognitive activity. Dr. Jones even more obviously exhibits intellectual virtues. She is excellent at medical diagnosis, we may assume, and so she has all the intellectual virtues a good doctor must have. She is attentive, careful, thorough, good at thinking up explanations for complex sets of data, etc. She has a true belief and the belief arises out of intellectual virtues. Still, she lacks knowledge. She is the victim of epistemic luck.

In order to see how Gettier problems can be avoided on the definition of knowledge I have given, let us examine the moral analogue of Gettier cases: instances in which a person acts out of moral virtues and has no operative moral vices but is morally successful only by accident. What I will do is to construct an ethical example that follows the directions for generating Gettier cases outlined in 3.1. I will start with a situation in which a person does what is right but fails in the end of the virtue through no fault of his own. This would be analogous to a justified false belief. The act fails by accident. We will then add a second accidental feature of the situation that cancels out the first, so the act successfuly reaches the desired end after all. This would be analogous to a Gettier case in which the truth is reached by a second accident that cancels out the effect of the justified false belief.

Suppose an Italian judge, weighing the evidence against an accused Mafia killer, determines by an impeccable procedure, motivated by justice and using an abundance of practical wisdom, that the man is guilty. The judge exhibits the virtues of justice and practical wisdom, and perhaps courage as well since he is undeterred by fear of Mafia reprisals. Nonetheless, let us suppose that the judge makes a mistake; the accused is the wrong man. The fact that the judge makes a mistake is not due to any defect in the judge, whether moral or intellectual; it is simply bad luck. Obviously, things have gone wrong and that is too bad, and if the judge found out later that he made a mistake, he would greatly regret it. Other persons would not actually blame the judge for the error, but they would not praise him either. That is, they would not give him the praise that would have been due him if he had made no mistake. The judge then suffers from bad moral luck in Nagel's sense. He may have exhibited numerous virtues in his act, including the virtue of justice, but we would not call the act *an act of justice.* Furthermore, it does not help to distinguish between the evaluation of the agent and the evaluation of the act because the act's lack of success leads to withholding a certain sort of moral praise from the agent. As we saw in Part II, we do not call an act an act *of* virtue unless it succeeds in reaching the internal or external aim of the virtue *in the particular case* through the operation of the features of the act that make the agent praiseworthy for doing it. The judge is just; he may even exhibit justice in his decision; we may even say that he acts justly; but the decision itself is not an act of justice.

As we have seen, the procedure for generating Gettier cases involves "double luck": an instance of good luck cancels out an instance of bad luck. We can use the same procedure in the moral case. Suppose that the actual killer is secretly switched with the man the judge thought he was sentencing so that the judge ends up accidentally sentencing the right man. One error cancels out the other; the right man is sentenced, but it is only accidental that the wrong man is not sentenced instead. In this case we may breathe a sigh of relief for the innocent man who barely escaped punishment, but our judgment of the judge is hardly better than in the former case, the one in which the judge makes the mistake. Again, it would be going too far to blame him, and it is possible our judgment would be somewhat less negative than it would be in the case in which the wrong man is punished. Nonetheless, the judge lacks the level of moral honor that would have been due him if he had been judging the right man in the first place. Once he found out what happened, he would not consider this case one of his great achievements, and even if he exhibited an impressive degree of virtue in hearing the case and rendering a verdict, no one would think to praise him for the decision, and I suggest that it would be inappropriate to call the decision an act of justice. If my appraisal of this case is right, it suggests that there are Gettier-style cases in ethics. The full achievement of the good of morality, like the achievement of the good of knowledge, requires that the good be reached by the right process, not just in general, but in the particular case. I venture the guess that the reason the epistemic cases are more noticeable than their ethical counterparts is that we are very demanding about the state of knowledge, requiring that everything work perfectly, both inside the agent's head and in his cognitive hookup with reality. For whatever reason, we are somewhat more forgiving when it comes to morally correct behavior, perhaps because an elaborate system of rewards and punishments is often involved. Nonetheless, I argued in Part II (6.2) that even in ethics there are good reasons for wanting to call attention to a category of acts that gets everything right, both in the agent's head and in his hookup with the moral reality he is trying to produce, and I called these acts "acts of virtue."

The distinction between exhibiting virtue and performing an act *of* virtue can help us resolve Gettier-style cases in a virtue theory. An act of virtue is virtuously motivated, is an act that a virtuous person is apt to do in the circumstances, and successfully leads to the ends of the virtue in question through the operation of these features of the act. The production of the goods that the virtuously motivated person aims to produce enhances the moral merit of the agent, and the production of evils that the virtuously motivated person aims to prevent detracts from the agent's merit, in spite of the fact that the level of the agent's virtue may be no different from what it is in the case in which his acts are morally successful. As we have said, this is because the aim of the moral life is not merely to *be* virtuous but to bring about the goods at which virtue aims by way of the sort of actions that usually result from virtue.

Gettier problems in virtue epistemology can be resolved by an analogous move. If we define knowledge simply as true belief exhibiting intellectual virtue, we will be faced with Gettier counterexamples. Consider again Dr. Jones and her diagnosis of Smith's virus. Dr. Jones may have all of the intellectual virtues a doctor can have, as well as any moral virtues that enhance the practice of medicine successfully. She has a true belief, and the belief arises out of intellectual virtue and exhibits such virtue. Nevertheless, her diagnosis is correct only by accident, and most of us hesitate to say that she *knows* Smith has virus X. Certainly, Dr. Jones has intellectual virtue and she exhibits it when she makes her diagnosis; we may even say she acts virtuously. Nonetheless, she does not reach an accurate diagnosis because of her intellectual virtues. She does not reach the truth through *an act of intellectual virtue.*

Similarly, in the case of the belief **Smith owns a Ford or Brown is in Barcelona,** the belief may exhibit intellectual virtue since it is acquired on good evidence and there is no reason to suspect Smith is lying about his new car, but the belief does not arise out of an act of intellectual virtue, because the truth is not acquired through virtuous motives or processes. The truth is not obtained *because of* the virtues. The truth is acquired because by accident Brown is in Barcelona.

Again, in the case of Mary's belief that her husband is in the living room, she may exhibit all the relevant intellectual virtues and no intellectual vices in the process of forming the belief, but she is not led to the truth through those virtuous processes or motives. So even though Mary has the belief she has because of her virtues and the belief is true, she does not have the truth because of her virtues.

The last statement may be puzzling since it might seem to be the case that if Mary has a belief B because of her virtues and B is true, it follows that Mary has the truth because of her virtues. But this inference is invalid. We cannot infer from the fact that M attains something S because of her trait V that she attains every property of S because of trait V. For example, Mary may be able to identify a fleeing figure because of her keen eyesight, and that figure may have a small birthmark on his arm, but it does not follow that she can identify a man with a small birthmark on his arm because of her keen eyesight. Similarly, Mary may be able to reach a certain belief because of her virtuous motives and acts, and the belief may be true, but it does not follow that she has reached the truth because of her virtuous motives and acts. There may be no more connection between her virtues and the belief's property of truth than there is between her keen eyesight and the man's birthmark.

Gettier problems can be avoided if we utilize the concept of an act of intellectual virtue. Acts of intellectual virtue are strictly analogous to acts of moral virtue, as we saw in Part II. An act of moral virtue is morally right in a very strong sense because it has all of the morally desirable characteristics of an act. It is virtuously motivated, it is what a morally virtuous person might do, *and* the external good of the virtue (if any) is successfully achieved through the operation of this motive and the act to which it gives rise. Similarly, an act of intellectual virtue is justified or epistemically right in a very strong sense. It is virtuously motivated, it leads to a belief that is acquired and sustained the way an intellectually virtuous person might do it, *and* the good of truth or cognitive contact with reality is successfully achieved by this motivation and process. Intellectual virtues, like such moral virtues as justice or compassion, include an aim that is partially external. We are ethically interested in success, as well as in the goodness of the heart, and we are particularly interested in there being a connection between these two aspects of ethical value. So we are interested in just motives and in the successful achievement of a just state of affairs through the operation of those motives, and for the same reason, we are interested in intellectually virtuous motives and in the successful achievement of cognitive contact with reality through these motives. We honor the resulting state by calling it "knowledge." That is to say, **knowledge is a state of cognitive contact with reality arising out of acts of intellectual virtue.** This definition of knowledge is immune to Gettier problems.

I concluded from the argument of 3.1 that the way to avoid Gettier problems is to define knowledge in such a way that truth is entailed by the other component(s) of the definition. That is, whatever knowledge is in addition to truth entails truth. My definition builds this entailment into it through the definition of an act of intellectual virtue. Other definitions of knowledge as warranted or justified true belief face a severe difficulty. It is intuitively implausible to interpret them in such a way that the truth condition is redundant. If a belief does not count as reliable unless it is true, this means that a reliable belief is not simply one that arises from a truth-conducive procedure; the procedure would have to be truth guaranteeing. Similarly, in Plantinga's theory, for a warranted belief to guarantee truth, it would have to arise not merely from properly functioning faculties but from perfectly functioning faculties. And in the case of accounts of justification as epistemic duty, a duty would have to be defined in such a way that a person following it cannot go wrong. In each case, it is very implausible to interpret the theory this way, and it is clearly not intended to be interpreted this way by its proponents. Given that whatever knowledge is in addition to truth must guarantee truth, the account of knowledge must explain that fact. Otherwise, the entailment between truth and the other component of knowledge is left completely implausible and mysterious. What we need is an account of knowledge that shows how truth is built into the rest of the components, that is plausible, and that is not ad hoc. My theory does that; the others I know of do not.

4 RELIABILISM

The accounts I have given of knowledge and of justified belief are derived from an account of intellectual virtue, and since intellectual virtue has an element that is at least weakly cognitively accessible (the component of motivation), as well as an element that may be inaccessible (the component of success in reaching the end of the virtuous motivation), my theory combines internalist and externalist elements. It is therefore neither purely externalist nor purely internalist, although it qualifies as externalist by the definition of externalism given by Laurence BonJour in the recent *Blackwell Companion to Epistemology*:

> [A] theory is *internalist* if and only if it requires that all of the factors needed for a belief to be epistemically justified for a given person be *cognitively accessible* to that person, *internal* to his cognitive perspective; and *externalist*, if it allows that at least some of the justifying factors need not be thus accessible, so that they can be *external* to the believer's cognitive perspective, beyond his ken. . . . [The distinction] has also been applied in a closely related way to accounts of knowledge. (P. 132; emphasis in original)

My theory counts as externalist by BonJour's definition, but its hybrid character sets it apart from the more strongly externalist theories in the contemporary literature, notably the popular theory of reliabilism and Plantinga's proper function theory, both of which have lately been labeled "virtue epistemology." In section 4, I will give some objections to a pure form of reliabilism and will then answer anticipated objections to my own theory from the viewpoint of the reliabilist.

4.1 Objections to reliabilism

I will begin with a general argument that any purely externalist theory of knowledge has the unwanted implication that the only thing valuable in an instance of knowledge is the value of the truth that is acquired. I will then turn to an argument that reliabilism does not give sufficient conditions for knowing. Since on my definition of knowledge reliability is entailed by the concept of an act of virtue, it follows that reliabilism does give necessary conditions for knowledge on my theory. This means that one important problem for reliabilism is a problem for my theory as well, and that is the generality problem, which I have already mentioned. One of the things I will do in this section is to explain how I think this problem should be handled.

Externalists often support their position with examples of apparent knowledge in which the element that converts true belief into knowledge is not accessible to the consciousness of the believer, not even in part. I will consider two of these cases as a way of bringing out a general problem in externalist theories that is parallel to an objection to rule utilitarianism.

The first is the chicken sexer case. I have maintained that too much of the debate between externalists and internalists has been driven by examples and counterexamples, and my use of this particular case presents a singular problem for me since I have already claimed that its most significant effect may simply be to call attention to the differences in intuition between internalists and externalists rather than to convince anyone to change her position. But I think the use of this example illustrates something about the way in which pure externalists think of knowledge that is worth investigating.

Let us review the case. Although I have no direct knowledge of the matter, it is apparently very difficult to determine the sex of a baby chick, yet reportedly there are people who are able to do so reliably, even though they themselves are not aware of how they do it, nor can observers find anything in their behavior that looks like a process. These people simply hold up the baby chick and the right answer comes to them – or so it appears. (Frankly, I'm skeptical about this whole thing, but I'll let that pass for the sake of argument.) Richard Foley (1987) says that the chicken sexer may have knowledge, although his belief is not rational. In that book Foley takes an internalist position on rationality but leaves open the possibility of an externalist position on knowledge. If it is thought that the chicken sexer has knowledge, the externalist concludes that it must be because his belief is produced by a reliable belief producing mechanism. The only difference between such a mechanism and other reliable belief-forming processes, such as simple perception, is that it is unusual.

The second case is mentioned by George Mavrodes (1988, pp. 37–8), who describes a person who wakes up in the morning with a firm conviction that there is a God, but without any awareness of the process by which the belief was acquired and without any independent support. As far as she knows, the belief just popped into her head. It could, however, have been implanted by God, who we may presume is reliable in his belief-creating activities. She therefore has knowledge according to the criteria of reliabilism. Now what should we say about these cases?

Virtually all philosophers now and in the past have agreed that knowledge is more than true belief. They have also agreed that knowledge is a more valuable state than true belief. It follows that the value of the knowing state is more than the value of the truth that is thereby possessed. So what knowledge has in addition to true belief has value. Let us now look at the two cases just described.

There is obviously something valuable in the ability that the chicken sexer has. His possession of a mechanism for determining the sex of a chick is a valuable thing. It is valuable because of its tendency to produce beliefs that are true. Its goodness can therefore be compared to the goodness of mechanisms for distributing goods fairly. Such mechanisms are valuable because of their tendency to produce fair (good) states of affairs. Now suppose some mechanism does reliably produce a fair state of affairs. That state of affairs could have been produced accidentally (we'll suppose). Is there anything more valuable in that state of affairs than there would have been if it had been produced accidentally? Surely not. There is, of course, value in the state of affairs itself; that is given. There is also value in the mechanism because, as we have already said, it is valuable to have such a reliable mechanism. However, that state of affairs has no *additional* value because of the fact that it was produced *by* that mechanism. Analogously, there is value in a true belief, whether acquired by guessing or by a reliable belief-producing mechanism or in some other way; there is value in the reliable belief-producing mechanism itself; there is no further value in the fact that some particular true belief was produced *by* the reliable mechanism. Since, as we have seen, whatever it is that converts true belief into knowledge has value, it cannot be the fact that the belief is produced by a reliable belief-producing mechanism, because there is no value in *that* fact at all.

The problem here parallels an objection to the preferability of rule utilitarianism over act utilitarianism. Let us suppose that an act is valuable when it produces good consequences. Rules are also valuable when they are reliable ways of producing good consequences. But, according to the act utilitarian, there is nothing valuable about the fact that some particular act is an instance of a rule the following of which *generally* leads to good consequences. If an act in the particular case has desirable consequences, there is no value added to it by the fact that it follows a rule, even though the rule is a valuable one. And if the act in the particular case does *not* have desirable consequences, it does not acquire value by following the rule.[16]

It follows that it is not sufficient for knowledge that a true belief is produced by a reliable belief-producing mechanism. There is nothing more valuable about that belief state than its truth. The chicken sexer has a valuable belief state insofar as he believes

---

[16] Of course, if the agent performs an act because it is an instance of a rule that generally produces good consequences, calculating that this makes it likely that the act will produce the desired consequence, he may be justified in doing the act even if the act is not right on utilitarian grounds. But that is a different matter.

what is true. He also has a valuable *ability*, because it is valuable to be able to reliably produce something valuable, namely, the truth. But this ability is valuable only in the sense that any means to something valuable is valuable. So the chicken sexer's *ability* is valuable, and the *truth* of his belief state is valuable, but the fact that his belief is produced via this ability does not increase the value of his true belief state. Hence, *if* his true belief state is a state of knowledge, its value must lie in something in addition to the value of the truth and in addition to his reliable mechanism for determining the sex of chicks and in addition to the fact that the truth was obtained in this case by the successful use of such a mechanism.

The same point applies to the case of the person inspired by God to believe some proposition. If a person believes *p* because of a God-given gift of prophecy whose mechanism is completely outside her consciousness and which she is unable to confirm, then if *p* is true, that state is valuable because of the truth of *p*. The prophecy gift is also a valuable thing to have. The fact that it is a reliable means for obtaining a good makes it epistemically valuable. There is, however, no *other* epistemic value in the fact that her true belief was produced *by* the gift of prophecy. That would be analogous to saying that a fair state of affairs is even better because it was produced by a mechanism that *in general* produces fair states of affairs. That is simply not very convincing.

What is valuable over and above the fairness of the state of affairs itself is probably something about the connection between such a state and certain inner states of the agent, such as his motive in producing it and the fact that he acted intentionally. The fact that a fair act arises from moral virtue or some component of moral virtue makes the act a moral achievement of the agent and it gives the production of fair states of affairs a value in addition to their external value. Analogously, the value of knowledge in addition to the value of the truth it acquires must be something analogous to the motives, feelings, and intentions that ground externally good states of affairs. This means the value of knowledge is connected with the components of intellectual virtue already identified. It is in part because knowledge arises out of acts of intellectual virtue that it is an achievement in a way that mere true belief cannot be. The value of the truth obtained by a reliable process in the absence of any conscious awareness of a connection between the behavior of the agent and the truth he thereby acquires is no better than the value of the lucky guess.

Why, then, are these cases so often accepted as examples of knowledge? I surmise that there must be a tendency to transfer the quite obvious value of the reliable mechanism to the product of that mechanism, the belief. This tendency may be natural and understandable, but I do not see that it is justified. In addition, the motive to avoid Gettier problems has led epistemologists to think of knowledge as nonaccidentally true belief, and there is a sense in which beliefs produced by a reliable mechanism obtain their truth nonaccidentally. But surely the moral of Gettier cases is not that just any nonaccidental way of obtaining the truth will merit the honor of being a state of knowledge. Nonaccidentality is necessary for knowledge, and that is demonstrated by Gettier examples, but we have seen no reason either in Gettier problems or elsewhere for thinking that it is sufficient.

Let us now turn to another argument that reliabilism does not give sufficient conditions for knowledge. The attempt to demonstrate this in the literature is usually done by examples, some of which are highly artificial. For instance, Alvin Plantinga invents a case of a person who is zapped by rays from outer space that give him a brain lesion that disrupts his normal cognitive processes but leads to a reliable process for forming beliefs in a very limited area (e.g., the belief that he has a brain lesion) (1993a, p. 199).[17] There are several reasons why we should be dubious of such an example. In the first place, I think that an epistemic theory has the methodological right to take for granted that the theory offers an account of the nature of human knowledge within a normal human environment. Counterexamples based on very abnormal conditions have much weaker force against such a theory than those that arise from normal circumstances, although this is not to say that they have no force at all. But more important, this example has the defect of relying on a very narrow interpretation of the

---

[17] Plantinga offers this example against the "old Goldman" and offers variations on the same example against other versions of reliabilism.

generality problem. Clearly, the brain lesion has the effect of preventing the operation of what would otherwise be reliable belief-forming processes, and only produces a reliable process in the formation of a single belief. A reliabilist could therefore reject the general reliability of the belief-forming process in the case of the belief **I have a brain lesion** because that belief is not produced by a process that produces a large enough set of true beliefs to count as reliable in the sense intended by reliabilists. What is really wrong with the brain lesion is that it interferes with the operation of a *more* reliable process for forming beliefs. We will look at a way to handle the generality problem later in this subsection, but we can conclude that Plantinga is partly right and partly wrong. His example no doubt misses the mark because of its excessively narrow interpretation of what counts as a reliable belief-forming process, but on the other hand, it calls attention to the fact that we shirk from calling an epistemic state knowledge when it arises from processes in which something has clearly gone wrong, whether or not the process is reliable. I believe this insight is important.

To show that reliabilism does not give sufficient conditions for knowledge it is desirable to have examples in which beliefs satisfy reliabilist criteria for knowledge but not other time-honored knowledge criteria. I believe we can find such cases in literature as well as ordinary life. Rather than to resort to such a recherché case as that of being zapped by rays from outer space, I will present a realistic and familiar case and will evaluate it on grounds which appeal not only to intuition but to actual normative epistemic criteria used within the history of philosophy.

The case concerns the unreflective acceptance of the opinion of others. This is a habit that not only is common but has been universally condemned by careful thinkers for millennia. Let us look at Tolstoy's description of Oblonsky in *Anna Karenina:*

> Oblonsky subscribed to and read a liberal paper, not an extreme liberal paper but one that expressed the views held by most people. And although he was not particularly interested in science, art, or politics, on all such subjects he adhered firmly to the views of the majority, as expressed by his paper, and

changed them only when the majority changed theirs; or rather he did not change them – they changed imperceptibly of their own accord.

Oblonsky never chose his tendencies and opinions any more than he chose the style of his hat or frock-coat. He always wore those which happened to be in fashion. Moving in a certain circle where a desire for some form of mental activity was part of maturity, he was obliged to hold views in the same way as he was obliged to wear a hat. If he had a reason for preferring Liberalism to the Conservatism of many in his set, it was not that he considered the liberal outlook more rational, but because it corresponded better with his mode of life. The Liberal Party maintained that everything in Russia was bad; and in truth Oblonsky had many debts and decidedly too little money. The Liberal Party said that marriage was an obsolete institution which ought to be reformed; and indeed family life gave Oblonsky very little pleasure, forcing him to tell lies and dissemble, which was quite contrary to his nature. The Liberal Party said, or rather assumed, that religion was only a curb on the illiterate; and indeed Oblonsky could not stand through even the shortest church service without aching feet, or understand the point of all that dreadful, high-flown talk about the other world, when life in this world was really very pleasant. . . . Thus Liberalism had become a habit with Oblonsky and he enjoyed his newspaper, as he did his afterdinner cigar, for the slight haze it produced in his brain.[18]

Oblonsky's behavior may remind us of the remark by Ralph Waldo Emerson quoted in Part II (4.1). If, as Emerson says, God offers to every mind a choice between truth and repose, Oblonsky has chosen repose, and he does not respect, in Emerson's words, "the highest law of his being." This is not yet a demonstration that Oblonsky does not have knowledge, but it definitely suggests that Oblonsky's epistemic state is deficient, even, perhaps, blameworthy. In this passage we see that Oblonsky has fallen prey to some of Bacon's Idols of the mind, and he violates all three

---

[18] *Anna Karenina,* trans. Rosemary Edmonds (New York: Penguin Books, 1954), pp 18–19.

of the ways Locke says that things can go wrong in the formation of our beliefs, quoted in Part II (end of sec. 3.2). Like the first sort of man Locke describes, Oblonsky seldom thinks for himself but borrows his ideas from others. Like Locke's second sort of man, he puts passion ahead of reason (insofar as he has passion at all) and lets his beliefs be governed by what suits his humor, interest, or political party. Unlike Locke's third sort of man, he does not follow reason, but like the third sort he does converse with only one sort of man and read only one sort of book. Yet in spite of the fact that Oblonsky's belief-forming processes are defective, it is possible that some significant subset of his beliefs are formed reliably. After all, it may be that the Liberal Party *is* generally on the track of the truth, although Oblonsky is in no position to know that. It is even possible that Oblonsky is lucky enough to have a circle of friends who are just the right sort of people from whom to take his beliefs. So the process by which Oblonsky arrives at some significant subset of his beliefs might actually be truth conducive. The important question, however, is whether these beliefs constitute knowledge.

Oblonsky's epistemic status would not fare well under the scrutiny of most philosophers from antiquity, not only Locke. Certainly his beliefs do not satisfy the conditions of Plato's *Meno* of being bound by an explanatory account (98a3). But it is even doubtful that he would satisfy the much looser conditions for knowledge of such lenient thinkers as Thomas Reid. Reid's famous policy of setting up common sense as an authority in epistemic matters was sometimes charged with canonizing "the judgment of the crowd," but such a criticism hardly does justice to the subtlety of Reid's thought. His appeal to common sense was fundamentally a response to philosophical skepticism, and he defended certain judgments that the skeptic would question by appealing to characteristics of these judgments that no crude Oblonskian believer could satisfy.[19] No, the verdict of philosophical history is against the position that Oblonsky has knowledge, no matter who his friends and newspapers are. If reliabilism is to

---

[19] See S. A. Grave's discussion of Reid in the Macmillan *Encyclopedia of Philosophy* (1967), p. 121, for a reading of Reid that supports this interpretation.

convince us that an accidentally reliable Oblonsky has knowledge, the theory is going to have to be presented to us in full awareness that it is an historical oddity.

It is therefore not necessary to construct cases as far from the actual world as those devised by Plantinga to see that reliability can go with bad epistemic procedures. The badness stressed by Plantinga is mechanical: it is a malfunctioning of human faculties closely allied to the malfunctioning of a machine. But other sorts of badness take away knowledge as well, including the badness of thinking like Oblonsky. Of course, if the concept of cognitive malfunction is interpreted broadly enough as covering, in effect, anything that is wrong in human thinking, then Plantinga could claim that Oblonsky's cognitive faculties are malfunctioning. But then there is no content to the concept of malfunction other than "behaving badly," or even "being bad," and as we will see in 4.2, the substantive work involved here is really done by the concept of intellectual vice.

Let us now turn to the generality problem, as promised. Richard Feldman (1985a) has called our attention to the fact that reliabilism is problematically vague as to the degree of generality used in describing the belief-forming process whose reliability is in question. To say that the process by which some particular belief is produced is reliable is to say that the same process leads to true beliefs in relevantly similar circumstances. But since similarity comes in degrees, we have a wide range of choice in determining the class of belief-forming processes that are similar to the one producing the belief in question. So if I read and believe a report in the newspaper on the increase in housing starts this year written by a person knowledgeable about the use of statistics in this area, my belief-forming process could be variously described as the process of believing what I read in the newspaper, the process of believing what I read in a particular newspaper, the process of believing what is written in the newspaper by an authority in the field of the report, the process of believing what is written in the newspaper by an authority who is merely reporting statistics that he is highly qualified to analyze, the process of believing an authority who has no reason to want the truth to be as reported, among many others. Some of these processes are more specific than others, but they do not all form subsets of more general processes. Clearly, the reliability of these different processes varies considerably.

I said earlier that the problem of generality arises with Plantinga's brain lesion counterexample to reliabilism because there are some ways to describe the belief-forming process in his example that make it unreliable. Certainly, a belief formed as the result of a brain lesion is formed by an unreliable process, even though a subsidiary process of forming the belief that the subject has a brain lesion is reliable.[20] The main effect of Plantinga's counterexample, then, may be to highlight the problem of generality in reliabilism rather than to demonstrate that the theory fails to give sufficient conditions for knowledge. So although I have agreed that Plantinga's example shows that we do not want to call a mechanism knowledge producing when its reliability is closely associated with a defect, it should be admitted that the claim that the mechanism in this case is reliable can be disputed by reliabilists on the grounds that Plantinga has improperly generalized the mechanism that is used. But then it is incumbent upon the reliabilist to explain how and why a certain way of generalizing is to be used. The generality problem appears in some of the other examples already mentioned, such as Mavrodes's religious believer and Tolstoy's Oblonsky. It is simply not reliable to believe whatever pops into your head, even though it is reliable to believe whatever God puts into your head. It is not reliable to be a conformist in beliefs, even if Oblonsky's own circle of friends at the moment are reliable. The way to properly generalize these cases is therefore important for a determination of the acceptability of reliability as a necessary condition for the normative element in knowledge. The generality problem is a problem for any theory that makes reliability a necessary condition for knowledge, including my theory and Plantinga's, so we should look now at a way to handle the problem.[21]

---

[20] Plantinga recognizes that the various brain lesion examples are vulnerable to the generality problem in 1993b, p. 29.

[21] Plantinga discusses the generality problem, particularly as an objection to

I have argued that the processes by which beliefs are formed soon become habits. This is relevant to the generality problem because habits form in ways that can be examined by psychological research. They probably favor the way the process appears on the inside rather than the outside, but my position does not require that this be the case. I suggest that the generality problem can be resolved by an empirical examination of habit formation. Does a person who believes what God puts into her head merely tend to believe whatever God puts into her head the next time, or does she instead tend to believe whatever pops into her head? If it is the former, her belief-forming process is reliable; if it is the latter, it is not. Does Oblonsky tend to conform his beliefs only to the opinions of his present circle of friends and his present newspaper? Or does he go on to believe whatever his friends and newspaper believe even when his newspaper and circle of friends gradually change? I suspect that it is the latter, in which case, Oblonsky's belief-forming process is less likely to be reliable. So even if conformity with Oblonsky's small circle of friends is reliable, conformity will probably lead him to believe in an unreliable fashion in the future. The unreliability of his future belief formation therefore infects the reliability of his present process. We can apply the same procedure to the newspaper reader. If I believe what I read in the newspaper concerning the number of housing starts because I have a habit of believing whatever I read in any newspaper, my belief-forming process will be considerably less reliable than if I believe it because I have acquired habits of belief formation that distinguish such things as the kind of information cited, the authority of the source, and the reputation of the newspaper. I suspect that habit formation tends to generalize rather broadly, but that no doubt varies from person to person and with the person's age; young people probably generalize much more broadly than educated adults. There no doubt are also significant

Goldman's paradigm reliabilism, in 1988, pp. 24–31; in 1993a, pp. 198–9; and in 1993b, p. 29. In the last he denies that the generality problem is a problem for his proper function theory also, but, as I have said, I am inclined to agree with Goldman that Plantinga faces a version of the problem also.

variations with subject matter. A study of the ways in which habits are formed in arriving at beliefs would be interesting, but it is an empirical matter that should be part of a different project than this one.

Anderson and Bower (1973) treat the process of forming a belief as the establishment of "associative links" between relevant conceptual representations in our brains, and Alvin Goldman (1978b) connects believing with habituation. I have not claimed that the state of believing is itself a habit of a certain kind, but I am suggesting that the processes by which beliefs are formed are habits,[22] and that this suggests a way of solving the generality problem empirically.

4.2 Anticipated objections to my theory from the perspective of reliabilism

We have seen that intellectual virtues are reliably truth conducive, but they are not virtues simply *because* they are reliable. They put us in touch with the truth in a qualitatively valuable way, a way that involves self-reflectiveness and other internal properties of the agent, including the motivation to obtain knowledge and the motivations distinctive of the individual virtues. I have defined knowledge as a state of cognitive contact with reality arising out of acts that are virtuously motivated, are what a person with intellectual virtue is apt to do in the circumstances, and are successful in leading to the epistemic ends of the virtuous motive because of these other features of the act. This does not require that a person actually have intellectual virtues in order to have knowledge, but to have knowledge, a person must imitate the behavior of intellectually virtuous persons and must at least be virtuously motivated. So the acts and processes leading to the

---

[22] It may not work to say that all beliefs are formed by habitual processes, because some beliefs are formed by processes that are too automatic and close to the instinctive to count as habits. Still, a large and important subclass of beliefs may be formed by habitual processes, and the generality problem as applied to those beliefs may be settled by a study of the pyschology of habit formation.

state of knowing are reliable, but the class of knowing states is more restricted than those that satisfy reliabilist criteria.

Let us now look at the sorts of cases a reliabilist would propose in criticizing my theory of knowledge. Since reliability is a component in my definition, the reliabilist would consider the state I define sufficient for knowledge but would deny that the components other than reliability are necessary. I have already argued that cases of reliability without any consciousness of reliability at all should be ruled out, and therefore, reliabilism allows too much into the fold of knowledge. But it could still be argued that I allow too little. Perhaps some consciousness of reliability must be present, at least weakly, but why think that the believer must go so far as to perform acts of intellectual virtue in the process of attaining knowledge?

One way to go about this thought experiment is to consider cases of belief arising from acts of intellectual virtue, and ask ourselves whether a person in this state would have knowledge if the reliability were the same but the feelings and motives or other aspects distinct from the reliability were different. There is, however, a problem in making sense of this thought experiment at the outset because the feelings and motives themselves are components of the reliable mechanism as I have defined intellectual virtue. If the motive for truth were not a reliable mechanism for attaining truth, we would be in much more serious trouble than simply having difficulty in defining knowledge! There would be little point in doing philosophy at all, or engaging in any other intellectual endeavor. But, of course, there are many reliable mechanisms for attaining truth, some of which are almost purely mechanical, such as perceptual processes or ordinary deductive procedures. I have argued that aside from those processes that are wholly involuntary, our belief-forming processes arise from and continue to operate from a foundation in the motive to know. And I have argued that in the form of virtue theory I call motivation-based, the value of reliability rests on the value of the motive for knowledge. There is no special value in the fact that a particular true belief arises from a reliable belief-forming process except insofar as the motive to know is a good thing and persons with such a motive use processes known to them to be reliable. So the motive to know operates in the background of those reliable procedures over which we have some degree of voluntary control, and the value of the epistemic state to which this motive leads is enhanced by the value of the motive itself. So I have claimed that the internalist feature of motive is both the usual accompaniment of reliable belief-forming processes and one whose value is important for the value we attach to the resulting state. Nevertheless, we can imagine situations in which a belief-forming mechanism is reliable but is not accompanied by the element of motivation, the element in my definition of knowledge that is at least weakly internalist.

Suppose that a medical researcher does what intellectually virtuous persons do in the conduct of her research. She is careful, attentive, thorough, evaluates her methods and results critically, is open to the criticism of others, is flexible, and *acts* as if she is unprejudiced, open-minded, and tolerant of conflicting views. Also, we can assume that she routinely reaches the truth through these procedures. She does not, however, have the motivations that we associate with the virtues of open-mindedness, tolerance, and lack of prejudice, nor does she particularly care about the truth. Her motive for following these procedures is simply that doing so is likely to enhance her reputation. Her procedures are reliable, and she is even *aware* that they are reliable, so she is aware that her procedures are likely to lead to the truth. But she does not *care* that they lead to the truth. She does what she does because she has learned that there is a close correlation between obtaining true results and the enhancement of her professional reputation. All of her research, then, is grounded in the basic motive for fame. She satisfies all the criteria for knowledge I have identified, with the exception of the motivational criterion, and thus she does not perform acts of intellectual virtue. But why deny that she has knowledge?

We can formulate even harder cases in which beliefs not only do not arise out of intellectually virtuous motives but actually arise out of vices. The problem is that vices seem to lead to reliable processes in some cases, and when they do, and when the truth is obtained in the particular case through such processes, it appears that the believer has knowledge. In this category we might think of the discoveries of a nosey neighbor, beliefs arising out of intellectual pride,[23] and Uncle Toby's intellectual acquisitiveness.

I wish to offer two ways of answering the objection arising from this set of examples. The first one involves denying that the believers in each of these cases have knowledge. The second, and my preferred way of handling these cases, is to accept these examples as cases of knowledge but to argue that they satisfy my definition.

First, it should be admitted that virtuous and vicious procedures can overlap. It would, in fact, be surprising if things were otherwise. Clearly, people can perform the same overt acts out of different motives, so it ought to be expected that they can also perform the same cognitive acts out of different motives. Some of these motives are praiseworthy; others are not. Some, in fact, may be blameworthy, and the examples just given may be in this category. So a nosey woman who snoops on her neighbor out of sexual envy will find out facts about her neighbor that are none of her business but that are facts nonetheless, and that she apparently knows. Similarly, some of the most successful minds are also the most prideful, and it definitely looks as if their discoveries are things they know. And the same goes for Tristram Shandy's charming Uncle Toby. I have already expressed reservations about claiming that Toby's intellectual acquisitiveness is a vice, but some readers may think so and still think that the result of this acquisitiveness is knowledge.

Each of these persons has done something epistemically irresponsible, but not to such an extent that it interferes with the reliability of their procedures, or so it appears. But here we need to be cautious since we encounter the generality problem once again. Nosiness arising out of envy includes a desire to believe something bad about the neighbor, and the snoop will no doubt jump to conclusions. If she sees a man emerging from her neighbor's home, she will hasten to believe that her neighbor is sexually involved with him; if she sees a lot of wine bottles in the

---

[23] The cases of the nosey neighbor and of beliefs arising from pride were suggested to me by Thomas D. Sullivan.

neighbor's trash, she will leap to the conclusion that her neighbor is an alcoholic, and so on. It is not at all clear, then, that beliefs formed out of envious nosiness are reliable, at least not if we examine a sufficiently large set of beliefs formed in this way. Beliefs formed out of pride are similar. Within a limited range, pride may have no deleterious effect on the proportion of truths obtained by the believer, but in the long run, prideful believing is not reliable. Pride leads a person to have an inordinate need to be right, and this means not giving up beliefs that have been disconfirmed by the evidence. In the case of the medical researcher, her desire for fame will lead her to believe in the same way as a person with a genuine love of truth in a limited range of cases, but eventually her desire for fame will lead her to aim to believe what others want to hear or what will get her name in the journals, and when that happens, her belief-forming processes will diverge from those of the genuine truth lover. I will not comment on the fourth example, Uncle Toby, since I am willing to say that his belief-forming processes are reliable. His defect is something else, which we will turn to next. My first line of defense, then, is to say that in each of these cases, with the exception of Uncle Toby, the person does not have knowledge because beliefs formed out of vices are not reliable as long as the reliability test is applied to a fairly wide set of beliefs.

But there is another problem with the epistemic states of the persons just described. Each of them will go wrong somewhere in his doxastic structure, even if he is epistemically successful in the particular case. Some intellectual virtues have to do more with the quality of the knowledge than with its quantity, and knowledge is also something that admits of higher and lower quality. Uncle Toby is probably lacking something doxastically even though he has gained a lot of knowledge. He is perhaps too focused on trivia, and although that is not such a terrible thing, it is a waste of intellectual talent. Toby's overall doxastic structure is out of balance, unintegrated, perhaps lacking in understanding of the particular facts with which he is so fascinated. Similarly, the intellectually proud person falls into ruin somewhere along the line, even if he makes no mistakes serious enough to lead to straightforward false beliefs. The nosey neighbor is going to overlook something more important sooner or later. She has lost a hold on the relative epistemic value of different portions of truth.

The case against counting these examples as instances of knowledge is therefore strengthened if we define knowledge in terms of cognitive contact with reality rather than true belief since this suggests that knowledge is a state whose value is holistic. The virtuous believer's entire doxastic structure is at a higher level than that of the believer whose beliefs arise from vices, even if both are equally reliable in the sense of reliable usually applied to individual items of belief. Her doxastic structure has such qualities as coherence, clarity, understanding, proper strength of conviction, etc. So one person may be epistemically better than another, even though she does not know more propositions. This approach may require some revision of the definition of knowledge I have given, emphasizing the "cognitive contact with reality" versions and eliminating the versions utilizing the ordinary notions of true belief.

I think that there is much to be said for the strict line on the nature of knowledge contained in the response I have just given, but my preferred way of handling the objection based on these cases is to go the other way. The conditions under which we are willing to say a person has knowledge are somewhat elastic, but then so are the conditions under which we are willing to say a person is performing acts of intellectual virtue. Could we say that the believers in each of these cases satisfy my definition of knowledge after all? All of these believers are motivated to get the truth, but not because they place intrinsic value on truth. They are also motivated to be open-minded, careful, attentive, etc., so they have some particular intellectually virtuous motives. Their problem is that they also have another motive, an ulterior one, one that is deplorable – envy, pride, or the desire for fame. But the above definition of knowledge is loose enough that beliefs arising from vicious motives need not be precluded from being cases of knowing so long as they also arise from the desire for truth and other virtuous motives. The problem here is that we have cases of mixed motives. Let us look more closely at the matter.

Aristotle discusses people like our medical researcher in the last chapter of the *Eudemian Ethics* when he distinguishes between people who are just plain good (*agathos*) and people who are both good and noble (*kalos kagathos*).

> There is also the civic disposition, such as the Laconians have, and others like them might have. This is a state of the following kind: there are people who think that one should possess virtue, but only for the sake of the natural goods. Such men are therefore good (for the natural goods are good for them), but they do not possess nobility as well as goodness [*kalokagathian*]. For the things that are noble do not belong to them for their own sake. (1248b38–1249a3)

In commenting on this passage Anthony Kenny (1992) says:

> The distinction between these two kinds of people depends on the distinction made above between the two kinds of intrinsic goods. Those goods that are praiseworthy are not merely good but noble. Nobody can be good without performing the virtuous actions which deserve praise. But it is possible to perform these actions for more than one motive. The actions may be done for their own sake; or they may be done with a view to gaining and retaining the nonpraiseworthy goods. (1992, p. 10)

Kenny remarks that this passage may appear to be inconsistent with those passages in the *Nicomachean Ethics* that deny that a person is good if he performs just acts for the sake of competitive advantage, but that would be a misreading. Kenny says:

> The Laconian, like any virtuous man, performs virtuous actions for their own sake, because they are the acts that virtue requires; where he differs from the noble person is in the answer he gives to the second-order question "What is the point of being virtuous?" The *kalos kagathos* gives the answer "Because virtue is splendid, fine, and noble"; the Laconian gives the answer "Because virtue pays." (p. 12)

The medical researcher motivated to attain fame is like the Laconian. She does act virtuously, that is, attentively, thoroughly, with perseverance, etc., because those are the acts that the various intellectual virtues require, and she is motivated by the *particular* motivational components of attentiveness, carefulness, and the rest. But these motivations do not arise out of a love of truth for its own sake, even though she is motivated to get the truth. To her the point of being intellectually virtuous is to become famous. She is, then, like the person Aristotle calls good but not noble. The question for us, however, is whether she performs acts of virtue. The answer, I think, is yes, as long as the motivational condition for performing acts of virtue does not preclude a second-order ulterior motive for having virtuous motives. If so, since she satisfies the other conditions for knowledge, she has knowledge. The medical researcher, then, is not an example of a person who we intuitively believe has knowledge but who does not satisfy the definition.

Now what about the nosey neighbor? Clearly she is not motivated to get the truth out of a love of truth for its own sake, but she cannot be compared with the Laconian, because her ulterior motive is not a natural good. Her desire to believe ill of someone is surely not a natural good or any sort of good. But she may also be able to perform acts of intellectual virtue for the same reason the medical researcher can perform such acts. As long as the definition of an act of intellectual virtue does not preclude ulterior second-order motives (even bad second-order motives such as envy or pride), she can perform acts of intellectual attentiveness, perseverance, etc. She must, of course, have the particular motives unique to each of these virtues, but there is no reason to think she lacks these motives. Her problem is the rationale for the motivations themselves.

Uncle Toby's case even more clearly satisfies the definition of knowledge since he really does have a love of truth for its own sake, and his vice, if he has one, is a matter of overlooking something of greater value. There is no reason to think that this prevents him from performing acts of intellectual virtue. I conclude that we do not yet have a case in which a belief satisfies reliabilist conditions for knowledge but not intellectual virtue conditions and yet is intuitively a case of knowledge.

Let us consider another type of objection to my theory. There is the problem that a virtuous process that is generally reliable may be unreliable in the particular case without ceasing to be virtuous, and in some of these cases we hesitate to call the resulting state knowledge. For example, I may form a belief out of the virtue of proper trust of authority in a field outside my area of expertise, but if the authority has based his own belief on weak evidence, and hence fails to attain knowledge, it seems to follow that his lack of knowledge is transferred to me even if the belief is true and I reach it by acts of intellectual virtue.[24] This case shows the importance of the social nexus of knowledge and the need to refine the account of an act of intellectual virtue accordingly. Virtue is a heavily social concept, both conceptually and in its historical usage. As I would put it, knowledge is transferred from person to person via a network of acts of intellectual virtue. To the extent that a person relies for knowledge on someone else, her resulting state is not knowledge if that someone else does not also have knowledge. This means that to perform an act of the virtue of proper reliance on others, one must get to the truth not only through one's own virtuous motivations and processes but through the virtuous motivations and processes of those others. Knowledge is the result of acts of intellectual virtue by both the agent and others in her epistemic community upon whom she relies in forming a subset of her beliefs. This aspect of knowledge makes it something for which we have social responsibility. And, in fact, it is one of the main reasons knowledge is something for which we are *morally* responsible. Others in our society have the moral right to expect us not to harm them, and passing on to them something that is not knowledge is one way of harming them.

5 PLANTINGA'S THEORY OF PROPER FUNCTION

Let us now investigate another major theory that has been categorized as a kind of "virtue epistemology": Alvin Plantinga's recent theory of proper function. This theory is better than straight reliabilism, and it is possible to interpret it in a way that is

24 This example was suggested to me by Alvin Plantinga.

similar to the theory I have proposed, but Plantinga's discussion and examples suggest that it is more externalist than is defensible, and this makes it vulnerable to some of the arguments we have already used against reliabilism.

Plantinga calls the property that in sufficient quantity converts true belief into knowledge "warrant." His definition of warrant is as follows:

> A belief *B* has warrant for *S* if and only if the relevant segments (the segments involved in the production of *B*) are functioning properly in a cognitive environment sufficiently similar to that for which *S*'s faculties are designed; and the modules of the design plan governing the production of *B* are (1) aimed at truth, and (2) such that there is a high objective probability that a belief formed in accordance with those modules (in that sort of cognitive environment) is true; and the more firmly *S* believes *B* the more warrant *B* has for *S*. (1993b, p. 19)

Notice that this definition makes reliability a necessary but not sufficient condition for knowledge.

Plantinga says that this definition is only an approximation, and he follows it up with a discussion of objections and refinements, but as the refinements do not bear on the objections I will give, and as the quoted definition is about as complex as it can be without becoming too cumbersome for discussion, I will treat the definition as a reasonable approximation of the theory Plantinga proposes.

Without the context of Plantinga's supporting examples and arguments, his definition of warrant may seem to be similar to my account of an intellectual virtue. After all, in classical Greek philosophy the concept of proper function was closely related to the concept of virtue since both were associated with the concept of a nature. But the classical concept of virtue includes numerous elements that are internal to the agent's consciousness (feelings, motives, self-conscious rational processes, intentions, etc.), whereas Plantinga's numerous examples suggest that his idea of a properly functioning human being is modeled more on that of a properly functioning machine. Throughout *Warrant and Proper Func-*

tion Plantinga compares properly functioning cognitive faculties with properly functioning cars, computers, linear accelerators, immune systems, digestive systems, and other highly mechanized objects and processes. Furthermore, his examples of warranted beliefs favor an externalist interpretation of proper function. Proper function according to a design plan is not really very close to the classical notion of behaving virtuously, it seems.

In one place, however, Plantinga explicitly mentions that faculties are not functioning properly when beliefs are formed as the result of such moral vices as "jealousy, lust, contrariness, desire for fame, or wishful thinking" (1984, p. 408). This is an especially curious remark since it takes quite a stretch to see any such beliefs as involving improperly functioning faculties. Which faculty is it that is not functioning properly when a person forms a belief as the result of a desire for fame or wishful thinking? Does a lustful belief really arise from the malfunction of a faculty? The most straightforward interpretation of these cases is simply that something is wrong with these beliefs because they arise out of vices, not because some faculty or other is not functioning properly. Perhaps if Plantinga had pursued this line of thought further, his theory might have turned out to be quite different in application, if not in substance.

Aristotle related the concept of virtue to the concept of proper functioning, but there are important differences that may bear on our present concern. A passage from Sarah Broadie's work on Aristotle's ethics shows the advantages of the concept of virtue over that of functioning well:

> These considerations show how crucial was the quiet step by which Aristotle, in defining happiness in *NE* I.7, moved from saying that happiness is nothing other than "functioning *well*" to saying that it is nothing other than "functioning *in accordance with virtue*" (1098a 14–17). It might have seemed reasonable to gloss the former with "doing what is right," or (given the definition) "doing what it is right that a rational being should do." Animals are functioning well when they are doing whatever creatures of their species naturally should be doing, and if we want to say that a well-functioning animal functions "in

accordance with the excellence of its kind" we may mean no more than that it is functioning healthily and effectively at this moment and can be reliably expected to do so at other moments. We may also imply the theory that its functioning well at all those moments is rooted in a single set of continuing empirical properties, which we may think of as constituting the relevant excellence. But this way of thinking could easily be misleading, for we should not be entitled to assert that at a given moment the animal's functioning is only fully good *because* it has and will continue to have the properties by which it functions well at this and other moments. Those properties (on the theory) make causally possible the functioning that is good, but their presence is not what makes it *good* functioning. By contrast, the human virtues, on Aristotle's account, do not stand to human good functioning as a set of properties that make causally possible a functioning whose goodness can be explained as complete without reference to them. On the contrary, the functioning is both possible and, by external standards, correct and good without virtue standing behind it, but is not in any instance completely good (hence not an instance of happiness) except when it issues from virtue. (1991, p. 84)

I do not know whether Broadie's interpretation here is faithful to Aristotle's intent, but I find this an illuminating way to compare the proper functioning of sensory and cognitive faculties with the proper functioning of intellectual virtues, and both with the idea of a human end. Properly functioning perceptual and cognitive faculties make causally possible good human epistemic functioning, the goodness of which can be explained without them, but not without the intellectual virtues. In contrast, the intellectual virtues are not causes of good epistemic functioning but are partially constitutive of it. To function well in the sense of using the right perceptual and cognitive mechanisms in the process of attaining truth may be just fine according to "external" standards, to borrow Broadie's way of speaking, and those are the standards used from a pure externalist standpoint in epistemology. On the externalist interpretation, proper function is possible without virtue standing behind it, but if warrant (and knowledge) is defined in terms of *this* sense of proper function, it is not an aspect of the human end or *eudaimonia*. For epistemic function to be proper in *that* sense ("completely good," as Broadie says), it must issue from intellectual virtue. Of course, the "quiet step" Aristotle made from defining happiness as "functioning well" to "functioning in accordance with virtue" is a step that could be made on behalf of Plantinga's theory. Nonetheless, the evidence strongly suggests that he did not make it. It is worth noting, however, that with a slight adjustment to the general idea of proper function, the whole theory can take on an entirely different cast – more internalist and with deeper roots in the history of normative inquiry.

If we accept the more strongly externalist interpretation of the theory intended by Plantinga himself, the theory has some advantages over reliabilism, but also some of the same problems. An advantage already noted in the section on reliabilism is Plantinga's insight that we ought to refrain from calling a belief knowledge when it is the result of malfunction, whether or not the process used is reliable. So Plantinga's idea that reliability is not good enough if something has gone wrong in the simple and straightforward sense in which brain lesions are things that have gone wrong is surely right. Adding the design feature seems to avoid the problems of accidental reliability that plague reliabilist theories, although we might question what is gained by adding the design feature to the concept of proper function.[25]

In spite of Plantinga's addition of some appealing features lacked by pure reliabilism, the general argument against externalism presented in the last section applies to Plantinga's theory as much as to reliabilism. The fact that one's faculties are working properly is a valuable thing, the value of which is virtually analytic, given what Plantinga means by "proper." There is also value in the product that usually results from the formation of beliefs by such faculties, namely, the truth. But there is no additional value in the fact that the truth is acquired *through* such properly functioning faculties. We can assume that the chicken sexer and the

---

[25] Ernest Sosa (1993) has proposed his swampbaby story to defend his claim that the design feature is an unnecessarily restrictive addition to the concept of proper function.

religious believer discussed in 4.1 have properly functioning faculties in the appropriate environment. At least the chicken sexer does not produce the correct belief by any sort of malfunction of his faculties. Thus, the chicken sexer's belief has warrant on Plantinga's theory, and as long as the degree of warrant is sufficiently high, he knows the sex of the baby chick according to Plantinga. Furthermore, we may assume that there is nothing malfunctioning in the Mavrodian believer's faculties. She may be singularly lacking in the *exercise* of her faculties since she does not seem to be exercising much of anything, but to the extent that she does, there is no malfunction. She also has knowledge as long as her proper functioning leads her to believe with a degree of firmness that brings the degree of warrant up to the level sufficient for knowledge according to Plantinga. We have seen, though, that it is a mistake to consider the epistemic state of either of these persons a state of knowledge. In each case, the believer has something valuable in having the truth and has something else valuable in her well-functioning epistemic faculties, but that is all the epistemic value she has.

Adding the element of design may eliminate the reliabilist's problem of accidental reliability in the faculties themselves, but it does not eliminate accidentality from the agent's perspective and, hence, does not distinguish between a person and a machine. This is not to deny that some human processes are machine-like or animal-like. The question is whether the state that results from such subhuman processes is knowledge, or whether knowledge is intrinsically related to the human capacity for self-reflection – processes that preclude a purely externalist theory of knowledge. The problem here is captured by Descartes:

> It is a supreme perfection in man to act voluntarily or freely, and thus to be in a special sense the author of his own actions, and to deserve praise for them. *We do not praise automata for carrying out all the movements for which they were designed,* since they carry them out by necessity; we rather praise the maker for fashioning such precise machines, because he fashioned them not by necessity, but freely. Similarly, it is more to our credit that we embrace the truth when we do, because we do this freely,

than it would be if we could not but embrace it. (Trans. Haldane
and Ross 1955, vol. 1, pp. 233–4; emphasis added)

On the other hand, not everyone has shared the Cartesian attitude towards involuntarily good behavior. T. H. Huxley is a striking example of the opposing viewpoint:

If some great Power would agree to make me always think
what is true and do what is right, on condition of being turned
into a sort of clock and wound up every morning before I got
out of bed, I should instantly close with the offer. (1896, pp.
192–3)

I will not offer a critique of Huxley's view, but it is worth
remarking that he expresses the same sanguine attitude about
giving up free will in the area of overt action as in the area of
cognitive activity. Plantinga, of course, distinguishes between the
responsibility that applies to the moral area of our lives and the
sort of credit that we get when we have epistemic warrant, and I
agree that there is a distinction between moral responsibility and
credit in the nonmoral sense. The difference between my position
and Plantinga's is that I claim that moral responsibility extends
rather widely throughout the realm of cognitive activity, embrac-
ing the areas to which the fundamental normative concepts used
in epistemology apply, whereas Plantinga's idea of moral responsibility is much more limited, and his idea of the nonmoral sense
of credit is proportionately greater. I will not now repeat my
arguments to the contrary but will merely point out the
difference.

The other set of arguments I used against reliabilism also apply
to Plantinga's theory. If, like Oblonsky, you read only newspapers
that support your own position, do not reflect critically on your
beliefs, borrow your views from others, and generally believe
what suits your fancy, is there anything wrong with your faculties? If so, what faculties are at fault? The argument here may
even be stronger against Plantinga's theory than against reliabilism because it is probably easier to mount an argument that,
contrary to appearances, Oblonsky's belief-forming processes are
unreliable than to maintain that they exhibit improperly function-

ing faculties. (Recall that I assumed in 4.1 that Oblonsky is lucky enough to read the "right" newspapers and to know the "right" people.)

I will mention only briefly several other problems with a theory based on proper function. One is that it is possible to take advantage of the ways people's faculties properly function in order to manipulate their beliefs, and when that happens, it is doubtful whether the resulting belief has warrant. In the example on the making of the movie *JFK* discussed in Part I, Oliver Stone described how he played upon the way human faculties naturally operate in order to get people to adopt a certain point of view. His use of high speed and vivid images borrowed from MTV editing techniques was intended to seduce the viewer into accepting Stone's view of the assassination of John F. Kennedy. It is natural for people to form beliefs or to believe more firmly by thinking of an idea over and over again. The vividness with which a proposition is imagined is connected with the strength of the belief in it, even if Hume is wrong that the belief just *is* the vivid imagining. Surely, there is nothing improper in the way this happens, and assuming that we were designed, it can hardly be denied that we were designed to think this way, because everyone does it, both good thinkers and bad. The difference between the good and the bad is that the virtuous believer is able to use his powers of self-reflection and to subject his beliefs to critical scrutiny; the nonvirtuous does not.

A couple of other problems with the proper function theory are the same as those mentioned in Part I as problems endemic to belief-based epistemology. Although Plantinga's theory is not actually belief-based,[26] it does focus evaluation on the single belief state of a single person at a single time, and it is as atomistic as belief-based theories. But if the worry expressed in Part I is sound, it is a mistake to focus evaluation on the isolated belief state because of the importance of the connection between the normative quality of the individual belief state and the normative qual-

---

[26] I thank John Greco for showing me that the difference between me and Plantinga is not the difference between belief-based and virtue-based epistemology but is really a difference in ethical models.

ity of other belief states of the same believer, or of belief states of other believers. An example of a way the first problem can arise for Plantinga's theory would be a case in which a woman's perceptual faculties alternate between functioning and not functioning, say, at five-minute intervals. I would think that true perceptual beliefs formed during the intervals when her eyesight is working properly have no more warrant than those formed during the intervals when it is malfunctioning for reasons analogous to the fake barn case (discussed in 3.1). In addition, many of the processes we rely upon in forming beliefs function in relation to other people. It is not enough that my belief-forming faculties are healthy and functioning well; those of my community must be also. This is because many processes do not merely relate the individual believer directly to an object of belief, as in cases of memory or perception, but operate via the testimony of others or the past learning of complex skills and information from others, as well as in the use of tools. For example, the conditions that make my plumber's belief in the location of the breakage in my sewer pipe warranted depend upon the people from whom he learned a complex set of skills, as well as the people who designed the instrument used for sounding the pipe above ground. In explaining warrant it is easier and more natural to relate the skills and virtues of one person to those of others than to attempt to relate the *faculties* of one person to the faculties of others. If my teacher does not have the right skills, neither do I; if she does not exercise her faculties properly, it is not at all clear that that damages *my* faculties. Yet it *should* diminish the warrant of any of my beliefs that depend upon that teacher.

A virtue theory also has an advantage over a proper function theory in solving the generality question. I have argued that the right way to describe the process used in forming a belief is to see how a belief-forming process in the individual case is naturally generalized in the formation of epistemic habits, and we must rely on psychological research to show us the patterns in which these habits are formed. So, for example, I would imagine that when the chicken sexer forms a correct belief, he begins to form an epistemic habit used in cases in which the sex of baby chicks is at issue, but he probably does not go on to form a habit of believing things that just "come" to him out of the blue. If he does the latter, the description of the process he is using in determining the sex of the chick changes, and its reliability clearly changes with it. The same question arises with respect to the Mavrodian believer. If a person who wakes up with the belief that there is a God tends to go on to form a habit of believing whatever pops into her head in the morning, then her theistic belief is an instance of the belief-forming process **believing whatever pops into her head first thing in the morning.** On the other hand, if she does not do this but only believes those beliefs inserted into her head by God overnight, then her belief is an instance of the belief-forming process **believing when she wakes up whatever God has put into her head.** Clearly, the reliability of these two processes is not the same. If I am right that the best way to solve the generality problem is through the idea of an epistemic habit, this favors a virtue approach since the concept of an epistemic habit is closely associated with the concept of intellectual virtue and is not so clearly related to the concept of proper epistemic function. So when we explicate the idea of a belief's arising from intellectual virtue, we are already talking about the formation of beliefs through habits. When we explicate the idea of a belief's arising from a properly functioning faculty, no relation to a habit is implied, at least not without a longer story on the nature of proper function than Plantinga has given us.

Let me end the discussion of Plantinga's theory of warrant by critiquing the last clause of his definition. According to that clause, "the more firmly S believes B the more warrant B has for S." It is easy to interpret this clause to indicate that as long as a belief B satisfies the conditions for warrant given in the first clause, then S gains in degree of warrant by believing B more firmly. So persons S and T in the same epistemic circumstances may both be warranted in believing, say, that Claremont is to the east of Los Angeles, but if S believes it more firmly than T, then S is more warranted in the belief than is T. This position is implausible and Plantinga has assured me that this is not what he intended. Instead, he says, his idea is that properly functioning faculties produce not only a belief but a certain degree or firmness of belief that is appropriate to a given set of epistemic circumstances. So if S and T differ in the strength of their respective beliefs in B in the same circumstances, then either S's or T's faculties are not functioning properly. But if S's properly functioning faculties produce a strong belief A and a weak belief B, then S's belief A is more warranted than his belief B.

As we have already seen, degree of conviction of a belief can be affected by factors that play upon the normal operation of cognitive faculties. To return to the interview with Oliver Stone, a vivid manipulation of images combined with high speed can intensify the degree of a belief. It is precisely the *normal* functioning of the believer's faculties that the moviemaker exploits. Of course, Plantinga can reply that what is normal need not be proper, but it is very difficult to see what, if anything, is improper in either the movie viewer's faculties or in his environment unless Stone's desire to produce beliefs in other people produces an improper environment for the faculties of those people. But surely that is far too strong a restriction. This is not to deny that there is something epistemically wrong with the movie viewer but only to say that it is quite a stretch to explain that wrongness in terms of faculty malfunction.

To conclude, the historical association of virtue with proper function may lead us to expect a similar closeness between Plantinga's theory and mine, but it is the concept of virtue that has been the primary focus of attention, and it has been much more fully developed and applied than has the concept of a human function, and it is therefore much more theoretically useful. In addition, the concept of proper function as applied to belief formation has problems that the concept of a virtue does not have.

6 HARMONIZING INTERNAL AND EXTERNAL ASPECTS OF KNOWING

I have remarked that Plantinga's definition of knowledge in terms of proper function can be interpreted in a way that is very much like the definition I have given, even if that is not Plantinga's intent. Similarly, my definition of knowledge in terms of acts of intellectual virtue can be interpreted in a more externalist way than I have intended, more like Plantinga. This could be done by modifying the motivational element in my account of virtue, making it weaker and farther removed from conscious awareness and control, although I do not think the internalist aspect can be eliminated entirely. The resulting notion of a virtue might look a lot like proper function. On the other hand, my theory can rather easily be adapted to a purely internalist one by modifying the concept of an intellectual virtue in the opposite direction. If an intellectual virtue is defined solely in terms of virtuous motivations and the success element is removed, we get an internalist notion of intellectual virtue, and the definition of knowledge that results is also internalist since the element of knowledge in addition to true belief would be wholly, even if weakly, accessible to the believer's consciousness. So the concept of intellectual virtue lends itself to adaptation either to Plantinga's externalist proper function theory or to an internalist theory. The concept can be bent either way. I mention this, not because I think it is a good idea to bend it either way, but because I want to indicate that what I have proposed here can be adapted by those whose intuitions about knowledge are either more strongly externalist or more strongly internalist than mine.

The relentless controversy between internalism and externalism has dominated epistemology, perhaps perversely, for some time now. I argued in Part I that one of the peculiarities of this debate is the fact that even though it concerns normative epistemic states such as justification and the normative aspect of knowledge, there is no debate in ethics that is exactly parallel, and in which the two sides to the dispute are as starkly divided as they now are in epistemology. There is, of course, more than one way to respond to this fact, if it is a fact, and not all of them are flattering to moral philosophers. It may be that ethicists are just more confused than contemporary epistemologists about the extent to which a *choice* must be made between internal and external grounds for evaluation. But there is enough discussion in ethics of the relation between "ought" and "can" and questions relating to the difference between subjective and objective grounds for evaluation that the more likely explanation is that ethicists are aware of the question in the theoretical sense but are simply not taken by it the way epistemologists are. The more intriguing dispute for moral philosophers appears to be the debate over the relation between motivation and moral justification. This dispute is the one that is called internalism/externalism in ethics. Roughly, ethical internalists maintain that there must be a close connection between what morally justifies an act and moral motivation, whereas ethical externalists claim that justification and motivation are separate issues. But although there is an association between this dispute and the dispute over the need for conscious access, it is not the same dispute. Some moral theorists, like epistemological externalists, take the position that what makes an act right or wrong need not be accessible to the consciousness of the agent, but this position is an exception in the history of ethics, and the fact that act utilitarianism is committed to it is generally regarded as one of the theory's problems. This is not to deny that external criteria of evaluation are almost always used by moral theorists. But although ethicists recognize and use external criteria for the evaluation of acts and personal traits, they generally take for granted that these criteria are internally accessible to a significant degree. Thus, persons are morally responsible for their acts because they ought to know the moral criteria and *can* know them, and they ought to know and can know how those criteria apply in their own case. This means that moral philosophers, for the most part, operate under an assumption of a coincidence between internal and external grounds for evaluation that is great enough to make the question of which one "really" counts largely immaterial. This position is based on a form of antiskepticism and is one of the ways in which the attitude toward skepticism can shape a theory decisively.

In 2.1 I mentioned the criteria for the possession of knowledge proposed by Hilary Kornblith (1985). Kornblith claims that the concept of knowledge must combine the idea that a belief is formed in an objectively correct manner and the idea that a belief is formed in a subjectively correct manner. This leads to the requirement that the knowing state must satisfy both external and internal criteria of evaluation. In virtue ethics, the concept of a virtue has almost always combined internally accessible and internally inaccessible criteria for its possession. I have done so myself in this book. On my account, a virtue has a component of motivation, which is the disposition to have a certain motive, and that motivation is internally accessible in the weak sense that motives and desires are internally accessible. The other component is success in reaching the ends of the motivational component. In a benign universe that one is largely accessible to consciousness also, but nothing in the definition requires that this be so, and I have been treating it as an external component. It is external in the same sense that reliabilist criteria in epistemology are external. But it is important to see that while the account of virtue in terms of motivation plus success is my own, the concept of virtue has almost always combined internally accessible and (potentially) internally inaccessible elements. So the blend of internal and external aspects is something that comes with the concept of virtue and that gives it an enormous advantage in epistemology, where it is becoming apparent that it is desirable to avoid both extreme externalism and extreme internalism.

I have argued that purely externalist accounts of the normative aspect of knowledge are unsuccessful because they do not give due regard to the place of motives and their governing virtues in the proper way to form beliefs in order to attain knowledge. One reason this is so is that we do not praise, admire, or even approve of true beliefs that are attained by nonvirtuous processes, and I have offered examples to illustrate this point. An even stronger reason for an internalist element in knowledge is that the concept of knowledge since antiquity has included the idea that the truth is not superficially grasped in the state of knowing but is *understood.* The neglect of understanding in the recent past has probably contributed to the success of reliabilism and other popular forms of externalism. The need for consciously accessible processes in attaining understanding is more obvious than is the need for consciously accessible processes in attaining truth. Understanding in antiquity included the ability to explain or to give an account of the truth known. It is difficult to see how such an ability could be the result of processes external to the subject's consciousness. But it is much easier to explain these processes as arising out of the conscious motive to understand and the virtues that aid understanding, such as insight, the ability to see the various ways beliefs are connected (not just their logical relations), and the ability to appreciate the relative value of different beliefs.

In "Thinking Subjectively," Robert Roberts (1980) discusses the Kierkegaardian vice of "objectivity," which, as Roberts explains it, is a kind of conceptual confusion in which a person theorizing about certain concepts does not understand that they are self-implicating – ethical and religious concepts such as honesty, justice, love, God, sin, and faith. If a writer on these topics leaves aside the way these concepts may apply to himself, he is leaving out an essential aspect of their use and hence is guilty of a conceptual error. I cannot say with any confidence just what is involved in the self-implicating feature of these concepts, but it seems to me that the point is largely right, and that furthermore, the concepts with this feature are not limited to the ones discussed by either Kierkegaard or Roberts. I have already said that we think of our knowing states as having a particularly intimate relation to our sense of self. We think of ourselves as partially constituted by our states of knowledge, and if so, knowledge is a self-implicating concept in the Kierkegaardian sense. Not only is it difficult to discuss knowledge without an awareness of its self-implicating aspect, but to do so would be to pervert its nature. If this is right, the need for an internalist element in knowledge is critical.

Although I have rejected purely externalist accounts of knowledge, I have also argued that a weaker form of externalism is right since "virtue" is a success term. Intellectual virtues are in part reliable mechanisms for producing true beliefs, or understanding of beliefs. If they were not reliable, they would not be virtues. Furthermore, in our discussion of Gettier problems we saw that we do not call a state knowledge unless the truth is achieved in the particular case through virtuous processes. This means that what is good about knowledge is not purely internal. There are both internal and external components of the normative aspect of knowledge. The concept of virtue is especially well suited to harmonize both aspects since in spite of the variations in the concept of virtue throughout the history of philosophy, it has almost always comprised both internally accessible and internally inaccessible elements.

In Part I we saw that contemporary epistemology faces some

serious difficulties. One is that a large part of the history of the concept of knowledge has been overlooked in the neglect of the idea of understanding. Another is that the concept of justification is in a conceptual muddle, and if Alston and Plantinga are right, it is unacceptably ambiguous. A third is that there is a stalemate between internalist and externalist accounts of knowledge. I have argued that an approach to epistemology based on a pure virtue theory is well suited to solving the first two problems. As for the third, I have claimed that both sides are partly right, but to resolve the controversy we would have to look more deeply into the connections between the internal aspects of intellectual virtue and of intellectually virtuous acts and their external aspects. This project would be partly empirical.

7 CONCLUSION TO PART III: ETHICS, EPISTEMOLOGY, AND PSYCHOLOGY

In a 1969 paper that ushered in the era of naturalized epistemology, W. V. Quine argued that knowledge ought to be treated as a natural phenomenon and examined the way any other such phenomenon is examined. This would mean, he said, that epistemology should be replaced by psychology, and so it would be a branch of the empirical sciences:

> Epistemology still goes on, though in a new setting and a clarified status. Epistemology, or something like it, simply falls into place as a chapter of psychology and hence of natural science. It studies a natural phenomenon, viz., a physical human subject. This human subject is accorded a certain experimentally controlled input – certain patterns of irradiation in assorted frequencies, for instance – and in the fullness of time the subject delivers as output a description of the three dimensional external world and its history. The relation between the meager input and the torrential output is a relation that we are prompted to study for somewhat the same reasons that always prompted epistemology; namely, in order to see how evidence relates to theory, and in what ways one's theory of nature transcends any available evidence. (1969, pp. 82–3)

334

Naturalistic epistemology is attractive in part because of the modern era's conspicuous triumph in attaining knowledge in a very circumscribed area – knowledge of the physical world. Assuming that we can have faith in this success as one of the marvels of human history, it is not unreasonable to think that a careful examination of how knowledge in this area arises might be useful as a way of finding out what knowledge *is*. One version of this approach treats knowledge as a natural kind on a par with such kinds as water and gold.[27] To find out the nature of water or gold, we do a careful empirical examination of its undisputed instances. Similarly, we might find out the nature of knowledge by doing an empirical investigation of the processes by which knowledge of the physical world has been gained with such rapidity in recent history. That, at least, is the suggestion.

This idea is an intriguing one, but one problem with it is that the area in which the natural human desire for knowledge has had resounding success is so limited that an empirical examination of our performance in that area alone is unlikely to yield an adequate analysis of the natural kind *knowledge*, as opposed to the kind *knowledge of the physical world*. Our efforts to obtain knowledge in philosophy and most of the humanities, as well as in at least some of the social sciences, have not been noted for their dramatic success or any kind of success, and are likely to remain so for some time. An empirical investigation of the ways in which we obtain knowledge about our physical environment is unlikely to illuminate the nature of knowledge in such areas as philosophy, history, and the arts, and hence, it is unlikely to illuminate the nature of knowledge itself. Of course, if it could be shown that the process of gaining knowledge about a literary text is no different than the process of gaining knowledge about physical particles, my objection would collapse, but as far as I know, that has not been shown, and it is hard to see how it could be shown by a purely empirical study.

The idea that knowledge is part of human science continuous with the natural sciences assumes that all forms of knowledge have the same direction of fit between mind and world. But many

---

[27] For a good recent explanation of this approach see Kornblith 1994.

of us believe that there is a fundamental difference in orientation between the natural scientist's struggle to acquire a conception of the world that fits the facts and the moral scientist's struggle to acquire a conception of how the facts can be made to fit his conception of what ought to be. The orientation of the investigator of knowledge is not clearly that of the former. If knowledge is connected with human fulfillment, as was maintained throughout most of philosophical history up to the work of Francis Bacon, it is much more like the latter. It would mean that knowledge is at root a moral notion. The separation of knowledge from moral concerns is a development inherited from Descartes, and although it has become familiar, it is important not to forget that there is a historically important alternative.

It is very difficult to explain why knowledge is valuable to us apart from its connection with something like the Aristotelian idea of *eudaimonia;* there are not many other options. One possible answer to the question of what makes knowledge valuable is just that it *is*. I do, in fact, take such an answer seriously, as I also take seriously the answer that it is valuable because that is what is desired by good persons. And that answer also links the value of knowledge with ethics. I see no way to explain the value of the state that is the primary concern of epistemology – knowledge – without linking it with the general study of value, and that means ethics.

Psychology and cognitive science have made important contributions to epistemology in the last two decades, and we have every reason to be grateful for this and to expect it to continue. Meanwhile, accomplishments on the normative side of epistemology have lagged, perhaps overshadowed by the more spectacular results on the empirical side. My purpose in writing this book is to draw more attention to the side of epistemology that overlaps with ethics and, in particular, to show how one form of ethical theory – a pure virtue theory – can be developed in ways that are rich enough to permit the kinds of evaluations of epistemic states that are crucial to epistemology. I suggest that cognitive psychology is related to normative epistemology as moral psychology is related to ethics. It is probably pointless to question whether moral psychology is a branch of ethics or is just an important neighboring field, and for the same reason it is probably pointless to question whether cognitive psychology is a branch of epistemology or is an important but distinct field that is highly useful to epistemology.

I believe one empirical study in particular would be helpful in understanding knowledge. I suspect that it would be useful to survey the history of ideas for major advances in order to find out what it is that allows human knowledge to make substantial gains. We might shed more light on the nature of knowledge by such a survey than by a survey of the history of epistemology. The question we would ask is "What intellectual traits (I would say virtues) permit such advances?" "What do discoveries, inventions, and the development of such abstract new ideas as the idea of freedom or of human rights show us about the conditions for increasing knowledge?" But the usefulness of such a procedure should not hide the fact that empirical studies are not the whole of epistemology. The fundamental questions of epistemology are varieties of the question "How ought we to go about finding out the truth?" or "What counts as a good belief?" or "What gives us understanding?" To answer such questions it is, of course, important to know how people *do* come to have and to maintain beliefs since belief formation is a natural phenomenon. For the same reason, it is important to know how people do characteristically act when they have conflicting desires or when fear inhibits them from doing what they think is right or when they become aware of moral disagreement with the members of another culture, and so on for a host of situations requiring ethical decision. It is especially important, I have argued, to know how a certain subset of persons make decisions, namely, those who have practical wisdom, and for the same reason I have urged that we look at the belief-forming processes of the practically wise. Making decisions, like forming beliefs, is a natural phenomenon, yet this does not make moral psychology ethics. Neither should the fact that belief formation is a natural phenomenon make cognitive psychology epistemology. At the same time, the importance to virtue theory of the way in which certain people behave clearly shows

337

that there is a strong empirical element in the process of evaluation in such a theory, perhaps more so than in other types of ethical theory.

Ultimately, both cognitive activity and more overt forms of behavior aim at the same end: the good. Knowledge is one form of good; happiness is another. If there are intimate connections between knowledge and happiness, it should not be surprising that the pursuit of one is not easily separable from the pursuit of the other. We have already noted several times that this attitude is familiar in classical Greek philosophy, but it even appears in the work of the modern American pragmatist C. S. Peirce, who bluntly asserts, "Truth, the conditions of which the logician endeavors to analyze, and which is the goal of the reasoner's aspirations, is nothing but a phase of the *summum bonum* which forms the subject of pure Ethics" (1931, p. 576). In addition to happiness, moral philosophers have sometimes named other goods as the ultimate or distinctively moral good, most prominently, in Kantian ethics, the goodness of a will motivated to be moral. Kant's approach suggests that the human end is not simply an external end but is partially constituted by the motive to get there. My argument in this book is that the goodness of knowledge is like that. The goodness of knowledge is partially constituted by the motive to get it. To switch again to virtue theory, the question of which comes first, end or motive, is the point at issue between a virtue theory that is happiness-based and an agent-based theory of the form I have called motivation-based. The former has the advantage of tradition; the latter has the advantage of novelty. I have given my reasons for thinking that either theory can be developed successfully for the purposes of epistemology, as well as for ethics.

In Part I I presented arguments that I hoped would motivate the reader to take a virtue theory seriously enough to want to investigate it seriously for the purposes of epistemology. But I said there that ultimately the question of whether a virtue-based epistemology is preferable to a belief-based epistemology must await the presentation of an actual example of the theory. I have done that in the rest of this book. At the conclusion of Part I, I said that ultimately the test of such a theory will be its fruitfulness in explaining a broad range of human life, and that at the end of the book I would ask whether the theory or range of theories I have presented here look like they are capable of doing this. So now that we are at the end, I hope that I have offered sufficient reasons for thinking that the answer is yes, or at least that it is likely enough to be yes to make further work on virtue theory in epistemology profitable. An enormous amount of work needs to be done on the virtues, most especially the intellectual virtues, and this includes their connection with the concepts given the most attention in epistemology – justification and knowledge and the neglected concept of understanding – as well as their connection with theoretical ethics. One of the most important directions for future work, I believe, is the broadening of ethical theory and the inclusion of normative epistemology within ethics proper. The benefits to both fields ought to be considerable.

> Now of all things good, truth holds the first place among gods and men alike. For him who is to know felicity and happiness, my prayer is that he may be endowed with it from the first, that he may live all the longer a true man. (Plato, *Laws*, trans. A. E. Taylor, V.730c)

Bibliography

Alderman, H. 1982. "By Virtue of a Virtue." *Review of Metaphysics* 36 (Sept.): 127–53. Reprinted in Kruschwitz and Roberts 1987.

Almeder, Robert. 1992. *Blind Realism*. Lanham, Md.: Rowman & Littlefield.

Alston, William P. 1983. "The Deontological Conception of Epistemic Justification." In *Philosophical Perspectives,* vol. 2, *Epistemology,* ed. James Tomberlin. Atascadero, Calif.: Ridgeview Press.

—— 1985. "Concepts of Epistemic Justification." *Monist* 68 (Jan.): 57–89.

—— 1986a. "Epistemic Circularity." *Philosophy and Phenomenological Research* 47, no. 1 (Sept.): 1–30.

—— 1986b. "Internalism and Externalism in Epistemology." *Philosophical Topics* 14 (Sept.): 179–221.

—— 1991. *Perceiving God.* Ithaca: Cornell University Press.

—— 1993. "Epistemic Desiderata." *Philosophy and Phenomenological Research* 53, no. 3 (Sept.): 527–51.

Anderson, J. R., and G. H. Bower. 1973. *Human Associative Memory.* Washington, D.C.: Winston.

Anscombe, G. E. M. 1958. "Modern Moral Philosophy." *Philosophy* 33 (Jan.): 1–19.

Aquinas, Thomas, 1947–8. *Summa Theologica,* 3 vols. Trans. Fathers of the English Dominican Province. New York: Benziger Brothers.

—— 1951. *Commentary on the "De Anima."* Trans. Kenelm Foster and Silvester Humphries. New Haven: Yale University Press.

—— 1964. *Commentary on the "Nicomachean Ethics,"* 2 vols. Trans. C. I. Litzinger. Chicago: Henry Regnery Co.

Aristotle. 1941a. *De Anima.* Trans. J. A. Smith. In McKeon 1941.

—— 1941b. *Metaphysics.* Trans. W. D. Ross. In McKeon 1941.

1941c. *Nicomachean Ethics*. Trans. W. D. Ross. In McKeon 1941.

1982. *Eudemian Ethics*. Trans. with commentary by Michael Woods. Oxford: Clarendon Press.

Armstrong, D. M. 1973. *Belief, Truth, and Knowledge*. Cambridge: Cambridge University Press.

Arnold, Magda B. 1960. *Emotion and Personality*. New York: Columbia University Press.

Audi, Robert. 1988. *Belief, Justification, and Knowledge*. Belmont, Calif.: Wadsworth Publishing.

1989a. "Internalism and Externalism In Moral Epistemology," *Logos: Philosophic Issues in Christian Perspective* 10:13–37.

1989b. *Practical Reasoning*. London and New York: Routledge.

1991. "Responsible Action and Virtuous Character." *Ethics* 101:304–21.

1994. "Acting from Virtue." Paper presented at conference on Virtue Ethics at Santa Clara University, 4 Mar.

Audi, Robert, and W. J. Wainwright. 1986. *Rationality, Religious Belief, and Moral Commitment*. Ithaca: Cornell University Press.

Aune, Bruce. 1965. *Knowledge, Mind, and Nature*. New York: Random House.

Ayer, A. J. *The Problem of Knowledge*. New York: St. Martin's Press.

Bacon, Francis. 1994. *Novum Organum*. Trans. and ed. Peter Urbach and John Gibson. Chicago: Open Court.

Baier, Annette. 1985. *Postures of the Mind: Essays on Mind and Morals*. Minneapolis: University of Minnesota Press.

1993. "Trust and Anti-trust." In Haber 1993.

Baron, Marcia. 1985. "Varieties of Ethics of Virtue." *American Philosophical Quarterly* 22, no. 1:47–54.

Bennett, Jonathan. 1964. *Rationality*. New York: Humanities Press.

Benson, John. 1987. "Who Is the Autonomous Man?" In Kruschwitz and Roberts 1987.

Berlin, Isaiah. 1978. *Russian Thinkers*. New York: Viking Press.

Bernstein, Mark. 1986. "Moral and Epistemic Saints." *Metaphilosophy* 17:102–8.

Blum, Lawrence A. 1980. *Friendship, Altruism and Morality*. London: Routledge & Kegan Paul.

1994. *Moral Perception and Particularity*. New York: Cambridge University Press.

Bonar, James M.A. 1894. *The Intellectual Virtues*. London: Macmillan and Co.

BonJour, Laurence. 1976. "The Coherence Theory of Empirical Knowledge." *Philosophical Studies* 30 (Nov.): 281–312.

1980. "Externalist Theories of Empirical Knowledge." In *Studies in Epistemology*. Midwest Studies in Philosophy, vol. 5. Notre Dame, Ind.: Notre Dame University Press.

1985. *The Structure of Empirical Knowledge*. Cambridge: Harvard University Press.

Boswell, James. 1934. *Life of Samuel Johnson*, vol. 1. Ed. George Birkbeck Hill. Oxford: Clarendon Press.

Braeton, Jane. 1990. "Towards a Feminist Reassessment of Intellectual Virtue." *Hypatia* 5, no. 3:1–14.

Brentano, Franz. 1969. *On the Origin of Our Knowledge of Right and Wrong*. New York: Humanities Press.

Brink, David. 1989. *Moral Realism and the Foundations of Ethics*. Cambridge: Cambridge University Press.

Broadie, Sarah. 1991. *Ethics with Aristotle*. New York: Oxford University Press.

Brown, David. 1985. "No Heaven without Purgatory." *Religious Studies* 44, no. 4:447–56.

Buck, Ross. 1976. *Human Motivation and Emotion*. New York: John Wiley & Sons.

1985. "Prime Theory: An Integrated View of Motivation and Emotion." *Psychological Review* 92:389–413.

Burnyeat, M. F. 1980a. "Aristotle on Learning to Be Good." In Rorty 1980.

1980b. "Aristotle on Understanding Knowledge." In *Aristotle on Science: The "Posterior Analytics,"* ed. E. Berti. Padua: Editrice Antenoire.

Burnyeat, M. F., and J. Barnes. 1980. "Socrates and the Jury." *Proceedings of the Aristotelian Society*, suppl. vol. 54, pp. 173–91.

Calhoun, Cheshire, and Robert Solomon, eds. 1984. *What Is an Emotion?* New York: Oxford University Press.

Carson, Thomas. 1984. *The Status of Mortality*. Dordecht: D. Reidel.

Casey, John. 1990. *Pagan Virtue*. Oxford: Clarendon Press.

Chapman, John W., and William A. Galston, eds. 1992. *Virtue*. Nomos, vol. 34. New York: New York University Press.

Charlton, William. 1988. *Weakness of Will*. Oxford: Basil Blackwell.

Chisholm, Roderick. 1968. "C. I. Lewis's Ethics of Belief." In *The Philosophy of C. I. Lewis*, ed. P. A. Schilpp. La Salle, Ill.: Open Court.

1969. *Perceiving: A Philosophical Study*. Ithaca: Cornell University Press.

1977. *Theory of Knowledge*. 2d. ed. New Jersey: Prentice-Hall.

1982. *The Foundations of Knowing*. Minneapolis: University of Minnesota Press.

1989. *Theory of Knowledge*. 3d ed. Englewood Cliffs, N.J.: Prentice-Hall.

Bibliography

Cicero. 1991. *On Duties,* Bk. I. 1991. Ed. M. T. Griffin and E. M. Atkins. Cambridge: Cambridge University Press.

Clarke, Murray. 1986. "Doxastic Voluntariness and Forced Belief." *Philosophical Studies* 50 (July): 39–51.

Clay, M., and K. Lehrer, eds. 1989. *Knowledge and Skepticism.* Boulder, Colo.: Westview Press.

Clifford, W. K. 1877. "The Ethics of Belief." Reprinted in Gerald D. McCarthy, ed., *The Ethics of Belief Debate* (Atlanta: Scholar's Press, 1986).

Code, Lorraine. 1984. "Toward a 'Responsibilist' Epistemology." *Philosophy and Phenomenological Research* 45, (Sept.): 29–50.

——— 1987. *Epistemic Responsibility.* Hanover, N.H.: University Press of New England for Brown University Press.

Cohen, Jonathan L. 1989. "Belief and Acceptance." *Mind* 98:365–89.

——— 1992. *An Essay on Belief and Acceptance.* Oxford: Clarendon Press.

Cohen, Stewart. 1984. "Justification and Truth." *Philosophical Studies* 46:189–98.

Conly, Sarah. 1988. "Flourishing and the Failure of the Ethics of Virtue." In *Ethical Theory: Character and Virtue.* Midwest Studies in Philosophy, vol. 13. Notre Dame, Ind.: University of Notre Dame Press.

Cook, Thomas. 1987. "Deciding to Believe without Self-Deception." *Journal of Philosophy* 84 (Aug.): 441–6.

Cooper, John. 1975. *Reason and Human Good in Aristotle.* Cambridge: Harvard University Press.

Cooper, Neil. 1994. "The Intellectual Virtues." *Philosophy* 69 (Oct.): 459–69.

Dahl, Norman O. 1984. *Practical Reason, Aristotle, and Weakness of Will.* Minneapolis: University of Minnesota Press.

Dancy, Jonathan, ed. 1985. *Contemporary Epistemology.* New York: Oxford University Press.

——— 1992. "Ethics and Epistemology." In Dancy and Sosa 1992.

——— 1995. "Supervenience, Virtues, and Consequences: A Commentary on *Knowledge in Perspective* by Ernest Sosa." *Philosophical Studies* 78 (June): 189–205.

Dancy, Jonathan, and Ernest Sosa, eds. 1992. *A Companion to Epistemology.* Oxford: Basil Blackwell.

Davidson, Donald. 1974. "On the Very Idea of a Conceptual Scheme." *Proceedings and Addresses of the APA* 47:5–20.

——— 1980. *Essays on Actions and Events.* Oxford: Oxford University Press.

——— 1984. *Inquiries into Truth and Interpretation.* Oxford: Oxford University Press.

Dearden, R. F., P. H. Hirst, and R. S. Peters, eds. 1972. *Education and the Development of Reason.* London: Routledge & Kegan Paul.

Deigh, John., ed. 1992. *Ethics and Personality.* Chicago: University of Chicago Press.

Dent, N. J. H. 1984. *The Moral Psychology of the Virtues.* New York: Cambridge University Press.

DeRose, K. Forthcoming. "Lewis on 'Might' and 'Would' Counterfactual Conditionals." *Canadian Journal of Philosophy.*

Descartes, René. 1955. *The Philosophical Works of Descartes.* Trans. Elizabeth S. Haldane and G. R. T. Ross. New York: Dover Press.

⎯⎯ 1964. *Rules for the Direction of the Mind.* In *Philosophical Essays,* trans. Laurence J. Lafleur. Indianapolis: Bobbs-Merrill, Library of Liberal Arts.

De Sousa, Ronald. 1987. *The Rationality of Emotion.* Cambridge: The MIT Press.

Dewey, John. 1930. *The Quest for Certainty.* London: George Allen & Unwin.

⎯⎯ 1933. *How We Think.* Boston: D. C. Heath & Co.

Dimnet, Ernest. 1928. *The Art of Thinking.* New York: Simon & Schuster.

Dretske, Frederick I. 1981. *Knowledge and the Flow of Information.* Cambridge: MIT Press.

Dunne, Joseph. 1993. *Back to the Rough Ground: "Phronesis" and "Techne" in Modern Philosophy and in Aristotle.* Notre Dame, Ind.: University of Notre Dame Press.

Engberg-Pedersen, Troels. 1983. *Aristotle's Theory of Moral Insight.* Oxford: Clarendon Press.

Erskine, John. 1921. *The Moral Obligation to Be Intelligent.* Indianapolis: Bobbs Merrill. Excerpt reprinted in *Gateway to the Great Books,* vol. 10, *Philosophical Essays* (Chicago: Encyclopaedia Britannica, 1963).

Ethical Theory: Character and Virtue (1988). Midwest Studies in Philosophy. vol. 13. Notre Dame, Ind.: University of Notre Dame Press.

Everson, Stephen. 1990. *Epistemology.* Companions to Ancient Thought, vol. 1. Cambridge: Cambridge University Press.

Feinberg, Joel. 1970. "Problematic Responsibility in Law and Morals." In *Doing and Deserving.* Princeton: Princeton University Press.

Feldman, Richard. 1985a. "Reliability and Justification." *Monist* 68, no. 2 (Apr.): 159–74.

⎯⎯ 1985b. "Subjective and Objective Justification in Ethics and Epistemology." *Monist* 71, no. 3 (July): 405–19.

Feldman, Richard, and Earl Conee. 1985. "Evidentialism," *Philosophical*

Studies 48:15–34. Reprinted in Moser and Vendernat 1987.

Fine, Gail. 1990. "Knowledge and Belief in *Republic* v–vii." In *Epistemology*, ed. Stephen Everson. Companions to Ancient Thought, vol. 1. Cambridge: Cambridge University Press.

Firth, Roderick. 1978. "Are Epistemic Concepts Reducible to Ethical Concepts?" In *Values and Morals*, ed. A. I. Goldman and J. Kim. Dordrecht: D. Reidel.

Fischer, John Martin, and Mark Ravizza, eds. 1993. *Perspectives on Moral Responsibility.* Ithaca: Cornell University Press.

Fitzpatrick, J. 1983. "Lonergan's Notion of Belief." *Method* 1 (Oct.): 101–13.

Foley, Richard. 1987. *A Theory of Epistemic Rationality.* Cambridge: Harvard University Press.

　　1993. *Working without a Net: A Study of Egocentric Epistemology.* New York: Oxford University Press.

Foot, Philippa. 1978. "Virtues and Vices." In *Virtues and Vices and Other Essays in Moral Philosophy.* Berkeley and Los Angeles: University of California Press.

　　1994. "The Rationality of Moral Action." Paper presented at conference on Virtue Ethics at Santa Clara University, 5 Mar.

Frankfurt, Harry. 1971. "Freedom of the Will and the Concept of a Person." *Journal of Philosophy* 68, no. 5 (Jan.): 5–20.

French, Peter. 1991. *The Spectrum of Responsibility.* New York: St. Martin's Press.

Geach, Peter. 1977. *The Virtues.* Cambridge: Cambridge University Press.

Gettier, E. L. 1963. "Is Justified True Belief Knowledge?" *Analysis* 23:121–3.

Gibbard, Allan. 1990. *Wise Choices, Apt Feelings.* Cambridge: Harvard University Press.

Ginet, Carl. 1975. *Knowledge, Perception, and Memory.* Dordrecht and Boston: Reidel.

Godlovitch, Stanley. 1981. "On Wisdom." *Canadian Journal of Philosophy* 11 (Mar.): 137–55. Reprinted in Sommers and Sommers 1985.

Goldman, Alvin I. 1978a. "Epistemics: The Regulative Theory of Cognition." *Journal of Philosophy* 75 (Oct.): 509–23.

　　1978b. "Epistemology and the Psychology of Cognition." *Monist* 61 (Oct): 525–35.

　　1980. "The Internalist Conception of Justification." In *Studies in Epistemology.* Midwest Studies in Philosophy, vol. 5. Notre Dame, Ind.: University of Notre Dame Press.

　　1986. *Epistemology and Cognition.* Cambridge: Harvard University Press.

1992. "Epistemic Folkways and Scientific Epistemology." In *Liaisons: Philosophy Meets the Cognitive and Social Sciences.* Cambridge: MIT Press.

Goodman, Nelson. 1978. *Ways of Worldmaking.* Indianapolis: Hackett Publishing.

Greco, John. 1990. "Internalism and Epistemically Responsible Belief." *Synthese* 85:245–77.

1992. "Virtue Epistemology." In Dancy and Sosa 1992.

1993. "Virtues and Vices of Virtue Epistemology." *Canadian Journal of Philosophy* 23:413–32.

1994a. "Review of Jonathan Kvanvig, *Intellectual Virtues and the Life of the Mind. Philosophy and Phenomenological Research* 54, no. 4 (Dec.): 973–6.

1994b. "Virtue Epistemology and the Relevant Sense of 'Relevant Possibility.'" *Southern Journal of Philosophy* 32:61–77.

Gutting, Gary. 1982. *Religious Belief and Religious Skepticism.* Notre Dame, Ind.: University of Notre Dame Press.

Haack, Susan. 1979. "Epistemology *with* a Knowing Subject." *Review of Metaphysics* 33 (Dec.): 309–35.

Haber, Joram Graf. 1993. *Doing and Being.* New York: Macmillan.

Hardie, W. F. R. 1980. *Aristotle's Ethical Theory.* 2d. ed. Oxford: Clarendon Press.

Hare, R. M. 1952. *The Language of Morals.* New York: Oxford University Press.

Harman, Gilbert. 1983. "Human Flourishing, Ethics, and Liberty." *Philosophy and Public Affairs* 12:307–22.

Heil, John. 1983a. "Believing What One Ought." *Journal of Philosophy* 80:752–64.

1983b. "Doxastic Agency." *Philosophical Studies* 43:355–64.

1983c. *Perception and Cognition.* Berkeley and Los Angeles: University of California Press.

1984. "Doxastic Incontinence." *Mind* 93 (Jan.): 56–70.

Hobbes, Thomas. *Leviathan,* pts. 1 and 2. 1958. New York: Macmillan, Library of Liberal Arts.

Hookway, Christopher. 1981. "Conscious Belief and Deliberation." *Proceedings of the Aristotelian Society,* suppl. vol. 55, pp. 75–89. (Response by K. V. Wilkes, pp. 91–107.)

1993. "Mimicking Foundationalism: On Sentiment and Self-Control." *European Journal of Philosophy* 1, no. 2:156–74.

1994. "Cognitive Virtues and Epistemic Evaluations." *International Journal of Philosophical Studies* 2, no. 2:211–27.

Hudson, Stephen D. 1986. *Human Character and Morality.* London: Routledge & Kegan Paul.

Hughes, Gerard J. 1990. "Ignatian Discernment: A Philosophical Analysis." *Heythrop Journal* 31:419–38.

Hume, David. 1967. *A Treatise of Human Nature.* Oxford: Clarendon Press.
1983. *An Enquiry concerning the Principles of Morals.* Ed. J. B. Schneewind. Indianapolis: Hackett Publishing.

Hurka, Thomas. 1993. *Perfectionism.* New York: Oxford University Press.

Hursthouse, Rosalind. 1991. "Virtue Theory and Abortion." *Philosophy and Public Affairs* 20:223–46.

Hutchinson, D. S. 1986. *The Virtues of Aristotle.* London: Routledge & Kegan Paul.

Huxley, T. H. 1896. "On Descartes' *Discourse on Method*" (1870). In *Methods and Results (Collected Essays).* New York: D. Appleton.

Ingham, Mary Elizabeth. 1995. "Practical Wisdom: Scotus' Presentation of Prudence." In *The Ethics and Metaphysics of John Duns Scotus,* ed. Rega Wood and Ludger Honnefelder. New York: Franciscan Publications.
1996. *The Harmony of Goodness: Mutuality and Moral Living According to John Duns Scotus.* New York: Franciscan Publications.

Irwin, T. H. 1980. "The Metaphysical and Psychological Basis of Aristotle's Ethics." In Rorty 1980.
1990. "Virtue, Praise and Success: Stoic Responses to Aristotle." *Monist* 73, no. 1 (Jan.): 59–79.

James, William. 1884. "What Is Emotion?" *Mind,* o.s., pp. 188–205.
1920. *The Letters of William James.* Ed. Henry James. Boston: Atlantic Monthly Press.
1937. "The Sentiment of Rationality." In *The Will to Believe and Other Essays.* London: Longmans, Green & Co.
1981. *Principles of Psychology.* 3 vols. Cambridge: Harvard University Press.

Kagan, Shelly. 1988. "The Additive Fallacy." *Ethics* 99 (Oct.): 5–31.

Kant, Immanuel. 1959. *Foundations of the Metaphysics of Morals.* Trans. Lewis White Beck. Indianapolis: Bobbs-Merrill.
1963. *Idea for a Universal History from a Cosmopolitan Point of View.* Trans. L. White Beck, R. E. Anchor, and E. L. Fackenheim. Indianapolis: Bobbs-Merrill.

Kearley, Carroll. n.d. "Callings: Personal and Communal." Book manuscript.

Kekes, John. 1976. *A Justification of Rationality.* Albany: State University of New York Press.

Kenny, Anthony. 1963. *Action, Emotion and Will*. London: Routledge & Kegan Paul.

1983. *Faith and Reason*. New York: Columbia University Press.

comp. 1986. *Rationalism, Empiricism, and Idealism*. Oxford: Clarendon Press.

1988. "Aristotle on Moral Luck." In *Human Agency: Language, Duty, and Value*, ed. Jonathan Dancy, J. M. E. Moravcsik, and C. C. W. Taylor. Stanford: Stanford University Press.

1992. *Aristotle on the Perfect Life*. Oxford: Clarendon Press.

Knaster, Stephen. 1984. "Chisholm, Deliberation, and the Free Acquisition of Belief." *Philosophical Studies* 46 (Nov.): 307–22.

Kornblith, Hilary. 1982. "The Psychological Turn." *Australasian Journal of Philosophy* 60 (Sept.): 238–53.

1983. "Justified Belief and Epistemically Responsible Action." *Philosophical Review* 92 (Jan.): 33–48.

1985. "Ever Since Descartes." *Monist* 68 no. 2 (Apr.): 264–76.

1993. "Epistemic Normativity." *Synthese* 94:357–76.

1994. "Naturalistic Epistemology and Its Critics." Invited paper, Eastern Division meeting of the American Philosophical Association, Boston, 30 Dec. Forthcoming in *Philosophical Topics*.

Kosman, L. A. "Being Properly Affected: Virtues and Feelings in Aristotle's Ethics." In Rorty 1980.

Kruschwitz, Robert and Robert C. Roberts, eds. 1987. *The Virtues: Contemporary Essays on Moral Character*. Belmont, Calif.: Wadsworth.

Kupperman, Joel J. 1991. *Character*. New York: Oxford University Press.

Kvanvig, Jonathan. 1992. *The Intellectual Virtues and the Life of the Mind*. Lanham, Md.: Rowman & Littlefield.

Lazarus, Richard. 1991. *Emotion and Adaptation*. New York: Oxford University Press.

Leeper, Robert Ward. 1970. "The Motivational and Perceptual Properties of Emotions as Indicating Their Fundamental Character and Role." In *Feeling and Emotions*, ed. Magda B. Arnold. New York: Academic Press.

Lehrer, Keith. 1974. *Knowledge*. Oxford: Clarendon Press.

1990. *Theory of Knowledge*. Boulder, Colo.: Westview Press.

Levy, Steven. 1977. "Defeasibility Theories of Knowledge." *Canadian Journal of Philosophy* 7 (Mar.): 115–23.

Lewis, C. I. 1946. *An Analysis of Knowledge and Valuation*. La Salle, Ill.: Open Court.

1969. "The Rational Imperatives." In *Values and Imperatives*, ed. John Lange. Stanford: Stanford University Press.

Lewis, David. 1973. *Counterfactuals.* Cambridge: Harvard University Press.

Locke, John. 1859. *Of the Conduct of the Understanding.* Ed. Bolt Corney. London: Bell & Daldy.

　　1975. *An Essay concerning Human Understanding.* Ed. Peter H. Nidditch. Oxford: Clarendon Press.

Lonergan, Bernard J. 1978. *Insight.* New York: Harper & Row.

Louden, Robert. 1987. "On Some Vices of Virtue Ethics." In Kruschwitz and Roberts 1987.

MacDonald, Scott, ed. 1991. *Being and Goodness.* Ithaca: Cornell University Press.

MacIntyre, Alasdair. 1984. *After Virtue.* Notre Dame, Ind.: University of Notre Dame Press.

Mann, William. 1993. "Hope." In *Reasoned Faith,* ed. Eleonore Stump. Ithaca: Cornell University Press.

Martin, Mike W., ed. 1985. *Self-deception and Self-understanding.* Lawrence: University of Kansas Press.

Mavrodes, George. 1988. *Revelation in Religious Belief.* Philadelphia: Temple University Press.

Mayo, Bernard. 1958. *Ethics and the Moral Life.* London: Macmillan; New York: St. Martin's Press.

McDowell, John. 1978. "Are Moral Requirements Hypothetical Imperatives?" *Proceedings of the Aristotelian Society,* suppl. vol. 52, pp. 13–29.

　　1979. "Virtue and Reason." *Monist* 62 (July): 331–50.

McKeon, R. P., ed. 1941. *The Basic Works of Aristotle.* New York: Random House.

McKinnon, Christine. 1991. "Hypocrisy, with a Note on Integrity." *American Philosophical Quarterly* 28, no. 4 (Oct.): 321–30.

Meilaender, Gilbert C. 1984. *The Theory and Practice of Virtue.* Notre Dame, Ind.: University of Notre Dame Press.

Meiland, Jack. 1980. "What Ought We to Believe? or The Ethics of Belief Revisited." *American Philosophical Quarterly* 17 (Jan.): 15–24.

Mele, Alfred R. 1986. "Incontinent Believing." *Philosophical Quarterly* 36 (Apr.): 215–22.

　　1987a. *Irrationality.* New York: Oxford University Press.

　　1987b. "Justification: Ethical and Epistemic." *Metaphilosophy* 18:187–99.

Merricks, Trenton. 1995. "Warrant Entails Truth." *Philosophy and Phenomenological Research* 55 (Dec.): 841–57.

Meyer, Susan Sauve. 1993. *Aristotle on Moral Responsibility.* Oxford: Blackwell.

Montaigne, Michel de. 1979. *Essays.* Harmondsworth, England, and New York: Penguin Books.

Montmarquet, James A. 1986a. "Epistemic Virtue." *Mind* 96:482–97.

1986b. "The Voluntariness of Believing." *Analysis* 46 (Jan.): 49–53.

1992. "Epistemic Virtue." In Dancy and Sosa 1992.

1993. *Epistemic Virtue and Doxastic Responsibility.* Lanham, Md.: Rowman & Littlefield.

Moravcsik, Julius. 1979. "Understanding and Knowledge in Plato's Philosophy." *Neue Hefte für Philosophie* 15/16:53–69.

1992. *Plato and Platonism.* Oxford: Blackwell.

Moser, Paul K. and Arnold Vandernat. eds. 1987. *Human Knowledge: Classical and Contemporary Approaches.* New York: Oxford University Press.

Murdoch, Iris. 1970. *The Sovereignty of Good.* London: Routledge & Kegan Paul. Title paper reprinted in Kruschwitz and Roberts 1987.

1992. *Metaphysics as a Guide to Morals.* New York: Allen Lane, Penguin Press.

Nagel, Thomas. 1970. *The Possibility of Altruism.* Princeton: Princeton University Press.

1974. "What Is It Like to Be a Bat?" *Philosophical Review* 83 (Oct.): 435–50.

1978. "Ethics as an Autonomous Theoretical Subject." In *Morality as a Biological Phenomenon,* ed. Gunther S. Stent. Berkeley and Los Angeles: University of California Press.

1979a. "Moral Luck." In *Mortal Questions.* Cambridge: Cambridge University Press.

1979b. "The Fragmentation of Value." In *Mortal Questions.* Cambridge: Cambridge University Press.

1986. *The View from Nowhere.* New York: Oxford University Press.

Needham, Rodney. 1972. *Belief, Language and Experience.* Oxford: Basil Blackwell.

Nelson, Daniel Mark. 1992. *The Priority of Prudence.* University Park: Pennsylvania State University Press.

Newman, John Henry. 1979. *An Essay in Aid of a Grammar of Assent.* Introduction by Nicholas Lash. Notre Dame, Ind.: University of Notre Dame Press.

Nietzsche, Friedrich. 1955. *Beyond Good and Evil.* Trans. Marianne Cowan. Chicago: Henry Regnery Co., Gateway.

1974. *The Gay Science.* Trans. Walter Kaufman. New York: Vintage Books.

Nowell-Smith, Patrick Horace. 1957. *Ethics.* New York: Philosophical Library.

Nozick, Robert. 1974. *Anarchy, State, and Utopia.* New York: Basic Books.
1981. *Philosophical Explanations.* Cambridge: Harvard University Press.
1993. *The Nature of Rationality.* Princeton: Princeton University Press.

Nussbaum, Martha. 1986. *The Fragility of Goodness: Luck and Ethics in Greek Tragedy and Philosophy.* Cambridge: Cambridge University Press.
1990. *Love's Knowledge.* New York: Oxford University Press.

O'Neill, Onora. 1986. "The Power of Example." *Philosophy* 61 (Jan.): 5–29.
1989. *Constructions of Reason.* Cambridge: Cambridge University Press.

Ortony, Andrew, Gerald L. Clore, and Allan Collins. 1988. *The Cognitive Structure of Emotion.* New York: Cambridge University Press.

Palmour, Jody. 1986. *On Moral Character.* Washington, D.C.: Archon Institute for Leadership Development.

Pappas, George, and Marshall Swain, eds. 1978. *Essays on Knowledge and Justification.* Ithaca: Cornell University Press.

Parfit, Derek. 1984. *Reasons and Persons.* Oxford: Oxford University Press.

Pascal, Blaise. 1981. *Pensees.* Trans. A. J. Krailsheimer. Harmondsworth, England, and New York: Penguin Books.

Passmore, John. "Locke and the Ethics of Belief." In Kenny 1986.

Peirce, C. S. 1877. "The Fixation of Belief." In Peirce 1992.
1878. "The Doctrine of Chances." In Peirce 1992.
1931. *Collected Papers,* vol. 1. Ed. C. Harsthorne and P. Weiss. Cambridge: Harvard University Press, Belknap Press.
1992. *The Essential Peirce,* vol. 1. Ed. Nathan Houser and Christian Kloesel. Bloomington: Indiana University Press.

Pence, Gregory. 1984. "Recent Work on Virtues." *American Philosophical Quarterly* 21 (Oct.): 281–93.

Penelhum, Terence. 1983. *God and Skepticism.* Dordrecht: D. Reidel.

Peters, R. S. 1972a. "Reason and Passion." In Dearden, Hirst, and Peters 1972.
1972b. "The Education of the Emotions." In Dearden, Hirst, and Peters 1972.

Petri, Herbert L. 1991. *Motivation: Theory, Research, and Applications.* 3d ed. Pacific Grove, Calif.: Brooks/Cole Publishing Co.

Phillips, Dewi Zephaniah. 1988. *Faith after Foundationalism.* London: Routledge & Kegan Paul.

Pieper, Joseph. 1963. *Belief and Faith.* Chicago: Henry Regnery Co.
1966. *The Four Cardinal Virtues.* Notre Dame, Ind.: University of Notre Dame Press.

Pincoffs, Edmund L. 1986. *Quandaries and Virtues*. Lawrence: University Press of Kansas.

Pitcher, George. 1965. "Emotion." *Mind* 74:326–46.

Plantinga, Alvin. 1984. "Justification and Theism." *Faith and Philosophy* 4 (Oct.): 403–26.

——— 1988. "Positive Epistemic Status and Proper Function." In *Philosophical Perspectives*, vol. 2, *Epistemology*, ed. James Tomberlin. Atascadero, Calif.: Ridgeview Press.

——— 1990. "Justification in the Twentieth Century." *Philosophy and Phenomenological Research* 50, suppl. (fall): 45–71.

——— 1993a. *Warrant: The Current Debate*. New York: Oxford University Press.

——— 1993b. *Warrant and Proper Function*. New York: Oxford University Press.

Plato. 1961. *The Collected Dialogues*. Ed. Edith Hamilton and Huntington Cairns. New York: Pantheon Books.

Plutchik, R. 1980. *Emotion: A Psychoevolutionary Synthesis*. New York: Harper & Row.

Pollock, John L. 1974. *Knowledge and Justification*, Princeton: Princeton University Press.

——— 1986. *Contemporary Theories of Knowledge*, Savage, Md.: Rowman & Littlefield.

Price, H. H. 1954. "Belief and Will." In *Proceedings of the Aristotelian Society*, suppl. vol. 28. Reprinted in Dearden, Hirst, and Peters 1972.

Prichard, H. A. 1912. "Does Moral Philosophy Rest on a Mistake?" *Mind* 21:23–37.

Provis, Chris. 1981. "Reason and Emotion." *Canadian Journal of Philosophy* 11:439–51.

Putnam, Hilary. 1976. "Realism and Reason." Presidential Address to the Eastern Division meeting of the American Philosophical Association, 29 Dec.. Reprinted in *Meaning and Moral Sciences* (London: Routledge & Kegan Paul, 1978).

Quine, W. V. O. 1969. "Epistemology Naturalized." In *Ontological Relativity and Other Essays*. New York: Columbia University Press.

Quinn, Philip L. 1985. "In Search of the Foundations of Theism." *Faith and Philosophy* 2 (Oct.): 469–86.

——— 1989. "Tragic Dilemmas, Suffering Love, and the Christian Life." *Journal of Religious Ethics* 17, no. 1:151–83.

Rawls, John. 1971. *A Theory of Justice*. Cambridge:Harvard University Press, Belknap Press.

——— 1974–5. "The Independence of Moral Theory." Presidential Address to the Eastern Division meeting of the American Philosophical Association. *Proceedings of the American Philosophical Association* 48:5–22.

Reid, Thomas. 1983. *Philosophical Works.* With notes by Sir William Hamilton. 8th ed. Hildesheim, Zurich, and New York: Georg Olms Verlag.

Roberts, Robert C. 1980. "Thinking Subjectively." *International Journal for Philosophy of Religion* 11, no. 2 (summer): 71–92.

———. 1984. "Will Power and the Virtues." *Philosophical Review* 93:227–47. Reprinted in Kruschwitz and Roberts 1987.

———. 1988. "What an Emotion Is: A Sketch." *Philosophical Review* 97, no. 2 (Apr.): 183–209.

———. 1989. "Aristotle on Virtues and Emotions." *Philosophical Studies* 56:293–306.

———. Forthcoming. *Emotions and Virtues: An Essay in Moral Psychology.*

Robertson, John, and Michael Stocker. 1991. "Externalism and Internalism." *Encyclopedia of Ethics.*

Robinson, Jenefer. 1983. "Emotion, Judgment, and Desire." *Journal of Philosophy* 80, no. 11 (Nov.): 731–41.

Rorty, Amelie Oksenberg. 1972. "Belief and Self-deception." *Inquiry* 15 (winter): 387–410.

———. 1978. "Explaining Emotions." *Journal of Philosophy* 75, no. 3 (Mar.): 139–61.

———. 1983. "Akratic Believers." *American Philosophical Quarterly* 20 (Apr.): 175–84.

———. 1988. *Mind in Action.* Boston: Beacon Press. See esp. "The Two Faces of Courage," pp. 299–313, and "Virtues and Their Vicissitudes," pp. 314–29.

———. 1994. "From Exasperating Virtues to Civic Virtues." Draft.

———, ed. 1980. *Essays on Aristotle's Ethics.* Berkeley and Los Angeles: University of California Press.

Ryle, Gilbert. 1949. *The Concept of Mind.* London: Hutchinson.

Scheffler, Israel. 1982. "In Praise of Cognitive Emotion." In *Science and Subjectivity,* app. B. 2d ed. Indianapolis: Hackett.

Schlossberger, Eugene. 1992. *Moral Responsibility and Persons.* Philadelphia: Temple University Press.

Schmitt, Frederick, ed. 1994. *Socializing Epistemology.* Lanham, Md.: Rowman & Littlefield.

Sher, George. 1992. "Knowing about Virtue." In Chapman and Galston, 1992.

Shope, Robert. 1983. *The Analysis of Knowing.* Princeton: Princeton University Press.

Siker, Louke Van Wensveen. 1993. "The Emergence of a Grounded Virtue
Ethic." In *Ecological Prospects,* ed. Christopher Chapple. Albany:
State University of New York Press.

Slote, Michael. 1983. *Goods and Virtues.* Oxford: Clarendon Press.

    1989. *Beyond Optimizing.* Cambridge: Harvard University Press.

    1992a. "Ethics Naturalized." In *Philosophical Perspectives, vol. 6, Ethics,*
ed. James E. Tomberlin. Atascadero, Calif.: Ridgeview Press.

    1992b. *From Morality to Virtue.* New York: Oxford University Press.

    1993. "Virtue Ethics and Democratic Values." *Journal of Social Philoso-
phy* 24, no. 2 (fall): 5–37.

    Forthcoming. "Agent-Based Virtue Ethics." In *Moral Concepts.* Mid-
west Studies in Philosophy, vol. 20.

Smith, Michael. 1994. *The Moral Problem.* Oxford: Blackwell.

Sommers, Christina, and Fred Sommers. 1985. *Vice and Virtue in Everyday
Life.* Harcourt Brace Jovanovich.

Sorabji, Richard. 1980. "Aristotle on the Role of Intellect in Virtue." In
Rorty 1980.

Sosa, Ernest. 1980. "The Raft and the Pyramid: Coherence versus Foundations in the Theory of Knowledge." In *Studies in Epistemology.*
Midwest Studies in Philosophy, vol. 5. Notre Dame, Ind.: University
of Notre Dame Press.

    1985. "Knowledge and Intellectual Virtue." *Monist* 68, no. 2 (Apr.):
226–45.

    1991. *Knowledge in Perspective.* Cambridge: Cambridge University
Press.

    1993. "Proper Functionalism and Virtue Epistemology." *Nous* 27, no. 1,
51–65.

    1995. "Perspectives in Virtue Epistemology: A Response to Dancy and
BonJour." *Philosophical Studies* 78, no. 3 (June): 221–35.

    Forthcoming. "Virtue Perspectivism: A Response to Foley and Fumer-
ton." *Philosophical Issues* 5.

Spinoza, Baruch. 1960. "Ethics." Trans. R. H. M. Elwes. In *The Rational-
ists.* New York: Doubleday, Dolphin Books.

Sterne, Laurence. 1967. *The Life and Opinions of Tristram Shandy.* Ed.
Graham Petrie. London and New York: Penguin Classics.

Stevenson, J. T. 1975. "On Doxastic Responsibility." In *Analysis and Metaphysics,* ed. Keith Lehrer. Dordrecht: Reidel.

Stich, Stephen. 1983. *From Folk Psychology to Cognitive Science: The Case
against Belief.* Cambridge: MIT Press.

    1990. *The Fragmentation of Reason.* Cambridge: MIT Press.

Stocker, Michael. 1976. "The Schizophrenia of Modern Ethical Theories."

Journal of Philosophy 73, no. 14 (12 Aug.): 453–66. Reprinted in Kruschwitz and Roberts 1987.

1980. "Intellectual Desire, Emotion, and Action." In *Explaining Emotions,* ed. Amelie Rorty. Berkeley and Los Angeles: University of California Press.

1982. "Responsibility Especially for Beliefs." *Mind* 91, no. 3 (July): 398–417.

1987. "Emotional Thoughts." *American Philosophical Quarterly* 24, no. 1 (Jan.): 59–69.

Strawson, Peter. 1962. "Freedom and Resentment." *Proceedings of the British Academy* 48:1–25.

Stroud, Barry. 1984. *The Significance of Philosophical Skepticism.* Oxford: Clarendon Press.

Stump, Eleonore. 1994. "Wisdom: Will, Belief, and Moral Goodness." Paper presented to the Society of Christian Philosophers, University of LaVerne, Calif., Jan.

Swain, Marshall. 1981. *Reasons and Knowledge.* Ithaca: Cornell University Press.

Swinburne, Richard. 1981. *Faith and Reason.* Oxford: Clarendon Press.

1986. *The Evolution of the Soul.* Oxford: Clarendon Press.

Taliaferro, Charles. 1985. "Divine Cognitive Power." *International Journal of Philosophy of Religion* 18:133–40.

Taylor, C. C. W. "Aristotle's Epistemology." In Everson 1990.

Taylor, Charles. 1982. "The Diversity of Goods." In *Utilitarianism and Beyond,* ed. A. Sen and B. Williams. New York: Cambridge University Press.

Taylor, Gabriele. 1981. "Integrity." *Proceedings of the Aristotelian Society,* suppl. vol. 55.

Taylor, Richard. 1985. *Ethics, Faith, and Reason.* Englewood Cliffs, N.J.: Prentice-Hall.

Taylor, Robert. n.d. "The Virtues and Freedom in Aquinas." Typescript.

Tiles, Mary, and Jim Tiles. 1993. *An Introduction to Historical Epistemology.* Cambridge, Mass.: Basil Blackwell.

Trianosky, Gregory. 1987. "Virtue, Action, and the Good Life: Towards a Theory of the Virtues." *Pacific Philosophical Quarterly* 68, no. 2 (June): 124–147.

Unger, Peter. 1968. "An Analysis of Factual Knowledge." *Journal of Philosophy* 65, no. 6 (21 Mar.): 157–70.

Urmson, J. O. 1988. *Aristotle's Ethics.* Oxford: Blackwell.

Vickers, John. n.d. "Belief." Typescript.

von Wright, G. H. 1963. *The Varieties of Goodness.* New York: Humanities Press.

Wainwright, William J. 1996. *Reason and the Heart: A Prolegomenon to a Critique of Passional Reason.* Ithaca: Cornell University Press.

Wallace, James D. 1978. *Virtues and Vices.* Ithaca: Cornell University Press.

Watson, Gary. 1984. "Virtues in Excess." *Philosophical Studies* 46:57–74.

    1990. "On the Primacy of Character." In *Identity, Character, and Morality: Essays in Moral Psychology,* ed. Owen Flanagan.Cambridge: MIT Press.

Welbourne, Michael. 1986. *The Community of Knowledge.* Scots Monograph Series. Aberdeen: Aberdeen University Press; Atlantic Highlands, N.J.: Humanities Press.

Wiggins, David. 1987. *Needs, Values, Truth: Essays in the Philosophy of Value.* Oxford: Basil Blackwell.

Wilkes, K. V. 1981. "Response to C. Hookway, 'Conscious Belief and Deliberations.'" *Proceedings of the Aristotelian Society,* suppl. vol. 55, pp. 91–107.

Williams, Bernard. 1973. "Deciding to Believe." In *Problems of the Self.* Cambridge: Cambridge University Press.

    1981. *Moral Luck.* Cambridge: Cambridge University Press.

    1985. *Ethics and the Limits of Philosophy.* Cambridge: Harvard University Press.

Wilson, B. R., ed. 1970. *Rationality.* Oxford: Basil Blackwell.

Winch, Peter. 1972. *Ethics and Action.* London: Routledge & Kegan Paul.

Wisdo, David. 1993. *The Life of Irony and the Ethics of Belief.* Albany: State University of New York Press.

Wittgenstein, Ludwig. 1967. *Philosophical Investigations.* Trans. G. E. M. Anscombe. 2d ed. Oxford: Blackwell.

    1971. *On Certainty.* Ed. G. E. M. Anscombe and G. H. von Wright. Trans. Dennis Paul and G. E. M. Anscombe. New York: Harper Torchbooks.

Woldheim, Richard. "The Good Self and the Bad Self." In Kenny 1986.

Wolf, Susan. 1982. "Moral Saints." *Journal of Philosophy* 79:419–39.

    1990. *Freedom within Reason.* New York: Oxford University Press.

Wolfson, Harry Austryn. 1970. *The Philosophy of the Church Fathers.* 3d ed. Cambridge: Harvard University Press.

Wolter, Allan B. 1986. *Duns Scotus on the Will and Morality.* Washington, D.C.: Catholic University of America Press.

Wolterstorff, Nicholas. 1988. "Once Again, Evidentialism – This Time, Social." *Philosophical Topics* 16, no. 2 (fall): 53–74.

Wong, David. 1991. "Relativism." In *A Companion to Ethics,* ed. Peter Singer. London: Blackwell.

Yearley, Lee A. 1990a. "Education and the Intellectual Virtues." In *Beyond the Classics? Essays on Religious Studies and Liberal Education,* ed. S. Burkhalter and Ann F. Reynolds. Mercer, Ga.: Scholars Press.

1990b. *Mencius and Aquinas: Theories of Virtue and Conceptions of Courage.* Albany: State University of New York Press.

1990c. "Recent Work on Virtue." *Religious Studies Review* 16, no. 1:1–9.

Young, Charles M. 1988. "Aristotle on Temperance." *Philosophical Review* 97, no. 4 (Oct.): 521–42.

1994. "Aristotle on Liberality." *Proceedings of the Boston Area Colloquium in Ancient Philosophy* 10.

1996. "The Doctrine of the Mean." *Topoi* 15: 89–99.

Zagzebski, Linda. 1993a. "Intellectual Virtue in Religious Epistemology." In *Faith in Theory and Practice: Essays on Justifying Religious Belief,* ed. Elizabeth Radcliffe and Carol White. Chicago and La Salle, Ill.: Open Court.

1993b. "Religious Knowledge and the Virtues of the Mind." In *Rational Faith: Catholic Responses to Reformed Epistemology,* ed. Linda Zagzebski. Notre Dame, Ind.: University of Notre Dame Press.

1994a. "The Inescapability of Gettier Problems." *Philosophical Quarterly* 44, no. 174 (Jan.): 65–73.

1994b. "Religious Luck." *Faith and Philosophy* 11, no. 3 (July): 397–413.

Forthcoming. "The Place of *Phronesis* in the Methodology of Theology." In *Philosophy and the Future of Christian Theology,* ed. Stephen T. Davis. London: Macmillan.

Name index

Almeder, Robert, 292
Alston, William P, 24, 31, 37, 38, 160, 234, 334
Anderson, J. R., 311
Anscombe, G. E. M., 17, 20, 86
Aquinas, Thomas, 64, 90, 91, 93, 141, 148, 198, 211–215, 217–219, 229, 230, 277
Archilochus, 45, 274
Aristotle, xiv, 4, 8, 11, 32, 33, 35, 36, 44, 57, 60, 67, 72, 81, 88, 96, 99, 102, 103, 105–107, 110–113, 116, 117, 119, 126–128, 138–145, 149–152, 155, 157, 158, 166, 190, 198, 200, 203–205, 211–217, 219, 221, 227–230, 233, 249, 250, 253, 255, 316, 318, 321, 323
Armstrong, D. M., 11
Augustine, 64, 95, 148, 262
Austen, Jane, 257

Bacon, Francis, 96, 163, 262, 277–278, 336
Bacon, Roger, 262
Bagehot, W., 52, 53
Baier, Annette, 161
Balzac, Honoré de, 123
Barnes, Jonathan, 48
Beard, Charles, 224
Benson, John, 159, 160
Berlin, Isaiah, 45, 274
Blake, David, 119
Blake, William, 282
Blum, Lawrence, 18

BonJour, Laurence, 4, 30, 42, 174, 299
Bower, G. H., 311
Braeton, Jane, 199
Brink, David, 38
Broadie, Sarah, 107, 110–112, 321–323
Brown, David, 121–123
Burnyeat, M. F., 35, 36, 48

Casey, John, 227, 228
Chisholm, Roderick, 1, 30, 35, 36
Clarke, Murray, 65
Clouston, T. S., 153
Code, Lorraine, xiii, 11, 12, 65, 152, 155
Cohen, L. Jonathan, 65
Conee, Earl, 30
Confucius, 211
Conly, Sarah, 202

Dancy, Jonathan, 2, 4, 39
DeRose, Keith, 233
Descartes, René, 31, 33–35, 63, 171, 262, 271, 278, 324, 336
Dewey, John, 100, 169, 171–173, 176, 179, 201, 272
Dimnet, Ernest, 123, 182, 183

Edwards, Jonathan, 167
Emerson, Ralph Waldo, 171, 193, 306
Endo, Shusaku, 240
Everson, Stephen, 36, 184, 262

Feinberg, Joel, 70, 71
Feldman, Richard, 30, 308

359

Name Index

Robinson, Jenefer, 57
Rorty, Amelie, 91, 100, 154, 180
Ross, W. D., 18, 19
Royce, Josiah, 211
Ryle, Gilbert, 108, 117

Saul of Tarsus, 123
Scheffler, Israel, 145
Scott, Sir Walter, 53, 183, 199
Scotus, John Duns, 242, 243
Scrooge, Ebeneezer, 123
Sher, George, 80
Slote, Michael, 16, 71, 75, 79, 80, 99, 100, 211, 232, 238, 254, 255, 258
Sosa, Ernest, xiii, 2, 4, 8–10, 12, 14, 39, 43, 102, 246, 279, 280, 323
Spinoza Baruch, 46, 128, 138, 169, 262, 292
Sterne, Lawrence, 196
Stich, Stephen, 51
Stocker, Michael, 3, 18, 40, 65, 138, 145
Stone, Oliver, 54, 56, 57, 103, 326, 329
Stump, Eleonore, 64, 66

Sullivan, Thomas D., 314
Swinburne, Richard, 56, 57, 62

Taliaferro, Charles, 26, 27
Tiles, Jim and Mary, 21, 184, 263, 278
Tomberlin, James, 292
Trianosky, Gregory, 15, 19, 24, 91, 93, 101, 106

von Wright, Georg, 16, 84, 104, 106, 115, 129

Wainwright, William, J., 21, 167
Wallace, James, 16, 107, 108, 110, 111, 149
Watson, Gary, 93, 196, ???
Williams, Bernard, 17, 57, 70
Wisdo, David, 21
Wittgenstein, Ludwig, 55–56
Wolfson, Harry, 218
Woodruff, Paul, 262

Young, Charles, 9, 57, 81, 94, 104, 105, 143, 145, 179, 233, 236, 250, 291

Subject index